W9-BIU-488

Working with the SAS® System

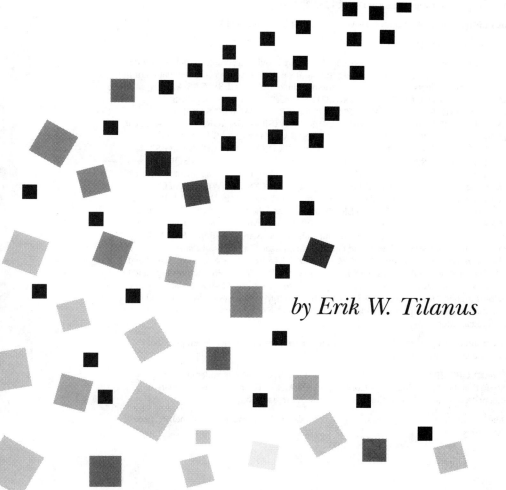

by Erik W. Tilanus

The correct bibliographic citation for this manual is as follows: Erik W. Tilanus, *Working with the SAS® System*, Cary, NC: SAS Institute Inc., 1994. 572 pp.

Working with the SAS® System

Authorized translation from the Dutch Language Edition. Original copyright © 1993 by SYBEX Uitgeverij b.v.

Translation copyright © 1994 by SAS Institute Inc., Cary, NC, USA.

ISBN 1-55544-645-0

All rights reserved. Printed in the United States of America. No part of this publication may be reproduced, stored in a retrieval system, or transmitted, in any form or by any means, electronic, mechanical, photocopying, or otherwise, without the prior written permission of the publisher, SAS Institute Inc.

Restricted Rights Legend. Use, duplication, or disclosure by the U.S. Government is subject to restrictions as set forth in subparagraph (c)(1)(ii) of the Rights in Technical Data and Computer Software clause at DFARS 252.227-7013.

SAS Institute Inc., SAS Campus Drive, Cary, North Carolina 27513.

1st printing, September 1994

The SAS® System is an integrated system of software providing complete control over data access, management, analysis, and presentation. Base SAS software is the foundation of the SAS System. Products within the SAS System include SAS/ACCESS® SAS/AF® SAS/ASSIST® SAS/CALC® SAS/CONNECT® SAS/CPE® SAS/DMI® SAS/EIS® SAS/ENGLISH® SAS/ETS® SAS/FSP® SAS/GRAPH® SAS/IMAGE® SAS/IML® SAS/IMS-DL/I® SAS/INSIGHT® SAS/LAB® SAS/NVISION® SAS/OR® SAS/PH-Clinical® SAS/QC® SAS/REPLAY-CICS® SAS/SESSION® SAS/SHARE® SAS/STAT® SAS/TOOLKIT® SAS/TRADER® SAS/TUTOR® SAS/DB2™ SAS/GEO™ SAS/GIS™ SAS/PH-Kinetics™ SAS/SHARE*NET™ SAS/SPECTRAVIEW™ and SAS/SQL-DS™ software. Other SAS Institute products are SYSTEM 2000® Data Management Software, with basic SYSTEM 2000, CREATE™ Multi-User™ QueX™ Screen Writer™ and CICS interface software; InfoTap™ software; NeoVisuals® software; JMP® JMP IN® JMP Serve® and JMP *Design®* software; SAS/RTERM® software; and the SAS/C® Compiler and the SAS/CX® Compiler; and Emulus™ software. MultiVendor Architecture™ and MVA™ are trademarks of SAS Institute Inc. SAS Institute also offers SAS Consulting® SAS Video Productions® Ambassador Select® and On-Site Ambassador™ services. *Authorline® Observations® SAS Communications® SAS Training® SAS Views®* the SASware Ballot® and *JMPer Cable®* are published by SAS Institute Inc. The SAS Video Productions logo and the Books By Users SAS Institute's Author Service logo are registered service marks and the Helplus logo is a trademark of SAS Institute Inc. All trademarks above are registered trademarks or trademarks of SAS Institute Inc. in the USA and other countries. ® indicates USA registration.

The Institute is a private company devoted to the support and further development of its software and related services.

AS/400® DB2® IBM® OS/2® and PS/2® are registered trademarks or trademarks of International Business Machines Corporation. ORACLE® is a registered trademark or trademark of Oracle Corporation. ® indicates USA registration.

Other brand and product names are registered trademarks or trademarks of their respective companies.

Contents

Preface

Introduction

In 1979, when I became acquainted with SAS Institute Inc. and the SAS System, I had the "privilege" that the documentation for the whole system was contained in a single book of only 500 pages. Reading and leafing through the material for a couple of evenings provided sufficient knowledge to get started using the system. At the present time, the language guide by itself is over 1000 pages. Then there is also a procedures guide of some 700 pages, a statistics guide in two parts and dozens of other handbooks. A beginner might be discouraged by such a quantity of material and could easily feel lost.

In 1980, I presented my first introductory course on the SAS System for a few colleagues. Since then, I have repeated that course many times for employees of various companies. While teaching these courses, I am frequently asked to publish my course material. When the time came to revise my material because of the advent of Version 6 of the SAS System, I summoned the courage to fulfill this request.
This book is the result.

To the reader

This book is designed to help you acquire and develop skills in using the SAS System regardless of whether you have previous experience with computers or programming.

The first chapter covers the essentials of computers, operating systems and programming which you will need to get started. The twelve chapters which follow cover the basics of the SAS System, and the remaining chapters cover more advanced topics.

What subjects to leave out is a major problem in writing a book of this type. I have not attempted to formally describe the SAS System or detail every facet of the SAS language, but rather to give a guidebook of system functions of practical benefit to the user. I have based the choice of material on my fourteen years of experience with the SAS System and on feedback from SAS users in various companies. If I have left out something you need, please accept my apology. More important, please let me know so that I can include it in a future edition.

This book contains much, but not all information about base SAS software. The more specialized SAS software products that are currently available are briefly described in appendix N. Others are under development. For more information, I refer you to SAS Institute.

I hope that this book can contribute to your understanding of the SAS System, that this understanding helps you to find better ways to do your work and new paths to follow. The SAS System grows through people like you who, through seeking and experimenting, uncover new horizons.

SAS documentation

The information in this book can serve as your first guide along the SAS path. Should you reach the point where it no longer provides you with sufficient tools, you will need to consult the SAS documentation. You can request the Publications Catalog from SAS Institute, which provides synopses of all users guides, reference guides and other books.
You should have these three books at hand from the start:

*   *SAS Language: Reference, Version 6, First Edition*
    ISBN 1-55544-381-8, SAS order number A56076

*   *SAS Procedures Guide, Version 6, Third Edition*
    ISBN 1-55544-378-8, SAS order number A56080

*   *SAS Technical Report P222: Changes and Enhancements to Base SAS Software, Release 6.07*
    ISBN 1-55544-466-0, SAS order number A59139

Some more books of general interest are listed in appendix N.

In addition to handbooks, SAS Institute also publishes a number of magazines and newsletters. SAS Communications is meant for every SAS user and contains announcements of new versions, descriptions of applications and tips from the SAS Technical Support Group. The quarterly journal Observations is specially aimed at advanced SAS System users and employees of information centers supporting SAS System users.

Conventions

This book uses the following conventions for displaying SAS statements, macro statements, and so on. SAS statements are always in upper case in THIS TYPEFACE. Macro statements are in THIS TYPEFACE.

Elements of statements which are optional are enclosed in angle brackets: <...>. It has been necessary to deviate from these conventions in a few places. Such exceptions will either be explicitly mentioned, or will be so obvious that confusion is impossible.

Acknowledgments

It is trite to say it, but you cannot write a book such as this alone. Many people have given me their direct or indirect assistance. It is impossible to name them all here. A few, however, I cannot leave out.

To begin with, Ton Bäcker and Rolf Steenge. I have worked with Ton and Rolf since the early 1980's in the development of my course material. The many hours we spent together dreaming up new tricks in using the SAS System have left me with many wonderful memories. Then there are my colleagues at KLM Royal Dutch Airlines: Desiree Hogguer, Wilma deRuyter, Ronald van Egmond, Piet van den Oever and Willie Prenen. In this book I have assimilated many of the practical examples of program problems and solutions which they provided me with.

I should also like to thank my "guinea pigs" for their positive feedback. They wished to learn the SAS System, but instead of a proper training course, they had to do with an unfinished manuscript! I thank them for their comments. The text is improved through their observations in many places.

I must also mention KLM itself. Without the availability of computer time to work out the examples, I could not have completed the draft of a book like this.

I offer my family my deepest apologies for the hours I spent in my attic in front of my computer instead of with them.

Preface with the English edition

Writing a book is quite an experience. Seeing it published is a thrill. But having it translated is again a completely different story!

When the subject came up at SUGI 19, my first reaction was one of astonishment: who is waiting for a book written by some Dutchman? But the weeks that followed made it quite clear that SYBEX, my Dutch publisher, and SAS Institute meant business!

There have been busy weeks since then. While the translator was working on the main text, I had to change all examples in such a way that people at the other end of the world would be able to grasp the notion. Then I had to integrate the text from the translator with the examples and in the mean time improve the text of some parts based on the reactions that came in from the Dutch readers. I was working in a language which is not my own; although I feel reasonably comfortable with English, it is obvious that one can miss the fine points of the language.

Several people have been most helpful in preparing this translation. First of all I would like to thank David Baggett of SAS Institute and George Kerstholt of SYBEX for their confidence that got the whole project started and completed in such a short time. Then thanks to Paul O'Brien who did the translation, which must have been a difficult job for somebody who is not familiar with the SAS System. Patsy Poole of SAS Institute deserves that her name be mentioned here in capitals. Her support and advice about the use of the English language have been essential to achieving good results. Léon Honings of SYBEX had the troublesome task of preparing the page layout of the whole book in just a few days. Well done!

Finally I thank my wife and sons for not complaining about all the hours I spent again in my attic. I won't do it again (at least for some months...)!

CHAPTER 1

Information Processing

Introduction

The SAS System is a computer based system for data analysis and information processing. Obviously, then, we are dealing with a computer system, data and information. The discussion of the SAS System and the use of SAS software begins with chapter 2. This chapter is devoted to making sure that you clearly understand the concepts 'computer system' (and its component elements), 'data', 'information' and 'information processing'. If you already understand and can apply these concepts, you may move ahead to the next chapter.

Information and information processing

Without being aware of it, we work with data and information all the time: when we look at a clock, we get the indicated time, from which we then derive information, such as: how late it is...

Information is a set of data which is meaningful by virtue of its interrelations.

If we apply this definition to the example of the clock, the meaning becomes clear. When we look at the clock, we get more data than the time indicated by the hands. We also instinctively verify that the clock is running. This too is data, along with the time.

Directly connected with the concept 'information' is the concept 'information processing': anything you do with the acquired information. In our clock example, the first thing we do is verify whether or not the time indicated can be correct: the sun is overhead but the clock reads 5:00. We draw a conclusion from this information: the clock is not working properly and the time indicated is not reliable. Once we have used the information for such tests and have determined that everything is probably in order, we can perform other actions: we can decide that it is time to prepare a meal.

In the above example, we can discern several important basics of information processing:

1.   collection of data;

2.   verification that the data is probably correct;

3.   combining the data into meaningful information;

4.   drawing conclusions;

5. determining follow up action.

In order to process information with computers, these same steps must be taken. The difference between us and a computer is that we perform these actions intuitively and unconsciously (testing that the clock is working properly), but for a computer, these steps must be explicit. Making them explicit is the essence of programming.

Information processing jargon

Information processing, like any specialty, has its own jargon, much of which is American English. In order to be able to use the SAS System or any other programming language, it is essential to understand a number of these terms. Once again, we shall make use of an example.

Suppose you are the representative of a business. You probably have a card file containing a card for each of your clients (figure 1.l).

On each card is, of course, the name of a business with its address and phone. There will be the name of a contact person as well. You also want to keep track of how important the client is to you, so you make a note of last year's turnover. Alongside, you might also make note of the date of the most recent order. Finally you jot down a note or two about your most recent visit to the client (date, any appointments made).

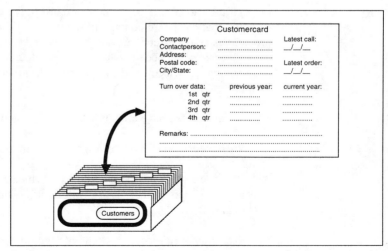

Figure 1.1: A card tray is the analogy to a computer data set, in this case filled with customer data. Every card is a "record" or "observation". Every field on the card is a "variable".

In computer jargon, such a card file is called simply a 'file', or a 'data set'. In SAS Institute documentation, a SAS file is usually referred to as a data set, while any other file is just called a file. In this book we shall follow the same usage.

In computer jargon, each client card would be called a record. The SAS System usually speaks of an observation when referring to a record in a SAS data set. As we go deeper into the details, we come to the individual data on the client card, such as the firm's name, postal code, previous year's turnover, and so on. Where we might speak of headings or categories on such a card, in computer jargon we speak of fields or variables. The SAS System uses the latter term.

Using the example of the card file, we can go deeper into the basic procedures of information processing. We can ask questions about the information in the card file, we can update the cards or add new cards, and we can perform specific analyses on the information.

Let us say that we want to plan a visit for the coming week to selected clients. The first thing we have to do is determine why a client should be visited: we must establish the processing criteria, for example: the client has not placed an order in over six weeks, or the turn-over for the last quarter was considerably lower than usual (For a computer this criterium is too vague. How much lower is too low? How should this be reckoned, in percentages or dollar figures?) or the client has not been visited in over eight weeks. Once the criteria have been established, then we can go through the card file to see which cards fit the criteria. It is naturally essential that each card contain all the data necessary to carry out the procedures and draw conclusions. If last visit date is not on a particular card, that card cannot be selected. Once the selection for the client visits has been made, then comes the next step in the process: working out the visit program.

As you can see, we have already taken several steps:

1. We have established our information requirements (whom to visit).

2. We have established the procedures by which the available data can be arranged to yield the desired information (when a visit should be planned).

3. We apply our procedures to the file (go through the card file) and extract the desired information.

4. We make a report on the results of the process (plan the visit).

If we want to take our client data with us on our visits, we make a temporary file containing only the cards for the clients we are going to visit. When we return from the visits, we must update these cards and return them to the main card file. This is file management.

5.   We make a new file based on the selection criteria (the cards we want to take with us).

6.   We alter this file (by updating the cards).

7.   We merge the two files (by replacing the cards).

The computer can be a great help to us in all these procedures, except for the first two. We must always work out for ourselves what our information requirements are and how these can be derived from the available data (or one step further, how we can acquire the required data). In summary, there are three basic elements: the information requirements, the rules by which these can be fulfilled and the relevant data.

If we wish to use a computer to meet our information needs, we must describe the above rules in a way that the computer can understand, which brings us to programming.

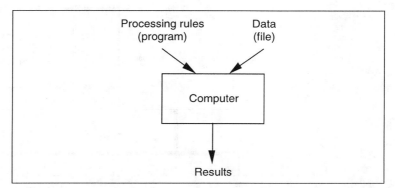

Figure 1.2: For information processing you always need two things: a program: the collection of all rules that should be applied and a file: the data upon which the rules should be applied.

Computer systems

General structure

You do not need to be a computer expert to work successfully with the SAS System. It is really only necessary for you to have some insight into the structure of a computer system, because this will make the SAS System easier to understand and use. All computer systems, whether microcomputers (PC's), minicomputers or mainframes, have in principal the same structure. Only the applied technology varies, as well as the size and the speed. There are no longer perfectly clear boundaries between these categories of systems. Today's microcomputers have a processing capacity which would shame a mainframe of ten years ago. To agree upon the names: by microcomputer we mean a device which can sit on or beside a desk, and to which usually only one terminal is connected (often it is an integrated unit, such as an IBM PC or PS/2 or an Apple Macintosh), by minicomputer we mean a computer to which a several tens of users can be connected via terminals (such as a Digital Equipment VAX) and by mainframe we mean a system which can accomodate hundreds or thousands of users at the same time (such as the IBM 4300 or 3090 systems or an Amdahl 5890 system).

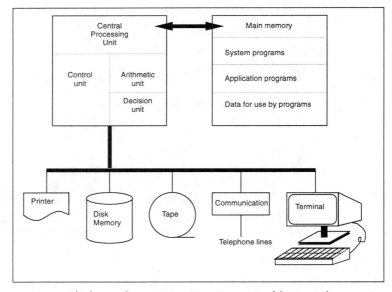

Figure 1.3: The heart of a computer system consists of the central processing unit in combination with the main memory. All peripheral equipment is connected to the CPU by a logical circuit which is normally called a "bus" in micro- or mini-computers. In mainframes it is generally referred to as a "channel".

The most important components of any computer system are the central processing unit (CPU) and the main memory. All processing takes place in the CPU: this is where all the procedures we have defined in our programs will be carried out. For this purpose, it is composed of two sections: an arithmetic unit, which carries out all calculations, and a control and decision-making unit where data are compared so that actions can be performed. In addition to these tasks, the CPU has the task of managing the entire computer system, which is the task of the control unit. Programs are stored in the computer's main memory from which they can be executed. While a program is running the related data is also maintained in main memory. During the execution of a program, the control unit calls up the program instructions one by one and interprets them: what is to be done and where the data is located. On this basis instructions will be issued to the arithmetic unit and data will be retrieved from memory. The control unit also regulates the activities of peripherals: printers, plotters, communications channels (for example, for connecting terminals) and peripheral memory devices: disks and magnetic tape. Peripheral memories store programs and data more permanently. These programs and data can be transferred when necessary to main memory for processing and then transferred back to peripheral memory. The reason for this is simple: when the power is turned off, the contents of the main memory of a computer system are lost; however, information on disk and tape is retained. The size of memory is measured in bytes. One byte is a location in memory which can store one symbol, such as a letter or a number. Main memories vary in capacity depending on the type of computer system. A microcomputer usually has a memory capacity of between 512 Kb (kilobyte = 1000 bytes; actually this is not quite correct: one kilobyte contains 1024 bytes and one megabyte equals 1024 kilobytes or 1048576 bytes) and 16 Mb (megabyte, million bytes); large systems can go as high as 256 Mb and beyond.

Peripheral memory devices have much greater capacity than main memory, but in contrast the time to access data on those devices is much longer than access to data in main memory. For example: the time needed to access a piece of data from main memory is a few tens of nanoseconds (1 nanosecond = 0.000000001 second) and from hard disk it takes a few to several tens of milliseconds (1 millisecond = 0,001 second). A hard disk unit consists of one or more disks coated with the same type of magnetic material as magnetic tape. A magnetic disk records information the same way as an audio or video tape recorder, except that it lays down information in concentric circles ('tracks').

Microcomputers often use the flexible, interchangeable diskette (or 'floppy'). The capacity of a diskette goes from 360 Kb to 2 Mb. When full, a blank diskette costing a dollar or so can take its place. It is not usually possible to interchange hard disks; the only means of expansion is by connecting an additional unit. The capacity of hard disks goes from 20 Mb to 1Gb (gigabyte = 1000 megabyte) and beyond.

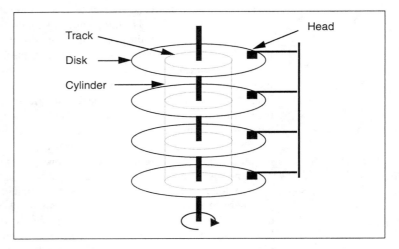

Figure 1.4: A disk storage unit consists of one or more rotating disks with a magnetizable surface, comparable to the surface of a video tape. Information is written onto these disks in concentric circles, called "tracks". Writing the information (and also reading back the information) is done by means of a read/write "head", which can move from track to track with high speed. All the corresponding tracks of all disks together are called a "cylinder".

Magnetic tape memory combines great storage capacity with small physical size. Tape is therefore highly suitable for archiving data. A tape costing a few dollars can hold the entire contents of a hard disk. The disadvantage of tape is that you have to run through the whole tape to access data, in contrast to the hard disk whose read/write head can locate and access data in a fraction of a second.

The method of encoding letters and numbers is different for IBM mainframes and for mini- or microcomputers. IBM coding is known as EBCDIC code, while other computers use what is known as ASCII code. You do not have to know these coding systems to work with the SAS System. For those interested, appendix B contains some notes on these codes.

Operating system

In a computer system, many similar tasks must be performed for each application, such as starting and stopping a printer, sending information to the monitor screen, reading keyboard input, transferring data from peripheral memory to main memory, and so on. These actions must all be programmed. In theory every program could do these jobs itself; but this is like reinventing the wheel. Therefore these sorts of general programs are installed as standard routines in the computer system. These programs together constitute the operating system. The operating system contains routines to control loading of a program from peripheral to main memory so that execution can begin. It also contains routines for accessing or storing data, and much more. The exact content of an operating system depends on the apparatus on which it runs. Thus every computer system has its own operating system. Often a computer can run more than just one operating system. There are three operating systems in use for the IBM mainframe computer system, called DOS/ VSE, VM and MVS/XA. Digital Equipment VAX most often uses the VMS operating system. The most common operating system for micro-computers is MS-DOS Windows, although other operating systems are gaining popularity (e.g. UNIX, OS/2).

Use of an operating system requires special command sets particular to that system. These are combined in a system specific command language. For IBM mainframes this is called 'Job Control Language' (JCL). For Digital VAX, it is called DCL (Digital Command Language) and for the PC it is simply referred to as DOS commands (or OS/2 commands). A description of the various command sets goes beyond the scope of this book. The most important part we are confronted with while dealing with the SAS System is file management: storing programs and files from computer to disk and recalling them for execution.

File allocation

One of the most used families of system commands (or JCL statements) concerns the allocation of files. These commands inform the operating system which files are to be processed and where they are located. In this context, programs are also files! This instruction usually occurs in an indirect manner. As part of the allocation command, a file is given a symbolic name which tells the operating system to use the file. This symbolic name is usually called the DD name or file reference (fileref). The SAS System uses for its own file structure ('SAS data libraries') the term 'library reference' (libref). Since the SAS System in general uses the terms 'fileref' or 'libref', they shall also be used throughout this book.

Once a fileref is defined you can use the symbolic file name throughout your program to locate data in that file.

You can compare the allocation process with the name of a house in relation to its official address. The formal address is 54 West Road, Smallville 28999. This defines its exact physical location. In the town, in the specific neighborhood, it is known however as 'the old house on the hill' and in the town everybody knows which house you mean. In the computer equivalent: the official address states the full name of the file on disk or tape. This includes an indication of which disk the file resides on (city), in which 'directory' (district), and what the file is called (street and number). For our own programs (in our own town), we can give a symbolic name (the local common description or house name), with which we can refer to data in our program.

The allocation process does more than just join the fileref to the file: it also tells the operating system if the file is only to be read, or if it can be altered as well. A new file can also be created through the allocation process.

It would be too ambitious here to give a full description of the allocation commands for every system environment. (Further information on SAS file allocation for various system environments is given in appendices H through M.) These can be found in the handbooks for the systems concerned. The following example is given only as an illustration.

The route from city via district to street and number is called 'path' in computer jargon. The path tells us how to physically reach the file we want. Usually the system contains a number of pre-specified access paths, so that to locate a file, a shortened address may be given instead of the full path. There is also usually an index present, which lists all files (or at least the files that are used most often). Then the full path name does not need to be used to locate a file.

Let us say that we have a file with the official name CLIENT.DATA and that the path to this file is named USERCAT. (Usually files have a name and an 'extension' or 'qualifier' indicating the type of file it is. The extension can be longer in one system than in another. In an IBM system, it can have 8 characters, while on a VAX or PC only 3. The extension DATA (DAT on VAX or PC) indicates that this is a simple data file.) Let us also say that for allocation we will use the symbolic name: BST01.

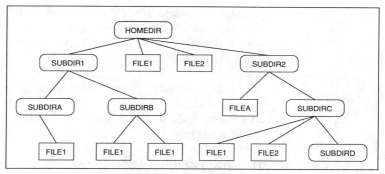

Figure 1.5: The directory structure as used on mini- and micro-computers. A file is completely and unambiguously pointed to by its access path: the chain of all directories and sub-directories. On IBM mainframes files are organized in "catalogs" rather than (sub-) directories. The path to a file starts in that case with a "catalog pointer".

In the IBM operating system MVS, allocation is controlled using the following commands:

```
//BST01 DD DSN=USERCAT.CLIENT.DATA,DISP=SHR
ALLOC DD(BST01) DA('USERCAT.CLIENT.DATA') SHR
```

The first form is used in so-called batch programs: programs run directly by the computer, the second variant is for on-line programs, programs executed during dialogue with a terminal (see TSO below). The first command is a so-called 'JCL statement'. All JCL statements are recognized by // in the first two positions. Then follows the symbolic name and the code for the type of JCL statement: DD (for Data Description), and then the path and the file name (DSN = data set name) and finally an instruction as to whether we want exclusive access to the file or that others can use it simultaneously. In general, you will want exclusive access if you intend to alter the file, and give others access if you only intend to read it. This instruction occurs in the DISP (disposition) parameter: DISP=OLD meaning that the program is creating a new version of the file; DISP=MOD meaning that this program is appending data to the file; DISP=SHR meaning that this program is only reading and that the file may be shared with other programs or users. DISP=NEW means that the program is creating a new file. To do this the program must also specify how much space is required for the file.

In the statement TSO ALLOC (the second form) the same terms recur. Further explanation is not necessary.

On a VAX, under the VMS operating system, the corresponding commands have a different look. We assume for comparison that the file is located in subdirectory USERCAT, which in turn is located in HOME. The VMS command is:

```
$ DEFINE BST01 [HOME.USERCAT]CLIENT.DAT
```

By comparing the VMS command with the IBM statements, the structure will be clear.

The VAX system makes extensive use of directories. Every user also has a so-called 'default directory': a directory where a file is placed if no other directory is indicated. Since no path is specified in the DEFINE command, the file is placed in the default directory. The same principle applies to PC's and UNIX systems.

SAS Institute has developed its own commands for file allocation so that files can be managed in a similar way regardless of the system environment: the FILENAME and LIBNAME statements, where FILENAME is intended for general use and LIBNAME is specific for SAS data libraries. More will be said about these statements in the relevant chapters. But here just for comparison is the FILENAME variant for the above allocation example:

```
FILENAME BST01 'USERCAT.CLIENT.DATA';
```

Processing methods

Application program

Say you want to write a program using the data 'article number', 'price exclusive of VAT (or sales tax)' and 'quantity sold', from which to calculate the article price VAT included, what the revenue per article is without VAT and the total revenue with VAT. The formulas in the program will be:

price incl. VAT = price excl. VAT x 1.175
                                          (assuming 17.5% VAT)

revenue excl. VAT = price excl. VAT x quantity sold

total revenue incl. VAT = sum for all articles of
(price incl. VAT x quantity sold)

In SAS statements this program could be written:

```
FILENAME TheData '<name of the input file>';
DATA REPORT;
    INFILE TheData;
    INPUT ART_NR PR_EXCL Q_SOLD;
    PR_INCL = PR_EXCL * 1.175;
    REV_EXCL = PR_EXCL * Q_SOLD;
    TOT_INCL + PR_INCL * Q_SOLD;

PROC PRINT;
```

This program can be interpreted as follows: DATA tells the SAS System to create a file with the name REPORT. The INFILE statement tells the SAS System where the data is located by referring to the FILENAME statement through the fileref. INPUT tells the SAS System which data to read. The subsequent statements implement the calculations. Only the statement TOT_INCL + PR_INCL * Q_SOLD needs a little explanation. It tells the SAS System to total the revenue for each article (calculated by PR_INCL*Q_SOLD) for all articles. The statement PROC PRINT prints the results in table form. (figure 1.6).

How do we get the computer to execute this program? First the program must be loaded into the computer, and then the proper commands must be given to start the execution.

INPUT file

ART_NR	PR_EXCL	Q_SOLD
1265	17.85	300
4363	46.00	165
7423	51.60	283
. . .	. . .	. . .

REPORT data set

ART_NR	PR_EXCL	Q_SOLD	PR_INCL	REV_EXCL	TOT_INCL
1265	17.85	300	21.15	5355.00	6345.00
4363	46.00	165	54.51	7590.00	15339.15
7423	51.60	283	61.15	14602.80	32644.60
. . .	. . .	. . .	. . .	. . .	. . .

Figure 1.6: The INFILE statement points to the file which contains in each record the relevant data for an article. For every record in this file the program will build an observation in the SAS data set REPORT. PROC PRINT will print the newly created data set.

Editor

To load a program that has already been written into the computer, a special program is used, either a standard program installed on the computer system, or a program supplied by the software producer. This program is known as the 'Editor', and is in fact a kind of word processor. When the editor is started up, the user will be asked to enter the program statements. In addition, there is a provision for adding statements later, changing statements or deleting statements. Once the program has been entered with the help of the editor, execution can begin. Usually the program is saved onto hard disk first, so that there is a backup copy for making alterations and corrections which show up at the time of execution.

The SAS System also has its own editor, which is part of the 'Display Manager'. This is covered in chapter 5.

Program execution

As the program is loaded, the legible text (statements as entered into the editor) must be converted into 'machine language'. This is done by a compiler: another standard program provided by the software supplier. The SAS compiler is integrated into the total system. After the program is typed in, the method of execution is selected and the program is started by means of the correct command. After that the SAS System will automatically call up the compiler to do the translation. Once compiling is successful, program execution normally proceeds. (It is possible to separate segments of an SAS program to be compiled and run at a later time, but the standard method is to compile and run the whole program.) The execution of such a program can take place autonomously; which means that once the program has started, the user does not need to take any further notice of it; it also means that he can have no further influence over it. Execution can also take place interactively, where the user remains in dialogue with the current program and can, for example, enter data from a terminal to be processed.

Batch processing

The type of processing where no contact is possible with the program while it is running is called 'non-interactive processing' or 'batch processing'. Often these programs are run in the background ('background processing'), during which the terminal can be used for other tasks. In contrast, there is 'foreground processing'. In foreground processing the terminal is blocked during the execution of the program. Batch processing has been used since the introduction of computers. For batch processing, all input data is placed in a file beforehand, the data is read by the program during processing.

On an IBM mainframe (MVS operating system) this is controlled by JCL statements, such as we have already seen with file allocation. The JCL statements are read by the operating system, and on this basis the system knows which programs to run. From installation to installation, there are a few variations in the exact form and content of the statements, and sometimes also the system itself creates statements, so that the user does not have to enter them. To load the previously described program into the MVS environment, we need to execute JCL statements which look more or less like:

```
//MYPROG   JOB   CLASS=8,MSGCLASS=(1,1),TIME=5,
//               ACCNT=(MYACC)
//         EXEC  SAS
//THEDATA  DD    DSN=MYSAS.INPUT.DATA,DISP=SHR
         .
         .
         .  (SAS program statements)
         .
```

The first statement tells MVS that a job (program) is to be executed and gives additional information to the system, for example about the 'job class' in which the program is to function (a way of maintaining priorities), the maximun allowable duration of the program, charge-out information and so on. The EXEC statement instructs the operating system to execute the SAS System, followed by specification of input data by means of the previously described DD statements. The statements of the real SAS program can also be stored in a separate file. In that case, you must enter a reference in the job's JCL:

```
//MYPROG   JOB   CLASS=8,MSGCLASS=(1,1),TIME=5,
//               ACCNT=(MYACC)
//         EXEC  SAS
//THEDATA  DD    DSN=MYSAS.INPUT.DATA,DISP=SHR
//SYSIN    DD    DSN=MYSAS.VATPROG.SASPGM,DISP=SHR
```

On a VAX system with the VMS operating system, the following DCL statements would execute the same program:

```
$ DEFINE THEDATA [MYSAS]INPUT.DAT
$ SAS [MYSAS]VATPROG.SAS
```

The first statement attaches the symbolic name (fileref) THEDATA to the input file, which is used in the SAS program. The second statement tells VMS that the SAS System should be started and that SAS should run the program contained in the file VATPROG.SAS in directory MYSAS.

On an IBM PC with OS/2, the SAS System starts in batch mode by the simple method of entering SAS after the OS/2 prompt, followed by the name of the SAS program. The allocation of the input file can be accomplished in this program by the SET command:

```
SET THEDATA C:\MYSAS\INPUT.DAT
SAS -SYSIN C:\MYSAS\VATPROG\SAS
```

The distinguishing feature of batch processing is that no interaction is possible between the start and finish of a program: everything is done in one process. Nor can faulty input be corrected; it is dumped onto an error list so that corrected data can be entered for the following run.

A batch program can be started from the so-called console terminal, the workstation where the system manager works, but often from other workstations as well which are connected to the system. In many cases it is also possible to start the program from a workstation in another location. This is referred to as 'Remote Job Entry'.

Online and interactive processing

If the communication between user and computer system takes place via a workstation (keyboard and monitor) there is yet another method of processing, namely that in which a direct 'dialogue' is maintained between the workstation and the computer. An instruction is sent from the workstation to start a certain program, and in turn the program asks the workstation to enter data line by line. The same program as above could go through a procedure as follows:

1. The program is started by the user.

2. The program asks for the first line of input data to be entered, in this case article number, price and quantity sold.

3. The program tests the input data (existing article number, likely price and quantity).

4. Any errors in the input data are listed and reported back to the terminal. The data can then be directly corrected or reentered before processing.

5. In case the input is correct, the required calculations are performed, following which the program asks for the next input data.

6. Once we inform the program that all input data has been processed, the program will stop and eventually print out the report.

There are many varieties of on-line and interactive processing. The differences lie mainly in the method by which dialogue between program and user is maintained. The SAS System also has various forms. These will be covered later.

CHAPTER 2

Introducing the SAS® System

The SAS System has its roots as a purely statistical programming package. Over the years it has developed into an all-round programming system for a vaste range of applications. It is used world-wide for reporting, on-line processing, statistical analysis and so on.

It is a complete programming system, and as such more than a programming language. Of course, the SAS programming language is at the heart of the system, but from there on it includes an integrated file management, report generator both in digital (tabular, for example) or graphic format, a 'data analysis toolbox' (a collection of procedures for data analysis and statistics) and finally a development and maintenance environment for SAS programs. The current version of the SAS System is Release 6.08 (for some system environments Release 6.09 or higher is already available). This version is available for a variety of hardware platforms, such as IBM mainframe under various operating systems, Digital VAX with VMS, PC with OS/2 and Windows, various UNIX workstations and so on. On all these systems, the SAS System has a similar look and feel. Therefore, this book is suitable for any aspiring SAS user, even though the examples have been generated on an IBM mainframe with MVS.

Some users are still running Version 5 of the SAS System. Most of what is in this book applies as well to Version 5 as to Version 6. Except where necessary, there will be no specific distinction made between V5 and V6.

A first example

The best way to learn the SAS System is through examples. The first example deals with the gasoline mileage of a car. For every fillup we log the odometer reading and how many liters we put in. Figure 2.1 shows part of such a log. On the basis of this log, we can calculate the mileage (expressed in kilometers per liter) and the average mileage over the whole log.

Odometer reading	Number of liters
9908	34.2
10227	35.2
10493	27.4
10855	34.8
11212	36.5
11515	30.4
...	...

Figure 2.1: The tankstops of a car are recorded in a log. This log contains the odometer reading of the car and the volume of gas (in liters) that was taken in.

The principle

To do this, the data must be entered into the SAS System. Data input takes place in a so-called DATA step. The printout of the results and the calculation of the average are done with PROC steps. The program looks like:

```
DATA CARDATA;
   INPUT KM LITERS;
   MILEAGE = DIF(KM)/LITERS;
CARDS;
 < here follow the input records >
PROC PRINT;
PROC MEANS;
```

The first statement is the DATA statement, which indicates that a DATA step has been initiated, and that a data set will be created with the name CARDATA. The INPUT statement specifies the input fields, in this case the odometer reading in kilometers (KM) and quantity of fuel in liters (LITERS). This is the simplest form of the INPUT statement; chapter 3 provides a more extensive discussion of this statement with several variants. Following the INPUT statement, the mileage is calculated. Mileage is defined as the number of kilometers driven per liter. Mileage is computed by taking the distance between two consecutive odometer readings and dividing this by the number of liters consumed. The DIFference between two odometer readings is indicated by DIF(KM). The result is then divided by LITERS and recorded in MILEAGE. The line CARDS tells the SAS System that lines of input data (odometer readings, liters) follow. PROC PRINT then prints the results and PROC MEANS calculates and prints the averages.

All these elements will be discussed in greater detail in following chapters.

The real thing

The above program is entered into the system and handed to the SAS System for execution. The SAS System reports on the execution of the program using 2 files: the SAS log and the SAS list. The SAS log records which statements have been processed and how the program has run. This means among other things that it prints out error messages, information about the files created or loaded and where the results of the invoked procedures (PROC's) can be found. The second file is the SAS list: the results of program execution. Figure 2.2 contains the SAS log of the program described above. In the SAS log you will easily recognize the program, although with a few differences. On lines 1, 2 and 3, you see one of the methods of entering comments into a SAS program: comments are enclosed between /* and */. Be very careful however. IBM once chose to make /* in positions 1 and 2 of a record to mean 'end of file'; the result is that program execution stops! Although this is not a serious problem in most system environments, it is a good idea to leave at least 1 space at the beginning of the line before using /*. A second method of inserting comments is with the comment statement *.......; This statement is used for comments after individual SAS statements. In practice, it is useful to use these two forms of comment statements for different purposes: the comment statement (*.....;) for permanent comments on the hows and whys of the program and /*...*/ for temporarily commenting out a whole segment of a program during program development and testing. On line 4 is a TITLE2 statement. This places a title at the top of the SAS list on the second line of each page. There are also the statements TITLE (or TITLE1) through TITLE9. The LABEL statements (lines 7 and 8) serve only for documentation: the labels are stored by the SAS System with variables as a description. The SAS commentary on the program is mentioned in the NOTEs. After the DATA step is a note stating that certain results could not be calculated because data was missing. In addition, each step includes data about the files created (name, number of variables and so on) and output produced, as well as data on the use of computer time and memory. In the log, all lines are numbered. The numbers are automatically assigned by the SAS System: they do not have to be entered. It is clear from the log that the SAS System also numbers the entered data lines: take note of the gap between lines 10 and 71.

Figure 2.3 is the SAS list produced by this program. First of all the result of PROC PRINT: a simple table of data. The lines which the SAS log reported it could not process due to missing data are clearly indicated by a point instead of a number. In SAS jargon these are called 'missing values'. Then follows the output of PROC MEANS. MEANS is a simple procedure to obtain several descriptive statistics on the input data. In its most elementary form (such as in the sample program) PROC MEANS provides the following data for all numeric variables in the file:

N	number of 'observations' (=lines or records) with a 'non-missing value'
MEAN	average value of the data (this variable)
STANDARD DEVIATION	measure of the variation around the average of the data
MINIMUM VALUE	lowest value present in the input
MAXIMUM VALUE	highest value present in the input

```
1                      The SAS System (6.08)
                                     16:45 Wednesday, June 1, 1994

NOTE: Copyright(c) 1989 by SAS Institute Inc., Cary, NC USA.
NOTE: SAS (r) Proprietary Software Release 6.08  TS405

NOTE: The initialization phase used 0.06 CPU seconds and 1092K.

NOTE: SAS job started on Wednesday 01JUN94 16:45 (199406011645)

1     /*------------------------------------------------------------*/
2     /* FIRST SAMPLE PROGAM -FUEL CONSUMPTION                      */
3     /*------------------------------------------------------------*/
4          TITLE2 'SAMPLE PROGRAM 1';
5          DATA CARDATA;                    * TEMPORARY DATASET;
6          INPUT KM LITERS;                 * INPUT CONTAINS THESE VAR.S;
7          LABEL KM='ODOMETER READING';
8          LABEL MILEAGE ='KM PER LITER';
9          MILEAGE =DIF(KM)/LITERS;         * KM'S BETWEEN FILLUP/LITERS;
10         CARDS;

NOTE: Missing values were generated as a result of performing an
      operation on missing values.
      Each place is given by: (Number of times) at (Line):(Column).
      8 at 9:17
NOTE: The data set WORK.CARDATA has 60 observations and 3 variables.
NOTE: The DATA statement used 0.02 CPU seconds and 1763K.

10                                          * INPUT FOLLOW THIS LINE;
71         PROC PRINT;                      * PRINT SURVEY OF DATA;

NOTE: The PROCEDURE PRINT printed pages 1-2.
NOTE: The PROCEDURE PRINT used 0.02 CPU seconds and 1817K.

72         PROC MEANS;                      * CALCULATE AVERAGE VALUES;

NOTE: The PROCEDURE MEANS printed page 3.
NOTE: The PROCEDURE MEANS used 0.01 CPU seconds and 1955K.

NOTE: The SAS session used 0.27 CPU seconds and 1955K.
NOTE: SAS Institute BV, 1217 KR Hilversum, The Netherlands
```

Figure 2.2: The SAS log (the "listing") of the SAS program from the previous paragraph. Some statements have been added to make the program more readable and understandable: a TITLE2 statement and two LABEL statements. Notice the NOTE's that the SAS System adds at the end of the DATA-step. There is a note that indicates that some input data was missing, a note describing in general how the SAS data set is structured and one that indicates the computer resources used to complete the task. At the end of each procedure you will find on which pages the results are printed.

```
              The SAS System, Version 6.08                     1
                     SAMPLE PROGRAM 1
                              17:06 Wednesday, June 1, 1994

          OBS      KM      LITERS     MILEAGE

           1      9908      34.2        .
           2     10227      35.2       9.0625
           3     10493      27.4       9.7080
           4     10855      34.8      10.4023
           5     11212      36.5       9.7808
           6     11515      30.4       9.9671
           7     11823      32.4       9.5062
           8     12150      30.0      10.9000
           9     12451      30.8       9.7727
          10     12812      37.2       9.7043
          11     13039      22.8       9.9561
          12     13398      37.3       9.6247
          13     13836      41.9      10.4535
          14     14154      32.7       9.7248
          15     14567        .          .
          16     14829      25.7      10.1946
          17     15210        .          .
          18     15488      28.2       9.8582
          19     15905        .          .
          20     16209      29.3      10.3754
          21     16471      26.0      10.0769
          22     16757      28.0      10.2143
          23     17102      33.5      10.2985
          24     17583      48.4       9.9380
          25     17978        .          .
          26     18366        .          .
          27     18661      29.2      10.1027
          28     18888      22.9       9.9127
          29     19243      35.2      10.0852
          30     19437      20.0       9.7000
          31     19776      30.6      11.0784
          32     20089      29.7      10.5387
          33     20440        .          .
          34     20694      27.9       9.1039
          35     20902      23.0       9.0435
          36     21158      26.4       9.6970
          37     21442      30.9       9.1909
          38     21716      30.6       8.9542
          39     22043      37.5       8.7200
          40     22474      46.5       9.2688
          41     22733      29.0       8.9310
```

Figure 2.3 (part 1): The SAS list with the output from PROC PRINT. The MISSING VALUES that were reported in the log are clearly recognizable by the . in the columns containing the number of liters and the fuel consumption.

```
                    The SAS System, Version 6.08                    2
                         SAMPLE PROGRAM 1
                                    17:06 Wednesday, June 1, 1994

            OBS      KM      LITERS     MILEAGE

            42     23061      37.0       8.8649
            43     23321      28.5       9.1228
            44     23624      34.5       8.7826
            45     23928      32.8       9.2683
            46     24264      37.4       8.9840
            47     24268        .          .
            48     24482      22.9       9.3450
            49     24804      35.4       9.0960
            50     25102      34.0       8.7647
            51     25427      35.3       9.2068
            52     25666      24.6       9.7154
            53     25886      23.9       9.2050
            54     26219      33.0      10.0909
            55     26508      30.0       9.6333
            56     26854      35.2       9.8295
            57     27194      36.3       9.3664
            58     27524      37.0       8.9189
            59     28078      60.1       9.2180
            60     28446      37.9       9.7098
```

Figure 2.3 (part 2): PROC PRINT output (continued).

```
                    The SAS System, Version 6.08                    3
                         SAMPLE PROGRAM 1
                                    17:06 Wednesday, June 1, 1994
  Variable  Label              N        Mean       Std Dev      Minimum
  ---------------------------------------------------------------------
  KM        ODOMETER READING  60     19311.50      5401.65      9908.00
  LITERS                      53    32.4132075    6.9426230   20.0000000
  MILEAGE   KM PER LITER      52     9.6340083    0.5648638    8.7200000
  ---------------------------------------------------------------------

            Variable  Label              Maximum
            ----------------------------------------------
            KM        ODOMETER READING    28446.00
            LITERS                       60.1000000
            MILEAGE   KM PER LITER       11.0784314
            ----------------------------------------------
```

Figure 2.3 (part 3): PROC MEANS output. If nothing else has been specified PROC MEANS will calculate for all numeric variables in the data set: the number of lines with a non-missing value, the average value, the standard deviation, the lowest value and the highest value.

Basic principles and basic concepts of the SAS System

The SAS program presented in the preceding section already incorporates many basic principles of the SAS System. In this section these principles will be examined and explained in more detail one at a time.

The SAS structure

In the sample program, you can see that the SAS System recognizes two types of so-called STEPs: the DATA step, beginning with the DATA statement, and the PROC step, beginning with a PROC statement (figure 2.4).

```
DATA step
     - reading in data
     - data manipulation
     - construction of data sets

PROC step
     - analysis of data sets
     - preparation of reports
     - supporting routines
```

Figure 2.4: The two basic building blocks of the SAS System are the DATA-step and the PROC-step. Each has its own specific field of application.

DATA and PROC steps can be regarded as the building blocks of a SAS program. They can occur in any quantity or sequence. The DATA step is primarily used for entering and processing data, particularly for manipulations between sets of data (variables). The PROC step deals primarily with what to do with the data once it has been entered, such as PRINT, MEANS, and so on.

In Version 6 of the SAS System there is also PROC SQL, which overlaps DATA and PROC somewhat. PROC SQL can be used to enter information into SAS data sets (or read from SAS data sets) by means of standard SQL commands (Structured Query Language, a standardized data retrieval or query language). The input for PROC SQL can come from SAS data sets, but also from other sources such as DB2 databases or TERADATA database computers.

A general principle when using the SAS System is to leave as much as possible to the system. For example, you could calculate the average value of fuel consumption yourself, but PROC MEANS saves time and effort.

SAS syntax

SAS statements have a standard structure: they all begin with a keyword and end with a semicolon(;):

```
Keyword  further specification ;
```

Because the beginning and the end of a statement are so clearly recognizable, one statement after another can be placed on a single line or one statement can extend over several lines for the sake of legibility.

Above all do not forget the semicolon. Without the semicolon, the SAS System can no longer tell where a statement ends, which gives rise to many possible errors. Figure 2.5 illustrates the structure with some examples.

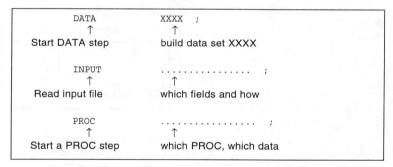

Figure 2.5: The SAS statement structure: a keyword, followed by further information about the what and how of the statement and finally a semicolon.

Variable and observation

The concepts *variable* and *observation* appear in the SAS log of the sample program. A variable is a certain type of data. Such a variable is labeled with a *name*. In the sample program we encountered KM and MILEAGE. The SAS System recognizes 2 kinds of variable: *character variable* meaning a string of text and *numeric variable* meaning a number, where it does not matter if it is an integer value or if there are fractions. Character variables can have a length of 1 to 200 characters. The SAS System determines the length by the first time such a variable is used, deriving it from the circumstances.

An observation is the set of specific values for all variables of an individual entity: to the odometer reading of 11823 is associated a fuel quantity of 32.4 liters and a mileage figure of 9.5062.

Together variables and observations form a matrix of information. The matrix can be thought of as rows and columns. The columns are the variables and the rows are the observations. For example, look back at the output of PROC PRINT, where this can be clearly seen.

The concepts variable and observation appear in all programming languages, sometimes under different names:

VARIABLE   field, column (SQL)

OBSERVATION   record, row (SQL)

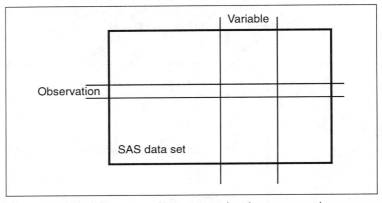

Figure 2.6: A SAS data set can be conceptualized as a rectangular structure of data, consisting of rows and columns. The rows are called observations, the columns represent the variables.

SAS names

The SAS System imposes some rules for the naming of SAS files and variables. They can be only 1 to 8 characters long and can be composed only of letters, numbers and the underscore sign (_). No spaces, no points. There is no difference between upper- and lowercase letters. It is best not to use any variable names in which the first and last position is an underscore, because the SAS System uses this convention for variables which it creates automatically (for example: _N_ whose value is the number of times the SAS System has begun executing the DATA step).

Because it can be difficult to give a clear name in 8 positions, the LABEL statement can be used to attach 40 positions of extra information to a variable. A similar thing applies to a data set name and a data set label. This will be explained in chapter 3.

It is often convenient to have a variable name in two segments. In this case, use the underscore to join the two segments, as in DEPT_NR for Department Number.

Structure of the SAS data set

Every SAS data set consists of 2 parts: a descriptive part and a data part. The descriptive part includes, among other things, what variables there are, if the variables are numeric or character, how many observations there are, when the data set was created and so on.

The descriptive part also includes the labels of the variables, so that it contains a complete, up-to-date documentation of the data set. (figure 2.7)

V6 has additional information about possible data set indexes and about data set sorting.

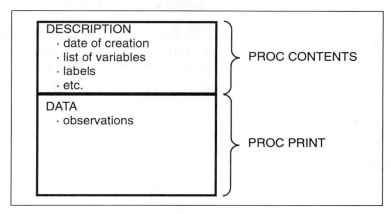

Figure 2.7: The SAS data set structure. A SAS dataset always contains two parts: a descriptive part and the actual data part. The descriptive part can be considered a simple information catalog: which data entities are there, how recent is the information, how many observations do exist. The data part contains the actual values of the variables for all observations.

The data part of the data set contains the values of all variables for all observations.

Note: the SAS data set structure has been revised in Version 6. SAS Version 6 can read and write SAS Version 5 data sets, but SAS Version 5 cannot work with Version 6 files.

We will return to the subject of SAS data storage in chapter 10.

Printing data set descriptions

In the sample program, you saw that PROC PRINT is used to print a data set. Note that it prints the data part of the data set. If you want to print the descriptive part of the data set, you must use another procedure: PROC CONTENTS. In figure 2.8 is the printout of the log of a variant of our original sample program. The DATA step is the same, but in place of PROC PRINT and PROC MEANS it contains PROC CONTENTS. Figure 2.9 shows its SAS list.

The PROC CONTENTS output consists of at least 3 parts: one part with general data about the data set: name, date of creation, number of observations and variables and so on, followed by another part containing more technical information, related to the system environment in which the SAS System is operating: actual name of the SAS library in which the data set is located (refer to SAS data sets and data libraries later in this chapter), space allocated and so on, and finally the functional description of the data set: the variables with their attributes (among other things their type, label and length).

The layout of the PROC CONTENTS output can be somewhat different from that shown in figure 2.9, depending on the system environment, but the same elements can always be found. The same is true for V5 contents.

```
1                    The SAS System (6.08)
                                    17:40 Wednesday, June 1, 1994

NOTE: Copyright(c) 1989 by SAS Institute Inc., Cary, NC USA.
NOTE: SAS (r) Proprietary Software Release 6.08   TS405

NOTE: The initialization phase used 0.06 CPU seconds and 1092K.

NOTE: SAS job started on Wednesday 01JUN94 17:40 (199406011740)

1    /*-------------------------------------------------------------*/
2    /* FIRST SAMPLE PROGAM - PROC CONTENTS                         */
3    /*-------------------------------------------------------------*/
4            TITLE2 'SAMPLE PROGRAM 1 VARIANT 2';
5            DATA CARDATA;              * TEMPORARY DATASET;
6            INPUT KM LITERS;           * INPUT CONTAINS THESE VAR.S;
7            LABEL KM='ODOMETER READING';
8            LABEL MILEAGE ='KM PER LITER';
9            MILEAGE =DIF(KM)/LITERS;   * KM'S BETWEEN FILLUP/LITERS;
10           CARDS;

NOTE: Missing values were generated as a result of performing an
      operation on missing values.
      Each place is given by: (Number of times) at (Line):(Column).
      8 at 9:17
NOTE: The data set WORK.CARDATA has 60 observations and 3 variables.
NOTE: The DATA statement used 0.02 CPU seconds and 1763K.

10                                     * INPUT FOLLOW THIS LINE;
71           PROC CONTENTS;            * PRINT DATA SET DESCRIPT.;

NOTE: The PROCEDURE CONTENTS printed page 1.
NOTE: The PROCEDURE CONTENTS used 0.03 CPU seconds and 1931K.

NOTE: The SAS session used 0.27 CPU seconds and 1955K.
NOTE: SAS Institute BV, 1217 KR Hilversum, The Netherlands
```

Figure 2.8: The same program as presented in figure 2.3, but this time PROC PRINT and PROC MEANS are replaced by PROC CONTENTS, which prints the description part of a SAS data set.

```
          The SAS System, Version 6.08                         1
              SAMPLE PROGRAM 1 VARIANT 2
                            17:40 Wednesday, June 1, 1994

                      CONTENTS PROCEDURE

Data Set Name: WORK.CARDATA              Observations:          60
Member Type:   DATA                      Variables:             3
Engine:        V608                      Indexes:               0
Created:       17:40 Wednesday, June 1, 1994   Observation Length: 24
Last Modified: 17:40 Wednesday, June 1, 1994   Deleted Observations: 0
Protection:                              Compressed:            NO
Data Set Type:                           Sorted:                NO
Label:

              -----Engine/Host Dependent Information-----

        Data Set Page Size:       30720
        Number of Data Set Pages: 1
        File Format:              607
        First Data Page:          1
        Max Obs per Page:         1272
        Obs in First Data Page:   60
        Physical Name:            SYS94152.T164528.RA000.TILANE.R0000097
        Release Created:          6.08
        Release Last Modified:    6.08
        Created by:               TILANE
        Last Modified by:         TILANE
        Subextents:               1
        Total Blocks Used:        5

        -----Alphabetic List of Variables and Attributes-----

        #   Variable   Type   Len   Pos   Label
        -------------------------------------------------------
        1   KM         Num     8     0    ODOMETER READING
        2   LITERS     Num     8     8
        3   MILEAGE    Num     8    16    KM PER LITER
```

Figure 2.9: The output of PROC CONTENTS. The first part presents a number of general attributes of the data set. The next part describes a number of technical details about the dataset, related to the system environment in which the SAS System operates. The bottom part shows the functional content of the data set.

SAS data sets and data libraries

SAS data sets are completely under the control of the SAS System. They are collected in SAS data libraries. In a SAS data library, many SAS data sets can be stored. In addition other SAS files can be included, such as the so-called catalogs. Catalogs are collections of special purpose information, generally of a descriptive nature. Thus FORMAT's (layout definitions for printing variables), SAS/AF and SAS/FSP screen definitions and PROC REPORT layout definitions are contained in catalogs.

Before a SAS data library can be used in a program, it must first be identified to the SAS System. This is done with a LIBNAME statement or an allocation command from the operating system.

All these statements join a symbolic name, the libref or DD name, with the actual name of the data library (see also chapter 1). In the original sample program this allocation is not directly visible. But you can see that it exists for the data library with libref work, because the data set created by the SAS System is called WORK.MILEAGE (see SAS log).

The physical form and structure of the data library depends on the system environment. In the IBM MVS environment it is an OS data set of type PS; on a Digital VAX or PC it is a subdirectory.

In figure 2.10 you see a data library schematic. It is represented by means of a libref or DD name linked to the physical data library on disk or tape. Such a data library contains a directory referencing all data sets, catalogs and other types of SAS files. A catalog is in turn referencing the various descriptions which it contains. Together all these elements form a 'path', similar to what is also used in MS-DOS. The elements of this path are separated by periods.

Thus MYLIB.AFCAT.MAIN .MENU refers to a SAS/AF menu called MAIN in the AF catalog called AFCAT in the data library identified by the libref (or DD name) MYLIB.

SAS data sets have only 2 levels in their names, for example, MYLIB.MY_D_SET refers to the data set MY_D_SET in the data library identified by the libref MYLIB. (Formally there is a third element: DATA, indicating which type of SAS file is involved, as opposed to the file type CATALOG. This DATA can normally be left out.)

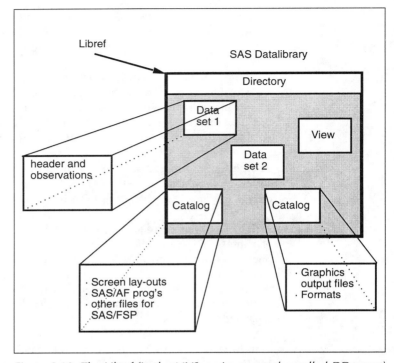

Figure 2.10: The Libref (in the MVS environment also called DD-name) establishes a link between the SAS session and the physical data library. The data library is the storage location for all SAS files, particularly data sets and catalogs. Each data set and every catalog entry are unambiguously named by the libref, followed by the data set or catalog name and after that (in case of a catalog) the name and type of the catalog entry.

Choice of variables

New SAS users often have a difficult time choosing between whether to enter information as variables or as observations. A guideline is: if more data of the same type are added, it is should lead to more observations, not more variables. A simple test is also whether or not the mean value of a numeric variable is meaningful. Figure 2.11 shows printouts of two small SAS data sets. We see that in the first variant both rules are violated (imagine the effect of adding figures for the third quarter), whereas in the second they are not.

```
(variant 1)

                ENTITY        QTR1        QTR2
(NORMALLY)      Turnover      126         133
WRONG           Cost          85          97
                Profit        41          36


(variant 2)
                QTR   TURNOVER  COST      PROFIT
(NORMALLY)      1     126       85        41
CORRECT         2     133       97        36
```

Figure 2.11: The choice between variables and observations. A good rule of the thumb is, that adding more information of the same kind (e.g. the results of the third quarter) should lead to more observations, not to more variables. Another rule is that normally the average value of a numeric variable should be something meaningful.

Be aware that this is a guideline and not a hard and fast rule. Sometimes it can be very handy to process a data set as in the first variant. Keep in mind that in a DATA step all variables are always available at the same time, but only for one observation (the DATA step works "horizontally" - think of the PROC PRINT output) and that PROC steps work by variables ("vertically").

You are not stuck to the variant you have. If it is necessary you can easily transpose the data sets (from variant 1 to variant 2 or vice versa) by means of PROC TRANSPOSE (see chapter 18). The following statements illustrate that for the data sets in figure 2.11,:

From variant 1 to 2:

```
PROC TRANSPOSE DATA=ONE OUT=TWO NAME=QTR;
    ID ENTITY;
    VAR QTR1 QTR2;
```

From variant 2 to 1:

```
PROC TRANSPOSE DATA=TWO OUT=ONE NAME=QTR;
    ID QTR;
    VAR TURNOVER COST PROFIT;
```

Graphical presentation

Besides tabular reporting, such as we have already encountered with
PROC PRINT, the SAS System also provides many facilities for
graphical presentation of results. The SAS/GRAPH product contains a
wide variety of advanced graphical features. But a graph can also be
created by very simple means. To conclude this introductory chapter, let
PROC PLOT take the place of PROC PRINT in our by now familiar
sample program. PROC PLOT is one of the SAS System's printer
graphics procedures: PLOT makes various plots, simply, on any printer.
Not nearly as nice looking as SAS/GRAPH or a PC graphics program
could make them, but fine for any printer or terminal. It also has the
advantage that it is easily included into batch processing jobs: it makes
rough graphs quickly in high volume, after that you could work out more
details for specific cases using the power of SAS/GRAPH. In our case
PROC PLOT is called with the following statements:

```
PROC PLOT;
   PLOT MILEAGE*KM;
```

Figure 2.12 shows you how this plot looks.

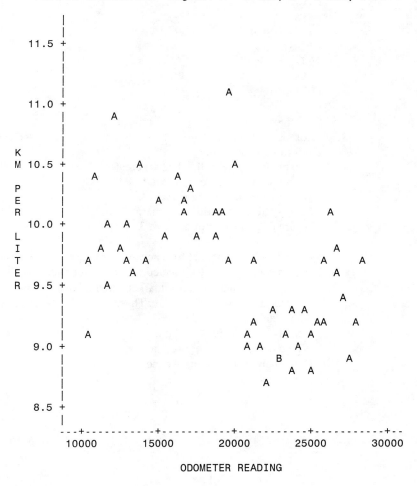

Figure 2.12: PROC PLOT makes it simple to present data graphically. For (far) more options and (far) more appealing results you can use SAS/GRAPH software.

Exercises

1. Which variable names are correct?
    NAME
    AGE
    RESIDENCE
    RESID.
    2ND_SCOR
    SCORE
    QTR ONE

2. Look again at the log of the sample program (figure 2.2) and answer
    the following questions:
    - What is the name of the data set created?
    - What are the variables in the data set?
    - Which variables are numeric?
    - How many observations are there?
    - Where does the output on page 3 come from?

3. Company ABC is looking for a new location for their business. For
    this purpose, they have collected the following data for 10 loca-
    tions: unemployment figures, market potential in the region, loca-
    tion costs and income per family. These data are to be entered into
    a SAS data set.
    - Which do you pick as variables?
    - Which do you pick as observations?
    - How many observations are there?

CHAPTER 3

Introduction to the DATA Step

As outlined in the previous chapter, the DATA step primarily creates SAS data sets and processes files by *observation*. The creation of SAS data sets can take place through the loading and processing of existing SAS data sets, but also on the basis of information in other (non-SAS) computer files. The possibilities are practically limitless.

The DATA statement

A DATA step always begins with a DATA statement, in which it is specified which SAS data sets shall be created in the step. The structure of the statement is as follows:

```
DATA datasetname<(options)> <dataset name<(options)> ... >;
```

Example:

```
DATA DSET   LABEL='Sample data set'
            DROP= VAR1 VAR2
            RENAME= (VAR3=VAR30));
```

The elements between <...> in a statement are optional. In the structure of a statement the syntax elements are written in uppercase letters and the other elements, your own working labels or values, are written in lowercase letters.

After the DATA keyword, all SAS data sets to be created are listed. Usually there is only one, but there can be a whole series. If there is no data set named in the DATA statement, the SAS System will name one automatically. The first is named DATA1, the second DATA2 and so on. A number of options can be specified for each SAS data set. These are given between parentheses after the data set name. The most important options are listed in figure 3.1.

The LABEL option links an explanatory text of up to 40 positions with the data set name, in the same way that the LABEL statement links explanatory text with a variable name.

```
LABEL= 'explanatory text'
KEEP= list of variables that should be written to the data set
DROP= list of variables that should be left out of the data set
RENAME=(old name=new name ...)


ALTER=password (no deletion, no replacement)
WRITE=password (no update of observations)
PROTECT=password (combination of ALTER and WRITE)
READ=password (no read access)
PW=password (combination of all other variants)
```

Figure 3.1: The most frequently used SAS data set options.

The KEEP and DROP options specify which variables are to be included in or excluded from the data set. By default, all variables which come up are included in the data set. By using the KEEP option, only those variables listed after KEEP are included, as likewise those listed after DROP are excluded. There exist also KEEP and DROP statements in the DATA step. These have a similar effect, but are valid for all data sets mentioned in the DATA statement. The data set option variant makes it possible to specify per data set which variables to store.

RENAME makes it possible to store variables in the data set under a different name from that used during the execution of the DATA step. The old name (the name used in the DATA step) and the new name (name under which the variable is to be stored) are placed between parentheses after RENAME.

Each of the 5 password options provides some aspect of security regarding the data set. It is possible for different aspects of the data set to have different passwords. ALTER works on the data set level: the data set can only be deleted or overwritten if the password is given. WRITE prevents the alteration of the contents of a data set, and thus prevents changing or adding to observations. READ blocks reading the data set. To do anything with the data set, the password must always be used. PROTECT and PW are combinations of the other password options. They can be used if there is no need to protect a specific aspect with a specific password.

It is also possible, of course, to use a separate security system, such as RACF or Top Secret under the IBM MVS operating system.

Reading data

To enter data from any source into an SAS data set, the SAS System has to know three things: which data, where the data are located, how the data are to be interpreted. The most important statements for entering data are the INFILE statement, which tells the SAS System where the data are located and what type of file is involved, and the INPUT statement, which specifies which variables exist and where and how they are to be located in the input record. To round off this section also the CARDS and the OUTPUT statements will be discussed.

List input

The INPUT statement recognizes three methods for specifying how data are to be read by the SAS System. The simplest is the list input method. This method however places several restrictions on the input format:

- Variables must be separated by at least one space;

- Character variables can be no longer than 8 positions and contain no spaces ('DEPT_NR' is acceptable, but 'DEPT NR' is not);

- There can be no 'missing' variables: the presence of 'missing' variables must be clearly indicated in the input record.

As long as these restrictions are observed, the list input method is extremely simple: list all variables in the INPUT statement in the same order as they appear in the input record. To indicate that a variable is a character variable add a $ sign after the variable name. Throughout SAS software the $ sign is an indication that a character variable is involved.

In list input, the SAS System locates the first non-blank position and begins reading the next variable from that point. The input field is presumed to end when a blank space is reached.

Figure 3.2 shows an example of list input and the record layout which can be read with it.

```
    INPUT NAME $ AGE WEIGHT SEX $;

would read the following input records correctly:

    input record postition
    1        10          20          30
    |---|----|----|----|----|----|-
    JOHN 12 38 M
    MARIA    11 32   F
            PETE   15    47          M
```

Figure 3.2: The list input statement in practice. All three input lines will be interpreted correctly.

In practice list input is primarily used when you want to enter some test data into a data set quickly. It is then easy to comply with all the restrictions as you have the layout of the input records in your own hands.

Column input

In column input the position of the field in the input record is also entered, by stating the first and last position after the variable in the INPUT statement. The SAS System automatically finds the entered value between the indicated columns. All character variables will be stripped of any leading blanks: the text will be 'left aligned'. Thus in the first 3 lines of the example in figure 3.3, the variable NAME will have the value JOHN and the variable AGE the value 12.

If an input field occupies only 1 column, you only need to specify that one position. Again: in case of a character field, place a $ sign after the variable.

The INPUT statement from the previous section will appear in column input as shown in figure 3.3.

Note that the variables can now be directly adjacent to one another, because the SAS System knows by means of the column specifications exactly where a variable begins or ends.

In the example it is clear that the variable AGE can take an arbitrary location in the input field: in the beginning, middle or end. The field will still be correctly interpreted.

```
    INPUT NAME    $ 1-8
          AGE       10-16
          WEIGHT  17-18
          SEX     $ 19;

would read the following input records correctly:

input record postition
1         10          20          30
|---|----|----|----|----|----|-
JOHN        12      38M
    JOHN        12    38M
        JOHN        1238M
MARIA       11        32F
    PETE            1547M
```

Figure 3.3: Column input: the name of the variable is followed by the position of the first and last column of the input field.

Pointer or formatted input

Using the pointer or formatted input method, the start position of a field in the input file is indicated by a pointer, placed before the variable. The most common method of doing this is to mark the location with an @ sign, followed by the start position. Be careful: the SAS System begins counting with position 1! After the variable comes information on how the input field is to be read, in the "informat". This informat also states the length of the field. For instance $8. means 'a character field of 8 positions' and 7. means 'a numerical field of 7 positions'. The general structure looks like this:

```
INPUT pointer variable informat
      pointer variable informat
      pointer variable informat
      ... and so on ;
```

To enter the data in figure 3.3 using pointer input, the following statement is required:

```
INPUT @1 NAME $8.
      @10 AGE 7.
      @17 WEIGHT 2.
      @19 SEX $1. ;
```

One of the advantages of the pointer method is that fields can be read in an arbitrary order. If the correct pointers are used, the SAS System will automatically read at the right locations.

The flexibility of this method lies in the fact that the pointer can also be governed by a numeric variable. If you place a variable name after @, then the value of the variable indicates the position where input begins. It is naturally the responsibility of the programmer to give the correct value to the variable. You can use this capability to read records in which the position of the next field depends on the length of the previous field.

Besides the absolute address pointer method (@pointer), there are two relative methods, one explicit and one implicit. A pointer indicator with a + sign means: advance ... positions. The implicit method is based on the fact that the informat information also contains a length specification of the field that is read using the informat. The SAS System uses this indication to position the pointer at the first column after the input field.

The statement

```
INPUT @12 LOCATION $6. +5 DATE DATE7.;
```

first reads a location from positions 12 through 17. As a result, the pointer stands at position 18. Then the pointer is advanced 5 positions (to position 23) and there a date 7 positions long will be read. The DATE input specification will be described in the next section.

For clarity and legibility of programs, it is advisable to use the absolute pointer (@) wherever possible.

Informat information

Informats are used to tell the SAS System how an input field should be read. For example 5. means that the field is numeric and that it is 5 positions long. The SAS System supplies many standard informats, and informats can also be user-defined. In figure 3.4 some of the most common informats are listed. For others, it is advised that you consult the Language Guide (chapter Informats).

Name of Format	Type and default length	Description
w.	numeric	w positions long
w.d	numeric	w positions long, decimal positions
COMMAXw.d	numeric (1)	decimal field with "," as decimal separator
IBw.d	numeric (4)	binary figures
$w.	character	w positions long, without "leading blanks"
$CHARw.	character (1)	w positions long, maintaining "leading blanks"
$VARYINGw.	character (8)	variable field length
DATEw.	numeric (7)	date in form 12JAN92
DDMMYYw.	numeric (6)	date in form 230991
MONYYw.	numeric (5)	date in form APR92
TIMEw.	numeric (8)	time in form 12:54:00

Figure 3.4: Some of the most commonly used SAS Informat's. The "w" represents the total field length, the "d" the number of decimal positions, if these cannot be derived explicitly from the input. The second column notes the w-value that will be used if no value is specified (the default value).

All informats (and as we shall see later, all formats) include a period in their name. This is how they can be distinguished from variables. And of course, all character informats begin with a $ sign.

If an informat is specified, the SAS System will also carry out data validation: thus if non-numerical data occurs in a field that is to be read with a numerical informat, an error message will be given.

In the table of figure 3.4 'w' always indicates the input field width. After the length specification comes the period, the hallmark of every informat. There is a minimum and maximum length for all informats. These limits do not normally cause problems. Many informats have also a default length, the length which applies if no 'w' value is given. These are given in the table. Thus 'DATE.' means the same as 'DATE7.'. The 'd' specification indicates the number of decimals that the SAS System can handle *if no decimal point (or comma, in the COMMAX. informat) appears in the input field.* The informat 8.2 indicates a numerical field 8 positions long with 2 decimal places. The 8.2 informat will thus read 12345 as 123.45, but 987.6 as 987.60. The $VARYING. informat reads fields of variable length. The condition is that the informat be followed directly by a numeric variable, which contains the actual length of the field. The length specification in $VARYING. indicates the maximum length of the field. If the input variable is already defined with a specific length, there does not need to be any additional length given in $VARYING: the length of the variable is fixed.

The informat information can be given in the INPUT statement, as already presented, but it can also be entered using an INFORMAT statement. The advantage of this latter method is that the informat will be stated in the descriptive part of the SAS data set and can thus be consulted via PROC CONTENTS. In the INFORMAT statement you specify the variable followed by the informat specification. Should the informat be applied to more variables, the whole series is entered at one time:

```
INFORMAT var1 var2 var3 ... $5.;
```

The following two variants are thus equivalent:

```
INPUT @10 DATE DATE7.;
```

```
INFORMAT DATE DATE7.;
INPUT @10 DATE;
```

Special features of the INPUT statement

The three above forms of the INPUT statement can be used interchangeably, even within one INPUT statement, but this is not recommended as it easily gets very confusing.

In some situations, it is desirable to use informat information in combination with list input. By just including an informat specification, the SAS System thinks that it has switched to pointer input so it does not look for the next non-blank position, and starts to read where the pointer is currently located. You can avoid this by preceding the informat with a colon (:). This is illustrated in figure 3.5.

```
input record postition
1      10       20        30
|---|----|----|----|----|----|-
MARIA  17DEC61
MARIA  17DEC61
MARIA     17DEC61


INPUT NAME $ BIRTH_DT DATE7.;
```

would result in:
line 1:   NAME=MARIA, BIRTH_DT=17DEC61
line 2:   NAME=MARIA, BIRTH_DT=17DEC06
line 3:   NAME=MARIA, BIRTH_DT=. (missing value!)

```
INPUT NAME $ BIRTH_DT :DATE7.;
```

would read all input lines correctly.

Figure 3.5: To use an informat in conjunction with list input, it must be preceded by a colon (:). Without that the SAS System assumes that you switched to pointer input and starts reading from the current pointer position: 7. In the second input line this has as a consequence that the second position of the year is not read while in the third input line the SAS System will only read 17D, which results in an error message.

There are a number of other options you can use in the INPUT statement for more specialized forms of input. One option is quite important: using the @ sign at the end of the input statement ('trailing @ sign'). With this, the SAS System knows that the input record must be retained for a further INPUT statement. You see it illustrated in the following example:

```
INPUT @1 TYPE $1. @2 POINT 2. @;
IF TYPE = 'A'
   THEN INPUT @POINT NAME $15.;
   ELSE INPUT @10 DATE DATE7.;
```

The first INPUT statement reads a record-type identification and some pointer information. The IF statement first tests whether we have record type A, in which case it reads the variable NAME on position POINT, otherwise it reads DATE on position 10. The IF statement will be explained in chapter 6: Programming of the DATA step.

A very useful application of this technique is the selective reading of a file: first only the variables are read which contain the information needed to determine whether or not to read the record. If the record meets the selection criteria, then the rest of the variables are read in a following INPUT statement. This may save substantial amounts of processing. Reading numeric data or date values requires relatively a lot of time.

INFILE statement

The INFILE statement serves in the first place to indicate which file should be read in the following INPUT statements. The form is:

```
INFILE fileref <options>;
```

Fileref

The fileref refers to an allocation statement. This will in many cases be a FILENAME statement, but it can also be a system command, such as a JCL DD statement in an IBM MVS batch environment or a SET command in the Windows or OS/2 environment. In many cases the FILENAME statement is preferable. In all cases the principle is the same: a temporary, symbolic name is given to a file on disk or tape: the fileref. The SAS System communicates with the computer's operating system by means of the fileref. If the SAS System gives the operating system the command 'read from file with fileref...', the operating system knows the physical location of the file on disk or tape and carries out the command. In the example in figure 3.6 the fileref is always FILE1, the choice is however completely arbitrary, as long as it fulfills the rules for SAS names. More information about the FILENAME statement in your system environment can be found in the system appendices (H through M).

It is also possible to place the physical file reference (the name known to the computer system, including any necessary directory information) directly in the INFILE statement. To make it easy to process another input file with the same program, it is recommended not to use this option but to choose a FILENAME statement or a system command external to the program.

After the specification of the fileref, a number of other options can be used in the INFILE statement, in which special instructions can be given on how the SAS System should read the file and how the SAS System should operate in special situations, such as instructions to rewind a tape after the read.

```
general:
 FILENAME  FILE1 'data set name';
 DATA XYZ;
  INFILE FILE1;
  INPUT ...........;
  ........


IBM-MVS batch:
 //ABC     JOB   ...................
 //        EXEC  SAS
 //FILE1   DD    DSN=datasetname,DISP=SHR
 //SYSIN   DD    *
 DATA XYZ;
  INFILE FILE1;
  INPUT ...........;
  ........


UNIX:
 FILE1=/datasetname
 export FILE1
 DATA XYZ;
  INFILE FILE1;
  INPUT ...........;
  ........
```

Figure 3.6: Examples of the INFILE statement in its context. Via an allocation statement a link is established between the fileref and the actual file name.

The total list of options for the INFILE statement is rather long and varies for each system environment. Figure 3.7 lists a few of the most used options.

END=	boolean variable,1 when reading the last record
EOF=	program label where end-of-file routine is located (see text)
FIRSTOBS=	first record number that will be read from a file
OBS=	last record number that will be read from a file
MISSOVER	prevents reading on in next record in case of "missing values"
FILENAME=	character variable loaded by SAS with the data set name

Figure 3.7: The most commonly used options of the INFILE statement.

End-of-file conditions

The END and EOF options are both instructions for what to do when the end of the input file is reached. After END= you specify a numeric variable. The value of this variable will be supplied by the SAS System. During file reading, the value is always 0; only when reading the last record does the value become 1. This can subsequently be tested *during* the processing of the last input record, for example, to activate special end-of-file routines. The EOF routine can do something similar: a program label is inserted after it: a location indicator in the program telling the SAS System where to go *after* reading and processing the last input record. Such a label goes before the first statement that should be executed if the SAS System jumps to that label. The label is followed by an ':' to separate it from the statement. In later chapters you will be shown more applications of these program labels. In the case of end-of-file processing its use could look more or less like this:

```
DATA ....;
    INFILE MYINPUT EOF=FINISH;
    ...
    (program statements)
    ...
    RETURN;
    FINISH:
    (end-of-file processing part)
```

The RETURN statement before the label prevents the SAS System from executing the end-of-file routine after each input line.

Starting and stopping reading of input

The FIRSTOBS and OBS options are used to indicate start and stop positions for reading an input file. FIRSTOBS=100 means start reading at the 100th input record, OBS=200 means stop at the 200th record.

MISSOVER means that the SAS System will not continue reading past the current input record if it cannot find values for all variables in the INPUT statement, but will assign a 'missing value' to any variable for which no value appears on the current line. This is especially important with list input.

Variables given in the FILENAME option shall be filled in by the SAS System with the name of the data set.

CARDS statement

The CARDS statement is only used to tell the SAS System that input records immediately follow and thus do not need to be read from an external file. In practice this is only used for test files. The CARDS statement functions as a separator between the DATA step and the input lines. Instead of CARDS you can also use DATALINES. The CARDS statement has no options. If it is necessary to use INFILE options, this can be done using an INFILE statement with the fileref CARDS.

Adding observations to the SAS data set

In the absence of any special instructions, the SAS System will write all variables (except a few 'automatic' variables maintained by the SAS System) as an observation to the data set after the last statement of a DATA step has been executed. As indicated in the beginning of the chapter, you can use KEEP and DROP options, respectively, to specify which variables should or should not be output.

RETURN statement

The RETURN statement also appears frequently as the last statement in the DATA step. If the SAS System encounters a RETURN statement in the main loop of the DATA step, it writes out the observation and returns to the beginning of the DATA step for the following input line. In the section about the INFILE statement on page 49 this is demonstrated in conjunction with the EOF option of the INFILE statement.

Output statement

The OUTPUT statement forces the output of an observation. It is used particularly if more than one data set is created in a DATA step or if more than one observation must be output on the basis of one input line. The automatic addition of observations when SAS reaches the end of the DATA step is suppressed if an OUTPUT statement appears in the DATA step. If there are more possible output data sets, the data set where the observation is to go should be stated in the OUTPUT statement. The following example illustrates this concept:

```
DATA MALE FEMALE;
 INFILE ....;
 INPUT .... @19 SEX $1. ....;
 ....
 (program statements)
 ....
 IF SEX='M'
      THEN OUTPUT MALE;
      ELSE OUTPUT FEMALE;
```

Structure of the DATA step

In this chapter you have seen how a DATA step can be used to import data from an external source into the SAS System. For each input line, the SAS System runs once through all the statements of the DATA step, as shown schematically in figure 3.8. In principle all variables are set at 'missing value' at the beginning of a new run. They are then gradually filled in during the run through the DATA step.

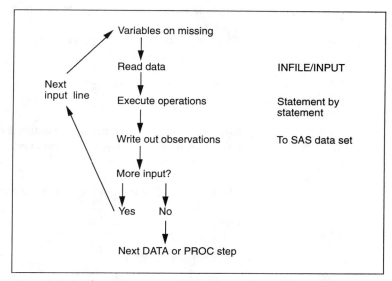

Figure 3.8: A schematic presentation of the working of the DATA step. For every line in the input file there will be a pass through the DATA-step, from the DATA statement till the end of the step. If all input lines are processed the SAS System will proceed to the next DATA or PROC step.

We have also seen that the RETURN statement can act as the end of the DATA step: it concludes the processing and outputs the variables with the values they have at that moment. If during processing a condition occurs in which no observations are to be output, the DELETE statement can be used. The DELETE statement halts the processing of the current record, outputs nothing and tells the SAS System to begin processing again at the next input record.

Exercises

1.   We want to read input records with the following layout:

```
input record postition
1        10        20        30
|---|----|----|----|----|----|-
IAN  292165 63   07MAR84
```

Give the values of the variables resulting from the following INPUT statements:

a.   INPUT NAME $ AGE SALARY DEPT JOINDATE DATE7.;

b.   INPUT NAME $ AGE 5-7 SALARY 5. @12 DEPT 3.
         JOINDATE DATE7.;

c.   INPUT @1 NAME $5. AGE 2. SALARY DEPT
         JOINDATE : DATE7.;

Note: these INPUT statements are cautionary examples of bad programming, all input styles are used in each, which produces a confusing result.

2.   Which of the following DATA steps are incorrect and why?

```
DATA ALPHA;
    INPUT A B C $;
    INFILE XYZ;

DATA BETA;
    INPUT A  1-4  B  5-6    C;

DATA GAMMA;
    INPUT  A  @3  B  6.  C  12-11;
    CARDS;
```

```
DATA DELTA;
    INFILE;
    INPUT A  1-4  B  5-6  C;

DATA EPSILON;
    INFILE XYZ;
    INPUT  A  @6  B  $4.  C;
    CARDS;

DATA ITHA;
    INFILE XYZ;
    INPUT  A  B  @15  3.  C;
```

3.   What is the difference between:

```
INPUT  A $ 3    B $ 6;
```

and

```
INPUT  A $ 3.   B $ 6.;
```

CHAPTER 4

Introduction to the PROC Step

The PROC step

The procedures in the SAS System (PROCs) provide ready-to-use processing tools for whole SAS data sets. The power of the SAS System lies precisely in the availability of so many procedures. These PROCs all begin with a PROC statement. Here is where the name of the procedure is stated as well as to which data set the procedure is to be applied.

```
PROC procedurename DATA=data set <options>;
    <specification statements>
```

With some procedures you specify a complete data library instead of a single data set and some procedures can also take a non-SAS data set as input. We confine ourselves here to the general case: one input data set is to be given in the DATA= specification of the PROC statement. If the DATA specification is left out and there is therefore no data set given, the SAS System uses the most recently created data set as input. Normally a number of additional options can be included in the PROC statement. These are PROC specific and will be dealt with in the descriptions of individual PROCs.

After the PROC statement, one or more specification statements can follow to tell the SAS System specifically what the PROC should do and how it should do it. In some PROCs certain specification statements are mandatory, in others they are purely optional. There are also a number of universal specification statements. These will be discussed here before the we go over to the specific PROCs (see figure 4.1).

The VAR statement

The VAR statement, specifying one or more variables, tells the SAS System which variables are to be involved in the procedure. Leaving it out has the consequence of involving all eligible variables, in PROC MEANS for example all numeric variables.

TITLE and FOOTNOTE statements

The TITLE and FOOTNOTE statements are used to format the output. TITLE produces title lines at the top, FOOTNOTE produces lines at the bottom of the page. There is a difference between the two statements in how they define which line the text should be printed on: TITLE6 always goes on line 6. FOOTNOTE3 does not automatically go on the third line

VAR variable list;	Specify which variables are included in the working of the procedure
TITLE 'text';	Title lines at the top of the output pages, max. 10 lines: TITLEn 'text on line n';
FOOTNOTE 'text';	Text at the bottom of the output pages, highest number (up to 10) at bottom line
LABEL variable='text';	Description of variable
BY variable list;	Processing of the procedure per BY-group
WHERE clause;	Procedure only processes observations that fulfill the conditions

Figure 4.1: General statements that are often used in the PROC step. TITLE and FOOTNOTE can be used anywhere, LABEL, BY and WHERE can be used in the DATA step as well.

from the bottom. FOOTNOTE statements employ a kind of 'push up' mechanism. The FOOTNOTE statement with the highest rank is placed on the bottom line of the page. Other lines are placed relative to this one. Thus with a FOOTNOTE1, FOOTNOTE2 and FOOTNOTE3 statement, FOOTNOTE3 goes on the bottom line and the FOOTNOTE1 statement two lines up. Titles and footnotes are not bound to a single procedure: they remain operative until another TITLE or FOOTNOTE statement is specified.

LABEL statements

The LABEL statement, the same one we encountered in chapter 2, can be used to label a variable for the duration of the procedure. This label takes precedence over any label for the variable that might be present in the SAS data set. Many procedures have the ability to print out variables with their labels.

BY statement

The BY statement tells the SAS System not to deal with the data set as a whole, but to group all observations for which the variables that are mentioned in the BY statement have the same values. In other words, the procedure carries out its processing by BY group.

In order to use the BY statement, the data set must be sorted according to the values of the BY variables. PROC SORT is the tool for properly sorting a SAS data set. It will be covered later in this chapter. Instead of sorting the data set may also be indexed on the BY variables. Creation of indexes will be discussed later.

The BY statement also has a few special options. DESCENDING, placed before a variable indictaes to the SAS System that the variable is sorted in descending order. NOT SORTED tells the SAS System that the data set is not sorted, but that every value change of a BY variable indicates the beginning of a new BY-group.

WHERE clause

WHERE processing is a simple means to select for inclusion in the procedure only those observations from a data set that meet the specified criteria. There is both a WHERE data set option and a WHERE statement. Using the data set option, the WHERE clause is placed in parentheses directly after the data set, as with all data set options and the clause itself is also placed in parentheses, as in this example:

```
PROC PRINT DATA=CLIENTS(WHERE=(CITY='AMSTERDAM'));
```

The principle of the WHERE clause is that only observations which satisfy the clause are processed. Observations which do not satisfy the WHERE clause are not read by the SAS System and are therefore not processed. The form of the statement is:

```
WHERE clause;
```

Usually such a clause has the form of a logical comparison as in:

```
WHERE CITY='AMSTERDAM';
```

But there are also a number of constructions specific to WHERE clauses.

Logical expressions and comparisons will be explored further in the chapter on programming the DATA step (chapter 6).

The specific WHERE clause constructions are shown in figure 4.2.

BETWEEN - AND	Specifies a range. Example: `WHERE AGE BETWEEN 18 AND 65;`
CONTAINS (for character strings)	Selects on presence of a string. Example: `WHERE CITY CONTAINS 'DAM';` selects AMSTERDAM ROTTER-DAM, DAMASCUS etc.
IS NULL or IS MISSING	Self explanatory
LIKE	Character comparison with "wild characters" _ for one character, % for string. Examples: `WHERE NAME LIKE 'ERI_';` selects ERIK, ERIC but not ERIKA `WHERE NAME LIKE 'WIL%';` selects WILBUR, WILLIE, WILMA, WILHELMINA
=* (Sounds like, Soundex algorithm)	`WHERE NAME =* 'JOHNSON';` selects JOHNSON, JANSEN, JENSZEN etc.

Figure 4.2: Some of the special WHERE clause constructions.

The BETWEEN-AND is nothing other than a reformulation: WHERE 18 <= AGE <= 65; will give the same result. The CONTAINS clause looks to see if the argument text (DAM in the example of figure 4.2) appears anywhere (it does not matter where) in the clause variable. IS ZERO or IS MISSING selects only the observations in which the given variable is zero or missing. This is also a direct reformulation of a logical equation: VAR = 0 or VAR = . The LIKE formulation provides pattern recognition: in principle a direct character comparison is made, but a wildcard facility is also available which uses the _ or the % signs in the comparison text to stand for any character or series of characters: the _ sign stands for any single character and the % sign stands for any series of characters.

Finally the =* operator ('sounds like') uses the patented Soundex algorithm to filter somewhat similar sounds. It is often used where names must be given by telephone, because in that situation, although a name might be phonetically clear, you might not know how to spell it. The test is not completely watertight, however. It is of course quite arbitrary that in the example 'JENTZEN' does not get filtered.

PROC SORT

In the section on the BY statement it has already been stated that, when using the BY statement, the data set as a rule should be sorted according to the BY variables. This is done with PROC SORT. Its basic form is:

```
PROC SORT DATA=dataset OUT=dataset <options>;
  BY variable list;
```

The PROC statement should in principle state both the input and the output data sets. If the output data set is left out, then the input data set will be replaced by the sorted data set. However, since there is no 'update in place', you must make sure that in the data library you are using there is enough room for both data sets. Available options in the PROC statement are NODUPKEY or NODUPLICATES. NODUPKEY removes observations which are identical to the BY variables. With this, each BY group will consist of only 1 observation. NODUPLICATES removes fully duplicated observations and inspects all variables, not only those in the BY statement. (as NODUPKEY does). However, NODUPLICATES is not completely watertight, as figure 4.3 shows. To avoid the problem as is shown there, all variables should be included in the BY statement which makes NODUPLICATES essentially the same as NODUPKEY.

```
PROC SORT DATA=IN OUT=NODUP NODUPLICATES;
BY KEY;
```

Dataset IN: Dataset NODUP:

OBS	KEY	OTHER		OBS	KEY	OTHER
1	1	45		1	1	45
2	2	52		2	2	52
3	2	52		3	2	12
4	2	12		4	2	52 (!)
5	2	52		5	3	31
6	3	31				

Figure 4.3: An anomaly of the NODUPLICATES option of PROC SORT. NODUPLICATES identifies observations 2 and 3 as duplicates, but overlooks observation 5.

Sorting in descending order is done simply by putting DESCENDING before the relevant variable in the BY statement, as in:

```
BY NAME DESCENDING AGE;
```

PROC PRINT

PROC PRINT was introduced already in chapter 2. It produces a simple tabular printout of a SAS data set. The form is:

```
PROC PRINT DATA=dataset <options>;
   <specification statements>
```

The options and specification statements are used to 'dress up' the reporting. The most important options and specifications are listed in figure 4.4.

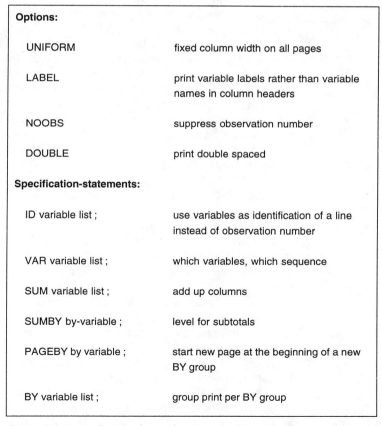

Options:	
UNIFORM	fixed column width on all pages
LABEL	print variable labels rather than variable names in column headers
NOOBS	suppress observation number
DOUBLE	print double spaced
Specification-statements:	
ID variable list ;	use variables as identification of a line instead of observation number
VAR variable list ;	which variables, which sequence
SUM variable list ;	add up columns
SUMBY by-variable ;	level for subtotals
PAGEBY by variable ;	start new page at the beginning of a new BY group
BY variable list ;	group print per BY group

Figure 4.4: Some frequently used options and specification statements of PROC PRINT.

Without specification statements, PROC PRINT prints an observation number preceding each line. After that can come as many variables as can fit on the line. Should there be more variables left in the data set, then the SAS System divides the output pages in two parts (even three or more) and prints the second half there, again with the observation number in front, so that it is easy to find the corresponding lines.

The NOOBS option suppresses the printout of observation numbers. If an ID statement is used, the SAS System also prints no observation numbers. The difference arises when there are so many variables that the SAS System cannot fit them all on one line. By using an ID statement, the SAS System prints the variables declared in it once again at the head of the line as a reminder of which observation the line belongs to. With NOOBS, nothing special is printed.

The UNIFORM option forces the SAS System to maintain the same column structure on each page. Without this option, the SAS System looks to see how many positions are needed to print a variable on the page so that it can fit as many variables on a line as possible, if the data set has too many variables to fit on one line. The effect of UNIFORM is that PROC PRINT uses many more print positions and therefore produces more output, as it must take into account the maximum length each variable can have. This effect shows most clearly with character variables. Say the variable NAME is defined as a character variable 30 positions long. If on a given page no name longer than 10 positions occurs, then without UNIFORM only 10 positions will be reserved. But UNIFORM reserves 30 positions, because that is the length which might occur anywhere in the printout.

The VAR statement with PROC PRINT states which variables to print and in which order to print them. Without the VAR statement, all variables would be printed in the order in which they occur in the data set, an order which it is difficult to influence from the outside. Variables which have already been declared in an ID statement naturally should not be repeated, or they would appear twice.

The SUM statement is used to add up a variable and print the total at the bottom of the column. When the SUM option is used in combination with a BY statement, subtotals are printed for each BY group. If that would be too much, the SUMBY statement can be used to specify a 'cutoff level': only if the BY variable mentioned in the SUMBY statement changes or some BY variable preceding it in the BY statement PROC PRINT will create a subtotal. This presumes multiple variables in the BY statement. Take the following BY statement: BY BRANCH DEPT; if you don't want subtotals at the department level but only at the branch level, then you must use SUMBY BRANCH;.

PAGEBY works in a similar manner. Using PAGEBY in the same situation would cause the printing to start on a new page every time output for a new branch starts.

The BY statement puts dividing lines in the printout at each transition to another BY group. If the same variables are declared in an ID statement as in a BY group, no dividing lines will be printed, but the transition to a new group will be shown at the beginning of the line. Try this!

PROC CONTENTS

PROC CONTENTS is primarily used to reproduce the explanatory section of a SAS data set. In addition it also provides information for the whole data library, such as size, occupied and free space, date of creation, overview of all files (members) in the data library (directory) and so on. The form is:

```
PROC CONTENTS DATA=dataset <options>;
```

A special data set name is _ALL_, which tells PROC CONTENTS to process all members in the data library. This can easily result in an overwhelming amount of output. A number of options are available for managing the amounts of information that PROC CONTENTS produces. Some of the most frequently used options are listed in figure 4.5.

DIRECTORY	print directory	
NODS	no detail listing (in combination with _ALL_)	
MEMTYPE=	specify member types (in combination with DATA = _ALL_)	
	ALL	default
	DATA	data sets
	CAT	catalogs
	PROGRAM	stored programs
	VIEW	views (e.g. SQL)
OUT=dataset	create output data set with meta data only data sets, not catalog info	

Figure 4.5: Options in PROC CONTENTS. Most of them are only used in combination with DATA=_ALL_ to limit the amount of output.

PROC CONTENTS prints the descriptive section of the data set. This includes an overview of all variables present and their characteristics, such as character versus numeric, length, (in)formats and place in the observation and also a summary of general characteristics of the data set, such as date of creation, label, number of observations, physical dimensions and so on.

NODS suppresses the description of details of the individual data sets (list of variables and their attributes).

MEMTYPE=... limits the output to only the SAS data sets of the specified type. Multiple types can be given between parentheses, such as MEMTYPE=(DATA VIEW). With MEMTYPE=ALL information on all existing SAS files, regardless of the type, like data sets, catalogs, stored programs, sources and views will be printed out.

The OUT= option makes it possible to store the information about a data set in another SAS data set. An ideal method of putting together a low-cost information catalog: create such data sets for all relevant data libraries, combine and print them, or make them accessible online!

Sample program 2

The previous material can now be applied to an extended variant of the sample program from chapter 2. Instead of a printout and averaging the whole input file, we now do it for increments of 5000 km. For this we enter a new variable INTERVAL with the value 1 for the interval from 5000 to 10000 km, 2 for 10000 to 15000 km and so on. In the printout, the total number of liters is added up and printed out for each interval. Finally, we use the capability of SAS software to specify a user defined layout for variables.

The SAS log is shown in figure 4.6. The first DATA step hardly needs further explanation. The statement on line 11 creates the INTERVAL variable, by dividing the number of kilometers by 5000 (KM=12647, then KM/5000 = 2.5294 and INTERVAL=2). The integer part of a number is isolated with the INT (integer) function.

PROC MEANS is now instructed to process only the variable MILEAGE and to calculate an average for each interval. The OUTPUT statement tells the SAS System to write the results to a SAS data set (ANALYSE) and put the average in the variable AVG. The data set ANALYSE will contain the variables INTERVAL and AVG, 1 observation per BY group. Besides these variables the SAS System also puts the variables _TYPE_ and _FREQ_ into the data set. These variables are not important for our application. The role of these variables will be explained in chapter 11, 'Descriptive Statistics'.

```
1                          The SAS System (6.08)
                                     11:54 Friday, June 3, 1994

NOTE: Copyright(c) 1989 by SAS Institute Inc., Cary, NC USA.
NOTE: SAS (r) Proprietary Software Release 6.08   TS405

NOTE: The initialization phase used 0.06 CPU seconds and 1092K.

NOTE: SAS job started on Friday 03JUN94 11:54 (199406031154)

1    /*---------------------------------------------------------------*/
2    /* SAMPLE PROGRAM 2: USE OF BY GROUPS                            */
3    /*---------------------------------------------------------------*/
4
5           TITLE2 'SAMPLE PROGRAM 2';
6           DATA CARDATA;                     * TEMPORARY DATASET;
7           INPUT KM LITERS;                  * INPUT CONTAINS THESE VAR'S;
8           LABEL KM='ODOMETER READING';
9           LABEL MILEAGE ='KM PER LITER';
10          MILEAGE =DIF(KM)/LITERS;          * KM'S BETWEEN FILLUP/LITERS;
11          INTERVAL=INT(KM/5000);            * RESULTS PER 5000 KM;
12          CARDS;

NOTE: Missing values were generated as a result of performing an
      operation on missing values.
      Each place is given by: (Number of times) at (Line):(Column).
      8 at 10:17
NOTE: The data set WORK.CARDATA has 60 observations and 4 variables.
NOTE: The DATA statement used 0.03 CPU seconds and 1769K.

12                                           * INPUT RECORDS FOLLOW HERE;
73          PROC MEANS;                      * CALCULATE MEAN VALUE;
74              VAR MILEAGE;                 * OF VARIABLE MILEAGE;
75              OUTPUT OUT=ANALYSE MEAN=AVG;* STORE RESULT IN DS ANALYSE;
76              BY INTERVAL;                 * FOR EACH INTERV. OF 5000 KM;

NOTE: The data set WORK.ANALYSE has 5 observations and 4 variables.
NOTE: The PROCEDURE MEANS printed page 1.
NOTE: The PROCEDURE MEANS used 0.02 CPU seconds and 2034K.

77          DATA RESULT;
78              MERGE CARDATA ANALYSE;       * COMBINE THE DATASETS;
79              BY INTERVAL;                 * MATCHING VARIABLE;

INFO: The variable INTERVAL on data set WORK.CARDATA will be
      overwritten by data set WORK.ANALYSE.
NOTE: The data set WORK.RESULT has 60 observations and 7 variables.
NOTE: The DATA statement used 0.02 CPU seconds and 2134K.

80          PROC FORMAT;                     * DEFINE LAY-OUT FOR INTERVAL;
81              VALUE PER 1='5000 TO 10000 KM'
82                        2='10000 TO 15000 KM'
83                        3='15000 TO 20000 KM'
84                        4='20000 TO 25000 KM'
85                        5='25000 TO 30000 KM';
NOTE: Format PER has been output.

NOTE: The PROCEDURE FORMAT used 0.01 CPU seconds and 2184K.
```

Figure 4.6 (part 1): The SAS log of sample program 2. Note that PROC MEANS creates a data set with 4 variables. Next to INTERVAL and AVG these are _TYPE_ and _FREQ_. For our sample these are irrelevant.

```
 2                        The SAS System (6.08)
                                          11:54 Friday, June 3, 1994

 86            PROC PRINT LABEL UNIFORM;     * PRINT DATASET RESULT;
 87               BY INTERVAL;               * DIVIDE PRINT INTO SECTIONS;
 88               SUM LITERS;                * ADD UP LITERS;
 89               ID KM;
 90               FORMAT INTERVAL PER.;      * COUPLE LAYOUT WITH VARIABLE;
 91               VAR LITERS MILEAGE AVG;    * ONLY THESE VARIABLES;

NOTE: The PROCEDURE PRINT printed pages 2-4.
NOTE: The PROCEDURE PRINT used 0.02 CPU seconds and 2237K.

 92            PROC CONTENTS DATA=_ALL_ ;

NOTE: The PROCEDURE CONTENTS printed pages 5-8.
NOTE: The PROCEDURE CONTENTS used 0.03 CPU seconds and 2395K.

NOTE: The SAS session used 0.34 CPU seconds and 2395K.
NOTE: SAS Institute BV, 1217 KR Hilversum, The Netherlands
```

Figure 4.6 (part2)

After PROC MEANS follows a second DATA step, in which the original data set (CARDATA) and the output data set of PROC MEANS (ANALYSE) are combined, for which INTERVAL serves as the 'linking pin'. PROC FORMAT, which follows, defines a FORMAT (comparable to INFORMAT) which will be used to print the variable INTERVAL: the output shall contain the explanatory text instead of the actual value of INTERVAL.

Next PROC PRINT is used to print out the data set. Here various options are used to improve the appearance of the output. A VAR statement is used to suppress the redundant variables (_TYPE_ and _FREQ_). After the options which were described in the previous section, you see a FORMAT statement: it couples the layout specification (the format) PER, which was created in the PROC FORMAT, with the variable INTERVAL. This way the SAS System knows that this layout should be used to print out INTERVAL.

At the end of the program, PROC CONTENTS is used to print the information about the datasets.

The details of PROC MEANS, the combining of SAS data sets and the details of PROC FORMAT come in later chapters.

The output of the program (the SAS list) is printed in figure 4.7. The output of PROC MEANS shows a strong resemblance to that which was already shown in chapter 2. Only now the calculation has been done for each BY group.

Note that PROC PRINT uses a different format than PROC MEANS: the number of decimals in the output is different. This is easy to correct by using FORMAT statements.

```
                    The SAS System, Version 6.08                    1
                     SAMPLE PROGRAM 2  11:54 Friday, June 3, 1994

      Analysis Variable : MILEAGE KM PER LITER


----------------------------- INTERVAL=1 -----------------------------


      N          Mean        Std Dev        Minimum        Maximum
      ------------------------------------------------------------
      0            .             .              .              .
      ------------------------------------------------------------

----------------------------- INTERVAL=2 -----------------------------


      N          Mean        Std Dev        Minimum        Maximum
      ------------------------------------------------------------
      14      9.9112532      0.4574040      9.0625000     10.9000000
      ------------------------------------------------------------

----------------------------- INTERVAL=3 -----------------------------


      N          Mean        Std Dev        Minimum        Maximum
      ------------------------------------------------------------
      11     10.1491252      0.3660175      9.7000000     11.0784314
      ------------------------------------------------------------

----------------------------- INTERVAL=4 -----------------------------


      N          Mean        Std Dev        Minimum        Maximum
      ------------------------------------------------------------
      16      9.1819815      0.4329196      8.7200000     10.5387205
      ------------------------------------------------------------

                     SAMPLE PROGRAM 2  11:54 Friday, June 3, 1994
----------------------------- INTERVAL=5 -----------------------------


      N          Mean        Std Dev        Minimum        Maximum
      ------------------------------------------------------------
      11      9.4235276      0.4062420      8.7647059     10.0909091
      ------------------------------------------------------------
```

Figure 4.7 (part 1): The output of PROC MEANS: per interval of 5000 KM the statistical attributes of MILEAGE are printed.

```
              The SAS System, Version 6.08                          2
                 SAMPLE PROGRAM 2  11:54 Friday, June 3, 1994

- - - - - - - - - - - - - - - - - - - -  INTERVAL=5000 TO 10000 KM  - - - - - - - - - - - - - - - - - - - - - -

           ODOMETER                     KM PER
            READING       LITERS        LITER          AVG

             9908          34.2           .             .


- - - - - - - - - - - - - - - - - - - -  INTERVAL=10000 TO 15000 KM  - - - - - - - - - - - - - - - - - - - -

           ODOMETER                     KM PER
            READING       LITERS        LITER          AVG

            10227          35.2         9.0625        9.9113
            10493          27.4         9.7080        9.9113
            10855          34.8        10.4023        9.9113
            11212          36.5         9.7808        9.9113
            11515          30.4         9.9671        9.9113
            11823          32.4         9.5062        9.9113
            12150          30.0        10.9000        9.9113
            12451          30.8         9.7727        9.9113
            12812          37.2         9.7043        9.9113
            13039          22.8         9.9561        9.9113
            13398          37.3         9.6247        9.9113
            13836          41.9        10.4535        9.9113
            14154          32.7         9.7248        9.9113
            14567           .             .           9.9113
            14829          25.7        10.1946        9.9113
                          - - - - - -
           INTERVAL        455.1


- - - - - - - - - - - - - - - - - - - -  INTERVAL=15000 TO 20000 KM  - - - - - - - - - - - - - - - - - - - -

           ODOMETER                     KM PER
            READING       LITERS        LITER          AVG

            15210           .             .          10.1491
            15488          28.2         9.8582        10.1491
            15905           .             .          10.1491
            16209          29.3        10.3754        10.1491
            16471          26.0        10.0769        10.1491
```

Figure 4.7 (part 2): The output of PROC PRINT. Try to explain the differences between this output and the output in figure 2.3 based on the used options and specification statements.

The SAS System, Version 6.08   *3*
                                    SAMPLE PROGRAM 2   11:54 Friday, June 3, 1994

-------------------- INTERVAL=15000 TO 20000 KM --------------------
                                (continued)

ODOMETER READING	LITERS	KM PER LITER	AVG
16757	28.0	10.2143	10.1491
17102	33.5	10.2985	10.1491
17583	48.4	9.9380	10.1491
17978	.	.	10.1491
18366	.	.	10.1491
18661	29.2	10.1027	10.1491
18888	22.9	9.9127	10.1491
19243	35.2	10.0852	10.1491
19437	20.0	9.7000	10.1491
19776	30.6	11.0784	10.1491

INTERVAL	331.3		

-------------------- INTERVAL=20000 TO 25000 KM --------------------

ODOMETER READING	LITERS	KM PER LITER	AVG
20089	29.7	10.5387	9.1820
20440	.	.	9.1820
20694	27.9	9.1039	9.1820
20902	23.0	9.0435	9.1820
21158	26.4	9.6970	9.1820
21442	30.9	9.1909	9.1820
21716	30.6	8.9542	9.1820
22043	37.5	8.7200	9.1820
22474	46.5	9.2688	9.1820
22733	29.0	8.9310	9.1820
23061	37.0	8.8649	9.1820
23321	28.5	9.1228	9.1820
23624	34.5	8.7826	9.1820
23928	32.8	9.2683	9.1820
24264	37.4	8.9840	9.1820
24268	.	.	9.1820
24482	22.9	9.3450	9.1820
24804	35.4	9.0960	9.1820

INTERVAL	510.0		

Figure 4.7 (part 3)

```
            The SAS System, Version 6.08                    4
              SAMPLE PROGRAM 2  11:54 Friday, June 3, 1994
---------------------- INTERVAL=25000 TO 30000 KM ----------------------

        ODOMETER                  KM PER
        READING      LITERS        LITER       AVG

          25102       34.0        8.7647      9.4235
          25427       35.3        9.2068      9.4235
          25666       24.6        9.7154      9.4235
          25886       23.9        9.2050      9.4235
          26219       33.0       10.0909      9.4235
          26508       30.0        9.6333      9.4235
          26854       35.2        9.8295      9.4235
          27194       36.3        9.3664      9.4235
          27524       37.0        8.9189      9.4235
          28078       60.1        9.2180      9.4235
          28446       37.9        9.7098      9.4235
                     ------
        INTERVAL      387.3
                     ======
                     1717.9
```

Figure 4.7 (part 4)

```
            The SAS System, Version 6.08                    5
              SAMPLE PROGRAM 2  11:54 Friday, June 3, 1994

                    CONTENTS PROCEDURE

                 -----Directory-----

    Libref:               WORK
    Engine:               V608
    Physical Name:        SYS94156.T113747.RA000.TILANE.R0000067
    Unit:                 VIO
    Volume:
    Disposition:          NEW
    Device:               3380
    Blocksize:            6144
    Blocks per Track:     7
    Total Library Blocks: 2310
    Total Used Blocks:    95
    Total Free Blocks:    2215
    Highest Used Block:   95
    Highest Formatted Block: 84
    Members:              5

              #  Name      Memtype   Indexes
              -----------------------------------
              1  ANALYSE   DATA
              2  CARDATA   DATA
              3  FORMATS   CATALOG
              4  RESULT    DATA
```

Figure 4.7 (part 5): The first part of the PROC CONTENTS output. This part describes the directory of the data library. Note that it contains a catalog, created autonomously by SAS software, next to the created data sets. FORMATS contains the defined format PER (see log in figure 4.6).

```
                    The SAS System, Version 6.08                       6
                    SAMPLE PROGRAM 2  11:54 Friday, June 3, 1994

                          CONTENTS PROCEDURE

Data Set Name: WORK.ANALYSE                 Observations:          5
Member Type:   DATA                         Variables:             4
Engine:        V608                         Indexes:               0
Created:       11:54 Friday, June 3, 1994   Observation Length:    32
Last Modified: 11:54 Friday, June 3, 1994   Deleted Observations:  0
Protection:                                 Compressed:            NO
Data Set Type:                              Sorted:                NO
Label:

              -----Engine/Host Dependent Information-----

    Data Set Page Size:        30720
    Number of Data Set Pages:  1
    File Format:               607
    First Data Page:           1
    Max Obs per Page:          955
    Obs in First Data Page:    5
    Physical Name:             SYS94156.T113747.RA000.TILANE.R0000067
    Release Created:           6.08
    Release Last Modified:     6.08
    Created by:                TILANE
    Last Modified by:          TILANE
    Subextents:                1
    Total Blocks Used:         5

        -----Alphabetic List of Variables and Attributes-----

            #     Variable    Type    Len    Pos
            ------------------------------------
            3     _FREQ_      Num     8      16
            2     _TYPE_      Num     8      8
            4     AVG         Num     8      24
            1     INTERVAL    Num     8      0
```

Figure 4.7 (part 6): After the directory part each of the data sets in the library are described in alphabetical order, with ANALYSE being the first. Here you can see that PROC MEANS adds the extra variables _FREQ_ and _TYPE_. Note also the default internal length of a numeric variable: 8.

```
1                        The SAS System, Version 6.08                    7
                         SAMPLE PROGRAM 2  11:54 Friday, June 3, 1994

                              CONTENTS PROCEDURE

Data Set Name: WORK.CARDATA                    Observations:            60
Member Type:   DATA                            Variables:                4
Engine:        V608                            Indexes:                  0
Created:       11:54 Friday, June 3, 1994      Observation Length:      32
Last Modified: 11:54 Friday, June 3, 1994      Deleted Observations:     0
Protection:                                    Compressed:              NO
Data Set Type:                                 Sorted:                  NO
Label:

                  -----Engine/Host Dependent Information-----

       Data Set Page Size:       30720
       Number of Data Set Pages: 1
       File Format:              607
       First Data Page:          1
       Max Obs per Page:         955
       Obs in First Data Page:   60
       Physical Name:            SYS94156.T113747.RA000.TILANE.R0000067
       Release Created:          6.08
       Release Last Modified:    6.08
       Created by:               TILANE
       Last Modified by:         TILANE
       Subextents:               1
       Total Blocks Used:        5

         -----Alphabetic List of Variables and Attributes-----

       #     Variable   Type    Len    Pos    Label
       ----------------------------------------------------------
       4     INTERVAL   Num       8     24
       1     KM         Num       8      0    ODOMETER READING
       2     LITERS     Num       8      8
       3     MILEAGE    Num       8     16    KM PER LITER
```

Figure 4.7 (part 7)

```
                    The SAS System, Version 6.08                    8
                    SAMPLE PROGRAM 2   11:54 Friday, June 3, 1994

                          CONTENTS PROCEDURE

Data Set Name: WORK.RESULT                  Observations:          60
Member Type:   DATA                         Variables:             7
Engine:        V608                         Indexes:               0
Created:       11:54 Friday, June 3, 1994   Observation Length:    56
Last Modified: 11:54 Friday, June 3, 1994   Deleted Observations:  0
Protection:                                 Compressed:            NO
Data Set Type:                              Sorted:                NO
Label:

              -----Engine/Host Dependent Information-----

     Data Set Page Size:         30720
     Number of Data Set Pages:   1
     File Format:                607
     First Data Page:            1
     Max Obs per Page:           547
     Obs in First Data Page:     60
     Physical Name:              SYS94156.T113747.RA000.TILANE.R0000067
     Release Created:            6.08
     Release Last Modified:      6.08
     Created by:                 TILANE
     Last Modified by:           TILANE
     Subextents:                 1
     Total Blocks Used:          5

        -----Alphabetic List of Variables and Attributes-----

     #    Variable    Type    Len    Pos    Label
     ------------------------------------------------------------
     6    _FREQ_      Num      8     40
     5    _TYPE_      Num      8     32
     7    AVG         Num      8     48
     4    INTERVAL    Num      8     24
     1    KM          Num      8      0     ODOMETER READING
     2    LITERS      Num      8      8
     3    MILEAGE     Num      8     16     KM PER LITER
```

Figure 4.7 (part 8)

Exercises

1. A department store has a quantity of sales information in an
    external file. The name of this file is SOURCE.DATA. Write a SAS
    program to perform the following tasks:

    a. On the basis of SOURCE.DATA, build a SAS data set with the
        name SALES. The data set should include the variables:

        SALESREP, DEPT, PRICE

        The layout of the input records is as follows:

FIELD	START POSITION	FIELD LENGTH
SALESREP (name)	1	15
DEPT (department description)	16	8
PRICE (of sold articles)	24	7

    Example:

    ```
    input record postition
    1          10         20          30
    |---|----|----|----|----|----|----|-
    STEVENSON      HARDWARE 124.95
    KING           TOYS       9.45
    NILSON         APPAREL   67.99
    ```

    b. Print the data set.

    c. Print only the variables SALESREP and PRICE and suppress
        the observation number.

    d. Make a grouped printout for SALESREP, in which the highest
        PRICE per sales representative is at the top.

    e. Print the data set description, as recorded by the SAS System.

2. A water utility company collects its data by punchcard. The cards contain the following data:

client code	column 1-8	character
previous reading	column 9-14	numeric
last reading	column 15-20	numeric
month of reading	column 21-23	character
year	column24-27	numeric
invoice amount	column 28-32	numeric

a. Build a SAS data set with the name WATER, containing the following variables: CLIENT, PREVIOUS, LAST, MONTH, YEAR, INVOICE. Give the variables a label, which corresponds to the category descriptions above.

b. Make a printout of the data set, in which the columns are defined with labels. Suppress the observation numbers. Print the total of the invoice amounts at the bottom.

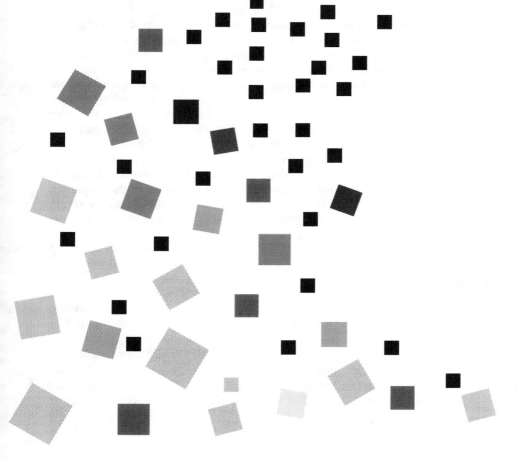

CHAPTER 5

The SAS® Display Manager

Introduction

In the previous chapters we became acquainted with the structure and syntax of the SAS System. Using this knowledge, it is possible to develop several simple programs. This chapter deals with the Display Manager, the universal development environment of the SAS System. The Display Manager brings together all the functions needed to interactively enter a SAS program into the computer and to test it. Although other development environments can be used to develop SAS programs, the Display Manager clearly has advantages. All activities take place within the SAS environment, with the result that it is extremely fast and efficient to go through the cycle of writing the program statements, running the program, assessing the results and going back to correct errors in the program statements. The Display Manager is a window oriented environment, consisting of 3 main and many supporting windows. (The SAS V5 Display Manager has only the 3 main windows. Almost everything in this chapter regarding the main windows applies to the V5 Display Manager as well.) The main windows are the PROGRAM EDITOR window (also called the PROG window), the LOG window and the OUTPUT window. You type the SAS program statements in the PROG window. After you have done so you give a 'Submit' command which loads, compiles and runs the statements you have entered. When the execution of the program is completed, the LOG window will show you the SAS log, with any potential NOTEs and ERRORs. If there is also procedure output, this will be displayed in the OUTPUT window.

The main windows

When the Display Manager starts up, two of the three main windows become visible: the PROG window and the LOG window (figure 5.1).

SAS programs can be typed in directly in the PROG window. At first you only see a few lines in the window. Often, to get a better overview, you might want to see more lines. Type in the ZOOM command on the command line and the PROG window expands to the whole screen (figure 5.2).

```
+LOG-------------------------------------------------------------------------+
| Command ===>                                                               |
|                                                                            |
|                                                                            |
|                                                                            |
|                                                                            |
|                                                                            |
|                                                                            |
|                                                                            |
|                                                                            |
|                                                                            |
|                                                                            |
|                                                                            |
| +------------------------------------------------------------------------+
+PROGRAM EDITOR--------------------------------------------------------------+
| Command ===>                                                               |
|                                                                            |
| 00001                                                                      |
| 00002                                                                      |
| 00003                                                                      |
| 00004                                                                      |
| 00005                                                                      |
| 00006                                                                      |
+----------------------------------------------------------------------------+
```

Figure 5.1: When you start the Display Manager you will first see the PROGRAM EDITOR (PROG) window and the LOG window. You enter your SAS statements in the PROG window.

```
+PROGRAM EDITOR--------------------------------------------------------------+
| Command ===>                                                               |
|                                                                            |
| 00001 data nosort;                                                         |
| 00002 input x y z;                                                         |
| 00003 cards;                                                               |
| 00004 1 2 3                                                                |
| 00005 1 2 3                                                                |
| 00006 1 2 4                                                                |
| 00007 2 3 4                                                                |
| 00008 1 2 3                                                                |
| 00009 ;                                                                    |
| 00010 proc sort noduplicates;                                              |
| 00011 by x;                                                                |
| 00012 run;                                                                 |
| 00013 proc print;                                                          |
| 00014 run;                                                                 |
| 00015                                                                      |
| 00016                                                                      |
| 00017                                                                      |
| 00018                                                                      |
| 00019                                                                      |
| 00020                                                                      |
+----------------------------------------------- ZOOM ----------+
```

Figure 5.2: To enter the progam it is handy to see as many lines as fit on the screen. The PF2 function key or the ZOOM command on the command line will enlarge the PROG window to cover the whole screen. Again PF2 or the command ZOOM OFF will reduce it to the original size.

As a rule the ZOOM command is assigned to a function key. In the IBM TSO environment it is PF2. (In this chapter the TSO function keys will always be treated as points of departure. The function keys available are different for different system environments. To find out which keys are available in your environment, call up the KEYS window using the KEYS command; see page 87). At the bottom of the window a ZOOM notice is given, as an indication that the screen is expanded and as a warning that other windows might be hidden behind it. The command 'ZOOM OFF' or again PF2 returns the screen to its original dimensions.

The PROG window

To demonstrate the way the Display Manager works, we shall run through the whole cycle of the program used for testing the anomalies of the NODUPLICATES option of PROC SORT (see chapter 4). The program will be typed in the PROG window, as shown in figure 5.2. To support the editing of your program source the necessary edit commands (copy, delete, insert and so on) are available. The edit facilities of the PROG window are based on the commands of IBM's ISPF editor. Those who are comfortable with the ISPF environment should find it easy to work with.

The most important edit commands are shown in figure 5.3. All these commands are so-called 'line commands', meaning that they are typed in on the line to which they apply (over the line number). A command consisting of a single letter is normally applied to a single line, and the commands consisting of two letters are applied to a 'block' of lines, marked by placing the command on the first and last line of the block. Figure 5.4 shows an example of how the commands are used. More effective than giving an extensive description of each command here is for you to go try them out on your computer.

Once the program has been typed in, the SUBMIT command (usually available as PF3) is used to compile the statements in the PROG window and execute the program, if compiling has been successful.

SUBMIT and all other commands which affect a whole window rather than just one or a few lines, are called 'command line' commands: they are typed in after the arrow on the command line. The progress of the program execution can be followed on the screen: in the upper righthand corner of the PROG window the SAS System displays how far along the execution is.

C	copy line
CC...CC	copy block from CC to CC
(CC on first and last line)	
M	move line
MM...MM	move block from MM to MM
Copy and move are combined with an indication of the target location:	
B	before
A	after
O	over
D	delete line
Dn	delete n lines
DD...DD	delete block
I	insert line
In	insert n lines
R	repeat line
Rn	repeat n times
RR...RR	repeat block

Figure 5.3: The most frequently used line commands while editing your source program.

OUTPUT window

As soon as output is created by a procedure, the SAS System brings up the OUTPUT window (figure 5.6). This causes a pause in the processing of the program. You can proceed though the output with PF8, which brings up the next page. With PF3 you jump to the last output page. With the standard scroll keys (PF7/PF8) you can move back and forth through the output. When the end of the output is reached, pressing PF3 (END command) again closes the output screen and the PROG window is once again active.

```
+PROGRAM EDITOR----------------------------------------------------------------+
| Command ===>                                                                 |
|                                                                              |
| R2001 After pressing ENTER this line will be repeated 2 times                |
| MM002 This text (line 2 - 6) will be moved.                                  |
| 00003 The new location is indicated with                                     |
| 00004 'A' (after) = after this line, or                                      |
| 00005 'B' (before) = before this line                                        |
| MM006 So in this example before line 8 (after 7)                             |
| 00007 this will be in front of the above text                                |
| B0008 this will be after the above text                                      |
| 00009                                                                        |
| 00010                                                                        |
| 00011                                                                        |
| 00012                                                                        |
| 00013                                                                        |
| 00014                                                                        |
| 00015                                                                        |
| 00016                                                                        |
| 00017                                                                        |
| 00018                                                                        |
| 00019                                                                        |
| 00020                                                                        |
+-------------------------------------------------------------- ZOOM ----------+
```

After Enter:

```
+PROGRAM EDITOR----------------------------------------------------------------+
| Command ===>                                                                 |
|                                                                              |
| 00001 After pressing ENTER this line will be repeated 2 times                |
| 00002 After pressing ENTER this line will be repeated 2 times                |
| 00003 After pressing ENTER this line will be repeated 2 times                |
| 00004 this will be in front of the above text                                |
| 00005 This text (line 2 - 6) will be moved.                                  |
| 00006 The new location is indicated with                                     |
| 00007 'A' (after) = after this line, or                                      |
| 00008 'B' (before) = before this line                                        |
| 00009 So in this example before line 8 (after 7)                             |
| 00010 this will be after the above text                                      |
| 00011                                                                        |
| 00012                                                                        |
| 00013                                                                        |
| 00014                                                                        |
| 00015                                                                        |
| 00016                                                                        |
| 00017                                                                        |
| 00018                                                                        |
| 00019                                                                        |
| 00020                                                                        |
+-------------------------------------------------------------- ZOOM ----------+
```

Figure 5.4: You can enter more than one line command at any time. Once you press enter they will all be applied.

```
+LOG--------------------------------------------------------------------------+
| Command ===>                                                                |
|                                                                             |
|                                                                             |
|                                                                             |
|                                                                             |
|                                                                             |
|                                                                             |
|                                                                             |
|                                                                             |
|                                                                             |
|                                                                             |
| +-------------------------------------------------------------------------+ |
+PROGRAM EDITOR---------------------------------------------DATA STEP running-+
| Command ===>                                                                |
| NOTE: 14 Lines submitted.                                                   |
| 00001                                                                       |
| 00002                                                                       |
| 00003                                                                       |
| 00004                                                                       |
| 00005                                                                       |
| 00006                                                                       |
+-------------------------------------------------------------- R  --------+
```

Figure 5.5: During execution you can follow the progress of the run: the active step is mentioned at the upper righthand corner of the PROG window.

```
+OUTPUT-----------------------------------------------------------------------+
| Command ===>                                                                |
| NOTE: Procedure PRINT created 1 page(s) of output.                          |
|                      The SAS System, Version 6.08                      1 |
|                                          17:47 Wednesday, June 1, 1994 |
|                                                                             |
|                   OBS    X    Y    Z                                        |
|                                                                             |
|                    1     1    2    3                                        |
|                    2     1    2    4                                        |
|                    3     1    2    3                                        |
|                    4     2    3    4                                        |
|                                                                             |
|                                                                             |
|                                                                             |
|                                                                             |
|                                                                             |
|                                                                             |
|                                                                             |
|                                                                             |
|                                                                             |
+-----------------------------------------------------------------------------+
```

Figure 5.6: The program is executed. If procedure output has been generated then the OUTPUT window will be displayed.

LOG window

After the return to the main screen, the PROGRAM EDITOR window
and the LOG window are again visible (figure 5.7). The LOG can be
examined by placing the cursor in the window and using PF7/PF8 to
scroll through.

```
+LOG--------------------------------------------------------------------------+
| Command ===>                                                                |
|                                                                             |
| NOTE: SAS sort was used.                                                    |
| NOTE: 1 duplicate observations were deleted.                                |
| NOTE: The data set WORK.NOSORT has 4 observations and 3 variables.          |
| NOTE: The PROCEDURE SORT used 0.01 CPU seconds and 1733K.                    |
|                                                                             |
| 13    proc print;                                                           |
| 14    run;                                                                  |
|                                                                             |
| NOTE: The PROCEDURE PRINT used 0.01 CPU seconds and 1733K.                  |
|                                                                             |
+-----------------------------------------------------------------------------+
+PROGRAM EDITOR---------------------------------------------------------------+
| Command ===>                                                                |
| NOTE: 14 Lines submitted.                                                   |
| 00001                                                                       |
| 00002                                                                       |
| 00003                                                                       |
| 00004                                                                       |
| 00005                                                                       |
| 00006                                                                       |
+-----------------------------------------------------------------------------+
```

*Figure 5.7: After inspecting the output the END command (PF3) will bring you back to the PROG
and LOG windows.*

Development cycle

In the previous section, the whole development cycle was demonstrated.
The only thing still left is to recall the program to the PROG window for
possible corrections and alterations. This is done using the RECALL
command (PF4). Each RECALL recalls the statements of the previous
SUBMIT. With this function you can keep moving back through the
already submitted statements.

Command line commands

In the description of the main windows we have already encountered a
number of commands which affect the whole window where they are
typed, such as SUBMIT which affects all the lines in the PROG window.
These commands are always typed on the command line after

'Command ===>', and they can also often be executed using the corresponding function keys.

```
+LOG--------------------------------+KEYS  <DMKEYS>------------------------+
|  Command ===>                      |  Command ===>                        |
|                                    |                                      |
|  NOTE: SAS sort was used.          |  Key      Definition                 |
|  NOTE: 1 duplicate observations w  |                                      |
|  NOTE: The data set WORK.NOSORT h  |  F1       help                       |
|  NOTE: The PROCEDURE SORT used 0.  |  F2       zoom                       |
|                                    |  F3       submit                     |
|  11    proc print;                 |  F4       pgm; recall                |
|  12    run;                        |  F5       rfind                      |
|                                    |  F6       rchange                    |
|  NOTE: The PROCEDURE PRINT used 0  |  F7        backward                  |
|                                    |  F8       forward                    |
+------------------------------      |  F9       output                     |
+PROGRAM EDITOR------------------    |  F10      left                       |
|  Command ===>                      |  F11      right                      |
|                                    |  F12      home                       |
|  00001                             |  F13      mark                       |
|  00002                             |  F14      smark                      |
|  00003                             |  F15      unmark                     |
|  00004                             |  F16      cut                        |
|  00005                             |  F17      paste                      |
|  00006                             |  F18      store                      |
+-----------------------------------+--------------------------------------+
```

Figure 5.8: The KEYS window is opened to inspect how the function keys are defined. You can change the definition simply by typing the new command.

The function keys are, depending on the system environment, assigned to F1, F2 and so on or PF1, PF2 and so on. With the KEYS command you open the KEYS window (figure 5.8). It displays which commands are assigned to which keys. In the KEYS window, key definitions can also be changed. One handy change could be, for example, to assign a ZOOM ON to F4 along with RECALL. To assign multiple commands to a single function key, they should be separated by a ';' (see F4 definition).

Scroll commands

Scroll commands are used to 'leaf through' the window. The four commands are:

FOR	(PF8)	forward
BAC	(PF7)	backwards
LEFT	(PF10)	left
RIGHT	(PF11)	right

In principle you scroll the entire height and breadth of a complete screen. However you can specify the number of lines or columns to scroll on the command line. 'M' on the command line indicates maximum scroll; thus FOR M means: go to the end of the contents of the window.

Find and change commands

As support for entering and modifying programs, there are also commands for finding and changing text in a window. These are the FIND and CHANGE commands. After the command comes what you want to find or change and in the CHANGE command you also add the replacement text:

```
CHANGE 'xxxx' 'yyyy' option <ALL>
FIND   'xxxx'        option
```

In which:
'xxxx': the text to be found
'yyyy': the replacement text
option: special search instructions

The option after the search text determines whether the text should be found as a separate word or as a portion of a word. Without any option every occurrence of the text will be sought. The option WORD specifies that the search text should appear as a separate word and the options PREFIX and SUFFIX search for the text respectively at the beginning and the end of a word. Finally, if the CHANGE command ends with ALL, the change is effected globally throughout the whole program. Without it the change is effected only at the first occurrence following the current cursor position. ALL does not work in combination with FIND, however a RFIND (repeat find command) can be done (usually with function key PF5) which finds the next occurrence.

Opening and closing windows

Opening a window or activating an open window is done by typing the name of the window on the command line. Thus LOG opens or activates the LOG window and KEYS the KEYS window. Figure 5.13 gives an overview of the most important windows. The END command (PF3) is used to leave a window. In many cases this is equivalent to closing the window (and where appropriate save the changes to it). In the PROG window, however, PF3 has another meaning, namely SUBMIT: the PROG window is deactivated and all statements are sent to the SAS System for compiling and executing.

The BYE command ends the Display Manager session. Watch out: there is no warning to save first any programs currently in the PROGRAM EDITOR window.

Calling and saving programs

In the section 'The main windows' we saw that after the SUBMIT command, statements disappear from the PROG window. They can be recalled with the RECALL command (PF4). Each RECALL calls up a previous program segment, back to the beginning of the session, and puts it at the top of the PROG window. Thus Recall works as a 'push down' mechanism: the most recently submitted statements are pushed down to the bottom of the PROG window.

You should of course be able to save programs typed into the PROG window for later use. This is done with the FILE command. Calling a program from disk and putting it into the PROG window is done with the INCLUDE command. The structure of both commands is the same:

```
INCLUDE <file specification> <options>
FILE    <file specification> <options>
```

```
+LOG--------------------------------------------------------------------+
| Command ===>                                                          |
|                                                                       |
|                                                                       |
|                                                                       |
|                                                                       |
|                                                                       |
|       +-----------------------------------------------------+         |
|       | WARNING: The file already exists.  Enter R to replace it, |   |
|       | enter A to append to it,  or enter C to cancel the FILE   |   |
|       | command.  NOTE:  If Replace or Append is selected, it will|   |
|       | become the default until another file is specified. _     |   |
|       +-----------------------------------------------------+         |
+-----------------------------------------------------------------------+
+PROGRAM EDITOR---------------------------------------------------------+
| Command ===> file                                                     |
|                                                                       |
| 00001 TITLE2 'SAMPLE PROGRAM 1 VARIANT 3';                            |
| 00002 DATA MILEAGE;              * TEMPORARY DATASET;                  |
| 00003 INPUT KM LITERS;           * INPUT CONTAINS THESE VAR'S;         |
| 00004 LABEL KM='ODOMETER READING';                                    |
| 00005 LABEL MILEAGE ='KM PER LITER';                                  |
| 00006 MILEAGE =DIF(KM)/LITERS;   * KM'S BETWEEN FILLUP/LITERS;         |
+-----------------------------------------------------------------------+
```

Figure 5.9: If you enter a FILE command for an existing file the Display Manager will open a confirmation dialog to make sure that you really want to overwrite the file. If you specified REPLACE or APPEND in the FILE command, then this dialog will not be displayed.

The file specification can take various forms: you can refer to a predefined fileref or straight to the name of the file. The latter should be placed in quotation marks.

IBM TSO users are reminded also that programs and files in their own libraries (where in TSO commands no user ID and no quotation marks are used) should be placed in quotation marks. This does not mean that the user ID needs to be given. Instead the file name is preceded by a period. When using a PDS (Partitioned Data Set) as program source, the member name can also be given. In the system appendices (H through M) additional information is given about specifying files in various system environments.

If the file specification is left out, the most recently referenced file will be used. Thus a FILE command in general refers to the file most recently included by INCLUDE. If the output file already exists, the SAS System will display a confirmation dialog in order to prevent accidentally overwriting the file. The dialog is suppressed with the option APPEND or REPLACE (see figure 5.9) with the FILE command. Other options are available, but these are not often used, so we will not go over them here.

Printing or storing information

The FILE command described above functions not only to save programs. In general it writes the contents of the window in which the command has been given (such as the LOG or OUTPUT window) to the indicated file. To print the contents of a window you use the PRINT command.

```
PRINT <FILE=file specification>
<FORM=form specification> <APPEND|REPLACE>
```

The operation of the PRINT command is dependent on the printing facilities available in the system. For printing, the SAS System can handle multiple paper sizes, working in both 'landscape' and 'portrait', with a choice of fonts. These functions are set down in FORMs which are stored in catalogs. We confine ourselves here to the standard form, so we do not have to state it. Through reference to the FILE= specification, the PRINT file is written to the indicated file, as with the FILE command. APPEND and REPLACE determine whether the existing contents of the file are to be saved or replaced.

FILE and PRINT operate on the total contents of the window, not only on the part which is visible. You can use a CLEAR command to first clear the window and then execute the final version of the program.

Other important commands

There are tens of other commands available in the Display Manager, some of them are used quite regularly and are mentioned here.

The CANCEL command closes a window without saving any changes.

The PREVCMD command (simply a question mark (?) on the command line) puts the previous command back on the command line. The SAS System keeps one list of all commands given in any window. By repeatedly entering the ? command you can leaf back through it.

The NEXT and PREVWIND commands are used to move back and forth through the windows which are open. However it is often easier to refer directly to the window you want by its name.

Support windows

The Display Manager is a complete windowing environment. Just as in Apple's Macintosh and the MS Windows environment there is a Notepad, Clock and so on. But more important are the windows for development support. All windows can be called up by typing their name on the command line.

DIR window

The DIR window displays the directory of a SAS data library, comparable to the output of PROC CONTENTS. See figure 5.10. The DIR window is not only for displaying information; a number of maintenance tasks can also be performed and detail windows can be accessed.

Typing an S (Select) before the file name opens either the VAR window or the CATALOG window for further examination of the file.

If the SAS/FSP product is installed, typing a B puts you in FSBROWSE mode for inspection of data set observations, while E puts you in FSEDIT mode.

Finally R and D, respectively, Rename and Delete a data set.

```
+LOG--------------  +DIR----------------------------------------------------------+
| Command ===>     | Command ===>                                                  |
|                  |                                                               |
| 29   libname gen | Libref: GEN                                                   |
| NOTE: Libref GEN | Type: ALL                                                     |
|       Engine:    |                                                               |
|       Physical N |      SAS File  Memtype    Indexed                             |
|                  |                                                               |
|                  |    _  AFD1      DATA                                          |
|                  |    _  AFD2      DATA                                          |
|                  |    _  AFD2      DATA                                          |
|                  |    _  ART_DES   DATA                                          |
|                  |    _  ART_UPD   DATA                                          |
+----------------  |    _  BANKNOTE  DATA                                          |
+PROGRAM EDITOR--- |    _  ORDER     DATA                                          |
| Command ===>     |    _  CANDIDAT  DATA                                          |
|                  |    _  CRISTAL   DATA                                          |
| 00001            |    _  DEVICES   CATALOG                                       |
| 00002            |    _  DIYCOMBI  VIEW                                          |
| 00003            |    _  ELECTION  DATA                                          |
| 00004            |    _  F_DETAIL  CATALOG                                       |
| 00005            |    _  FLIGHT    DATA                                          |
| 00006            |    _  FORMATS   CATALOG                                       |
+----------------  +--------------------------------------------------------------+
```

Figure 5.10: The DIR window displays the directory of a SAS data library, comparable to the output of PROC CONTENTS. Individual data sets can be renamed or deleted, but you can also from here edit or browse the data set or call up the VAR window.

VAR window

The VAR window (figure 5.11) displays the descriptive section of a SAS data set, similar to using PROC CONTENTS. At the same time, you can also make changes in the description.

All attributes of a variable can be adjusted: the name, the label, the formats and informats. However it is not possible to remove variables from the data set using the VAR window. To change variables, type in the R command before the variable. It is of course necessary to have write authority for the data set if you want to do that.

Remaining windows

There are many other windows available in the Display Manager. It is impossible to show an example for each window. It is more appropriate to try them out using the table in figure 5.13.

```
+LOG------------- +VAR----------------------------------------------------------+
| Command ===>   | Command ===>                                                 |
|                |                                                              |
|                | Libref: GEN                                                  |
|                | Dataset: ORDER                                               |
|                |                                                              |
|                |     Variable Length Format          Informat        Ke |
|                |                                                              |
|                |   _  ART_CAT  $8                                    N  |
|                |   _  ART_NR    8                                    N  |
|                |   _  COUNT     8                                    N  |
|                |   _  DESCRIP  $10                                   N  |
|                |   _  PRICE     8                                    N  |
|                |                                                              |
+----------------+                                                              |
+PROGRAM EDITOR---|                                                              |
| Command ===>   |                                                              |
|                |                                                              |
|  00001         |                                                              |
|  00002         |                                                              |
|  00003         |                                                              |
|  00004         |                                                              |
|  00005         |                                                              |
|  00006         |                                                              |
+----------------+ +----------------------------------------------------------+
```

Figure 5.11: The VAR window. In this window you can rename variables, assign new formats or informats and other attributes. You cannot delete variables from a data set in this window.

HELP screens

The SAS System has an extensive on-line HELP system. The main menu is called up by typing HELP on the command line (figure 5.12). You then choose a category by placing the cursor on its name and pressing Enter. If you have a workstation with a mouse, you only need to click your choice. You can also jump directly to a specific section of the help files by calling it directly, for example HELP FILENAME sends you directly to information about the FILENAME statement and the FILENAME command. When you find the information you want, you can use PF3 to move back out, one screen at the time. With the command =X, you leave the help screens altogether, regardless of where you are in the help system.

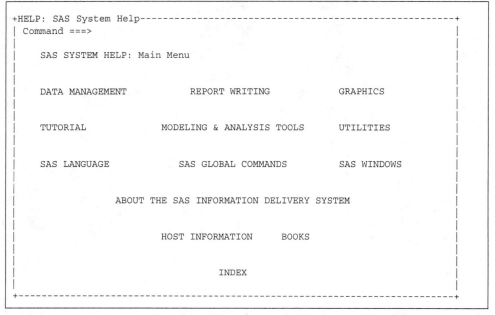

Figure 5.12: The main menu of the SAS Help files. You select a subject on which you want help by placing the cursor over it and pressing enter. If you have a mouse attached to your workstation, simply clicking on the subject will take you to the specified section. You can leave the help system using PF3 or the =X command line command.

Other aspects

So far in this chapter we have sketched a picture of the capabilities of the Display Manager. Learning to use the Display Manager from a book is like learning to swim on dry land. You really have to get wet to learn it!

Especially in the beginning it could be difficult to remember all the commands. For those who are having this problem, you might try switching over to a Macintosh or Windows sort of environment, even without a graphics terminal and mouse. You do this with the PMENU command. This command suppresses the command line and replaces it with 'pull down' menus (figure 5.14). If there is no mouse, do the same thing as in the HELP environment: place the cursor on the option you want and press Enter. Place the cursor outside the menu box and press Enter to cancel. In some system environments in which pull-down menus are the rule, such as MS Windows, OS/2, X Windows or DECwindows, the Display Manager normally starts up with pull-down menus instead of a command line. To get back from pull down menus to the command line format, go to the 'Command' option under 'Globals'.

There you can give the command PMENU OFF in a command line window in order to remove the menus from all windows.

CATALOG	Displays and updates the contents of a Catalog
DIR	Displays the directory of a SAS data library
OUTPUT MANAGER (MGR)	Displays a table of contents of the OUTPUT window
TITLE FOOTNOTE	Displays the current TITLE and FOOTNOTE statements. You can also enter TITLEs and FOOTNOTEs in this window
FILENAME	Displays a list of the files which are currently assigned using FILENAME statements
FNAME	Displays a list of all allocated files, also those that were allocated using system commands
LIBNAME	Displays a list with all allocated SAS data libraries
DSINFO	Displays physical aspects of a data set
VAR	Displays the descriptive part of a SAS data set

Figure 5.13: An overview of the most important supporting windows of the Display Manager.

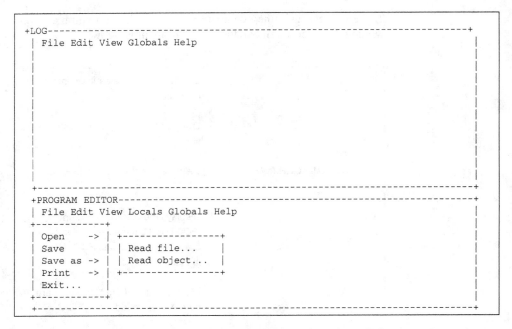

Figure 5.14: The PMENU command replaces the command line by pull-down menus. Without a mouse the cursor keys are used for navigation and the ENTER key replaces the mouse button. Via 'Command' in the 'Globals' menu you can return to the command-line version of the window.

CHAPTER 6

Programming the DATA Step

The previous chapters have given a first introduction to the DATA step and the PROC step. This and the following chapters will go more deeply into the programming capabilities of the DATA step. This chapter covers, among other things, the assignment of values to variables by means of calculations, the making of comparisons and program flow control, such as loops and conditional processing.

The two subsequent chapters cover SAS functions and the use of SAS files as input.

Programming within the DATA step for the most part follows the reading of the input, thus in many cases the structure of the DATA step will look like this:

```
DATA ....;
 INFILE ....;
 INPUT ....;
     | assignments
     | transformations
     | (logical) comparisons
     | program flow control
```

Assignment

An assignment statement assigns a value to a variable. If the variable has not yet been created, it will be created on the fly. The value assigned by the statement is the result of working out an expression. An expression can be as simple as a constant, but complex calculations are also possible.

```
variable = expression ;
```

When the SAS System has to create a new variable, it uses the result of the expression to determine what kind of variable should be created: a numeric variable from a numerical expression and a character variable from a character expression. The length of the text in the expression ultimately determines the length of the variable.

Figure 6.1 shows examples of a number of assignment statements. You see, among others, the TODAY function which gives today's date and the MEAN function which calculates the average value of a number of variables.

```
VAT = .175;                     numerical constant
NAME = 'JOHN';                  character constant
DATE = TODAY();                 function
PROFIT = REVENUE - COST;        existing variables
AVERAGE = MEAN (A,B,C);         function and variables
TOMORROW =TODAY() + 1;          function and constant
```

Figure 6.1: Examples of assignment statements. The expression on the right side of the equal sign is evaluated and the resulting value assigned to the variable on the left.

Arithmetic processing

The numerical expressions in an assignment statement usually contain one or another form of calculation. Figure 6.2 gives the basic types of calculation with their formulas. The order of processing is as usual raising to a power (**), multiplication (*), division (/), addition (+), subtraction (-). The same usual rules also indicate that first parts of the expression within parentheses are evaluated, from the inside out. So the most deeply embedded parts first. An expression can contain constants, functions or variables in every imaginable combination.

```
A = B;                  copy
A = B+C;                adding
A = B-C;                subtraction
A = B*C;                multiplication
A = B/C;                division
A = B**C;               raise to the power
```

Figure 6.2: The elementary arithmetic operations. B and C could be variables, functions or any combination thereof.

Functions

The concept 'function' has been mentioned several times already in the preceding sections. Chapter 7 contains the discussion of a number of frequently used functions, but it is useful to become acquainted with them here because it will be necessary to use a number of functions in this chapter.

A function is in fact a special separate program with which you can carry out complex operations on input data. Complex is relative: many functions could be programmed with just a few 'normal' lines of code, such as a function to calculate averages. The advantage of using functions is twofold: they are more efficient than the same routine written in normal SAS statements and they are already developed and tested. There exists a large library of functions in many different areas. Whatever complex calculation you want to make, always consider whether it is absolutely unique or whether it is likely that someone else has already done it (especially considering that there are over two million SAS users in the world); in the latter case look in the Language Guide to see if what you need is already available as a function. A function can appear anywhere in an expression. Often in assignments, but also in the conditions of IF statements as you shall see in the next section of this chapter. The form of a function is: function name, followed by the input arguments in parentheses. These parentheses are essential: this way the SAS System knows that it is dealing with a function and not with a variable. The result is a number value or some text string which will then be used in the further processing of the expression.

Character operations

Most character operations take place by means of functions, and therefore the subject comes up in chapter 7. Along with the direct assignment of text to a character variable, there is the very important process of 'concatenation': joining of multiple character strings (as constants or as character variables) to form a new text string. This is done with the concatenation operator: ||. So

```
F_NAME = 'JOHN';
D_NAME = F_NAME||'-'||'PAUL';
```

assigns the value 'JOHN-PAUL' to the variable D_NAME.

Program flow control

SAS processing is by sequential instructions, as are most programming languages, beginning with the DATA statement and on to the end of the DATA step. There are also, as in most programming languages, possibilities for repeated processing of statements or portions of programs. For conditional processing, the SAS System has the IF and SELECT statements. Inasmuch as the SELECT statement can always be written as a collection of IF statements, we will pass over it here and come back to it in chapter 15 (Advanced DATA step features). For looping program segments there are several variations of the DO-END statement combination (also called DO-END group).

IF statement

The IF statement is used, as we have already seen, to process statements on specific conditions. The form is:

```
IF condition THEN statement;
              ELSE statement;
```

This is simply interpreted as: If ... is true, then do ...; if not, do .... The heart of the matter is the condition and whether it is true (TRUE) or not (FALSE). TRUE and FALSE are expressed numerically in the SAS System. If an equation is true, the SAS System gives it a value of 1, and if false a value of 0. This gets generalized in that, if a numerical expression is used as a condition and has the value of 0 or missing (the concept 'missing value' will be dealt with later in this chapter), the condition is FALSE and the statement after ELSE is processed. Non-0, non-missing is TRUE, which causes the THEN branch to be processed.

In the treatment of the INFILE statement we saw the END option: with this a variable is defined to which the SAS System assigns the value 0 in the process of reading the input, except during the last input record when the value is 1. This can be used directly in an IF statement:

```
INFILE .... END=FINISH;
...
(statements to reading in and process)
...
IF FINISH THEN .... ;* end-of-file processing;
```

Only one statement can come after THEN or ELSE. A DO-END group counts as a single statement in this context, effectively making it possible to include many statements in a single branch:

```
IF .... THEN
     DO;
         the THEN-branch statements
     END;
ELSE
     DO;
         the ELSE-branch statements
     END;
```

The indention you see above is not required, but is highly recommended so that you can see at a glance which statements belong where.

The ELSE statement does not need to be present. If there is no action required for the ELSE situation, this part can be left out.

Logical comparisons

The TRUE or FALSE of a condition is usually the result of an evaluation of an expression or a comparison. The standard logical (comparison) operators are listed in figure 6.3. Their use is simple: the operators are placed between the expressions to be compared, either as a two-letter abbreviation or as a symbol. For example:

```
Assume A = 12
A >= 10      TRUE
A EQ 3*4     TRUE
A NE 12      FALSE
```

The IN operator (not in V5) is used to see if a specific value occurs in a list of possibilities. This makes it unnecessary to create long lists of OR combinations. The list must consist of constants, as in:

```
IF CITY IN ('CARY','HUIZEN','HEIDELBERG','NORTH YORK')
     THEN .... ;
IF CHOICE IN (1,3,5,7,9) THEN .... ;
```

If two or more conditions must be tested in order to ultimately judge whether the THEN or the ELSE applies, then these tests can be joined together by means of OR and AND. With OR, at least one condition must be fulfilled to make the total TRUE, but with AND the conditions on both sides of the equation must be fulfilled. For example:

```
IF STATE = 'NC' OR STATE = 'SC' THEN REGION = 'SE';
IF AGE GE 18 AND AGE LT 65 THEN .... ;
```

There are strict rules for the priorities by which the evaluation of complex conditions takes place, but in practice it appears not to be intuitive for most people and it is easy to make mistakes. For this reason, it is advisable always to use parentheses when using OR and AND to make the various groups clearly visible and keep the priorities of the evaluation straight. The sample program in the following section reveals how easy it is to make mistakes in constructing conditions, especially in combination with AND and OR.

LT	<	less than
GT	>	greater than
EQ	=	equal to
LE	<=	less than or equal to
GE	>=	greater than or equal to
NE	=	not equal to
IN		equal to one of a list

Figure 6.3: The comparison operators of the SAS System. The operators are placed between the expressions that should be compared.

Subsetting IF

Besides the general IF statement there is also an abbreviated form, the 'Subsetting IF statement'. It consists of only IF and a condition. The function of the subsetting IF statement is to process the rest of the DATA step only for observations whose conditions are fulfilled. Other observations are thrown out. Of course the same thing can be accomplished with normal IF statements, although with more code.

Figure 6.4 shows an example of the use of the subsetting IF statement and two variants of a normal IF statement in which the same results are achieved. The DELETE statement which is used has the effect that the processing of the observation is terminated, that the observation is thrown out and the program goes back to the beginning of the DATA step to read and process the subsequent observation.

The subsetting IF statement has lost some if its value through the introduction of the WHERE statement and the WHERE data set option, with which the same kinds of selections are possible. The most important differences between WHERE and subsetting IF are:

- WHERE can only be used in combination with SAS data sets, subsetting IF can also be used in combination with the reading of external files using INPUT statements.

- WHERE takes effect before the observation is read in, subsetting IF after.

- This last point has the consequence that the FIRST. and LAST. options (discussed later) continue to work in combination with the WHERE statement.

- WHERE can also be used in procedures, while subsetting IF is purely a DATA step statement.

```
Process only observations with SALARY > 6000

   IF SALARY GT 6000;

   IF SALARY LE 6000 THEN DELETE;

   IF SALARY GT 6000 THEN
      DO;
         ... (rest of the program)
      END;
   ELSE DELETE;
```

Figure 6.4: The three constructions in this figure all have the effect that the remainder of the DATA step is only executed for observations where SALARY is greater than 6000. All other observations are thrown out.

Sample program using IF statements

Figures 6.5 and 6.6 illustrate the IF condition at work, particularly with OR and AND constructions, in log and list printouts. The point of the exercise is to make selections from an airline company file of passenger data. For the sake of clarity, the input is printed out in the log, by means of the LIST statement (line 6). This statement prints out the whole input line as the SAS System gets it. On line 15 you see a FORMAT statement. The FORMAT statement complements the INFORMAT statement: it defines the layout of a variable in the printout. In the example the FORMAT statement causes the variable DATE to be printed as a recognizable date. Without it, the SAS System would print the date as a number. In statement 29 the format for DATE is changed and in the related printout you can see the numerical nature of a SAS date.

The first IF statement (line 7) simply selects the lines with flight number KL631. In the second IF statement, this is combined with a date. The following IF statements try to select a flight on two dates. On line 10, this runs up against the priority rules of AND and OR. 15 May is evaluated in combination with flight number (the AND condition) but for 22 May the AND restriction is not applicable. Thus every flight on 22 May is selected. On line 11 the effect is worse still: non-0, non-missing means TRUE in the SAS System. And since, internally for the SAS System, a date is a number which is non-0 and non-missing, the OR condition always gives a TRUE result and all input lines get selected. Only the statement on line 13 gives the desired result, because now, thanks to the parentheses, it is clear both to the reader and to the SAS System that the test of the dates belong together.

```
1                          The SAS System (6.08)
                                         11:27 Friday, June 3, 1994

NOTE: Copyright(c) 1989 by SAS Institute Inc., Cary, NC USA.
NOTE: SAS (r) Proprietary Software Release 6.08   TS405

NOTE: The initialization phase used 0.06 CPU seconds and 1092K.

NOTE: SAS job started on Friday 03JUN94 11:27 (199406031127)

1              * SAMPLE PROGRAM IF STATEMENTS ;
2
3              TITLE2 'IF STATEMENTS WITH AND AND OR OPERATORS';
4              DATA ONE TWO THREE FOUR FIVE;
5                INPUT FLIGHTNR $ FLDATE:DATE7. CAP PASS;
6                LIST;
7                IF FLIGHTNR = 'KL631' THEN OUTPUT ONE;
8                IF FLIGHTNR = 'KL631' AND FLDATE='15MAY91'D THEN OUTPUT TWO;
9                IF FLIGHTNR = 'KL631' AND FLDATE='15MAY91'D OR
10                  FLDATE='22MAY91'D THEN OUTPUT THREE;
11               IF FLIGHTNR = 'KL631' AND FLDATE='15MAY91'D OR '22MAY91'D
12                  THEN OUTPUT FOUR;
13               IF FLIGHTNR = 'KL631' AND (FLDATE='15MAY91'D OR
14                  FLDATE='22MAY91'D) THEN OUTPUT FIVE;
15               FORMAT FLDATE DATE7.;
16             CARDS;

RULE:          ----+----1----+----2----+----3----+----4----+----5----+----6-
17             KL519 12MAY91 124 112
18             KL519 15MAY91 124 124
19             KL519 22MAY91 168 138
20             KL631 13MAY91 289 254
21             KL631 15MAY91 289 212
22             KL631 22MAY91 212 164
23             KL632 15MAY91 289 234
24             KL632 22MAY91 212 199
NOTE: The data set WORK.ONE has 3 observations and 4 variables.
NOTE: The data set WORK.TWO has 1 observations and 4 variables.
NOTE: The data set WORK.THREE has 4 observations and 4 variables.
NOTE: The data set WORK.FOUR has 8 observations and 4 variables.
NOTE: The data set WORK.FIVE has 2 observations and 4 variables.
NOTE: The DATA statement used 0.05 CPU seconds and 2238K.

25             PROC PRINT DATA=ONE;

NOTE: The PROCEDURE PRINT printed page 1.
NOTE: The PROCEDURE PRINT used 0.01 CPU seconds and 2292K.

26             PROC PRINT DATA=TWO;

NOTE: The PROCEDURE PRINT printed page 2.
NOTE: The PROCEDURE PRINT used 0.01 CPU seconds and 2292K.

27             PROC PRINT DATA=THREE;

NOTE: The PROCEDURE PRINT printed page 3.
NOTE: The PROCEDURE PRINT used 0.01 CPU seconds and 2292K.
```

Figure 6.5 (part 1): This program shows the working of the conditions in the IF statement, especially in combination with AND and OR.

```
2                          The SAS System (6.08)
                                            11:27 Friday, June 3, 1994

28            PROC PRINT DATA=FOUR;
29               FORMAT FLDATE 7.;

NOTE: The PROCEDURE PRINT printed page 4.
NOTE: The PROCEDURE PRINT used 0.01 CPU seconds and 2292K.

30            PROC PRINT DATA=FIVE;

NOTE: The PROCEDURE PRINT printed page 5.
NOTE: The PROCEDURE PRINT used 0.01 CPU seconds and 2292K.

NOTE: The SAS session used 0.31 CPU seconds and 2292K.
NOTE: SAS Institute BV, 1217 KR Hilversum, The Netherlands
```

Figure 6.5 (part 2): Note the PROC PRINT of data set FOUR: by means of a FORMAT statement the layout of variable DATE is changed into a general numerical form. From this the numerical nature of a date in the SAS System is visible.

```
              The SAS System, Version 6.08                  1
        IF STATEMENTS WITH AND AND OR OPERATORS
                                    11:27 Friday, June 3, 1994

     OBS      FLIGHTNR      FLDATE     CAP     PASS

      1        KL631        13MAY91     289      254
      2        KL631        15MAY91     289      212
      3        KL631        22MAY91     212      164


              The SAS System, Version 6.08                  2
        IF STATEMENTS WITH AND AND OR OPERATORS
                                    11:27 Friday, June 3, 1994

     OBS      FLIGHTNR      FLDATE     CAP     PASS

      1        KL631        15MAY91     289      212


              The SAS System, Version 6.08                  3
        IF STATEMENTS WITH AND AND OR OPERATORS
                                    11:27 Friday, June 3, 1994

     OBS      FLIGHTNR      FLDATE     CAP     PASS

      1        KL519        22MAY91     168      138
      2        KL631        15MAY91     289      212
      3        KL631        22MAY91     212      164
      4        KL632        22MAY91     212      199
```

Figure 6.6 (part 1): The PROC PRINT output. Compare the selected observations with the input lines and the related IF statement.

```
                    The SAS System, Version 6.08                      4
        IF STATEMENTS WITH AND AND OR OPERATORS
                                    11:27 Friday, June 3, 1994

        OBS    FLIGHTNR     FLDATE     CAP    PASS

         1     KL519        11454      124    112
         2     KL519        11457      124    124
         3     KL519        11464      168    138
         4     KL631        11455      289    254
         5     KL631        11457      289    212
         6     KL631        11464      212    164
         7     KL632        11457      289    234
         8     KL632        11464      212    199


                    The SAS System, Version 6.08                      5
        IF STATEMENTS WITH AND AND OR OPERATORS
                                    11:27 Friday, June 3, 1994

        OBS    FLIGHTNR     FLDATE     CAP    PASS

         1     KL631        15MAY91    289    212
         2     KL631        22MAY91    212    164
```

Figure 6.6 (part 2): In the printout of data set FOUR the numerical nature of a date value is clearly visible.

DO-END groups

DO-END groups are used to mark groups of statements and eventually process them in a loop. Such a group consists of a DO statement, in one of its four basic forms, then all 'normal' statements and finally an END statement. The simplest form is used in the IF statement to attach an entire program segment as a whole to a THEN or ELSE branch. This technique is handled as before.

Repeated DO-END groups form a loop in the program: the 'DO loop'.

Iterative DO statement

The iterative DO statement repeats the statements in the DO-END group a predefined number of times. For this, an index variable is defined and start, end and stop values are used. The index variable (N in the following example) begins at the start value ('start') and each run through the DO-END group it is incremented by the step value ('step') until the end value is reached:

```
DO N = start TO end BY step;
```

In practice, the step value is quite often 1. In this case, the last part of the statement can be left out, as in the sample program (page 109).

A variant of the iterative DO statement is a form in which a number of discrete values are given for the index variable:

```
DO N = 1,2,3,7,11;
DO MONTH = 'JAN','APR','JUL','OCT';
```

The last example shows that in this case character variables can also be used as index variables.

DO WHILE statement

The DO WHILE statement processes the statements between DO and END as long as the condition after WHILE is true. The condition is placed in parentheses:

```
DO WHILE (condition);
```

The condition is evaluated before each pass though the DO-END group. If it yields TRUE, the statements are processed. As soon as the evaluation comes out FALSE, the processing continues with the first statement after the END statement. If the condition comes out FALSE already the first time, the statements of the group will never be processed.

DO UNTIL statement

The DO UNTIL statement is in a certain sense the complement of DO WHILE: the statements of the DO-END group are executed just until the condition TRUE comes out.

The most important difference between DO WHILE and DO UNTIL, however, is that DO WHILE tests the condition before processing of the DO group and DO UNTIL tests the condition afterwards. In other words the statements in a DO UNTIL group will always be processed at least once.

CONTINUE and LEAVE statement

It often happens in practice that a DO loop must be broken before it is finished running. This is what the CONTINUE and LEAVE statements are for. The CONTINUE statement stops the loop and goes back to the DO statement for the following pass. The LEAVE statement breaks the processing of the DO-END group completely and the program execution continues with the statement after the END statement.

Example of a DO-END group

Figure 6.7 shows the printout of the LOG of a program in which three DATA steps always give the same result, by means of three different DO-END group constructions. There is always an index variable X which can have the value of 0 through 10 and a variable Y which is X squared. In the first loop X gets its value directly assigned as an index variable. In the other two DO loops X is initialized before the DO loop and gets incremented by 1 with each pass. In all DO-END groups an OUTPUT statement is used to output an observation to the data set for each pass.

```
1                           The SAS System (6.08)
                                        11:32 Friday, June 3, 1994

NOTE: Copyright(c) 1989 by SAS Institute Inc., Cary, NC USA.
NOTE: SAS (r) Proprietary Software Release 6.08   TS405

NOTE: The initialization phase used 0.06 CPU seconds and 1092K.

NOTE: SAS job started on Friday 03JUN94 11:32 (199406031132)

1              * SAMPLE PROGRAM DO LOOPS ;
2
3              DATA DOLOOP1;
4                 DO X = 0 TO 10;
5                    Y = X**2;
6                    OUTPUT;
7                 END;

NOTE: The data set WORK.DOLOOP1 has 11 observations and 2 variables.
NOTE: The DATA statement used 0.02 CPU seconds and 1759K.

8              DATA DOLOOP2;
9                 DO WHILE (X LE 10);
10                   Y = X**2;
11                   OUTPUT;
12                   X+1;
13                END;

NOTE: The data set WORK.DOLOOP2 has 11 observations and 2 variables.
NOTE: The DATA statement used 0.01 CPU seconds and 1759K.

14             DATA DOLOOP3;
15                DO UNTIL (X GT 10);
16                   Y = X**2;
17                   OUTPUT;
18                   X+1;
19                END;

NOTE: The data set WORK.DOLOOP3 has 11 observations and 2 variables.
NOTE: The DATA statement used 0.01 CPU seconds and 1759K.

NOTE: The SAS session used 0.26 CPU seconds and 1813K.
NOTE: SAS Institute BV, 1217 KR Hilversum, The Netherlands
```

Figure 6.7: The DATA steps in this program all produce the same result: an X variable which runs from 0 to 10 and a Y variable which equals X squared.

Date and time

SAS date and SAS time

It has already been mentioned that the SAS System's internal date is a numeric value: the internal SAS date is the number of days since 1 January 1960. This is not to say that the system cannot handle a date before 1 January 1960; dates before 1960 have a negative value. The SAS calendar runs from 1582 till 20000.

SAS time works on a similar principle: time of day is the number of seconds since midnight. For a date/time combination, the SAS System counts the number of seconds since midnight, 1 January 1960. The advantage of this method is that both dates and times are calculated in the same simple way. If you want to know the number of days between two dates, you just subtract one from the other. It does not have to deal with cycles of months and years. The same applies for time calculations. Externally, the internal value becomes a date or a time again by means of the appropriate formats, comparable to the informats for reading date values which we encountered earlier.

Date or time constant

The text '01APR92' will be recognized by the SAS System as a character constant and not as a date. To enter a date as a constant into a program, it must be followed by a D, as in '01APR92'D. In the same way, a time constant must be identified with a T, as in '13:43'T. You can guess the date/time constant: '01APR92:13:43'DT.

When a piece of text is tagged in this manner as a date or a time, the system automatically converts it to an internal SAS date, time or date/time combination.

Date and time formats

As has been said, dates are only displayed as dates and times as times if the variable involved has been formatted accordingly. This can best be done in a FORMAT statement, such as:

```
FORMAT DATE DATE7.;
```

DATE7. translates the numeric variable DATE in a layout as 15APR93, 7 positions long. If the format is applied, the numerical value of the variable (the number of days since 1960) will be converted into the DATE7. form. Take note that just as informats, formats always have a

'.'. This is normally in the final position, although in some formats a user-defined number of decimals can follow the point. Figure 6.8 gives an overview of the more common date/time formats.

When you use the default length, the length indicator (w) need not be given. DATE. is automatically interpreted as DATE7.. Decimals mean a decimal fraction of the smallest unit; thus, the decimal in HHMM8.2 means hundredths of a minute, not seconds.

Name of format	possible length (default)	layout sample
DATEw.	5-9 (7)	21SEP90
DATETIMEw.d	7-40 (16)	21SEP90:13:53:25
DDMMYYw.	2-8 (8)	21/09/90
JULIANw.	5-7 (5)	90264
MMDDYYw.	2-8 (8)	09/21/90
MONYYw.	5-7 (5)	SEP90
QTRw.	1-32 (1)	3
WORDDATXw.	2-32 (18)	21 September 1990
YYMMDDw.	2-8 (8)	90-09-18
YYQw.	4-32 (6)	1990Q3
HHMMw.d	2-20 (5)	13:53
MMSSw.d	2-20 (5)	833 (MMSS6.: 833:25)
TIMEw.d	2-20 (8)	13:53:25

Figure 6.8: Some of the standard date and time formats of the SAS System. In all samples the date of September, 21 1990 is used and a time of 13:53:25. The layout sample is based on the default value.

If such a FORMAT statement is used in the DATA step, the information will be put with the variable in the descriptive section of the data set, so that all succeeding PROC steps can use the information. The FORMAT statement can also be used in a procedure, in which case the specification is valid only for that procedure. In either case however, the date or time variable remains a number value internally as usual. Therefore there is no problem at all with first using one date/time format and later on another.

Date/time functions

The date/time capabilities are supported by a variety of functions, a number of which are given in figure 6.9. TODAY() and TIME() have no arguments, only the parentheses to indicate that they are functions. The majority of the other functions have a single date, date/time or time as argument. Only INTCK and INTNX have three arguments. Both functions work on time intervals. The first argument gives the type of interval (such as 'DAY', 'WEEK', 'MONTH', 'HOUR', 'MINUTE', and so on), the second argument gives a 'starting from' reference and the third argument an 'until'. For INTCK this 'until' is a second date: INTCK calculates the number of intervals of the given type between two dates. For INTNX the 'until' is a number of intervals counted from 'starting from' while INTNX calculates a new date a given number of intervals ahead (or back). In principle, the result of INTNX is always the first day of the interval involved. The result of SUNDAY=INTNX('WEEK',TODAY(),0); is thus the date of the Sunday of the current week.

Starting with Release 6.07 it is also possible to use these functions to work with "shifted periods "; for example, for many businesses the week begins on Monday and the fiscal year on 1 April. For this, the shift is given in the logical subunits of the primary unit. The shift is placed after the primary unit, separated by a period. Thus, a year beginning on April 1 is 'YEAR.4'.

ISO week number

You can use INTCK and INTNX to calculate the ISO week number. According the ISO standard, the week count of a year begins with the week in which the first thursday of the year falls, and the week runs from Monday through Sunday. In other words, if January 1 falls between a Monday and a Thursday, then January 1 falls in week 1, and if January 1 falls between a Friday and a Sunday, then January 1 belongs to week 52 or 53 of the previous year. Similarly the last days of the previous year could belong to week 1 of the new year. In the following formula the last days of the year always fall in week 52 or 53 and January 1 falls either in week 0 or in week 1. The calculation to find the week number for the datevalue in theDate looks like this:

```
WEEK = INTCK('WEEK.2',INTNX('YEAR',theDate,0,theDate) +
        (WEEKDAY(INTNX('YEAR',theDate,0)-1) < 5);
```

The first term calculates the number of one-week intervals between the input date (theDate) and January 1. 'WEEK.2' shifts the first day of the week from Sunday to Monday. The second term increments by 1 for the years in which January 1 falls on Monday through Thursday. This construction makes use of the fact that the SAS System evaluates a logical expression as 0 (FALSE) or 1 (TRUE). If the WEEKDAY function returns a value lower that 5 for January 1, then the week number in the first term will be incremented by 1!

Such an intricate construction as this lends itself to being written as a macro. Macros are discussed in chapter 14. For the macro user, it would look like this:

```
WEEK = %ISOWEEK(theDate);
```

Appendix F describes a macro for a complete ISO week calculation, with the correct spill over of days into the previous or following year.

'Vertical' processing

So far we have used the concept that the DATA step works observation by observation. This is the general rule. Before the SAS System starts processing the DATA step it establishes which variables appear, and sets these all to 'missing value'. It repeats that every time it begins processing the next observation.

It is easy to imagine situations where you would like to save a value from a previous observation, for example for comparison or totaling.

RETAIN statement

The RETAIN statement is used to specify that a variable should keep its value across iterations of the DATA step, i.e. the variable will not be reset to missing each time the DATA step starts processing a new observation. The form is simple: RETAIN followed by the list of variables to be retained. You can use the RETAIN statement also to assign an initial value to the retained variable. For instance:

```
RETAIN DATE TOTAL 0;
```

SUM statement

The SUM statement increments an 'accumulator' (a normal numeric variable) with the value of an expression. The form is:

```
accumulator + expression ;
```

The SUM statement only increments (adds to the accumulator); to decrement (subtract), you have to make a little detour: A + (-1). The SUM statement incorporates a RETAIN and an initialization at 0.

So
```
A + B;
```

is equivalent to:

```
RETAIN A 0;
A = SUM(A,B);
```

The LAG and DIF functions

The LAG function is used to take a value of a variable from a previous observation, as far back as 99 observations. DIF does the same but returns the difference between the value of the variable in the current observation and the value of the variable in the previous observation. The form is:

```
LAG(argument) or LAGn(argument)          (n = 1 .. 99)
DIF(argument) or DIFn(argument)          (n = 1 .. 99)
```

SAS builds an internal stack when LAG and DIF are used: at each execution of the function the value of the variable is appended to the bottom of the stack and the value at the top row is returned as the function result and that row is then dropped. As a result, you must be very careful when using LAG and DIF: it should be executed only once (not more, not less) per DATA step iteration for each variable, under penalty of getting out of sync!

Missing values

In the previous chapters we have come across the concept 'missing value' from time to time. A missing value is simply the value of a variable which has not yet been given another (normal) value. For numeric variables this is indicated by a period. If mathematical operations are attempted on missing values they result again in missing values. Functions normally operate only on non-missing values. The effect can be clearly seen in the following example. In the calculation of C with the SUM function, you might think that missing value and zero are the same thing, but the MEAN function in the example clearly shows that missing values are excluded from the calculation.

```
A = .;
B = 2;
C = A+B;            * C is missing! ;
C = SUM(A,B);       * C = 2;
C = MEAN(A,B);      * C = 2;
```

The first statement in this example also shows how a numeric variable can be assigned a missing value explicitly.

For character variables, a missing value is indicated by a single space (blank).

When a data set is sorted using PROC SORT, all missing values always move to the beginning of the data set: they are smaller than the smallest 'normal' (non-missing) value.

There are also such things as "special missing values". These are only used in restricted situations, so we will not go into them any further here. The purpose of the special missing values is to be able to make distinctions between different causes of missing values. In an inquiry, for instance, you can use it to make a distinction between 'do not know', 'no answer' and 'incorrect answer'.

Exercises

1. A computer center records all executed programs in a file. Each record of the file contains an account number, the execution date (as a SAS date value), and other pertinent data about the executed program. The file is created monthly. When the month is over, a report must be prepared. A complicating factor is that sometimes records from the previous months are in the file. These must be skipped in the report. It is required that the program with which the report is made can run on any day of the month following the month covered by the report. Write a routine by which records from older months can be excluded from the analysis.

2. The following program reads in data and must keep count of how many records it has read.

    ```
    DATA COUNT;
    INFILE MYDATA;
    INPUT @1 NAME $15. @16 ADDRESS $25.;
    N+1;
    ```

    a. Does N give the correct number of records read?

    b. Replace the last statement with N=N+1; does N now give the correct number?

    Note: In this exercise, you could have used the 'automatic SAS variable' _N_. This contains the number of iterations of the DATA step and thus in this program the number of input records read.

3. The weather service has collected data on temperature and rainfall per state for a period of one year. The records have the following layout:

FIELD	START POSITION	LENGTH	TYPE	COMMENTS
State	1	2	CHAR	NC TX MN etc.
Month	3	3	CHAR	MAR MAY etc.
Rainfall	6	5	NUM	millimeters
Max. temp.	11	5	NUM	1 decimal
Min. temp.	16	5	NUM	1 decimal
Average temp.	21	6	NUM	2 decimals

Decide for yourself whether these data are already on disk or tape, or will be included in the program as input records. The model solution however will assume the records are in a file named WEATHER.DATA.

a. Make a SAS data set containing the above data.

b. Add a variable containing the difference between minimum and maximum temperature.

c. Add a variable containing a measure for the rainfall: The measure is 'DRY' for less than 5 centimeters of rainfall and 'WET' for all other cases.

d. Add a variable containing a measure for the temperature according to the following rules (temperatures in celcius):

TROPICAL   average temperature higher than 23 °. maximum temperature above 30 °.

HOT   average temperature between 18 °. and 23 °., minimum temperature above 15 °., maximum temperature under 30 °.

MILD   average temperature between 10 °. and 18 °.

COOL   minimum temperature above 0 °, maximum temperature under 15 °.

COLD   minimum temperature under 0 deg or maximum temperature under 5 °.

In case any of the above criteria overlap, the warmest appropriate qualification should be given. If the month falls outside any of the criteria, the result should be a 'missing value'.

CHAPTER 7

Functions

In chapter 6, 'Programming the DATA step', we came across the concept of functions and their role in the SAS language. In this chapter we shall introduce a number of frequently used functions and illustrate them with examples.

Character functions

Character functions perform manipulations on text strings, which may or may not be contained in a character variable. The result is again a text string, which might be assigned to a character variable.

SUBSTR function

SUBSTR is used to lift a segment from a text string. The user specifies how long the segment should be and where it is in the text. The segment to be lifted begins at position 'start' and covers 'length' positions.

```
SUBSTR(text string,start,length)
```

If the length parameter is not specified, then the function covers the segment from 'start' to the end of the input text.

SUBSTR is a somewhat peculiar function: it can also appear to the left of the = sign in an assignment statement. This changes the way the function works. The specified segment is not lifted, but changed. This is demonstrated below:

```
NAME = 'MARIE THERESE';
SEGMENT = SUBSTR(NAME,1,5);
SUBSTR(NAME,7,7) = 'HELENE ';
```

After these statements, the variable SEGMENT has the value 'MARIE' and the variable NAME now has the value 'MARIE HELENE ' (note the space at the end).

LENGTH function

The LENGTH function returns the length of a text string (in the function argument) through the last non-blank position. The form is:

```
LENGTH(argument)
```

The result of the function is numeric. For instance if:

```
TEXT = 'This is text with trailing blanks
L_STRING = LENGTH(TEXT);
```

then L_STRING will have the value 33.

TRIM function

The TRIM function removes spaces at the end of a text string.

```
TRIM(argument)
```

This function is often used in combination with the concatenation operator. The SAS System always fills out a character variable with spaces to the length of the variable. If two character variables are to be joined by concatenation, the resulting text can have many intermediate spaces. Say that SEGMENT1 and SEGMENT2 are character variables with a length of 10 positions and COMBI1 and COMBI2 have a length of 15 positions:

```
SEGMENT1 = 'SAS';
SEGMENT2 = 'SYSTEM';
COMBI1 = SEGMENT1||SEGMENT2;
COMBI2 = TRIM(SEGMENT1)||SEGMENT2;
```

After these statements are processed, COMBI1 and COMBI2, respectively, have the values 'SAS   SYSTE' and 'SASSYSTEM   '.

COMBI1 takes the first 10 positions of SEGMENT1, including the 'trailing blanks', This leaves only 5 positions for the first 5 characters of SEGMENT2. When creating COMBI2 first the spaces from SEGMENT1 are removed and then SEGMENT2 is appended to it.

SCAN function

The SCAN function searches the input argument for words and gives as the result the text of a single word from the input argument:

```
SCAN(argument, n, separators)
```

The first argument contains the input text, the second argument, 'n', gives the position number of the object word: the result of the function is thus the 'n'th word of the input. The separators parameter can be used to define what characters should be recognized as separators between the words of the input string. The third parameter is optional. If this is left out, then all signs which are used for punctuation in normal language are recognized as acceptable separator, such as ,.!?space.

```
THIRD = SCAN('SCAN THIS TEXT FOR WORDS',3)
CITY = SCAN('AMSTERDAM AVENUE,NEW YORK',2,',');
```

THIRD will have the value 'TEXT' and CITY the value 'NEW YORK'.

INDEX function and INDEXC function

Both INDEX and INDEXC search for the occurrence of a specific text or set of characters in the input argument:

```
INDEX(input argument,search text)
INDEXC(input argument,search characters,
       search characters,..);
```

The INDEX function searches for the whole text in 'search text' occurring anywhere in the input argument. If the search is successful (if 'search text' is found), the result of the function is the position number in the input argument of the beginning of the search text. The INDEXC function searches at the character level: if any character from the 'search character' parameters is found, its position is given as a result. Both functions return 0 as a result if the searches are unsuccessful.

The following program segment extracts all the spaces from a text string and replaces them with underscores '_':

```
DO WHILE (INDEX(INPUTSTR,' ') > 0);
 SUBSTR(INPUTSTR,INDEX(INPUTSTR,' '),1) = '_';
END;
```

A DO WHILE has been used in this example to evaluate whether or not a space is present before executing the statement with the SUBSTR function. The example also makes it clear that functions can be used as arguments of functions.

The above example could have been carried out with INDEXC as well, because the search string was only one character. An easier method would have been to use the TRANSLATE function.

LEFT function and RIGHT function

The LEFT and RIGHT functions are used to align text. LEFT removes spaces at the beginning of a text, thus shifting the text to the left margin, and RIGHT removes spaces at the end and fills out the beginning, in other words shifting the text to the right margin. The example with the TRIM function can also be realized using LEFT and RIGHT, although it is more complicated:

```
COMBI = LEFT(RIGHT(SEGMENT1)||SEGMENT2);
```

The text SAS of SEGMENT1 is first shifted to the right, so that it will be directly connected by the concatenation to the text SYSTEM of SEGMENT2. Then the whole text is shifted back to the left.

COMPRESS function and COMPBL function

The COMPRESS function removes characters from an input argument.

```
COMPRESS(input argument,characters)
```

Usually COMPRESS is used to suppress spaces from the input, in which case the second function argument ("characters") does not need to be given. If in the second argument one or more characters are given, these characters will be removed. Take note: characters are removed, not segments of text. Thus if the second argument consists of 'DOG', all Ds, all Os and all Gs will be removed. Example:

```
STRING = 'ABC     19352 X Y Z';
PRESS1 = COMPRESS(STRING);
PRESS2 = COMPRESS(STRING,'123');
```

After the execution of these statements, PRESS1 will have the value 'ABC19352XYZ' and PRESS2 the value 'ABC   95 X Y Z'.

The COMPBL function removes only multiple spaces. One space is left over. Thus COMPBL(STRING) would result in:

```
'ABC 19352 X Y Z'
```

TRANSLATE function and TRANWRD function

With the TRANSLATE function you can replace characters in the input text with other characters. This takes place in a character-by-character manner. TRANWRD on the other hand replaces complete words (or combinations of letters) with other words. The structure is:

```
TRANSLATE(input string,new1,old1,new2,old2,...)
TRANWRD(input string,old word,new word)
```

The following example shows the difference between the way the two functions work:

```
STRING = 'we bought a new television set';
TR1 = TRANSLATE(STRING,'b','n','i','e','g','w');
TR2 = TRANWRD(STRING,'new','big');
```

TR1 now has the value 'gi bought a big tilivisiob sit' and TR2 the value 'we bought a big television set'.

General numeric functions

Under this umbrella the functions are gathered which have no clear arithmetic tasks, such as rounding off.

ROUND function

The ROUND function rounds off the number in the first argument. The rounding unit goes in the second argument.

```
ROUND(argument,rounding unit)
```

If the second argument is left out, rounding is to whole numbers. The rounding rule is: 5 or higher in the position after the rounding position, round up, otherwise round down:

```
ROUND(123.68)              results in: 124
ROUND(123.68,0.1)          results in: 123.7
ROUND(123,68,10)           results in: 120
```

INT, FLOOR and CEIL functions

The INT, FLOOR and CEIL functions give a whole number as a result.

```
INT(argument)
FLOOR(argument)
CEIL(argument)
```

The differences can be explained easily when you imagine the number line. INT searches the whole number in the direction the 0 point of the line, FLOOR always goes to the left and CEIL to the right:

negative numbers	0	positive numbers
INT→ CEIL→ FLOOR←		INT← CEIL→ FLOOR←

Thus CEIL always returns a number larger than the argument, FLOOR a number smaller than the argument and INT 'cuts off' the argument:

`INT(123.68)` and `FLOOR(123.68)`	result in: 123
`CEIL(123.68)`	results in: 124
`INT(-123.68)` and `CEIL(-123.68)`	result in: -123
`FLOOR(-123.68)`	results in: -124

ABS function

The ABS function gives the absolute value of the input argument, thus stripping the number of any minus signs:

```
ABS(argument)
```

Hence ABS(-5) returns 5.

Arithmetic functions

The arithmetic functions include a number of complex arithmetic operations, such as logarithms, root extraction and so on.

LOG function

In the SAS System, several logarithmic functions are available, with various bases.

```
LOG(argument)
LOG2(argument)
LOG10(argument)
```

The LOG function yields the 'natural base' e ($e \approx 2.71828$). LOG2 yields base 2 and LOG10 base 10. All these functions require as an argument a number larger than 0, otherwise the result is a missing value.

`LOG(10)`	results in: 2.30259
`LOG2(10)`	results in: 3.32193
`LOG10(10)`	results in: 1.00000

EXP function

The EXP function raises the number e to the power in the function argument:

```
EXP(argument)
```

As per definition $e^{\ln(x)} = x$, in which ln stands for the natural logarithm. So the following holds:

```
A = LOG(10);
B = EXP(A);
```
results in: A=2.30259
results in: B=10

The maximum input argument for the EXP function on IBM mainframe computers is 174.673. The function result is a number of 76 digits! Other limits apply in other systems.

SQRT function

The SQRT (SQuare RooT) function takes the square root of the argument:

```
SQRT(argument)
```

For example:

```
SQRT(25)
```
results in: 5

The input argument for the SQRT function must be 0 or positive, otherwise the result is a missing value (you cannot take the square root of a negative number).

MOD function

The MOD (modulo) function calculates the division remainder of two arguments:

```
MOD(argument1,argument2)
```

The division remainder of argument1/argument2 is the result.

```
A = MOD(10,3)
B = MOD(-65,31)
```
results in: A=1
results in: B=-3

In the second example, you can see the processing of negative numbers: - 65 : 31 = -2, remainder -3.

Statistical functions

There are many statistical functions available in the SAS System. These include a wide variety of probability functions. In this book we will only go into the most "mundane" statistical functions. For the more specialized functions, please refer to the Language Guide and the SAS/STAT Reference Guide.

MEAN function

The MEAN function calculates the average value of the input argument:

```
MEAN(argument1,argument2,...)
```

The number of arguments is in principle unlimited. For the calculation of the average, only non-missing arguments are considered. If there is a very large number of arguments, it can be useful to make a 'variable list'. This is done by preceding the arguments with the keyword OF, followed by the range of the variables. Thus if you want to calculate the average from variables X1 through X10, you could write MEAN(OF X1-X10). This construction with OF can also be used in combination with specific individual variables, in which case you do not put a comma between the variables.

```
A = 3; B = 5; C = 9;
D = MEAN(A,B,C, . ,10)              results in: D=6.75
```

Take note: the functions within the DATA step work per observation, not on the DATA step as a whole. The MEAN function can therefore calculate the average of the values of a number of variables in a single observation. PROC MEANS calculates the average value of a variable, taken over all observations (or possibly per BY group). The same distinction holds for all other functions.

MIN function and MAX function

The MIN and MAX functions return as a result the lowest or highest value, respectively, of any of the input arguments.

```
MIN(argument1,argument2,...)
MAX(argument1,argument2,....)
```

Here too, the number of arguments is in principle unlimited, and here too the variable list construction with OF can be used.

```
A = 3;  B = 5;  C = 9;
D = MIN(A,B,C,  .  ,10);          results in: D=3
E = MAX(A,B,C);                   results in: E = 9
```

STD function

The STD function calculates the standard deviation of the argument.

```
STD(argument1,argument2,...)
```

The same remarks made about the other statistical functions apply here
as well.

```
A = 3;  B = 5;  C = 9;
D = STD(A,B,C,  .  ,10);          results in: D=3.30404
```

Other functions

In addition to the function categories already described, there are many
others: trigonometric functions, financial and econometric functions,
'random number generators' and so on. For all these functions, please
refer to the SAS Language Guide. Here we will only take a quick look
at a few examples of these functions.

UNIFORM function

UNIFORM is a 'random number generator'. Random number generators
are functions which generate arbitrary numbers whose chances of
coming up are determined by a probability distribution function. In this
way UNIFORM generates an arbitrary number between 0 and 1 for
which any value between the two limits has an equal chance of occurring.

```
UNIFORM(0)
```

A random number generator always needs some value to start. This is
called the 'seed value'. By specifying zero as the seed value as done
above, the SAS System uses the value of the system clock as seed.

The following example uses UNIFORM to generate a random (whole)
number in the range from 0 through 20:

```
FIGURE = INT(21 * UNIFORM(0));
```

Here is how to take a random sample of about 5 percent from a file:

```
IF UNIFORM(0) LT .05;
```

We on purpose say 'around 5 percent' because UNIFORM naturally has a 5 percent chance of yielding a value smaller that 0.05, but that of course does not mean that exactly 5 percent of the observations will pass the subsetting IF statement.

NORMAL function

The NORMAL function is also a random number generator. NORMAL yields a number drawn from a so-called 'normal distribution', which is a bell curve distribution: a large chance of the value lying near the average and a rapidly decreasing probability of greater deviation. The rapidity with which the chance of deviation from the average decreases is determined through the standard deviation.

```
NORMAL(0)
```

NORMAL returns a value from a distribution with average 0 and standard deviation 1. To take an arbitrary number from a normal distribution of average 150 and standard deviation 10, write:

```
SAMPLE = 150 + 10*NORMAL(0);
```

UNIFORM and NORMAL are two of the simplest random number generators. There are also random number generators available based on other probability distributions, including the Poisson distribution and the binomial distribution.

Financial functions

For financial analyses, there are functions available which all have a similar structure. The functions have 4 parameters, 3 of which must be given; the fourth is 'missing'. The function figures out the missing parameter and gives its value as the function result.

```
MORT(principal,instalment,interest,number of instalments)
```

MORT calculates a loan on an annuity basis. Given, for example, principal, installment and interest, the function calculates how many installments are to be paid. The interest must be expressed as a fraction per period. 10% interest per year is thus given in monthly periods as 0.1/12.

```
ANNU = MORT(50000,  .  ,0.10/12,30*12);
```

calculates the monthly payment for a loan with a principal of 50000 over 30 years at 10% interest (ANNU=438.7858).

The following functions work in a similar manner:

COMPOUND   Calculation of compound interest. Arguments: initial
                  amount, final amount, interest per period (as fraction,
                  see MORT function) and number of periods.

SAVING   Future value of periodic deposits. Arguments: final
                  amount, amount of deposit, interest per period (as
                  fraction) and number of periods.

Three sorts of arguments play a role in establishing a net cash value: interest, number of payments per interest period and the amount of payment. A function is available in two variants for calculating net cash value (net present value): NPV, which expects interest expressed as a percentage, and NETPV, which expects interest expressed as a fraction, as in the functions described earlier:

```
NPV(interest percentage,number of payments,
    amount1,amount2,...amountn)
NETPV(interest fraction,number of payments,
    amount1,amount2,...amountn)
```

If interest is calculated per quarter based on 9% per year and payments are monthly, the function looks like this:

```
NETPV(.09/4,3,  ...)
```

INPUT function

The INPUT function is similar to the INPUT statement. It reads a value, applying a given informat, and returns the value read as function result.

```
INPUT(argument,informat)
```

The function is used most of all to read and interpret (segments of) character variables according to a layout specification.

```
A = '12APR85';
B = INPUT(A,DATE7.);
```
results in B=9233
(SAS date value)

In the above, variable A contains a date, but as text. The INPUT function reads this text and interprets it as a date.

PUT function

The PUT function does precisely the opposite of the INPUT function: a value in the input argument is transformed into a segment of text, according to a given format specification.

```
PUT(argument,format)
```

The PUT function is often used to validate input data on the basis of a table of permitted codes. We will come back to this in the chapter on PROC FORMAT.

In the SAS Procedures Guide (description of PROC FORMAT) a format is defined which translates the two-letter codes of the American states into the complete names of the states. The example below shows how the PUT function can be used to get the name of a state:

```
LENGTH STATE $20;
CODE = 'MA';
STATE = PUT(CODE, $STATE.);
```

If the variable CODE should not contain any valid state code, the format does not apply and the result of the function is the same as the input. This can be used to test the correctness of the value of the variable CODE:

```
IF CODE = PUT(CODE,$STATE.) THEN
  DO;
      * CODE contains an invalid value;
  END;
```

Warning

In this and previous chapters many building blocks have been described for the construction of expressions and calculations in the SAS System. In principle, you can make expressions as complex as you wish, with any combination of calculations and functions, including the use of functions as arguments for other functions. Be very careful to keep your programs legible and understandable. The following is formally correct, but practically impossible for an outsider to understand:

```
ROUND(MEAN(MIN(0,A),MAX(0,B),MEAN(A,B,C)))
```

If A=3, B=5, C=9, then this expression can be evaluated as follows:

ROUND(MEAN(0,5,5.6667)) = ROUND(3.5556) = 4

Exercises

1. Study the vollowing SAS program and answer the questions:

```
DATA RATING;
    INPUT ID_NO RATE1 RATE2 RATE3;
    AVE1 = (RATE1 + RATE2 + RATE3)/3;
    AVE2 = MEAN(RATE1,RATE2,RATE3);
CARDS;
03 6 6 6
26 3 2 7
18 8 7 .
```

   a. Which variables does the SAS System define during the compilation phase of the program?

   b. What are the values of the variables at the end of the first pass through the DATA step during the execution phase?

   c. How many passes does the DATA step run?

   d. Are AVE1 and AVE2 always the same? Explain your answer.

   e. The variable HIGHEST should contain the highest value of the RATE variables. Write a routine to calculate HIGHEST. State where this routine should be inserted.

2. A light bulb factory collects daily data on production per machine and machine breakdown. These data are contained in input records with the following layout:

Category	Start position	Length	Description
date	1	8	as in 07/18/84
repairs	9	2	number of machine repairs
production	11	4	number of produced light bulbs
defect	15	4	faulty light bulbs
machine	19	1	machine code, A, B or C

a. Create a data set of only those records which indicate a failure rate of more than 10%.

b. During the reading of the data, print those records in which production contains no number greater then 0. (Hint: use the LIST statement.)

c. Accumulate the total number of repairs in a variable TOT_REP.

d. Put the total number of repairs for machine A in A_REP, for B in B_REP, for C in C_REP.

The bulbs made on A, B and C are different. A good bulb made on A yields a profit of $ 0.55, a good bulb from B yields a profit of $ 0.35 and a good bulb from C $ 0.19. Defective bulbs on the contrary give a loss: on A $ 0.23, on B $ 0.21 and on C $ 0.11.

e. Total the profit per machine on good bulbs and the loss on defects. Put the results into variables PROFIT_A, PROFIT_B, PROFIT_C and LOSS_A, LOSS_B, LOSS_C.

f. After reading the last record, calculate the total net proceeds for all machines together (total profit minus total loss) and the percentage of the gross profit lost through defects.

g. Write the total net proceeds calculated in f. into a data set PROFIT. (Hint: use the data set option KEEP.)

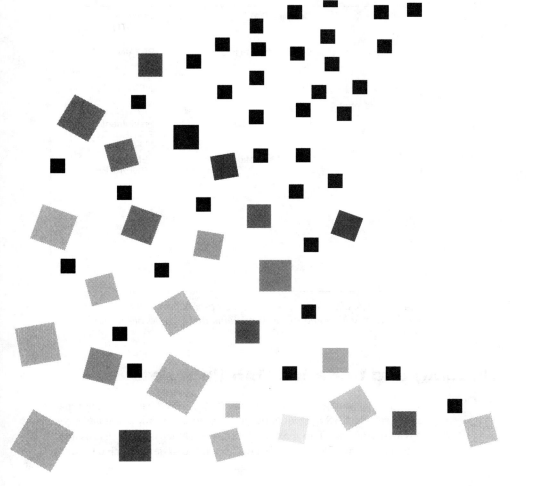

CHAPTER 8

SAS® Data Sets as Input

In figure 8.1 once again the flow of the execution of the DATA step is charted. The SAS System begins by reading in the source statements, from DATA to 'step boundary', i.e. until the SAS System recognizes the end of the DATA step. This end is formed by a following DATA or PROC statement, the CARDS statement or the RUN statement. After reading the source statements, the SAS System compiles the DATA step. During the compilation a buffer is set up in the computer memory to store all the variables. In SAS books, this is referred to as the 'Program Data Vector'. After successful compiling, the DATA step starts execution. First all variables are set to missing, unless blocked by a RETAIN statement. Then the SAS System reads a record and performs all desired operations. Finally in general an observation is written to the data set. If there is any further input, execution is repeated from the point where the variables are set to missing.

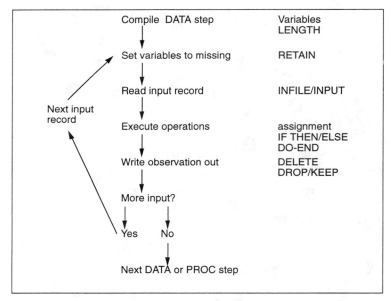

Figure 8.1: A schematic drawing of the compilation and execution of the DATA step, with some of the statements that play a role in each of the phases.

Reading and updating SAS data sets

The great advantage of using SAS data sets is that during the creation of a data set, the SAS System builds a complete description of it and saves it with the data set. This makes a SAS data set much easier to use as input than an external file. You only need to tell the system which data set to read and it knows immediately which variables are there, their types, possible format information, and so on.

Once data are in a SAS data set, you no longer use the INFILE and INPUT statements, but in their place the SET, MERGE, and UPDATE statements.

The SAS System does a RETAIN by default for variables which are read in using these statements. Only when changing BY group or transferring to another data set variables are set to missing. In practice this phenomenon is rarely seen, only in special constructions can this retain come as a surprise. In the exercises at the end of this chapter are a few examples of these hidden surprises.

Sample programs

This chapter is built around the example of a Do-It-Yourself shop. Each department of this shop has a list of articles that can be ordered and this information is stored in SAS data sets. Figure 8.2 shows the PROC PRINT output of the various order lists.

Department 1: Woodproducts etc.

OBS	ART_CAT	ART_NBR	QUANTITY
1	timber	10020	4
2	timber	10030	9
3	timber	10050	12
4	sheet	11030	8
5	sheet	11070	16

Department 2: Hardware and tools

OBS	ART_CAT	ART_NBR	QUANTITY
1	tools	40090	4
2	tools	45030	9
3	hardware	50010	15
4	hardware	50030	17

Department 3: Paint etc.

OBS	ART_CAT	ART_NBR	QUANTITY
1	paint	20060	17
2	paint	20100	8
3	paint	21090	9
4	paint	22001	3

Figure 8.2: These order lists of the departments in a Do-It-Yourself shop form the heart of our examples in this chapter.

SET statement

The principle of the SET statement

The SET statement is used for the simple reading of data stored in a SAS data set. In this statement you name the data set(s) to be read and any possible options for affecting the process of reading in one way or another.

```
SET dataset1 <dataset2 dataset3 ...> <options>;
```

If no data set name is given after SET, the SAS System uses the most recently created data set.

Figure 8.3 shows this in a simple example. A data set DISTANCE is read, containing the variables FROM, TO and MILE, the distance between FROM and TO in miles. In the DATA step, a new SAS data set is created: DISTKM. To create DISTKM the data set DISTANCE is read observation by observation, and a new variable (KM) is added which is calculated as MILE*1.609. The new data set DISTKM contains all the observations of DISTANCE and also all the variables of DISTANCE + the variable KM which is created in the DATA step.

```
data set DISTANCE contains the variables
    FROM
    TO
    MILE

task: create a new dataset containing distances measured in KM

  DATA DISTKM;
   SET DISTANCE;
   KM = MILE*1.609;
                DistKm
data set DISTANCE contains the variables
    FROM
    TO
    MILE
    KM
```

Figure 8.3: If the input data are already in a SAS data set, then using it is quite simple. Mention the data set in a SET statement and the SAS system has all the information about the data set at hand.

Concatenating and interleaving data sets

In the majority of cases, the SET statement will read only one data set, although a whole series of data sets can be included and read in at the same time with one SET statement. The limiting factor is system memory. If multiple data sets are specified, they are read in the order in which they are listed in the SET statement and the observations are written to the output data set in the same order. This process is known as 'concatenation'.

It is also possible to interweave data sets with one another ('interleaving'), where the observations of different data sets are woven together according to a specified key. To do this a few conditions must be fulfilled:

1.   the data sets must have one or more common variables;

2.   a BY statement must be used to create the sorting order (and consequently the weaving order);

3.   the data set must be sorted according to the variables in the BY statement. For this PROC SORT can of course be used.

The output data set will always contain all the variables which appear anywhere in one of the input data sets, unless manipulated by DROP and KEEP options or statements.

Example: combination of order lists

The three individual data sets (figure 8.2) can be read and combined into a single data set by using a SET statement. If no BY statement is used, then the observations from the three data sets are simply placed one after the other. Figure 8.4 shows how it works.

To combine data sets according to article number, a BY statement must be used with the SET statement. The use of the BY statement implies that the data sets are arranged in order of BY variable. To get the input data sets in the correct order, they must first be sorted. Then, by using the BY statement after the SET statement, the observations from various data sets are woven together in the correct order. In this example the same result was achieved by later sorting the unsorted data set TOTAL. There are however many situations in which this is not practical or even possible.

```
DATA COMBINED;
    SET DEPT1 DEPT2 DEPT3;
PROC PRINT;

OBS     ART_CAT     ART_NBR     QUANTITY

 1      timber      10020          4
 2      timber      10030          9
 3      timber      10050         12
 4      sheet       11030          8
 5      sheet       11070         16
 6      hardware    50010         15
 7      hardware    50030         17
 8      tools       45030          9
 9      tools       40090          4
10      paint       20060         17
11      paint       20100          8
12      paint       21090          9
13      paint       22001          3
```

Figure 8.4: The DATA step combines the three separate order lists into one: they are just one after the other.

```
PROC SORT DATA=DEPT1;
    BY ART_NBR;
PROC SORT DATA=DEPT2;
    BY ART_NBR;
PROC SORT DATA=DEPT3;
    BY ART_NBR;
DATA SORT_TOT;
    SET DEPT1 DEPT2 DEPT3;
    BY ART_NBR;
PROC PRINT;

OBS     ART_CAT     ART_NBR     QUANTITY

 1      timber      10020          4
 2      timber      10030          9
 3      timber      10050         12
 4      sheet       11030          8
 5      sheet       11070         16
 6      paint       20060         17
 7      paint       20100          8
 8      paint       21090          9
 9      paint       22001          3
10      tools       40090          4
11      tools       45030          9
12      hardware    50010         15
13      hardware    50030         17
```

FIGURE 8.5: When combining the SET statement with a BY statement the observations are woven together in the order of the BY variables. The condition is that the datasets are properly sorted.

MERGE statement

How the MERGE statement works

MERGE integrates observations from two or more data sets into a new observation in which the variables from all the data sets are included.

```
MERGE dataset1 dataset2 ...;
```

In practice the MERGE statement is almost always used in combination with a BY statement. This is inherently logical: the very fact that the variables must come together into a single observation shows that a logical connection exists between the data sets. This connection usually shows up as a common variable in the data sets. Those are typically the variables which are listed in the BY statement. If there are more common variables that those listed in the BY statement, then as a rule the value from the last data set listed in the MERGE statement will be carried over to the output.

To ensure that the merging operation goes smoothly, the values of the BY variables should only be repeated in one data set at a time. The SAS System will not consider it an error if repetitions appear in more than one data set, but it will give a warning. In practice the appearance of the warning ('repeat of BY values in more than one data set') is tantamount to an error message. If multiple observations with the same values as the BY variables occur in one of the data sets, all of them will be combined with the observations with the same value from the other data sets.

Although the BY statement is very useful in combination with the MERGE statement, it is not required. Without a BY statement, the SAS System will apply a 'one to one merging'. This means that the first observation from each data set will be combined, then the second observation from each data set, and so on.

Figure 8.6 shows a merging of two data sets, in which practically all the points described so far are involved. There are two input data sets: A and B. The 'linking pin' between the data sets is formed by the variable X. Hence this is stated in the BY statement. In addition, the variable Y is common. For corresponding observations, the value of Y from data set B will turn up again in the merged data set.

Caution! The result of the merge in this case will be different if the data sets are listed in the opposite order: MERGE B A;

Data set A					Data set B			
Obs	X	Y	Z		Obs	X	Y	B
1	1	3	NBC		1	2	5	34
2	1	4	CNN		2	2	3	36
3	2	5	HBO		3	2	.	73
4	3	6	WDR		4	3	8	31
5	3	9	BBC		5	3	6	78
6	4	7	MTV		6	3	3	66
					7	5	6	70

```
DATA COMBINED;
MERGE A B;
BY X;
```

Data set COMBINED

Obs	X	Y	Z	B
1	1	3	NBC	.
2	1	4	CNN	.
3	2	5	HBO	34
4	2	3	HBO	36
5	2	.	HBO	73
6	3	8	WDR	31
7	3	6	BBC	78
8	3	3	BBC	66
9	4	7	MTV	.
10	5	6		70

Figure 8.6: Data sets A and B are combined using a MERGE statement. Note that the value of the Y variable comes from B, if a fitting observation is present in B.

The order of the merge is based on the value of variable X. Seeing that the first value of X (1) occurs only in data set A, first of all observations A-1 and A-2 are output to data set COMBINED. Thereby, of course, variable B is missing. The X-value 2 occurs in both data sets. So a merge is made of all appropriate observations, thus A-3 with B-1, then A-3 with B-2 and finally A-3 with B-3. With X-value 3, there is repetition of BY variables in both data sets. The consequence is that the SAS System applies a kind of 'one to one merge' until the last observation in one of the data sets with this X-value is reached. From this point the merge again proceeds normally. Thus the following combinations now arise: A-4 with B-4, A-5 with B-5 and A-5 with B-6. Finally A-6 and B-7 are added.

Repetition of BY values

The previous section already contains a warning over errors which can arise when using the MERGE statement, in the case where a BY variable is repeated in multiple data sets. The SAS System then goes over to a 'one to one merging'.

The example in this section shows how errors get introduced and how they can be avoided.

A data set JOBS contains a number of tasks to be executed. Each task consists of a number of subtasks whose run times are known. The subtasks and their run times are contained in data set NORMS. You are quested to develop a program which calculates the total time for the tasks in JOBS. Figure 8.7 shows the SAS log of the program, with both faulty and correct processing. Figure 8.8 shows its output. For convenience, the data sets JOBS and NORMS were created with CARDS input.

The first (faulty) attempt executes a direct merge between the data sets JOBS and NORMS. Task A occurs twice in WORK and since task A also consists of two subtasks, there is the situation of 'repeat of BY values'. The consequence is that the SAS System cannot calculate properly the total time for the two A-tasks, as is clearly shown in the PROC PRINT output (figure 8.8).

The correct method is to first calculate the total time per task, and store that in an intermediate data set TOTNORM. This DATA step uses the FIRST. and LAST. options, which are explained in a later section, to determine the beginning and end of each task (BY group).

The merge of JOBS and TOTNORM does not produce any 'repeat of BY values', because in TOTNORM now each BY group consists of only 1 observation. The total task time can then be correctly calculated in the final DATA step.

```
1                        The SAS System (6.08)
                                              13:45 Monday, June 6, 1994

NOTE: Copyright(c) 1989 by SAS Institute Inc., Cary, NC USA.
NOTE: SAS (r) Proprietary Software Release 6.08   TS405

NOTE: The initialization phase used 0.06 CPU seconds and 1092K.

NOTE: SAS job started on Monday 06JUN94 13:45 (199406061345)


1           /*--------------------------------------------------*/
2           /* MERGE WITH REPEAT OF BY VALUES                   */
3           /*--------------------------------------------------*/
4
5           DATA TASKLIST;
6               INPUT TASK $;
7           CARDS;

NOTE: The data set WORK.TASKLIST has 3 observations and 1 variables.
NOTE: The DATA statement used 0.01 CPU seconds and 1759K.

11          PROC PRINT;
12          TITLE 'DATA SET TASKLIST';
13          RUN;

NOTE: The PROCEDURE PRINT printed page 1.
NOTE: The PROCEDURE PRINT used 0.01 CPU seconds and 1813K.

14          DATA NORMS;
15              INPUT TASK $ SUBTASK $ DURATION;
16          CARDS;

NOTE: The data set WORK.NORMS has 5 observations and 3 variables.
NOTE: The DATA statement used 0.01 CPU seconds and 1813K.

22          PROC PRINT;
23          TITLE 'DATA SET NORMS';
24          RUN;

NOTE: The PROCEDURE PRINT printed page 2.
NOTE: The PROCEDURE PRINT used 0.01 CPU seconds and 1813K.

25          DATA WRONGTOT;
26              MERGE TASKLIST NORMS;
27              BY TASK;
28              TOT_MIN + DURATION;
29          RUN;

INFO: The variable TASK on data set WORK.TASKLIST will be overwritten
      by data set WORK.NORMS.
NOTE: MERGE statement has more than one data set with repeats of BY
      values.
NOTE: The data set WORK.WRONGTOT has 5 observations and 4 variables.
NOTE: The DATA statement used 0.02 CPU seconds and 2021K.
```

Figure 8.7 (part 1): The data sets TASKLIST and NORMS contain tasks to be performed and a breakdown of those tasks by subtask. Per subtask the required labor is known. The first (faulty) attempt to calculate the total required labor for all tasks is calculated in a simple MERGE action. The time required for 2x task A is incorrect due to a "repeat of BY values" See note in the log.

```
2                          The SAS System (6.08)
                                          13:45 Monday, June 6, 1994

30              PROC PRINT;
31              TITLE 'WRONG CALCULATION';
32              RUN;

NOTE: The PROCEDURE PRINT printed page 3.
NOTE: The PROCEDURE PRINT used 0.00 CPU seconds and 2021K.

33              DATA TOTNORM (KEEP = TASK MINUTES);
34                 SET NORMS;
35                 BY TASK;
36                 IF FIRST.TASK THEN MINUTES = 0;
37                 MINUTES + DURATION;
38                 IF LAST.TASK THEN OUTPUT;
39              RUN;

NOTE: The data set WORK.TOTNORM has 2 observations and 2 variables.
NOTE: The DATA statement used 0.01 CPU seconds and 2021K.

40              PROC PRINT;
41              TITLE 'TOTAL TIME PER TASK';
42              RUN;

NOTE: The PROCEDURE PRINT printed page 4.
NOTE: The PROCEDURE PRINT used 0.01 CPU seconds and 2021K.

43              DATA CORRECT;
44                 MERGE TASKLIST TOTNORM;
45                 BY TASK;
46                 TOT_MIN + MINUTES;
47              RUN;

INFO: The variable TASK on data set WORK.TASKLIST will be overwritten
      by data set WORK.TOTNORM.
NOTE: The data set WORK.CORRECT has 3 observations and 3 variables.
NOTE: The DATA statement used 0.01 CPU seconds and 2053K.

48              PROC PRINT;
49              TITLE 'CORRECT TOTAL JOBTIME';
50              RUN;

NOTE: The PROCEDURE PRINT printed page 5.
NOTE: The PROCEDURE PRINT used 0.01 CPU seconds and 2053K.

NOTE: The SAS session used 0.35 CPU seconds and 2053K.
NOTE: SAS Institute BV, 1217 KR Hilversum, The Netherlands
```

Figure 8.7 (part 2): The correct way starts with the calculation of the total amount of time needed for a task. This total is merged with the tasklist. Now there is no repetition of BY values.

```
                    DATA SET TASKLIST                          1
                              13:45 Monday, June 6, 1994

               OBS      TASK

                1        A
                2        A
                3        B
```

```
                    DATA SET NORMS                             2
                              13:45 Monday, June 6, 1994

          OBS     TASK     SUBTASK     DURATION

           1       A         A1          10
           2       A         A2           5
           3       B         B1          20
           4       B         B2          15
           5       B         B3          10
```

```
                    WRONG CALCULATION                          3
                              13:45 Monday, June 6, 1994

    OBS     TASK     SUBTASK     DURATION      TOT_MIN

     1       A         A1          10            10
     2       A         A2           5            15
     3       B         B1          20            35
     4       B         B2          15            50
     5       B         B3          10            60
```

```
                    TOTAL TIME PER TASK                        4
                              13:45 Monday, June 6, 1994

               OBS      TASK     MINUTES

                1        A         15
                2        B         45
```

```
                    CORRECT TOTAL JOBTIME                      5
                              13:45 Monday, June 6, 1994

          OBS     TASK     MINUTES     TOT_MIN

           1       A         15          15
           2       A         15          30
           3       B         45          75
```

Figure 8.8: The contents of the data sets TASKLIST and NORMS and the result of the direct MERGE. Due to the repetition of BY values the total required time for the A tasks is calculated incorrectly. By first calculating the total required time per task and after that, merge this with the TASKLIST data set you obtain the correct answers.

Example of MERGE in practice

To show MERGE in practice, we go back to the Do-It-Yourself shop. In addition to the data sets with order information, such as those demonstrated with the SET statement, there is also a data set with article descriptions and prices (ART_DES). This data set is printed in figure 8.9. Prices are exclusive of VAT.

OBS	ART_NBR	DESCRIPT	PRICE
1	10020	plank 3x5	10.60
2	10030	plank 2x3	4.95
3	10050	profile pl	7.80
4	11030	chipwood 8	12.95
5	11070	plywood 18	64.50
6	20060	glos white	8.40
7	20100	acrylwhite	12.70
8	21090	brush 2x1	4.50
9	22001	abbr p 180	0.90
10	40090	el drill	149.00
11	45030	handsaw	29.90
12	50010	screw 1x5	21.50
13	50030	nail 1.75	12.60

Figure 8.9: The data set with descriptions and prices.

```
DATA ORDER;
    MERGE SORT_TOT ART_DES;
    BY ART_NBR;
    VAT = .175 * PRICE;
    AMOUNT = QUANTITY * (PRICE + VAT);
PROC PRINT;
    SUM AMOUNT;
```

OBS	ART_CAT	ART_NBR	QUANTITY	DESCRIPT	PRICE	VAT	AMOUNT
1	timber	10020	4	plank 3x5	10.60	1.8550	49.82
2	timber	10030	9	plank 2x3	4.95	0.8663	52.35
3	timber	10050	12	profile pl	7.80	1.3650	109.98
4	sheet	11030	8	chipwood 8	12.95	2.2662	121.73
5	sheet	11070	16	plywood 18	64.50	11.2875	1212.60
6	paint	20060	17	glos white	8.40	1.4700	167.79
7	paint	20100	8	acrylwhite	12.70	2.2225	119.38
8	paint	21090	9	brush 2x1	4.50	0.7875	47.59
9	paint	22001	3	abbr p 180	0.90	0.1575	3.17
10	tools	40090	4	el drill	149.00	26.0750	700.30
11	tools	45030	9	handsaw	29.90	5.2325	316.19
12	hardware	50010	15	screw 1x5	21.50	3.7625	378.94
13	hardware	50030	17	nail 1.75	12.60	2.2050	251.69
							=======
							3531.52

Figure 8.10: A MERGE of SORT_TOT and ART_DES. In the same DATA step VAT and total amount including VAT are calculated.

The order list must now be completed with the article descriptions and prices. Besides this, the total order amount per article including VAT must be calculated. The total amount for all articles is also calculated. The 'linking pin' between the SORT_TOT data set (see figure 8.5) and the ART_DES data set is the article number (ART_NBR). This variable will also be mentioned in the BY statement. That is also the reason for using SORT_TOT as input: before using the BY statement the data sets must be sorted.

The SUM statement in the PROC PRINT is, in this case, the simplest way to determine the total order amount for all articles together.

UPDATE statement

Principle of the UPDATE statement

The purpose of the UPDATE statement is to transfer new data into a masterfile. The new data exist in a transaction file.

```
UPDATE masterfile transactionfile;
```

The way it works is similar to the way the MERGE statement works, however with a few fundamental differences. In the first place, the UPDATE statement always involves two data sets, the first is the master file followed by the transaction file. A BY statement must be used and each observation in the master file must have unique BY variable values. Repeated values may occur in the transaction file, but that does not lead to repeated values in the output data set (the new master): just after the final observation of the BY group in the transaction file, an observation in the master is updated or appended. Update only works for variables with a non-missing value in the transaction data set.

Example of UPDATE

Say that a few alterations must be made in the ART_DES data set: a few prices have changed, a few articles must be added and one description must be improved. The data set ART_UPD (see figure 8.11) contains the desired changes. Only the data for the changes are present, the rest is missing.

OBS	ART_NBR	PRICE	DESCRIPT
1	10050	8.15	
2	11060	48.50	plywood 12
3	20060	8.95	
4	20105	12.70	acrylyello
5	45030	24.90	
6	50030	.	nail SP 2

Figure 8.11: The ART_UPD data set. These updates are to be made to the ART_DES data set.

```
DATA NART_DES;
    UPDATE ART_DES ART_UPD;
    BY ART_NBR;
PROC PRINT;
```

OBS	ART_NBR	DESCRIPT	PRICE
1	10020	plank 3x5	10.60
2	10030	plank 2x3	4.95
3	10050	profile pl	8.15
4	11030	chipwood 8	12.95
5	11060	plywood 12	48.50
6	11070	plywood 18	64.50
7	20060	glos white	8.95
8	20100	acrylwhite	12.70
9	20105	acrylyello	12.70
10	21090	brush 2x1	4.50
11	22001	abbr p 180	0.90
12	40090	el drill	149.00
13	45030	handsaw	24.90
14	50010	screw 1x5	21.50
15	50030	nail SP 2	12.60

Figure 8.12: By means of the UPDATE statement the changes to the ART_DES data set are applied, leading to a new data set: NART_DES.

By means of an UPDATE, changes are made in the article description data set. Be aware that the missing variables of the ART_UPD data set remain unchanged in the master data set. The new generation of the master data set is now called: NART_DES. In practice it is inconvenient to give the data set another name. That can be resolved by working through 'generation data sets'. First the old master is renamed to another name and the new one again gets the name ART_DES. This technique can be executed simply with the help of PROC DATASETS, which is described in greater detail in chapter 10.

Options for SET/MERGE/UPDATE

Dataset options

The general data set options can also be used with SET, MERGE and UPDATE. In practice, DROP, KEEP and RENAME are used most often. DROP and KEEP of course establish which variables are to be used in the processing. It is sensible to always remove all redundant variables to avoid problems with overlapping variables, other than the BY variables (see also the section on the MERGE statement). If there are other variables, apart from the BY variables, with the same name and they are all to be preserved, they should be renamed with the RENAME option to eliminate the overlaps.

Besides the above data set options, the IN= option is very important. IN= creates a variable with value 1 if that data set contributes an observation in the current iteration, otherwise the value is 0.

```
IN = variable
```

Note: IN= is a data set option and thus is placed in parentheses after the data set to which it belongs. With IN= it is very easy to test where a given observation comes from. Two versions of a data set can be quickly compared for differences. This is shown in figure 8.13 with a small program that shows changes between two versions of a catalog: discontinued and newly added articles.

```
DATA DIFFER;
    MERGE OLD_CAT(IN=IN_O) NEW_CAT(IN=IN_N);
    BY ART_NBR;
    IF IN_O AND IN_N THEN DELETE;
    IF IN_O THEN STATUS = 'DISCONTINUED';
            ELSE STATUS = 'ADDED';
```

Figure 8.13: With this simple DATA step you can create a report about the differences between two editions of a catalog.

Continued articles are in both OLD_CAT and NEW_CAT and therefore do not come through the first IF statement (both IN_O and IN_N have the value 1). What remains is found either in OLD_CAT (IN_O=1, IN_N=0) or in NEW_CAT (IN_O=0, IN_N=1). Thus only one of these conditions needs to be tested.

END= option

The END= option works with SET, MERGE and UPDATE similar to the END option for the INFILE statement.

```
END = variable
```

The variable thus has the value 1 for the final observation and 0 in all other cases. If multiple data sets are called, then the END variable comes up 1 after the reading of the final observation of the final data set. The END= option is not a data set option, but a specific SET, MERGE and UPDATE option. The option therefore does not go in parentheses, but as normal at the end of the statement.

FIRST. and LAST. variables

When using the BY statement, the SAS System creates two more important variables which mark the first and last observation of a BY group. These variables are named FIRST.variable and LAST.variable, where variable is the name of the BY variable.

The FIRST.variable has a value 1 if the related BY variable (or a BY variable higher in the BY hierarchy, i.e. earlier in the BY statement) has changed value, and otherwise is 0. The LAST.variable just has a value 1 for the last observation of a BY group and otherwise 0. The following statements can be used to test whether a BY group consists of only one observation:

```
...
BY BY_VAR;
IF FIRST.BY_VAR AND LAST.BY_VAR THEN ...;
```

In the section 'Repetition of BY values' on page 143 and figures 8.7 and 8.8 another application of FIRST. and LAST is demonstrated.

Example of SET/MERGE with options

If the SORT_TOT data set and the NART_DES data set are merged just like that, then there will be an observation for each article number, even for the numbers which are not ordered. These would show missing values in the variables ART_CAT and QUANTITY. By using the IN= option (figure 8.14) you can test whether an observation has really been read from SORT_TOT and the article thus really should appear on the order list. The subsetting IF statement removes all other observations.

The results will then be the same as in figure 8.10.

```
DATA ORDER;
    MERGE SORT_TOT(IN=IN_ORD) NART_DES;
    BY ART_NBR;
    IF IN_ORD;
```

Figure 8.14: By using the IN= option you can make sure that only those observations are included in data set ORDER, that are also in SORT_TOT.

Finally a summary is created with an overview of the number of items ordered per article category (figure 8.15). Note the use of NOTSORTED here: the data set was sorted in ART_NBR. Therefore the articles are already grouped by category, although the categories do not appear in alphabetical order.

Instead of the DATA step, such as was used in figure 8.15, these calculations can also be done with PROC MEANS or PROC SUMMARY. We will go into these in chapter 11.

```
DATA SUMMARY(KEEP=ART_CAT ITEMS);
    SET ORDER;
    BY ART_CAT NOTSORTED;
    IF FIRST.ART_CAT THEN ITEMS=0;
    ITEMS + 1;
    IF LAST.ART_CAT THEN OUTPUT;
PROC PRINT;

OBS    ART_CAT       ITEMS

 1     timber          3
 2     sheet           2
 3     paint           4
 4     tools           2
 5     hardware        2
```

Figure 8.15: By counting the number of observations per BY group you can determine how many different articles are ordered per category.

Exercises

1. For the following two data sets:

A				B		
ID	X	Y		ID	X	Z
01	12	11		01	.	4
02	15	.		03	17	6
				03	18	.

describe what data set C looks like after:

   a. `DATA C; SET A B;`

   b. `DATA C; SET A; SET B;`

   c. `DATA C; SET A B; BY ID;`

   d. `DATA C; MERGE A B;`

   e. `DATA C; MERGE A B; BY ID;`

   f. `DATA C; UPDATE A B; BY ID;`

   g. `DATA C; SET B; IF X=. THEN SET A;`

   h. `DATA C; SET B; IF X NE . ;`

   i. `DATA C; SET B; IF X EQ . THEN DELETE;`

   j. `DATA C; MERGE A(IN=IN_A) B(IN=IN_B);`
       `BY ID;`
       `IF IN_A AND IN_B;`

2. Data on candidates for the American presidential elections are in data sets ELECTION and CANDIDATE. ELECTION contains the names of the winners and losers in each election year, CANDIDATE contains the name of the candidate, his party and the state he comes from.

ELECTION:	YEAR	NAME	LOSER
	1952	EISENHOWER	STEVENSON
	1956	EISENHOWER	STEVENSON
	1960	KENNEDY	NIXON
	1964	JOHNSON	GOLDWATER
	1968	NIXON	HUMPHREY
	1972	NIXON	MCGOVERN
	1976	CARTER	FORD
	1980	REAGAN	CARTER
	1984	REAGAN	MONDALE
	1988	BUSH	DUKAKIS
	1992	CLINTON	BUSH

CANDIDAT:	NAME	PARTY	STATE
	EISENHOWER	R	TX
	STEVENSON	D	IL
	NIXON	R	CA
	KENNEDY	D	MA
	GOLDWATER	R	AR
	JOHNSON	D	TX
	HUMPHREY	D	MN
	MCGOVERN	D	SD
	FORD	R	MI
	CARTER	D	GA
	REAGAN	R	CA
	MONDALE	D	CO
	DUKAKIS	D	MA
	BUSH	R	TX
	CLINTON	D	AR

a. Make a data set which for every election year contains the winning party and the president's home state.

b. Find for each candidate the last election in which he took part and express whether or not he won. (Hint: make a copy of the ELECTION data set and sort it on LOSER.)

c. Count for each candidate the number of times he has won an election.

d. Look for which candidates both won and lost.

3. In a laboratory test, measurements must be evaluated by multiple weight factors. The measurements are stored in data set MEASURE, The weight factors in the data set WEIGHING.

MEASURE contains the variables IDENT (identification of the test) and MEASRMNT, the WEIGHING data set contains the variables IDENT and WEIGHT. For each observation of MEASURE multiple observations are present in WEIGHING.

Create a data set in which observations occur with the measurements multiplied with each weight factor.

CHAPTER 9

Layout Definitions

Introduction

In the previous chapters we have seen how data from an external source can be read into an SAS program, how data can be written into SAS data sets and also how SAS data sets can be used as input. Figure 9.1 charts the statements used in these processes.

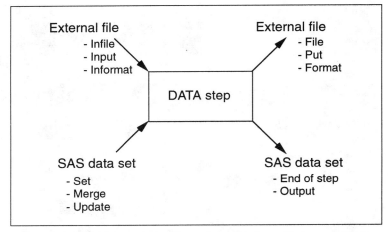

Figure 9.1: The DATA step is the place where data is read in from and written to files. These files can be both external (= non SAS) files and SAS data sets. The drawing indicates the related statements.

In this chapter we come to the last part of this quartet: writing data to an external file and defining the layout of the file. This includes both formatting variables and defining records. The focus is on creating print files, thus reporting although these same techniques are also valid for other external files.

However many standard reporting facilities there are in the SAS System (in their simplest form PROC PRINT), you will still regularly need to define the complete layout of a report. This can be done using the techniques described in this chapter.

Layout of variables: FORMAT

We have already dealt with the concept format in the section on date and time in chapter 6. We have also already dealt with its counterpart informat in chapter 3. To recall: a format is a layout specification for printing a variable. To print a variable according to a specified format, that format must be linked to the variable. This is usually done with the

FORMAT statement. In the FORMAT statement one or more variables are declared, followed by the format to be applied.

```
FORMAT variable format.;
```

or

```
FORMAT variable1 variable2 ... format.;
```

or

```
FORMAT variable1 format1. variable2 format2. ...;
```

In this way you can use the DATE format to print a numeric variable as a date, and with the WORDS format a number can be written as text (for example THREE HUNDRED).

Refer to the SAS Language Guide for the many different standard formats. Figure 9.2 gives a summary of the most used formats, and the common Date/Time formats are given in figure 6.8. Once again you should realize that the format works only on the outside: the internal value of the variable does not change. Remember that the format name always includes a period, in most instances in the final position. In the format a length specification is also given: the number before the period. Many format specifications have a default length. When using a default length, the length does not have to be specified. Thus DATE. and DATE7. are the same. In numerical formats, you can if you want specify the number of decimal places in a number after the period. Thus 10.2 means a numerical format of 10 positions of which 2 are decimal places (for example 1234567.89). In the SAS manuals, length is referred to by the code w and decimal places by the code d. We shall use the same codes here.

In spite of the fact that many standard formats already exist, there is always the chance that there is no standard version of the layout you want. In that case you can use PROC FORMAT to define your own layout.

Format name	length range (default)	description
$CHARw. $w.	1-200	standard text, including leading blanks
$VARYINGw.	1-200	variable length character output
BESTw.	1-32 (12)	standard numerical, exponential notation if field too narrow
COMMAXw.d	2-32 (6)	numeric, with periods between thousands and comma as decimal separator (European notation)
Ew.	7-32 (12)	exponential notation
IBw.d	1-8 (4)	binary "word", not for print, intended for files
PERCENTw.d	3-32 (6)	writes value as a percentage (= x 100) including % sign
ROMANw.	2-32 (6)	writes value as Roman numeral
w.d	1-32	normal numeric value, including decimals, right aligned
WORDSw.	5-200 (10)	value written as text
Zw.d	1 -32 (1)	as w.d, but padded with leading zeros

Figure 9.2: Some of the many standard formats the SAS System provides. They can be linked to a variable using a FORMAT statement, like FORMAT NUM_VAR Z4.;

PROC FORMAT

Introduction

In its most commonly used and simplest form, PROC FORMAT defines text strings (labels) which are used to print variables. These labels are defined in the VALUE statement of PROC FORMAT. First after the keyword VALUE comes the name of the format being created and then the values (of the variable to which the format is about to be applied) and the label which will be printed as a result:

```
PROC FORMAT;
   VALUE formatname
       value1 = 'label1'
       value2 = 'label2'
       ... ;
```

You can define as many formats as you like in a single run of PROC FORMAT.

In figure 9.3 a format is defined that correlates a person's age with an age group. Be careful to put the whole series of values and their labels together in a single VALUE statement, in other words generate the whole format in a single statement. Once you have the format defined, you could use it for instance in a PROC PRINT. Assume you have a data set with a variable AGE. By applying the declared format by means of the FORMAT statement to variable AGE, the SAS System will print the labels (and thus the age groups) instead of the age numbers.

```
PROC FORMAT;
    VALUE AGEGRP
        0-1= 'BABY'
        2-3= 'INFANT'
        4-5= 'TODDLER'
        6-12= 'CHILD'
        13-19= 'TEENAGER'
        20-HIGH= 'ADULT';

Assume data set PEOPLE contains variable AGE:

 PROC PRINT DATA=PEOPLE;
 FORMAT AGE AGEGRP.;

OBS      ...      ...      AGE    ...
1        ...      ...      INFANT         ...
2        ...      ...      TEENAGER   ...
```

Figure 9.3: The format AGEGRP is defined with PROC FORMAT. This format is linked to the variable AGE. As a consequence PROC PRINT does not print the numerical value of AGE, but the corresponding label.

The VALUE statement

In the VALUE statement, the name of the format to be created is declared first of all. This name follows the general rules of SAS names (letters, numbers, underscore, no number at the beginning), with two exceptions:

a character format begins with a $ sign and the name of a format may not end on a number. The first of these corresponds to the rules which apply also for standard SAS formats and informats. The reason for the last one is that a number at the end of a format specifies a length, e.g. $CHAR10. indicates: a character format 10 positions long.

In declaring values and labels, all character values and labels must be enclosed in quotation marks. Both character and number values can be declared as a range; for example "AAA"-"AZZ" = "A" "BAA"-"BZZ" = "B" or 1-10 = "<=10". When values are declared as ranges, there can be gaps included, but there can be no overlaps among ranges. If there are gaps in the range description, the format will not apply if the variable on which the format is used has that value, meaning that the variable will be printed unformatted. Ranges are inclusive by default, in other words 1-2 means 1 through 2. Connecting ranges can lead to overlapping. Therefore in this case the interpretation is adapted so that 1-2 and 2-3 means 1 through 2 and 2.00000001 through 3. If the ranges are not connected, you can specify a range of 'to' rather than 'through' by putting a 'less than' sign before the end of the range (for example 1-<2). Three special indicators can save a lot of writing: LOW, HIGH and OTHER. LOW specifies an unlimited lower value, for example LOW-<0 = "NEGATIVE", just as HIGH specifies an unlimited upper value: 100-HIGH = ">100". OTHER is the set of all values not in any declared range.

If, for example, a set of standard codes is declared as values, with their description as label, you could add OTHER = "INCORRECT CODE". The special indicators LOW, HIGH and OTHER are not placed in quotation marks. They are SAS keywords and not normal text strings. In Version 5 of the SAS System the maximum length of range definitions and labels was 16 and 40 positions respectively; in V6 these have been extended to 200 positions.

Examples of the VALUE statement

In figure 9.4 you see some of examples of a special application of PROC FORMAT. Both examples show how through use of formats specific values of a variable can be highlighted. In the first case through just giving the normal value of a variable a label, in the second case through accenting the value with a number of asterisks.

```
PROC FORMAT;
   VALUE FEVER 36.5 - 37.5 ='NORMAL';
   VALUE EXCEPT
      1-5     = "*"
      5-10    = "**"
      10-20   = "***"
      20-50   = "****"
      50-HIGH = "*****";

PROC PRINT DATA=.....;

   OBS        ...   ...   TEMP      LEVEL    ...
   1          ...   ...   36.3      16.3     ...
   2          ...   ...   36.8      36.8     ...
   3          ...   ...   37.0      97.0     ...
   4          ...   ...   38.6       8.6     ...
   5          ...   ...   37.2       3.2     ...

PROC PRINT DATA=.....;
   FORMAT TEMP FEVER. LEVEL EXCEPT.;

   OBS        ...   ...   TEMP      LEVEL    ...
   1          ...   ...   36.3      ***      ...
   2          ...   ...   NORMAL    ****     ...
   3          ...   ...   NORMAL    *****    ...
   4          ...   ...   38.6      **       ...
   5          ...   ...   NORMAL    *        ...
```

Figure 9.4: FORMATs can be used to put emphasis on specific values of the related variable. The first example highlights a normal body temperature (in °Celcius). The second example indicates a simple means to group values and makes them visible.

The PICTURE statement

In addition to converting variable values into text, such as with the VALUE statement, PROC FORMAT can also format the layout of numerical values. As an example you might think of the formatting of monetary figures in European notation: period between thousands and comma as decimal point or the formatting of phone numbers: 2 groups of 3 digits and one group of 4 digits, the first group in parentheses the others separated by a hyphen.

We will use these two examples in discussing the PICTURE statement (see figure 9.5). The PICTURE statement has the following form:

```
PICTURE formatname
 range1 = template1 (options)
 range2 = template2 (options)
 ... ;
```

The kernel of the PICTURE statement is a template (the 'picture') by which the method of printing of the number is specified. This picture consists of digits (0 and 9, but might be any other digit as well) and other characters. When the picture is applied to some number, the 0 and 9 in the picture are substituted by the digits in the number. When the number is printed, the other characters lying in between are also printed. The difference between the use of 0 and 9 lies in the 'significance' of the position: with 0, only significant digits are printed, and with 9 all digits are printed, even a non-significant 0.

Only the integer part of the input number gets put into the picture; the unit position of the input line goes in the final place of the picture. Thus decimals will not be included in the input line. If you want to print decimals, you must use the MULTIPLIER option (MULT=) to bring the significant decimals into the whole number part. A complication arises if there are periods specified in the picture. Then the SAS System regards the first period as the decimal point and the input line will automatically be multiplied by such power of 10, that the unit position will be put in the corresponding position of the picture. If you do not want the system to interpret the first point as the decimal point, you must use the MULTIPLIER option to instruct the system to do something else.

```
PICTURE CREDIT
 LOW-<0='00.009,99 D'(MULT=100)
 0-HIGH='00.009,99'(MULT=100);

PICTURE PHONE
 0-HIGH =' 999) 999-9999'(PREFIX='(');
```

Figure 9.5: The first PICTURE statement defines a layout for printing figures in European notation. The second defines a layout for printing phone numbers.

The picture CREDIT (figure 9.5) defines the European notation you want. In the example we use a D (for debit) after the number rather than a minus sign before the number. In this context you see two ranges: one for negative values and one for positive values. Because one digit must always be printed in the unit position ("Price 0,98"), a 9 is used in the template. Before that, only the positions that are actually significant will be printed.

The number of decimals to be included in the picture form the basis of the multiply: a factor of 10 for each decimal. In the example, there should be 2 decimals (the cents positions), thus a multiply of 10x10=100. What actually happens in the SAS System is that the number to be printed is multiplied by the multiply factor and then the whole number section is put in the picture. Figure 9.6 shows this process schematically. All positions which fall outside the picture (thus the decimals which are left after the multiply and positions in the front, if the picture is too narrow) do not get printed. This way the left over number does not get rounded, unless this is specified in the PICTURE statement with the ROUND option. This ROUND option is new in Release 6.07.

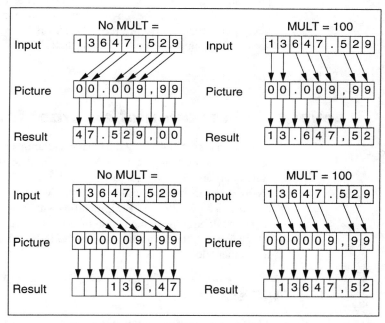

Figure 9.6: The principle of editing by means of a picture format. If the picture frame contains a period, the SAS System will consider that to be the decimal point and the unit position will be positioned accordingly. Without a period in the picture, the last position is the unit position. If you want it to be somewhere else you have to use the MULT= option: a factor 10 for each decimal position.

The following examples show the printed result of a numeric variable, with and without the CREDIT format:

without format	with format
27135.6	27.135,60
-68	68,00 D
0.737	0,73

In the case where a ROUND option was specified in the CREDIT format, the last number is formatted as 0,74.

The phone number picture uses the PREFIX option to generate the opening parenthesis. This cannot be done inside the picture, because significance is not yet started: it starts with the first significant print position, which is the first digit of the area code. The space before the first digit is to define the length of the picture one position longer, to make place for the opening parenthesis. Instead you could also have specified a length when using the format:

```
FORMAT PHONENBR PHONE14.;
```

Layout and creation of external files

Creating a report of original design and creating an external (non-SAS) file is an activity in the DATA step. For this, the FILE and PUT statements are of central importance. FILE and PUT are to output what INFILE and INPUT are to input; in other words, FILE specifies where data are to be written and PUT specifies what is to be written and how it is to be done (in which position of the line, or in the record, and with which format). It does not actually matter if the output is printed or goes to another file.

The FILE statement

The form of the FILE statement is

```
FILE filereference options;
```

The file reference refers to the desired output file. There are a few standard file references, such as LOG and PRINT to send the output to the SAS log and the standard procedure output file respectively, but any other destination can also be specified. In V6, this can be done directly by entering the file name (between quotation marks) or indirectly by giving a DD name or fileref. The DD name or fileref must first be defined by means of an allocation or a FILENAME statement before you can reference it in a FILE statement. For more information on the FILENAME statement, refer to the system appendices (H through M).

After the file specification come possible options. A number of these options are specific for report creation (print files), others are intended primarily for creating 'normal' files.

In figure 9.7 the most important options are defined for creating print files. The PRINT option is used for adding ANSI printer control codes. This option only needs to be applied if the file characteristics are not really those of a printer file. The HEADER=label option refers by means of the label to a section of the DATA step where the header for each output page is created. This is explained later in greater detail. The N=PS option holds a full page of output in the print buffer, which makes it possible to criss-cross the page using the PUT statement. LINESLEFT= declares a variable whose value is the number of lines left on the current page. The NOTITLES option suppresses the standard title lines, such as those created using TITLE statements. The page numbering and date are also suspended.

PRINT	adds ANSI printer control characters on the first position of each line
HEADER=label	program label of header routine
N=PS	keeps whole output page in a buffer
LINESLEFT=variable	SAS loads this variable with the number of lines left on the current page
NOTITLES	suppresses the standard SAS title lines

Figure 9.7: Options in the FILE statement, for use while creating custom made reports (print files).

NOPRINT	no printer control characters in the first print position
OLD	empty the output file before writing new data to it
MOD	append new data after existing data
N=	number of records that should be kept in the output buffer.

Figure 9.8: Options in the FILE statement, primarily used for creation of external data sets. For special data sets and techniques tens of other options are available, enabling you to construct virtually any type of file.

PUT statement

The PUT statement is subsequently used to write variables and/or text to output. Just as with the INPUT statement, the PUT statement has LIST, COLUMN and POINTER modes. In practice, only the POINTER mode is actually used. The form is similar to that of the INPUT statement:

```
PUT pointer variable format.
    pointer variable format.
    ... ;
```

There are a few other important variants of the PUT statement:

```
PUT pointer "text";
PUT variable= ... ;
PUT _PAGE_;
```

The first form shows how text is printed: it sets the pointer to the position from which text is to be printed. The 'PUT variable=' form is the so-called 'named output' as opposed to 'pointer output'. Named output is not often used in reporting, but is very handy for program development: without a preceding FILE statement, this PUT statement writes the value of the given variable(s) to the SAS log, preceded by the name of the variable. With this it is often quick to spot where possible errors appear in the DATA step, as a result of incorrect values in variables. Finally, PUT_PAGE_; tells the system that the construction of the current page is complete and that it can be sent to the printer. The next PUT statement will then go to the following page.

In principle each PUT statement moves to the next line. If however the PUT statement ends with an @ sign, the following PUT statement appears on the same line; this is similar to the 'trailing @' in an INPUT statement: the input record is retained for the following INPUT statement. You can use a slash (/) to move to a new line within the PUT statement .

If you have declared N=PS in the FILE statement then the whole output page is available in a buffer as mentioned before. You can then use the special line pointer (#) to indicate which line to print on. With N=PS you can skate all over the page which makes it impossible for the SAS System to know when you are through. Therefore you use PUT_PAGE_; to signal the completion of the page.

You encounter a number of the previously discussed tools in the following PUT statement:

```
PUT @10 'TOTAL EXPENSES IN' /
    @24 MONTH MONYY.
    @32 AMOUNT CREDIT. ;
```

It starts with the printing of the fixed text, then it jumps to a following line and prints two formatted variables (the CREDIT format is dealt with on page 164, figure 9.5).

Structure of DATA step for reporting

FILE and PUT processing takes place in the DATA step. One of the basic tasks of the DATA step is to create SAS data sets. This is often not needed in combination with creating reports or external files. By declaring _NULL_ as a special data set name in the DATA statement, no data set is created. This makes the step also work faster, since no information has to be output (other than to the report or file).

The basic DATA step structure when using it for creating reports is sketched in figure 9.9. At the beginning of each new page, the FILE statement forces a jump to the routine indicated with "HEAD:". Then the statements are executed which are needed to create the header lines. The RETURN statement causes a jump back to the statement after the FILE statement.

Then the main part of the program will execute up to the RETURN statement before the label HEAD. This RETURN statement functions as a divider between the main program and the subroutine HEAD. There the DATA step ends and the SAS System starts again at the DATA statement and the SET statement to read and process the next observation. If a special end-of-routine is needed, it can be done using the END option in the SET statement.

For the most part, the same structure is valid for DATA steps which are specially adapted for creating external files. Only the HEADER option is not used.

Files for downloading to PCs

Many PC programs, in particular spreadsheet programs and database programs can read, in addition to their own file structures, files of type TSV(Tab Separated Values) or CSV(Comma Separated Values). Creating these types of files is simple: between all variables always print the dividing marks as text. On IBM mainframes (EBCDIC character set) the tab character has the hexadecimal value 05. Systems with an ASCII character set (VAX, PC) the hexadecimal value is 09. Starting from an IBM mainframe, a TSV file can be created in the following manner:

```
PUT variable1 "05"X variable2 "05"X variable3 ... ;
```

The specification "05"X tells the SAS System that the text in quotes is not normal text, but a hexadecimal number, namely hexadecimal 05, the tab mark. A more elegant method is to use the RETAIN statement with an initial value:

```
RETAIN TAB '05'X;
PUT variable1 TAB variable2 TAB variable3 ... ;
```

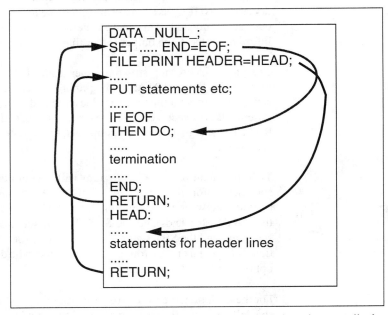

Figure 9.9: The basic structure of a DATA step developed especially for creation of reports.

Sample program with FILE and PUT statements

In this sample program we will draw a so-called sine curve the width of the paper. The sine curve is a concept from geometry, and is also much used in electronics. It is an oscillating line of which the value varies with the size of an angle. The value runs from 0 (angle of 0°) to 1 (right angle, 90°), then again back to 0 (180°), down to -1 (270°) and finally back to 0 (360°), a complete circle. Because of this oscillation, the N=PS option is used, so that we have complete freedom of movement over the paper. The SAS log of this program is printed in figure 9.10 and the result is printed in figure 9.11.

```
1                        The SAS System (6.08)
                                    18:43 Tuesday, June 7, 1994

NOTE: Copyright(c) 1989 by SAS Institute Inc., Cary, NC USA.
NOTE: SAS (r) Proprietary Software Release 6.08  TS405

NOTE: The initialization phase used 0.06 CPU seconds and 1092K.

NOTE: SAS job started on Tuesday 07JUN94 18:43 (199406071843)

1          /*------------------------------------------------------*/
2          /* CREATION OF A SINE CURVE                             */
3          /*------------------------------------------------------*/
4
5          TITLE2 'SAMPLE PROGRAM CHAPT 9: SINE CURVE';
6          DATA _NULL_;                 * NO CREATION OF DATA SET;
7            FILE PRINT N=PS;           * KEEP WHOLE PAGE IN BUFFER;
8            C=1;
9            DO UNTIL (C=72);           * 72 COLUMNS OUTPUT REQUIRED;
10             ARC=2*3.14*C/72;         * CONVERT C TO RADIANS 72 = 2 PI;
11             SIN=SIN(ARC);            * SINUS FUNCTON;
12             L=ROUND(20-15*SIN);      * POSITION ON THE PAGE;
13             PUT #L @C '*';           * WRITE POINT OF SINE CURVE;
14             PUT #20 @C '-';          * WRITE BASE LINE;
15             C+1;                     * NEXT COLUMN. SUM STATEMENT;
16           END;
17         PUT _PAGE_;

NOTE: 30 lines were written to file PRINT.
NOTE: The DATASTEP printed page 1.
NOTE: The DATA statement used 0.04 CPU seconds and 1667K.

NOTE: The SAS session used 0.25 CPU seconds and 1667K.
NOTE: SAS Institute BV, 1217 KR Hilversum, The Netherlands
```

Figure 9.10: This program creates a sine curve on paper. By using N=PS in the FILE statement the whole output page is available at any time, enabling to print on any line.

The heart of this program is the SIN function (statement 11), which gives the sine of an angle. The angle must be given in radians. An angle of 360° (circle) is 2π(2 x 3.14) radians. Starting with 72 positions on a line, the angle can be calculated for each position (statement10). If the sine must have value 1 we naturally go to the top of the page, and for value -1 to the bottom. The output lines however count from top to bottom. This is solved in statement 12. The middle of the page is line 20 and subsequently we subtract 15x the sine. If the sine has value 1, we come to line 5 and with -1 to line 35. The ROUND function is used because we only want to arrive at whole line positions. Subsequently the PUT statement is used printing one point of the curve and one point of the zero line. For this the line pointer (#) is used for vertical positioning and the column pointer (@) for horizontal positioning.

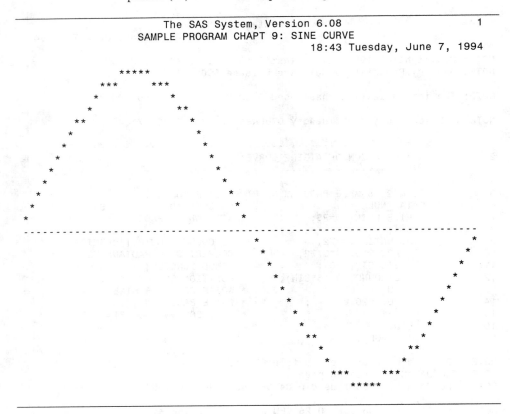

```
                    The SAS System, Version 6.08                      1
                 SAMPLE PROGRAM CHAPT 9: SINE CURVE
                                      18:43 Tuesday, June 7, 1994
```

Figure 9.11: The result of the program in figure 9.10: the sine curve.

Exercises

1. A real estate agent has his house file stored in a SAS data set. The data library is allocated with libref REALEST, the data set is called HOUSES.

    PROC CONTENTS DATA=REALEST.HOUSES; produces among other things the following output:

VARIABLE	TYPE	LENGTH	LABEL
BATHROOM	CHAR	6	BATH SHOWER
GARAGE	NUM	8	0=NO 1=YES
LAND	NUM	8	SQ. FEET
ROOMS	NUM	8	NBR OF ROOMS
CELLAR	NUM	8	0=NO 1=YES
FIREPL	NUM	8	0=NO 1=YES
CITY	CHAR	15	CITY OR COMMUNITY
PRICE	NUM	8	PRICE IN DOLLARS
STREET	CHAR	15	NUMBER AND STREET
TYPE	CHAR	12	MANSION APARTMENT CONDOMINIUM

a. Print the data set. The prices should have European notation ($ 123.456,--). Replace the codes for fireplace, cellar and garage with the appropriate text.

b. Print the data set so that each house is on a separate page, with layout as described below. Hint: a quote in a text (Extra's) can be created in two ways: place the text in double quotation marks ("Extra's") or insert two quotes ('Extra"s').

City:	Street:
Type:	Price:
Land:	Sq. feet
Number of rooms:	
Bathroom facilities:	

Extra's: Fireplace
                Garage   (these lines only if appropriate)
                Cellar

2. A company telephone directory has to be made. For each employee the following should be mentioned in the directory: name of the employee, department code and telephone number. The company has a SAS data set containing, by department, all employees with their room numbers. There is also a SAS data set with all names and telephone numbers. However, it is not known what the variables in the data sets are called, or if the data sets contain any more information.

Requirements for the layout of the telephone directory:

- Page layout in three columns;

- At the start of a new initial (marking an alphabetical section), three lines should be skipped, unless the new section begins at the top of a column, then the new initial (section header) should be printed, after which one line should be skipped

- If, after starting a new alphabetical section there is room for fewer than four names in the column, the column should be interrupted and the new initial (header) printed at the top of the next column;

- On line 2 at the top right of the page, the first three letters of the first and last name on the page should be printed. If the page begins with a new letter, only that letter should be printed;

- A column header goes on line 3;

- The body of the list begins on line 5 and has 50 lines.

a. How do you know which variables are in the data sets?

b. Write a program to make the telephone directory.

    Hint 1: first make a number of assumptions about what you discovered in exercise a.

    Hint 2: use LINK and RETURN statements (consult chapter 15 of this book or the SAS Language Guide) for transferring to a new column or a new page.

CHAPTER 10

Storage and Maintenance of SAS® Files

So far we have given little attention to the storage of information, once it has entered the SAS System, through recording in a SAS data set or in the form, for example, of a format. In chapter 2 we went into the concept of the SAS data library. In this chapter we will go deeper into the principle of data libraries and the SAS System's provisions for the management of data libraries.

SAS data libraries

The data library is the central storage point for all SAS files. The two most used SAS files are the SAS data set and the catalog. Within the data library the various types of files are marked with a so-called 'member type'. For data sets the member type is 'DATA' and for catalogs the member type is 'CATALOG'. Later in this book we will also encounter the member types 'PROGRAM' and 'VIEW'.

The organization of a data library is an internal SAS matter. It is enough to know that a data library can contain many SAS data sets, catalogs and other files. The data library itself is a structure which is dependent on the host system environment. In the IBM mainframe environment (MVS) the data library is a special OS data set, in the minicomputer (such as Digital VAX) and PC environments the data library is a subdirectory. For more information on the data library structure in your environment, refer to the system appendices.

Data sets

We have already gone into the concept of the data set extensively, so we will not go over it again here. Consult chapter 2 once more if needed. There can be many SAS data sets in a data library: each with its own unique name. The complete formal name for a SAS data set in a data library is: membername.DATA. The extension DATA is only needed if there is some potential for confusion, for example a catalog with the same name.

Catalogs

In contrast to the SAS data set, we have hardly touched on the concept of the catalog. A catalog is a collection point for a lot of support information, such as formats, screen definitions of for example the SAS/ FSP package, function key definitions and so on. The catalog is a member in the data library and within the catalog are 'entries', members of the catalog, with an 'entry type': an identifier for the type of catalog entry.

In the sections of the previous chapter dealing with PROC FORMAT, a number of formats were defined as examples. These become entries in the catalog FORMATS which the SAS System automatically creates for the storage of formats. The entry name in the catalog is the format name, without the $ sign which is used as the first sign in the name for character formats, and the entry type is FORMATC for character formats and FORMAT for numerical formats.

The complete formal name for the CREDIT format reads then: <data library reference>.FORMATS.CREDIT.FORMAT. In normal activity this complete name is hardly ever needed; it is only used for management and maintenance activity within data libraries.

Accessing SAS data libraries

To use a SAS data set, for example as input in a SET or MERGE statement, in the DATA= option in a PROC statement, or as output in a DATA statement, two things must be specified: what the data set is called and which data library it resides in. The same goes for catalogs, but adding entry names and entry types where needed.

Accessing the data library is done using a 'library reference', in short 'libref'. This libref can be defined within the SAS System by means of the LIBNAME statement, but also in many cases with the aid of operating system commands, such as the SET command in Windows or OS/2 and the JCL DD statement in the MVS batch environment. We will have more to say about the LIBNAME statement in the section 'LIBNAME statement' on page 181. In the system appendices you will find supplementary information on the LIBNAME statement in your system environment. A SAS data set is referenced with the reference to the data library (the libref) followed by the name of the data set. These are declared one after the other, separated by a period.

Figure 10.1 illustrates some possibilities for assigning and using data libraries.

```
Universal example:

  LIBNAME  SASDB1   'MYDATA.SASLIB' ACCESS=READONLY;
  LIBNAME  SASDB2   'NEWDATA.SASLIB';
  DATA SASDB2.NEW;
      SET SASDB1.OLD;

MVS-batch example:

  //MYJOB   JOB       ..................
  //        EXECSAS
  //SASDB1 DD        DSN=MYDATA.SASLIB,DISP=SHR
  //SASDB2 DD        DSN=NEWDATA.SASLIB,DISP=OLD
  //SYSIN  DD        *
  DATA SASDB2.NEW;
      SET SASDB1.OLD;
```

Figure 10.1: Before you can use a SAS data library you have to assign it first. This can be done within the SAS environment by means of a LIBNAME statement, or outside the SAS environment with host system allocation commands, as shown above for the IBM MVS environment. A reference to a SAS data set consists of two parts: the libref of the data library followed by the data set name, with a period in between as separator.

Temporary data sets

During the start up of the SAS System, a temporary data library is automatically set up with libref WORK. This functions as 'default' library, meaning that if no other library is indicated, all data set and catalog references will be in WORK. This is clear in the sample programs we have seen so far: in each case there is only a data set name declared and no libref. The SAS System itself supplies the libref WORK (which is also mentioned in the log). Also formats go into the WORK data library, if no other specification with respect to storage is given in the PROC FORMAT statement. The SAS System creates the catalog FORMATS in WORK at first use.

Permanent data sets

The difference between temporary and permanent data libraries and also between temporary and permanent SAS files (data sets, catalogs) is only in the way the data library is set up. In a data library all information is permanent as long as it is not explicitly removed. Thus by setting up a permanent data library, all information stored into it is permanent and through the proper allocation can be used again in a later SAS session.

Multiple Engine Architecture

Conceptual design of the SAS data set

In the development of Version 6 of the SAS System, SAS Institute has aimed for a universal design for data storage. Not only have they attempted to implement a data library which functions similarly for all system platforms on which the SAS System operates, but also to define a universal access path to other database systems present on the platforms. To this end the concept of the SAS data set has been broadened in V6. The kernel of the concept remains the same: a description of available variables and a repository for the values of these variables: the observations. In V6, however, the physical form can vary. Figure 10.2 shows the extended SAS data set concept. In the first place there is still the 'native' form, which is similar to the Version 5 data set, although the physical structure has been modified. Besides this, there is the 'interface' form, by means of which files from other systems can be read directly. Completely new in V6 is the concept 'View'. A View contains only the description of the data set and a reference to the storage location of the data. The consequence of this is that you can work with Views as if they were normal SAS data sets. Views are employed primarily so that the SAS System can be used with other database systems, such as DB2. By means of PROC SQL, however, it is also possible to create Views which are based on one or more normal SAS data set. With this you can construct an access safeguard which goes beyond normal password security. Say that there is a large central data set, but not everyone can see all the variables or someone can only see observations which fulfill certain criteria. In that case a VIEW is defined for the data set with only those variables (use DROP or KEEP) and those observations which fulfill the criteria (use WHERE).

Engines

In order to assimilate all these different physical forms of SAS data sets, different access methods are needed. They are implemented in the form of 'Engines' (figure 10.3). There is an engine which can read and modify V5 data libraries, an engine for reading and modifying Version 6 data libraries, an engine for reading and creating SAS data libraries on tape and so on. As a rule the user does not have to concern himself with these engines: the system itself selects the ones which it needs. The SAS System reports in the LIBNAME statement and PROC CONTENTS, among others, which engine is being applied.

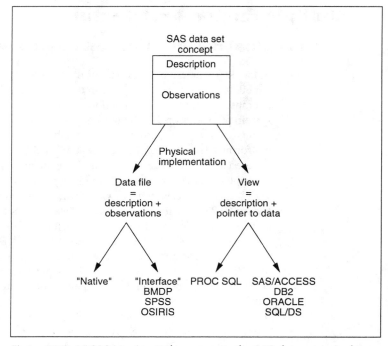

Figure 10.2: In SAS Version 6 the concept of a SAS data set is no longer limited to the physical implementation (the native data set) but can be used also to describe other physical structures. From a functional point of view these will work as SAS data sets.

Only in special cases might it be necessary to explicitly state the engine, for example if a tape format data set needs to be created on disk, then it must be explicitly stated that the tape engine should be used.

Engine tasks

Not every physical form of a SAS data set has the same capabilities with regard to reading and writing. Obviously with a SAS data set on tape, only sequential reading is possible.

The engine used determines which manipulative capabilities there are for the data set. Most engines can both read and write a SAS data set, but there are special engines which can only read, for instance the engine for consulting SPSS files. Some engines, such as those which process SAS data sets on tape, can only move through the data set sequentially, others can move through at random. The standard engine for V6 data libraries can also index a SAS data set or compress a data set. The engines also determine to what degree SAS data sets can be modified by multiple users simultaneously. The possibilities vary from no common use to excluding only simultaneous updates at the observation level. It is not necessary to learn all the possibilities of the engines.

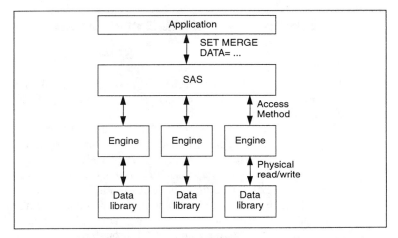

Figure 10.3: The broadening of the SAS data set concept (aimed for direct access to other database environments) necessitated to define several access methods. These are contained in so called Engines. This makes it possible for the SAS System to handle all physical implementations of data sets in a universal manner, seen from the point of view of the user.

Mostly you will be working with the V6 engine or with the V5 compatibility engine (for reading and updating of V5 data sets). With the V6 engine it is important to know that for large files you have at your disposal indexing techniques for making quick selections from files and the ability to compress data sets by which a substantial saving of memory can be realized, but which is restricted to sequential processing.

LIBNAME statement

The LIBNAME statement is one of the possibilities for allocating a data library and establishing a connection between the SAS program and the data library, through the assigning of a 'libref'.

The use of the LIBNAME statement for allocation, rather than a host system allocation command, has definite advantages. The allocation takes place within the SAS System, and the SAS System has control over the allocation. So at the end of a SAS session all allocations are automatically undone, which you would have to do yourself using host commands. Also, the libraries which have been allocated via LIBNAME can be consulted in the Display Manager, using the DIR window.

By means of the macro variable SYSLIBRC a test can be made in the
program to see if the allocation has been successful. More about this in
chapter 14, The SAS macro language.

Form of the LIBNAME statement

The basic form of the LIBNAME statement is:

```
LIBNAME libref <engine> 'data library name'
        <ACCESS=READONLY> <host options>;
```

After the keyword LIBNAME and the libref you have chosen, an engine
marker could follow, but this is usually not necessary, because the SAS
System normally decides itself which engine is required. The name of
the data library goes in quotation marks. This can be a complete data set
name, including the access path, but in most system environments a
partial name is also possible. Then the system searches from the user
directory to the data library. You will find more information on this in
the system appendices (H through M).

If you only want to read from the data library and not make any
modifications, you can append the ACCESS=READONLY option.
Other possible options depend on the system environment and will
therefore be dealt with in the system appendices.

LIBNAME...CLEAR

The LIBNAME statement can also be used to cancel the libref and break
the connection to the data library (deallocate the library). For this, the
following form is used:

```
LIBNAME libref CLEAR;
```

By using the special libref _ALL_, all libraries are deallocated.

The LIBNAME...CLEAR statement works only for data libraries which
have also been allocated by a LIBNAME statement. If this is not the case,
the libref gets canceled but the allocation continues to exist.

LIBNAME...LIST

The form:

```
LIBNAME libref LIST;
```

prints the characteristics of the library concerned in the SAS log, such as engine used, size, complete name and so on. Here too using the libref _ALL_ gives information on all libraries allocated via LIBNAME statement.

Data library management and maintenance

For the management and maintenance of SAS data libraries there are four important procedures.

PROC CONTENTS gives a summary of the contents of a data library. We have already had a look at this procedure (see chapter 4).

PROC COPY is used to copy data sets, catalogs and other SAS files from one data library to another.

PROC DATASETS is the 'Swiss Army Knife' of library management. Besides deleting or renaming data sets, it can also be used in the management of generation data sets, or in V6 for the indexing of SAS data sets.

PROC CATALOG is to catalogs what PROC DATASETS is to data sets.

PROC COPY

The form of PROC COPY is:

```
PROC COPY IN=libref OUT=libref <options>;
    EXCLUDE member1 <member2 ...> </MEMTYPE=... >;
    SELECT  member1 <member2 ...> </MEMTYPE=... >;
```

The IN and OUT librefs point the data libraries from where and to where the data sets and catalogs (the 'members') are to be copied. In the PROC statement 2 further options can be declared: MEMTYPE=... and MOVE. The MEMTYPE= option tells the SAS System that only specific types of files may be copied, for example MEMTYPE=(DATA CATALOG) copies all the data sets and the catalogs, but not other types of files (VIEWs, for example). If this option is left out, then every type of file is marked for copying. If the MOVE option is declared, then the file is deleted from the input data library after copying.

Without further specification statements, PROC COPY copies all files in the input data library, ultimately limited to the declared member types. If you only want to copy a part of the members, then you can use SELECT or EXCLUDE statements to state which members you want to copy. Only one or the other can be used. You can include a member type specification in the SELECT or EXCLUDE statement: this has priority over the member type declaration in the PROC statement. The following statements:

```
PROC COPY IN=fromlib OUT=tolib MEMTYPE=DATA;
   SELECT A B C;
   SELECT C FORMATS /MEMTYPE=CATALOG;
```

copy data sets A, B and C from the data library with fileref 'fromlib' to the data library with fileref 'tolib' and subsequently also the catalogs C and FORMATS, with all their entries.

PROC DATASETS

PROC DATASETS is a versatile procedure for the management of data libraries. A simple, much used application is for deleting or renaming SAS data sets, but you can do much more with it. In V6 PROC DATASETS has the unified capabilities of PROC COPY, PROC CONTENTS and PROC APPEND.

The procedure begins with the PROC statement:

```
PROC DATASETS LIBRARY=libref <options>;
```

The most important (and most dangerous!) option is the KILL option, which deletes the complete contents of the data library. There is no way back!

In an interactive environment, such as the Display Manager, PROC DATASETS remains active after the submit. Thus new maintenance tasks can be submitted and executed over and over. The procedure is ended by a QUIT statement or a following DATA or PROC statement.

Deleting members from a data library

In addition to the KILL option which deletes all the files in the data library, selected members of the data library can be deleted with PROC DATASETS using the DELETE statement or SAVE statement:

```
DELETE member1 <member2 ...> </MEMTYPE=...>;
SAVE   member1 <member2 ...> </MEMTYPE=...>;
```

Obviously the DELETE statement deletes the declared members, and the SAVE statement deletes all members except for those declared. By default, the DELETE statement only deletes data sets (MEMTYPE= DATA). To delete other types of files, then you must specify this using the MEMTYPE= option. The default for the SAVE statement is MEMTYPE=ALL.

Renaming a member

The CHANGE statement is used for renaming. Here too the MEMTYPE= option can be used to restrict the action to members of the declared type:

```
CHANGE oldname1=newname1 <oldname2=newname2 ...>
        </MEMTYPE=...>;
```

With the EXCHANGE statement:

```
EXCHANGE name1=name2 <name3=name4 ...> </MEMTYPE=...>;
```

the names of members are exchanged. Thus member 'name1' becomes 'name2' and 'name2' becomes 'name1' and so on.

Generation data sets

PROC DATASETS can also manage 'generation data sets'. The 'generation data set' principle is also known as the 'grandfather, father, son' system. The advantage is that in a program a data set is always created with the same name (the 'son') while older versions ('father', 'grandfather') are saved as back-up. The management of such a group of generation data sets is done with the AGE statement:

```
AGE membernames from new to old </MEMTYPE=...>;
```

Say that you are working with 3 generations, with the names CURRENT, OLD and VERYOLD (see figure 10.4). The processing is then as follows: first the data set VERYOLD is deleted. Then the data set OLD is renamed to VERYOLD and CURRENT is renamed to OLD. There is now no longer a CURRENT data set. A new CURRENT can now be created in the program.

```
LIBNAME MYLIB 'data library';
PROC DATASETS DD=MYLIB;
   AGE CURRENT OLD VERYOLD;
DATA MYLIB.CURRENT;
   SET MYLIB.OLD;
   * and what else has to be done;
RUN;
```

Figure 10.4: The principle of the generation data set. PROC DATASETS first removes VERYOLD, then renames OLD to VERYOLD and CURRENT to OLD. THE DATA step can create a new CURRENT data set.

Should something go wrong with the program, it can be rerun, without PROC DATASETS, now that OLD is still the push off point, or the data sets can be renamed again using the CHANGE option from OLD and VERYOLD to CURRENT and OLD, after which the whole program including AGE can be run again. If PROC DATASETS does not encounter VERYOLD, then nothing is deleted. This generation data set principle is most often used with normal data sets, but you can do the same thing with other files, such as catalogs. For this the MEMTYPE= option definitely must be declared.

Modifying the description of a data set

The MODIFY statement gives you access to the descriptive part of a SAS data set, where you can for example link formats to variables, rename variables, and so on. You cannot modify the contents of observations by adding or deleting variables. The modifications must usually be declared in a group of statements. This group always begins with a MODIFY statement:

```
MODIFY datasetname <LABEL='data set label'>;
   FORMAT variable format. ...;
   INFORMAT variable informat. ...;
   LABEL variable = 'variable label';
   RENAME oldvariablename=newvariablename ...;
```

The tasks of the various statements within the MODIFY group are self-evident. You should be aware however that no verification takes place whether or not specified formats or informats are really available. This will show up when using the data set (and create an error message if they are not).

Indexing data sets

In the discussion of engines, we already mentioned the possibility of constructing indexes for large SAS data sets, in order to gain quick access to observations which fulfill certain criteria. Creating indexes for SAS data sets is also a task for PROC DATASETS. You can construct multiple indexes for a data set. An index can refer to the value of a single variable (simple index), but you can also make a "composite index", which consists of a combination of variables. Such a composite index gets a special name. Say for example that we want to make indexes for a data set ADRSFILE, a simple index for the variable CITY and a composite index ADDRESS composed of postal code (POSTALCD) and house number (HOUSENBR). Seeing that an index is also a data set modification, the INDEX statement is preceded by a MODIFY statement:

```
MODIFY ADRSFILE;
    INDEX CREATE CITY ADDRESS=(POSTALCD HOUSENBR);
```

The INDEX statement can have the following options: UNIQUE and NOMISS. These options are separated from the rest of the statement by a '/'. UNIQUE indicates that no repeated values can occur in the index and NOMISS excludes observations with a missing value from the index.

An index can also be created during the creation of the data set with the INDEX=data set option. The indexes CITY and ADDRESS (see above) would then be created in the following way:

```
DATA ADRSFILE(INDEX=(CITY ADDRESS=(POSTALCD HOUSENBR)));
```

The WHERE data set option or the WHERE statement use the index whenever appropriate. With a composite index, the individual variables which make it up are stated and not the index name. In the previous example, this would be:

```
SET ADRSLIST (WHERE=(POSTALCD='2010AA' AND HOUSENBR < 10));
```

Or with the WHERE statement:

```
SET ADRSLIST;
WHERE POSTALCD='2010AA' AND HOUSENBR < 10;
```

The use of WHERE clauses has already been dealt with in chapter 4.

Copying of data sets to other libraries

Copying of data sets within PROC DATASETS is analogous to the way PROC COPY works. The COPY statement takes the place of the PROC COPY statement. The IN= option does not have to be declared if the input data library is the same as the library which is specified in the PROC DATASETS statement. After the COPY statement comes either the SELECT or EXCLUDE statement as required.

Appending observations to a data set

If the observations from two data sets are to be placed one after the other in a single data set, this can naturally be done by means of a SET statement:

```
DATA TOTAL;
   SET TOTAL ADDITION;
```

First all the observations of TOTAL will be read and output to a new TOTAL data set and then all the observations of ADDITION will be appended. Using the APPEND statement of PROC DATASETS, it goes like this:

```
APPEND BASE=TOTAL DATA=ADDITION;
```

The advantage is that the whole data set TOTAL does not first have to be read; the observations of ADDITION will be appended directly to TOTAL.

Making a back-up copy of a data set

The APPEND statement can also be used to make a copy of a data set under a different name, in the same or another data library, as a backup for example. If the data set declared in the BASE option does not exist, it will be created. The following statement creates a backup of the data set TOTAL:

```
APPEND BASE=TTL_BU DATA=TOTAL;
```

Without specifying a libref TTL_BU and TOTAL will naturally be in the data library which occurs in the PROC DATASETS statement; if a 2-level data set name is used (libref.datasetname), then the specified data library is used.

PROC CATALOG

What has been said up to now about PROC DATASETS also applies to PROC CATALOG as long as you keep in mind that you are dealing with catalogs and entries within a catalog rather than data libraries and members within a library. PROC CATALOG too is an interactive procedure which is ended with a QUIT statement. The procedure begins with:

```
PROC CATALOG CATALOG=libref.catalogname <options>;
```

Here too the most important option is the KILL option, which deletes all entries in the catalog.

Deleting entries from a catalog

Using a DELETE or SAVE statement, selected entries can be deleted from a catalog:

```
DELETE entry1 <entry2 ...> /ENTRYTYPE=...;
SAVE   entry1 <entry2 ...> /ENTRYTYPE=...;
```

ENTRYTYPE	Description
FORMAT	numeric format created by PROC FORMAT
FORMATC	character format created by PROC FORMAT
KEYS	function key definitions
MACRO	defines macros (ref. chapter 14)
MSYMTAB	macrovariable information (SAS internal)
REPT	report layout definition of PROC REPORT (ref. chapter 17)
SCREEN	screen layout definition of PROC FSEDIT (ref. chapter 19)
GSEG	SAS/GRAPH output (ref. chapter 20)
TEMPLATE	SAS/GRAPH templates (ref. chapter 20)
TITLE	text of TITLE-, FOOTNOTE- and NOTE-statements

Figure 10.5: Some of the many entry types that can be stored in catalogs. The entry type must be specified before you can manipulate the entries in PROC CATALOG.

The ENTRYTYPE indicates what type of entries in the catalog you mean, such as FORMAT or FORMATC. The SAS System recognizes many catalog entry types. A few of the most general entry types are listed in figure 10.5. Since no default values are valid for entry types, as for member types in PROC DATASETS, the entry type must be stated.

Renaming an entry

The name of an entry can be changed using the CHANGE statement and the names of entries can be exchanged using the EXCHANGE statement:

```
CHANGE oldname1=newname1 <oldname2=newname2 ...>
       /ENTRYTYPE=...;
EXCHANGE name1=name2 <name3=name4 ...>
       /ENTRYTYPE=...;
```

Note: CHANGE and EXCHANGE here work on the entry type level. To change the name of the catalog, you must use the CHANGE statement in PROC DATASETS.

Copying catalog entries to other catalogs

Copying catalog entries to another catalog is done with the same statements you would use in PROC DATASETS:

```
COPY OUT=libref.catalog <options>;
    SELECT entry1 <entry2 ...> </ENTRYTYPE=...>;
    EXCLUDE entry1 <entry2 ...> </ENTRYTYPE=...>;
```

In the COPY statement, an input catalog (IN = libref.catalog) can also be declared, if the entries copied are from another catalog than the one declared in the PROC CATALOG statement. The MOVE option deletes the entry from the input catalog after copying. The ENTRYTYPE option used in the COPY statement has a default entry type for the SELECT and EXCLUDE statements. However, an ENTRYTYPE= option can be specified in the SELECT or EXCLUDE statement. Just as in PROC COPY, only the SELECT or the EXCLUDE statement can be used in a COPY group, not both.

Table of contents of a catalog

The CONTENTS statement produces a summary of the entries in a catalog. Without further specification, this summary is placed in the SAS list, but it can be output to an output data set if so instructed.

```
CONTENTS <OUT=dataset> <FILE=fileref>;
```

The data set indicated in the OUT option will contain 6 variables: LIBNAME, the libref; MEMNAME, the catalog name; NAME, the entry name; TYPE, the entry type; DATE, date of the most recent modification; DESC, a description. The file which is declared in the FILE option contains only a copy of that which will be printed in the SAS list.

Exercises

1. In exercise 2 of chapter 8, the ELECTION data set must be copied under another name, whereby the variable LOSER is renamed to NAME. Try to create this data set in the correct form using PROC DATASETS.

2. In chapter 9 a number of formats are defined with PROC FORMATS. The SAS System places these in the catalog FORMATS of the WORK data library by default. Set up a new data library and copy the format PHONE to the catalog FORMATS in this library.

CHAPTER 11

Descriptive Statistics

fame with the power of its
primarily about general use
nto its many and extensive
:edures in descriptive statis-
for management reporting.
it. Those who will be using
s should read through the
SAS/ETS reference guides
) offer in the areas of linear
time series analysis and so

gistration at the check-out
is kept of the arrival time
long the transaction took.
...et. The information has
aireaqy been stored in an SAS data set with the name REG. Figure 11.1
shows a printout of a bit of the data set, which gives an idea of the kind
of information it contains.

The data set contains the log of arrival time at the check-out, transaction
time and check-out number in random order. Arrival time is formatted
with HHMM5. and transaction time with MMSS5. The first observation
therefore reveals that at 10:13 a fast customer arrived at check-out 7.
He was done in 47 seconds.

PROC MEANS - introduction

PROC MEANS has already been introduced in chapter 2 as a procedure
to quickly and easily calculate a number of statistical characteristics of
variables in a data set.
The basic form is:

```
PROC MEANS DATA=dataset <options> <statistics>;
    BY variables;
    VAR variables;
    FREQ variable;
    OUTPUT OUT=dataset
           statistic = variables
           statistic = variables
           ... ;
```

All statements and options in PROC MEANS are optional. They only serve to give greater control over the process.

The statistics which PROC MEANS is to include in its report should be declared in the PROC statement. If PROC MEANS is used without specification of the required statistics, the following data are calculated: N: the number of observations with a non-missing value for the analysis variable; MEAN: the mean value of the variable; STD: the standard deviation, a measure of the spread of the values, MIN and MAX, the lowest and highest occurring values of the variable. The capabilities of MEANS, however, do not stop with these five statistics, although they are the most often used. The complete list of available statistics is given in figure 11.4.

Of the options in the PROC statement the following are most commonly used: MAXDEC=.. and NOPRINT. The MAXDEC= option specifies in how many decimals the procedure should print results. Without the MAXDEC specification, the default is 6 decimal places. NOPRINT supresses the printout of MEANS. You will use it in combination with the OUTPUT statement which outputs the statistics to a SAS data set.

OBS	TIME	DURATION	CHECKOUT
1	10:13	0:47	7
2	9:58	1:00	4
3	11:57	1:06	3
4	10:51	0:51	2
5	9:42	1:21	5
6	11:11	1:05	2
7	10:04	1:08	4
8	9:46	2:46	2
9	12:18	1:34	4
10	9:59	0:47	1
11	11:37	0:38	5
12	13:15	0:37	3
13	10:39	0:50	4
14	10:26	2:01	3
15	10:09	0:53	6
16	11:06	12:51	9
17	12:10	0:43	4
18	11:33	5:55	7
19	9:56	0:51	2
20	13:03	0:36	4

Figure 11.1: The examples in this chapter are based on a registration of customers at check-out counters of a supermarket. For each customer it has been registered at what time he/she arrived at the counter, and how long the transaction took. TIME (the arrival time) has a format HHMM5., DURATION (the transaction time) is formatted with MMSS5.

Statements in PROC MEANS

As with virtually all PROCs, PROC MEANS can use a BY statement. The effect of using the BY statement is that the statistical characteristics are calculated separately for each BY group (the set of observations with equal values for BY variables).

Also the commonly occurring VAR statement applies here. By using the VAR statement, the statistics will be calculated only for the declared variables. If no VAR statement is used, MEANS will process all numeric variables in the data set.

The FREQ statement put a weight on the observation to be used during the calculation. In the FREQ statement a numeric variable is declared. The value of this variable makes it look as if the observation were present that number of times in the data set. If the value of the FREQ variable is less than 1, the observation is ignored in the calculation.

The OUTPUT statement specifies that the results are to be output to a SAS data set. In the OUTPUT statement you first of all state to which SAS data set the data should go, followed by the statistics to be calculated, followed in turn by the name of the variables in which these data are to be stored in the output data set. These variables correspond to variables in the VAR statement.

The first declared variable will contain the characteristic corresponding to the first variable in the VAR statement, and so on. In V6 there are also other methods to specify output, methods which in previous versions existed only in PROC SUMMARY. This will be covered in the next section.

The following example:

```
PROC MEANS DATA=... NOPRINT;
    VAR SALARY AGE;
    OUTPUT OUT=STAT MEAN=AVE_SAL MAX=MAX_SAL MAX_AGE;
```

contains an analysis of the variables SALARY and AGE. PROC MEANS provides no printout, but the results are output to data set STAT. The variable AVE_SAL in the data set will contain the mean value of the SALARY variable, and the variables MAX_SAL and MAX_AGE which contain respectively the maximum values of SAL-ARY and AGE. Be careful that in this way you do not process a statistic for AGE separately; the output variables must have a one-to-one correspondence with the variables in the VAR statement.

Example of PROC MEANS

In the first sample program based on the theme of this chapter, a number of characteristics are calculated for the variable DURATION, the time needed for a customer to complete a transaction at the check-out. The SAS log of the program is in figure 11.2 and the SAS list follows in figure 11.3.

With the first PROC MEANS, the mean, standard deviation and several other characteristics of DURATION are calculated. The required characteristics are in the PROC statement (line 6).

Then analysis is done per check-out counter. This is done with a BY statement. To use the BY statement, the data set must first be sorted. Note that with the sort (line 8) the data set is copied to the WORK library at the same time, so that the original permanent data set remains unaltered.

```
1                      The SAS System (6.08)
                                 19:04 Tuesday, June 7, 1994

NOTE: Copyright(c) 1989 by SAS Institute Inc., Cary, NC USA.
NOTE: SAS (r) Proprietary Software Release 6.08  TS405

NOTE: The initialization phase used 0.06 CPU seconds and 1092K.

NOTE: SAS job started on Tuesday 07JUN94 19:04 (199406071904)

1          /*------------------------------------------------------*/
2          /* SIMPLE USE OF PROC MEANS                             */
3          /*------------------------------------------------------*/
4          LIBNAME F1 '.GENERAL.SASLIB' DISP=SHR;
NOTE: Libref F1 was successfully assigned as follows:
      Engine:       V608
      Physical Name: TILANE.GENERAL.SASLIB
5          TITLE2 'PROC MEANS EXAMPLE';
6          PROC MEANS DATA=F1. REG MEAN STD SKEWNESS MIN MAX STDERR
MAXDEC=2;
7              VAR DURATION;

NOTE: The PROCEDURE MEANS printed page 1.
NOTE: The PROCEDURE MEANS used 0.02 CPU seconds and 1949K.

8          PROC SORT DATA=F1.REG OUT=REG;
9              BY CHECKOUT;

NOTE: SAS sort was used.
NOTE: The data set WORK.REG has 803 observations and 3 variables.
NOTE: The PROCEDURE SORT used 0.02 CPU seconds and 2216K.

10         PROC MEANS DATA=REG NOPRINT;
11             VAR DURATION;
12             OUTPUT OUT=RESULT MEAN=MEANDUR;
13             BY CHECKOUT;

NOTE: The data set WORK.RESULT has 10 observations and 4 variables.
NOTE: The PROCEDURE MEANS used 0.02 CPU seconds and 2248K.

14         PROC PRINT;
15             ID CHECKOUT;

NOTE: The PROCEDURE PRINT printed page 2.
NOTE: The PROCEDURE PRINT used 0.01 CPU seconds and 2302K.

NOTE: The SAS session used 0.32 CPU seconds and 2302K.
NOTE: SAS Institute BV, 1217 KR Hilversum, The Netherlands
```

Figure 11.2: A simple application of PROC MEANS. The first PROC step prints the specified statistics in the SAS list. The second PROC MEANS does not create printed output, but writes the results to a SAS data set: one observation per BY group.

```
                    The SAS System, Version 6.08                        1
                         PROC MEANS EXAMPLE
                                    19:04 Tuesday, June 7, 1994

Analysis Variable : DURATION


        Mean        Std Dev      Skewness        Minimum       Maximum
    ---------------------------------------------------------------------
       116.58         87.50          3.55          49.00        881.00
    ---------------------------------------------------------------------


                             Std Error
                         ----------------
                                3.09
                         ----------------



                    The SAS System, Version 6.08                        2
                         PROC MEANS EXAMPLE
                                    19:04 Tuesday, June 7, 1994

           CHECKOUT      _TYPE_      _FREQ_      MEANDUR

               1            0           91       104.703
               2            0           93       125.312
               3            0          111       119.009
               4            0           98       112.980
               5            0          100       126.470
               6            0           80       103.050
               7            0           79       128.354
               8            0           75       112.280
               9            0           45       118.289
              10            0           31       108.742
```

Figure 11.3: The output of the first PROC MEANS and PROC PRINT output of the data set created by the second PROC MEANS.

In the second PROC MEANS the option NOPRINT is used, so there is no printout. Instead the OUTPUT statement is used (line 12) to output the statistics to a SAS data set. In Version 5 the SAS System outputs two variables: the BY variable CHECKOUT, as identifier for the observation, and MEANDUR, the calculated mean. In Version 6 there are four. There are two additional variables with additional information: the _TYPE_ and the _FREQ_ variable.

TYPE is a variable which is used in PROC SUMMARY to indicate the level of the class variable. Since no class variable is used in the example (CLASS is not dealt with either), _TYPE_ always has the value 0. _FREQ_ indicates the number of observations that are present in the relevant BY group.

PROC MEANS and PROC SUMMARY

Having introduced PROC MEANS in the previous section, we now give a more complete description of PROC MEANS and PROC SUMMARY. In Version 5 PROC SUMMARY was a fundamentally different procedure from PROC MEANS, even though SUMMARY provided the same sort of statistical characteristics as MEANS. In V6 SUMMARY and MEANS have been fully integrated and the difference lies only in the default values of the options, by which MEANS primarily tends toward printed output and SUMMARY toward output to a SAS data set (in Version 5 SUMMARY could not create a printout on its own).

The PROC statement

The form of the PROC statement is:

```
PROC MEANS   DATA=... <options> <statistics>;
PROC SUMMARY DATA=... <options> <statistics>;
```

The options can be split into a number of groups, as shown in figure 11.4. The PRINT and NOPRINT control the printing of procedure results in the SAS list. In this context the MAXDEC option specifies the number of decimal places to be used in the printout. The default depends on the number of print positions available (see also option FW=), but MAXDEC can set it between 0 and 8. Take note: MAXDEC is valid only for print output of the procedure; any potential output data set always records the maximum number of decimal places.

After the general options follow the specification of the statistics to be printed. Figure 11.5 gives a summary of the possibilities. The order in which the statistics are entered in the PROC statement establishes at the same time the order in which they appear in the printout.

If no statistics are specified with PROC MEANS, then MEANS prints N, MEAN, STD, MIN and MAX by default.

PROC options	Description
Print control	
PRINT	creates printed output with PROC SUMMARY, is default with PROC MEANS
NOPRINT	suppresses printed output with PROC MEANS, is default with PROC SUMMARY
MAXDEC=	specifies the number of decimals in printed output
FW=	specifies the column width in printed output, default 12.
With CLASS statement	
DESCENDING	descending order of _TYPE_ values
MISSING	Missing values accepted as class-group
NWAY	only use highest _TYPE_ value
ORDER=	determines order of class groups (<u>INTERNAL</u>, DATA, FORMATTED, FREQ)
With WEIGHT statement	
VARDEF=	determines basis for calculation of (co-) variances (<u>DF</u>, N, WDF, WGT)
With ID statement	
IDMIN	lowest value of ID variable in the group is written to output data set, instead of the highest
With CLM statistics	
ALPHA=	specification of confidence interval, as fraction that is not included e.g. ALPHA=0.05 results in a 95% confidence interval.

Figure 11.4: Options that can be used in the PROC MEANS or PROC SUMMARY statement. The underscored values are defaults.

Statistic keyword	Description
N	number of observations with non-missing value
NMISS	number of observations with missing value
MIN	minimum value
MAX	maximum value
RANGE	difference between minimum and maximum value
SUM	sum of all non-missing values
MEAN	mean value
CLM	2-sided confidence interval
LCLM	1-sided lower confidence limit
UCLM	1-sided upper confidence limit
CSS	corrected sum of squares
USS	uncorrected sum of squares
VAR	variance
STD	standard deviation
STDERR	standard error of mean
CV	coefficient of variation
SKEWNESS	skewness
KURTOSIS	kurtosis
T	Student's T test (test population mean = 0)
PRT	probability of greater absolute value for T

Figure 11.5: A summary of the available statistics in PROC MEANS and PROC SUMMARY. They are specified in the PROC STATEMENT when required.

The VAR statement

The VAR statement indicates which variables are to be involved in the procedure. If this statement is left out, PROC MEANS will process all numeric variables. PROC SUMMARY reacts differently; it provides only the count of the number of observations.

The BY and the CLASS statements

Both the BY and the CLASS statement are used by PROC MEANS and PROC SUMMARY to create processing groups. The form for both is identical:

```
BY variables;
CLASS variables;
```

There are great differences, however. For the BY statement the data set must be sorted and the calculation for each unique combination of BY variable is output. To use the CLASS statement the data set does not have to be sorted, however the construction of whole sets of all class groups takes place in memory, where problems can arise if you are dealing with large data sets with many groups. Each variable in the CLASS statement is handled separately in the calculation: the first calculation takes place for the whole data set, thus without regard to the value of the class variables. Only the last declared variable in the CLASS statement is involved in the second calculation; therefore groups are generated for each value of the last variable, whether or not any more class variables exist. The third calculation takes the next to the last variable as the basis of the groups, regardless of the rest. The fourth calculation takes the last and the next to last together as basis, and so on. The calculations which are output (which class variables have or have not been declared to form groups) are indicated in the _TYPE_ variable.

TYPE=0 is the calculation for the whole data set, _TYPE_=1 is the calculation based only on the last class variable and so on. Figure 11.6 gives a schematic rendering. If the NWAY option is used, then all level-calculations are suspended and only the highest level is used: the combination of all class variables. This is the same grouping you can get with the BY statement.

For each value of a class variable a separate group is defined. It is logical then that the number of different values of a class variable must be limited. If this does not happen 'naturally', it can be simulated using formats, since the classification takes place on the basis of formatted values. See also the example on page 206, in which the variable TIME is used as classification, but formatted in whole hours.

A	B	C	_TYPE_
-	-	-	0
-	-	X	1
-	X	-	2
-	X	X	3
X	-	-	4
X	-	X	5
X	X	-	6
X	X	X	7

Figure 11.6: This table shows the relationship between the _TYPE_ variable and the class variables that are used to group observations. A CLASS statement: CLASS A B C; has been assumed here. An X means that the class variable is used to define a group and - that it is not. The NWAY option would only make the calculation for _TYPE_ = 7.

The FREQ and WEIGHT statements

The FREQ and WEIGHT statements both indicate the weight of the observation in the calculation of means, et cetera. The form is:

```
FREQ variable;
WEIGHT variable;
```

In both cases the declared variable must be numeric. The processing of the two statements is somewhat different however. Say that the value of the variable is 'n'. Then the observation will be regarded as INT(n) observations by the FREQ statement and in the WEIGHT statement the value of the analysis variable will first be multiplied by n. The sum of the weight factors is used as denominator in calculations of mean. In the calculation of a weighed variance you can specify (using the VARDEF option in the PROC statement) on which basis the calculation should take place.

For both the FREQ and WEIGHT variables the value must be greater than 0. Otherwise FREQ will not record the observation and WEIGHT will give an weight factor of 0.

The ID statement

The ID statement:

```
ID variable1 variable2 ...;
```

indicates what other than the class, BY or statistical variables must be included in the output data set.

Since only one observation per BY or class group is output, it must therefore be determined which values of the ID variable come under consideration. The default is the maximum value occuring in the relevant group, unless IDMIN is specified in the PROC statement. In that case only the minimum value is used. If multiple variables are declared, then the values all come from the same observation and the value of the first declared variable is used to determine which observation.

The OUTPUT statement

The OUTPUT statement is used to record the results of PROC MEANS and PROC SUMMARY in an output data set. The form is:

```
OUTPUT OUT=dataset
      statistic specifications
      <MINID (analysisvariable(IDvariable))=outputvariable>
      <MAXID (analysisvariable(IDvariable))=outputvariable>
      ;
```

OUT= specifies the output data set (libref.dataset), after that follow the specifications of the statistics to be output to the output data set. Many variations are possible, but the following two are the most used and are prone to the fewest errors:

```
keyword = output variables
keyword(analysis variables) = output variables
```

The first form has already been described in the section PROC MEANS introduction. The output variables correspond one-to-one with the variables in the VAR statement. The second variant gives a list of the analysis variables to which the output variables correspond one-to-one.

With the MAXID and MINID specifications it is possible to associate another variable with the highest and lowest values of the specified analysis variable as identification of the relevant observation, and the value of that ID variable (the ID variable which is declared in the MINID or MAXID, not to be confused with the ID statement) is then placed in the output variable.

Example of PROC MEANS and PROC SUMMARY

TIME and CHECKOUT are used as classification variables to get an insight into the total time per hour that a check-out counter was really active and into the average transaction time per check-out per hour. The confidence interval (90% interval) will also be calculated with this average. Figure 11.7 gives the SAS log and figure 11.8 the SAS list.

The printout of PROC MEANS has the average transaction time with its confidence interval (assuming that the data set contains a representative sample). When using the CLM statistics the ALPHA option should also be specified to give the interval. The OUTPUT statement requires other statistics. The variable TIME is consolidated into whole hours with a FORMAT statement, in order to limit the number of classification levels (otherwise each observation would form its own group!). Formats are assigned for the variables that PROC MEANS creates. This information is stored in the output data set. Note however the warnings in the log.

The PROC SUMMARY output statement is identical to that of PROC MEANS. Consequently the contents are also identical.

```
1                            The SAS System (6.08)
                                    19:19 Tuesday, June 7, 1994

NOTE: Copyright(c) 1989 by SAS Institute Inc., Cary, NC USA.
NOTE: The initialization phase used 0.06 CPU seconds and 1092K.

NOTE: SAS job started on Tuesday 07JUN94 19:19 (199406071919)

1            /*-------------------------------------------------------*/
2            /* EXAMPLE PROC MEANS / PROC SUMMARY                     */
3            /*-------------------------------------------------------*/
4            LIBNAME GEN '.GENERAL.SASLIB' DISP=SHR;
NOTE: Libref GEN was successfully assigned as follows:
      Engine:        V608
      Physical Name: TILANE.GENERAL.SASLIB
5
6            TITLE2 'MEANS AND SUMMARY';

NOTE: The data set WORK.REG has 803 observations and 3 variables.
NOTE: The DATA statement used 0.03 CPU seconds and 1811K.

7            PROC MEANS DATA=GEN.REG ALPHA=.1 FW=8 MAXDEC=3 MEAN CLM;
8            CLASS TIME CHECKOUT;
9            VAR DURATION;
10           OUTPUT OUT=OUTMEANS SUM(DURATION)=TOT_BUSY
11                  MEAN(DURATION)=C_O_TIME;
12           FORMAT TIME HOUR.;
13           FORMAT TOT_BUSY MMSS. C_O_TIME MMSS.;
WARNING: Variable TOT_BUSY not found in data set WORK.REG.
WARNING: Variable C_O_TIME not found in data set WORK.REG.
14           RUN;

NOTE: The data set WORK.OUTMEANS has 109 observations and 6 variables.
NOTE: The PROCEDURE MEANS printed pages 1-5.
NOTE: The PROCEDURE MEANS used 0.08 CPU seconds and 2316K.

15           PROC SUMMARY DATA=    REG;
16           CLASS TIME CHECKOUT;
17           VAR DURATION;
18           OUTPUT OUT=OUTMEANS SUM(DURATION)=TOT_BUSY
19           MEAN(DURATION)=C_O_TIME;
20           FORMAT TIME HOUR.;
21           FORMAT TOT_BUSY MMSS. C_O_TIME MMSS.;
WARNING: Variable TOT_BUSY not found in data set WORK.REG.
WARNING: Variable C_O_TIME not found in data set WORK.REG.
22           RUN;

NOTE: The data set WORK.OUTMEANS has 109 observations and 6 variables.
NOTE: The PROCEDURE SUMMARY used 0.04 CPU seconds and 2316K.

NOTE: The SAS session used 0.39 CPU seconds and 2370K.
NOTE: SAS Institute BV, 1217 KR Hilversum, The Netherlands
```

Figure 11.7: In PROC MEANS the average transaction time per hour is calculated for each check-out, including the 90% confidence interval. Compare the options to control the printed output with the result in figure 11.8. The OUTPUT statements in PROC MEANS and PROC SUMMARY are identical, hence the created data sets as well. The data set is printed in figure 11.8 parts 6 through 8.

```
                        The SAS System, Version 6.08                        1
                             MEANS AND SUMMARY
                                         19:19 Tuesday, June 7, 1994

Analysis Variable : DURATION


TIME    CHECKOUT  N Obs      Mean  Lower 90.0% CLM  Upper 90.0% CLM
-------------------------------------------------------------------
 9             1      6    93.333           86.301          100.365

               2      4    87.500           50.558          124.442

               3      6   146.000           22.529          269.471

               4      9    95.111           68.067          122.155

               5      6    92.500           61.137          123.863

               6      4    86.250           65.237          107.263

               7      2    89.000           70.059          107.941

               8      2   134.000         -175.374          443.374

               9      2   102.500           86.716          118.284

              10      2   101.000           44.176          157.824

10             1      9   135.333           66.476          204.190

               2     14   114.857           65.078          164.637

               3     14   119.357           69.748          168.967

               4     11   136.636           93.366          179.906

               5     15   176.067          129.308          222.826

               6      9    97.556           75.123          119.988

               7      7   126.429           16.518          236.339

               8      4    81.750           51.806          111.694
-------------------------------------------------------------------
```

Figure 11.8 (part1): For each combination of time (whole hours) and check-out PROC MEANS has calculated and printed the mean transaction time and its confidence limits.

```
                    The SAS System, Version 6.08                    2
                         MEANS AND SUMMARY
                                        19:19 Tuesday, June 7, 1994

Analysis Variable : DURATION


TIME    CHECKOUT   N Obs     Mean   Lower 90.0% CLM   Upper 90.0% CLM
------------------------------------------------------------------------
10             9       6   124.667            84.768           164.565

              10       5   106.800            44.342           169.258

11             1      19   112.737            89.676           135.797

               2      13   139.231            78.007           200.455

               3      12   121.250            88.704           153.796

               4      13    89.385            64.201           114.569

               5      19   142.053           109.088           175.018

               6      13    89.462            69.242           109.681

               7      10   139.700            31.143           248.257

               8      12   104.667            62.086           147.247

               9       7   197.571            -6.034           401.177

              10       5   152.200            37.315           267.085

12             1       7    82.857            57.964           107.751

               2      13   173.692           130.422           216.963

               3      16    82.000            70.202            93.798

               4       9   116.778            75.524           158.031

               5      10   108.500            60.111           156.889

               6       5    82.200            58.823           105.577
------------------------------------------------------------------------
```

Figure 11.8 (part 2)

The SAS System, Version 6.08   3
MEANS AND SUMMARY
19:19 Tuesday, June 7, 1994

Analysis Variable : DURATION

TIME	CHECKOUT	N Obs	Mean	Lower 90.0% CLM	Upper 90.0% CLM
12	7	13	179.385	98.567	260.202
	8	10	92.000	76.198	107.802
	9	7	105.286	59.304	151.267
	10	5	97.200	49.386	145.014
13	1	12	99.583	75.288	123.879
	2	6	71.000	55.680	86.320
	3	16	127.625	64.156	191.094
	4	9	101.889	66.898	136.879
	5	12	80.500	63.484	97.516
	6	8	82.750	54.045	111.455
	7	14	86.357	71.446	101.268
	8	11	90.636	68.363	112.910
	9	4	75.000	66.247	83.753
	10	3	102.667	52.533	152.800
14	1	10	122.000	47.163	196.837
	2	13	91.077	72.985	109.169
	3	12	105.333	87.143	123.524
	4	8	99.125	75.002	123.248

Figure 11.8 (part 3)

```
                    The SAS System, Version 6.08              4
                        MEANS AND SUMMARY
                                   19:19 Tuesday, June 7, 1994

Analysis Variable : DURATION


TIME     CHECKOUT  N Obs     Mean  Lower 90.0% CLM  Upper 90.0% CLM
-----------------------------------------------------------------
14          5        7    130.000           40.047          219.953

            6        7    105.714           44.393          167.035

            7        7    176.714          103.604          249.824

            8        6    159.167           63.216          255.117

            9        5    100.800           67.463          134.137

           10        3     78.667           66.706           90.627

15          1       13    104.923           81.931          127.915

            2       15    119.467           91.318          147.616

            3       13    117.385           82.749          152.021

            4       13     95.154           78.304          112.004

            5       10    147.800           90.340          205.260

            6       16    112.750           89.269          136.231

            7       10     85.200           77.044           93.356

            8       14    140.929          108.681          173.176

            9        3     65.667           41.805           89.528

           10        3     98.000           32.685          163.315

16          1       10     70.000           60.974           79.026

            2       12    153.083           97.232          208.935
-----------------------------------------------------------------
```

Figure 11.8 (part 4)

The SAS System, Version 6.08   5
MEANS AND SUMMARY
19:19 Tuesday, June 7, 1994

Analysis Variable : DURATION

TIME	CHECKOUT	N Obs	Mean	Lower 90.0% CLM	Upper 90.0% CLM
16	3	19	121.737	95.097	148.377
	4	19	92.105	78.522	105.689
	5	15	110.667	72.899	148.434
	6	15	111.000	74.366	147.634
	7	9	138.444	76.590	200.299
	8	12	117.917	78.160	157.674
	9	10	114.200	81.376	147.024
	10	5	110.000	85.871	134.129
17	1	5	109.800	48.674	170.926
	2	3	129.667	-89.859	349.193
	3	3	250.333	-61.947	562.614
	4	7	257.571	48.849	466.293
	5	6	108.833	62.888	154.779
	6	3	192.000	-57.250	441.250
	7	7	114.857	71.740	157.974
	8	4	77.500	59.032	95.968
	9	1	107.000	.	.

Figure 11.8 (part 5)

```
                        The SAS System, Version 6.08                        1
                             MEANS AND SUMMARY
                                          19:25 Tuesday, June 7, 1994

     OBS     TIME     CHECKOUT    _TYPE_     _FREQ_     TOT_BUSY      C_O_TIME

      1       .          .           0        803        1560         1:57
      2       .          1           1         91         158         1:45
      3       .          2           1         93         194         2:05
      4       .          3           1        111         220         1:59
      5       .          4           1         98         184         1:53
      6       .          5           1        100         210         2:06
      7       .          6           1         80         137         1:43
      8       .          7           1         79         169         2:08
      9       .          8           1         75         140         1:52
     10       .          9           1         45       88:43         1:58
     11       .         10           1         31       56:11         1:49
     12       9          .           2         43       73:15         1:42
     13      10          .           2         94         200         2:08
     14      11          .           2        123         253         2:04
     15      12          .           2         95         186         1:58
     16      13          .           2         95         150         1:35
     17      14          .           2         78         150         1:56
     18      15          .           2        110         208         1:54
     19      16          .           2        126         237         1:53
     20      17          .           2         39       99:02         2:32
     21       9          1           3          6        9:20         1:33
     22       9          2           3          4        5:50         1:28
     23       9          3           3          6       14:36         2:26
     24       9          4           3          9       14:16         1:35
     25       9          5           3          6        9:15         1:33
     26       9          6           3          4        5:45         1:26
     27       9          7           3          2        2:58         1:29
     28       9          8           3          2        4:28         2:14
     29       9          9           3          2        3:25         1:43
     30       9         10           3          2        3:22         1:41
     31      10          1           3          9       20:18         2:15
     32      10          2           3         14       26:48         1:55
     33      10          3           3         14       27:51         1:59
     34      10          4           3         11       25:03         2:17
     35      10          5           3         15       44:01         2:56
     36      10          6           3          9       14:38         1:38
     37      10          7           3          7       14:45         2:06
     38      10          8           3          4        5:27         1:22
     39      10          9           3          6       12:28         2:05
```

Figure 11.8 (part 6): PROC PRINT output of the data set as created by PROC SUMMARY. Inspect the relationship between the _TYPE_ variable and the indicated value of the class variables. A missing value for a class variable means that the variable was not used when forming a class group.

OBS	TIME	CHECKOUT	_TYPE_	_FREQ_	TOT_BUSY	C_O_TIME
40	10	10	3	5	8:54	1:47
41	11	1	3	19	35:42	1:53
42	11	2	3	13	30:10	2:19
43	11	3	3	12	24:15	2:01
44	11	4	3	13	19:22	1:29
45	11	5	3	19	44:59	2:22
46	11	6	3	13	19:23	1:29
47	11	7	3	10	23:17	2:20
48	11	8	3	12	20:56	1:45
49	11	9	3	7	23:03	3:18
50	11	10	3	5	12:41	2:32
51	12	1	3	7	9:40	1:23
52	12	2	3	13	37:38	2:54
53	12	3	3	16	21:52	1:22
54	12	4	3	9	17:31	1:57
55	12	5	3	10	18:05	1:49
56	12	6	3	5	6:51	1:22
57	12	7	3	13	38:52	2:59
58	12	8	3	10	15:20	1:32
59	12	9	3	7	12:17	1:45
60	12	10	3	5	8:06	1:37
61	13	1	3	12	19:55	1:40
62	13	2	3	6	7:06	1:11
63	13	3	3	16	34:02	2:08
64	13	4	3	9	15:17	1:42
65	13	5	3	12	16:06	1:21
66	13	6	3	8	11:02	1:23
67	13	7	3	14	20:09	1:26
68	13	8	3	11	16:37	1:31
69	13	9	3	4	5:00	1:15
70	13	10	3	3	5:08	1:43
71	14	1	3	10	20:20	2:02
72	14	2	3	13	19:44	1:31
73	14	3	3	12	21:04	1:45
74	14	4	3	8	13:13	1:39
75	14	5	3	7	15:10	2:10
76	14	6	3	7	12:20	1:46
77	14	7	3	7	20:37	2:57
78	14	8	3	6	15:55	2:39

Figure 11.8 (part 7)

Th(

OBS	TIME	CHECK(				
79	14	9				
80	14	10				
81	15	1				
82	15	2				
83	15	3				
84	15					
85	15					
86	15					
87	15					
88	15					
89	15					
90	15					
91	16					
92	16					
93	16					
94	16	4				
95	16	5	3			
96	16	6	3	15	27:45	..
97	16	7	3	9	20:46	2:18
98	16	8	3	12	23:35	1:58
99	16	9	3	10	19:02	1:54
100	16	10	3	5	9:10	1:50
101	17	1	3	5	9:09	1:50
102	17	2	3	3	6:29	2:10
103	17	3	3	3	12:31	4:10
104	17	4	3	7	30:03	4:18
105	17	5	3	6	10:53	1:49
106	17	6	3	3	9:36	3:12
107	17	7	3	7	13:24	1:55
108	17	8	3	4	5:10	1:18
109	17	9	3	1	1:47	1:47

216

Next to simple freq
other statistics
should refer

The PROC

Figure 11.8 (part 8)

PROC FREQ

PROC FREQ is designed to make frequency tables: how often does a given situation occur (for example the value of a variable). If one variable is involved, we speak of a one-way frequency table and if two or more variables are involved, we refer to them as crosstabulation tables. The form is:

```
PROC FREQ DATA=dataset <options>;
    TABLE variable1 </options>;
    TABLE variable1*variable2 </options>;
    WEIGHT variable;
```

uency counts PROC FREQ can also calculate several
(e.g. Chi-square). For these advanced features you
to the Procedures Guide.

statement

he most important options in the PROC statement are ORDER=
(similar to the ORDER= option in PROC MEANS, refer there) and the
PAGE option which indicates that each table should be on a separate
page. Without this last option the SAS System will put as many tables
together as possible on one page.

The TABLE statement

The frequency count is specified in the TABLE statement. Multiple
TABLE statements can be used in PROC FREQ. If a single variable is
declared in the TABLE statement, then a one-way calculation is done
simply to see how often each value occurs. If multiple variables are
declared, linked by an asterisk (*), a cross tabulation is done.

Be careful: the output of PROC FREQ can grow extremely rapidly with
cross tabulations. Say that we are dealing with three variables, each of
which has twenty different values. A one-way tabulation of each of these
variables produces twenty numbers; a cross tabulation of two of the
variables produces 20 x 20 = 400 numbers and a cross tabulation of all
three variables produces 20 x 20 x 20 = 8000 numbers!

Next to the pure frequency counts, the SAS System also calculates
percentages and cumulative frequencies unless otherwise instructed.

Calculating on the basis of Formatted Values

Before frequency calculation can take place, the SAS System formats
the analysis variables and PROC FREQ then uses these formatted values
in its calculations. Thus by attaching another format to the analysis
variables (include a FORMAT statement in PROC FREQ), the tables
can be grouped in another way. The formats which are used for this can
of course be the standard SAS formats, but PROC FORMAT can also be
used to define the levels that make up the groups for the frequency
calculation.

Options in the TABLE statement

PROC FREQ can also send the results to a SAS data set. This can be done with an OUTPUT statement, but usually it is simpler to do it with the OUT= option, which together with various other options are declared after a '/' in the TABLE statement. Other options fix the layout and contents of the tables. NOFREQ, NOPERCENT, NOROW and NOCOL all suppress one part of the standard output. NOFREQ and NOPERCENT speak for themselves, NOROW and NOCOL suppress row and column totals in the event of a cross tabulation. NOPRINT, to be used in combination with OUT=, suppresses the printout completely. The LIST option finally prints the results not as a table, but more in the style of PROC PRIN

The WEIGHT statement

A WEIGHT statement can also be given with PROC FREQ for making weighed frequency tables. The value of the variable in the WEIGHT statement establishes the weight of the observation in the calculation. Only one WEIGHT statement can be given, which has an effect on all TABLE statements.

Example of PROC FREQ

The example is again the supermarket check-outs. Figure 11.9 has the SAS log of the program and the corresponding list is in figure 11.10. The first example requires a simple frequency tabulation of the number of customers per unit of time. The unit of time is set to hours by using the FORMAT statement (line 14). The second TABLE statement calculates how often each check-out is approached. Then comes a cross calculation: how many customers pass through each check-out each hour. The fourth TABLE statement shows the same, but this time in LIST form. Finally the same data, although in a different sequence and written to the data set FREQOUT. The PROC PRINT output shows that no cumulative calculations have occurred. That is logical seeing that they are purely dependent on the sorting of the data set.

```
1                          The SAS System (6.08)
                                          10:32 Thursday, June 9, 1994

NOTE: Copyright(c) 1989 by SAS Institute Inc., Cary, NC USA.
NOTE: SAS (r) Proprietary Software Release 6.08  TS405

NOTE: The initialization phase used 0.07 CPU seconds and 1092K.

NOTE: SAS job started on Thursday 09JUN94 10:32 (199406091032)

1              /*--------------------------------------------------*/
2              /* PROC FREQ EXAMPLE                                */
3              /*--------------------------------------------------*/
4              LIBNAME GEN '.GENERAL.SASLIB' DISP=SHR;
NOTE: Libref GEN was successfully assigned as follows:
      Engine:        V608
      Physical Name: TILANE.GENERAL.SASLIB
6
7              TITLE2 'PROC FREQ EXAMPLE  ';
8              PROC FREQ DATA=GEN.REG;
9                 TABLE TIME;
10                TABLE CHECKOUT;
11                TABLE TIME*CHECKOUT;
12                TABLE TIME*CHECKOUT/LIST;
13                TABLE CHECKOUT*TIME/OUT=FREQOUT NOPRINT;
14                FORMAT TIME HOUR.;

NOTE: For table location in print file, see
      page 1 for TIME
      page 1 for CHECKOUT
      page 2 for TIME*CHECKOUT
      page 4 for TIME*CHECKOUT
      page 5 for CHECKOUT*TIME
NOTE: The data set WORK.FREQOUT has 89 observations and 4 variables.
NOTE: The PROCEDURE FREQ printed pages 1-5.
NOTE: The PROCEDURE FREQ used 0.07 CPU seconds and 2154K.

15             +PROC PRINT DATA=FREQOUT;

NOTE: The PROCEDURE PRINT printed pages 6-7.
NOTE: The PROCEDURE PRINT used 0.02 CPU seconds and 2207K.

NOTE: The SAS session used 0.35 CPU seconds and 2207K.
NOTE: SAS Institute BV, 1217 KR Hilversum, The Netherlands
```

Figure 11.9: You can invoke more than one table in a single PROC FREQ run. The SAS System puts as many tables on one page as will fit, unless you specify the PAGE option in the PROC statement.

```
                    The SAS System, Version 6.08                        1
                    PROC FREQ EXAMPLE
                                        10:32 Thursday, June 9, 1994

                                      Cumulative  Cumulative
         TIME    Frequency   Percent   Frequency    Percent
         - - - - - - - - - - - - - - - - - - - - - - - - - - - - - -
          9         43        5.4         43         5.4
         10         94       11.7        137        17.1
         11        123       15.3        260        32.4
         12         95       11.8        355        44.2
         13         95       11.8        450        56.0
         14         78        9.7        528        65.8
         15        110       13.7        638        79.5
         16        126       15.7        764        95.1
         17         39        4.9        803       100.0


                                      Cumulative  Cumulative
      CHECKOUT   Frequency   Percent   Frequency    Percent
      - - - - - - - - - - - - - - - - - - - - - - - - - - - - - - - -
          1         91       11.3         91        11.3
          2         93       11.6        184        22.9
          3        111       13.8        295        36.7
          4         98       12.2        393        48.9
          5        100       12.5        493        61.4
          6         80       10.0        573        71.4
          7         79        9.8        652        81.2
          8         75        9.3        727        90.5
          9         45        5.6        772        96.1
         10         31        3.9        803       100.0
```

Figure 11.10 (part 1): The simple one-way frequency tables created by the first two TABLE statements.

Figure 11.10 (parts 2 and 3, next pages): The two-way frequency table as defined in the third TABLE statement. Not the row and column totals.

```
                    The SAS System, Version 6.08                    2
                         PROC FREQ EXAMPLE
                                        10:32 Thursday, June 9, 1994

                    TABLE OF TIME BY CHECKOUT

TIME        CHECKOUT

Frequency|
Percent  |
Row Pct  |
Col Pct  |      1|       2|       3|       4|       5| Total
---------+--------+--------+--------+--------+--------+
     9 |      6 |      4 |      6 |      9 |      6 |     43
       |   0.75 |   0.50 |   0.75 |   1.12 |   0.75 |   5.35
       |  13.95 |   9.30 |  13.95 |  20.93 |  13.95 |
       |   6.59 |   4.30 |   5.41 |   9.18 |   6.00 |
---------+--------+--------+--------+--------+--------+
    10 |      9 |     14 |     14 |     11 |     15 |     94
       |   1.12 |   1.74 |   1.74 |   1.37 |   1.87 |  11.71
       |   9.57 |  14.89 |  14.89 |  11.70 |  15.96 |
       |   9.89 |  15.05 |  12.61 |  11.22 |  15.00 |
---------+--------+--------+--------+--------+--------+
    11 |     19 |     13 |     12 |     13 |     19 |    123
       |   2.37 |   1.62 |   1.49 |   1.62 |   2.37 |  15.32
       |  15.45 |  10.57 |   9.76 |  10.57 |  15.45 |
       |  20.88 |  13.98 |  10.81 |  13.27 |  19.00 |
---------+--------+--------+--------+--------+--------+
    12 |      7 |     13 |     16 |      9 |     10 |     95
       |   0.87 |   1.62 |   1.99 |   1.12 |   1.25 |  11.83
       |   7.37 |  13.68 |  16.84 |   9.47 |  10.53 |
       |   7.69 |  13.98 |  14.41 |   9.18 |  10.00 |
---------+--------+--------+--------+--------+--------+
    13 |     12 |      6 |     16 |      9 |     12 |     95
       |   1.49 |   0.75 |   1.99 |   1.12 |   1.49 |  11.83
       |  12.63 |   6.32 |  16.84 |   9.47 |  12.63 |
       |  13.19 |   6.45 |  14.41 |   9.18 |  12.00 |
---------+--------+--------+--------+--------+--------+
    14 |     10 |     13 |     12 |      8 |      7 |     78
       |   1.25 |   1.62 |   1.49 |   1.00 |   0.87 |   9.71
       |  12.82 |  16.67 |  15.38 |  10.26 |   8.97 |
       |  10.99 |  13.98 |  10.81 |   8.16 |   7.00 |
---------+--------+--------+--------+--------+--------+
    15 |     13 |     15 |     13 |     13 |     10 |    110
       |   1.62 |   1.87 |   1.62 |   1.62 |   1.25 |  13.70
       |  11.82 |  13.64 |  11.82 |  11.82 |   9.09 |
       |  14.29 |  16.13 |  11.71 |  13.27 |  10.00 |
---------+--------+--------+--------+--------+--------+
    16 |     10 |     12 |     19 |     19 |     15 |    126
       |   1.25 |   1.49 |   2.37 |   2.37 |   1.87 |  15.69
       |   7.94 |   9.52 |  15.08 |  15.08 |  11.90 |
       |  10.99 |  12.90 |  17.12 |  19.39 |  15.00 |
---------+--------+--------+--------+--------+--------+
    17 |      5 |      3 |      3 |      7 |      6 |     39
       |   0.62 |   0.37 |   0.37 |   0.87 |   0.75 |   4.86
       |  12.82 |   7.69 |   7.69 |  17.95 |  15.38 |
       |   5.49 |   3.23 |   2.70 |   7.14 |   6.00 |
---------+--------+--------+--------+--------+--------+
Total          91       93      111       98      100      803
            11.33    11.58    13.82    12.20    12.45   100.00
```

```
                   The SAS System, Version 6.08                    3
                        PROC FREQ EXAMPLE
                                     10:32 Thursday, June 9, 1994

                    TABLE OF TIME BY CHECKOUT

TIME      CHECKOUT

Frequency|
Percent  |
Row Pct  |
Col Pct  |      6|      7|      8|      9|     10|  Total
---------+-------+-------+-------+-------+-------+
     9   |    4  |    2  |    2  |    2  |    2  |     43
         | 0.50  | 0.25  | 0.25  | 0.25  | 0.25  |   5.35
         | 9.30  | 4.65  | 4.65  | 4.65  | 4.65  |
         | 5.00  | 2.53  | 2.67  | 4.44  | 6.45  |
---------+-------+-------+-------+-------+-------+
    10   |    9  |    7  |    4  |    6  |    5  |     94
         | 1.12  | 0.87  | 0.50  | 0.75  | 0.62  |  11.71
         | 9.57  | 7.45  | 4.26  | 6.38  | 5.32  |
         |11.25  | 8.86  | 5.33  |13.33  |16.13  |
---------+-------+-------+-------+-------+-------+
    11   |   13  |   10  |   12  |    7  |    5  |    123
         | 1.62  | 1.25  | 1.49  | 0.87  | 0.62  |  15.32
         |10.57  | 8.13  | 9.76  | 5.69  | 4.07  |
         |16.25  |12.66  |16.00  |15.56  |16.13  |
---------+-------+-------+-------+-------+-------+
    12   |    5  |   13  |   10  |    7  |    5  |     95
         | 0.62  | 1.62  | 1.25  | 0.87  | 0.62  |  11.83
         | 5.26  |13.68  |10.53  | 7.37  | 5.26  |
         | 6.25  |16.46  |13.33  |15.56  |16.13  |
---------+-------+-------+-------+-------+-------+
    13   |    8  |   14  |   11  |    4  |    3  |     95
         | 1.00  | 1.74  | 1.37  | 0.50  | 0.37  |  11.83
         | 8.42  |14.74  |11.58  | 4.21  | 3.16  |
         |10.00  |17.72  |14.67  | 8.89  | 9.68  |
---------+-------+-------+-------+-------+-------+
    14   |    7  |    7  |    6  |    5  |    3  |     78
         | 0.87  | 0.87  | 0.75  | 0.62  | 0.37  |   9.71
         | 8.97  | 8.97  | 7.69  | 6.41  | 3.85  |
         | 8.75  | 8.86  | 8.00  |11.11  | 9.68  |
---------+-------+-------+-------+-------+-------+
    15   |   16  |   10  |   14  |    3  |    3  |    110
         | 1.99  | 1.25  | 1.74  | 0.37  | 0.37  |  13.70
         |14.55  | 9.09  |12.73  | 2.73  | 2.73  |
         |20.00  |12.66  |18.67  | 6.67  | 9.68  |
---------+-------+-------+-------+-------+-------+
    16   |   15  |    9  |   12  |   10  |    5  |    126
         | 1.87  | 1.12  | 1.49  | 1.25  | 0.62  |  15.69
         |11.90  | 7.14  | 9.52  | 7.94  | 3.97  |
         |18.75  |11.39  |16.00  |22.22  |16.13  |
---------+-------+-------+-------+-------+-------+
    17   |    3  |    7  |    4  |    1  |    0  |     39
         | 0.37  | 0.87  | 0.50  | 0.12  | 0.00  |   4.86
         | 7.69  |17.95  |10.26  | 2.56  | 0.00  |
         | 3.75  | 8.86  | 5.33  | 2.22  | 0.00  |
---------+-------+-------+-------+-------+-------+
Total         80      79      75      45      31      803
            9.96    9.84    9.34    5.60    3.86   100.00
```

The SAS System, Version 6.08   4
                            PROC FREQ EXAMPLE
                                                 10:32 Thursday, June 9, 1994

TIME	CHECKOUT	Frequency	Percent	Cumulative Frequency	Cumulative Percent
9	1	6	0.7	6	0.7
9	2	4	0.5	10	1.2
9	3	6	0.7	16	2.0
9	4	9	1.1	25	3.1
9	5	6	0.7	31	3.9
9	6	4	0.5	35	4.4
9	7	2	0.2	37	4.6
9	8	2	0.2	39	4.9
9	9	2	0.2	41	5.1
9	10	2	0.2	43	5.4
10	1	9	1.1	52	6.5
10	2	14	1.7	66	8.2
10	3	14	1.7	80	10.0
10	4	11	1.4	91	11.3
10	5	15	1.9	106	13.2
10	6	9	1.1	115	14.3
10	7	7	0.9	122	15.2
10	8	4	0.5	126	15.7
10	9	6	0.7	132	16.4
10	10	5	0.6	137	17.1
11	1	19	2.4	156	19.4
11	2	13	1.6	169	21.0
11	3	12	1.5	181	22.5
11	4	13	1.6	194	24.2
11	5	19	2.4	213	26.5
11	6	13	1.6	226	28.1
11	7	10	1.2	236	29.4
11	8	12	1.5	248	30.9
11	9	7	0.9	255	31.8
11	10	5	0.6	260	32.4
12	1	7	0.9	267	33.3
12	2	13	1.6	280	34.9
12	3	16	2.0	296	36.9
12	4	9	1.1	305	38.0
12	5	10	1.2	315	39.2
12	6	5	0.6	320	39.9
12	7	13	1.6	333	41.5
12	8	10	1.2	343	42.7
12	9	7	0.9	350	43.6
12	10	5	0.6	355	44.2
13	1	12	1.5	367	45.7
13	2	6	0.7	373	46.5
13	3	16	2.0	389	48.4
13	4	9	1.1	398	49.6
13	5	12	1.5	410	51.1
13	6	8	1.0	418	52.1
13	7	14	1.7	432	53.8

Figure 11.10 (part 4): PROC FREQ output in LIST format

```
                    The SAS System, Version 6.08                    5
                    PROC FREQ EXAMPLE
                                   10:32 Thursday, June 9, 1994

                                        Cumulative  Cumulative
     TIME   CHECKOUT   Frequency  Percent  Frequency    Percent
     ------------------------------------------------------------
       13       8         11       1.4       443        55.2
       13       9          4       0.5       447        55.7
       13      10          3       0.4       450        56.0
       14       1         10       1.2       460        57.3
       14       2         13       1.6       473        58.9
       14       3         12       1.5       485        60.4
       14       4          8       1.0       493        61.4
       14       5          7       0.9       500        62.3
       14       6          7       0.9       507        63.1
       14       7          7       0.9       514        64.0
       14       8          6       0.7       520        64.8
       14       9          5       0.6       525        65.4
       14      10          3       0.4       528        65.8
       15       1         13       1.6       541        67.4
       15       2         15       1.9       556        69.2
       15       3         13       1.6       569        70.9
       15       4         13       1.6       582        72.5
       15       5         10       1.2       592        73.7
       15       6         16       2.0       608        75.7
       15       7         10       1.2       618        77.0
       15       8         14       1.7       632        78.7
       15       9          3       0.4       635        79.1
       15      10          3       0.4       638        79.5
       16       1         10       1.2       648        80.7
       16       2         12       1.5       660        82.2
       16       3         19       2.4       679        84.6
       16       4         19       2.4       698        86.9
       16       5         15       1.9       713        88.8
       16       6         15       1.9       728        90.7
       16       7          9       1.1       737        91.8
       16       8         12       1.5       749        93.3
       16       9         10       1.2       759        94.5
       16      10          5       0.6       764        95.1
       17       1          5       0.6       769        95.8
       17       2          3       0.4       772        96.1
       17       3          3       0.4       775        96.5
       17       4          7       0.9       782        97.4
       17       5          6       0.7       788        98.1
       17       6          3       0.4       791        98.5
       17       7          7       0.9       798        99.4
       17       8          4       0.5       802        99.9
       17       9          1       0.1       803       100.0
```

Figure 11.10 (part 5)

```
                    The SAS System, Version 6.08                        6
                         PROC FREQ EXAMPLE
                                       10:32 Thursday, June 9, 1994

       OBS      CHECKOUT      TIME       COUNT      PERCENT

        1           1           9           6       0.74720
        2           1          10           9       1.12080
        3           1          11          19       2.36613
        4           1          12           7       0.87173
        5           1          13          12       1.49440
        6           1          14          10       1.24533
        7           1          15          13       1.61893
        8           1          16          10       1.24533
        9           1          17           5       0.62267
       10           2           9           4       0.49813
       11           2          10          14       1.74346
       12           2          11          13       1.61893
       13           2          12          13       1.61893
       14           2          13           6       0.74720
       15           2          14          13       1.61893
       16           2          15          15       1.86800
       17           2          16          12       1.49440
       18           2          17           3       0.37360
       19           3           9           6       0.74720
       20           3          10          14       1.74346
       21           3          11          12       1.49440
       22           3          12          16       1.99253
       23           3          13          16       1.99253
       24           3          14          12       1.49440
       25           3          15          13       1.61893
       26           3          16          19       2.36613
       27           3          17           3       0.37360
       28           4           9           9       1.12080
       29           4          10          11       1.36986
       30           4          11          13       1.61893
       31           4          12           9       1.12080
       32           4          13           9       1.12080
       33           4          14           8       0.99626
       34           4          15          13       1.61893
       35           4          16          19       2.36613
       36           4          17           7       0.87173
       37           5           9           6       0.74720
       38           5          10          15       1.86800
       39           5          11          19       2.36613
       40           5          12          10       1.24533
       41           5          13          12       1.49440
       42           5          14           7       0.87173
       43           5          15          10       1.24533
       44           5          16          15       1.86800
       45           5          17           6       0.74720
```

Figure 11.10 (part 6): PROC PRINT output of the data set which has been created with the last TABLE statement in the program of figure 11.9.

OBS	CHECKOUT	TIME	COUNT	PERCENT
46	6	9	4	0.49813
47	6	10	9	1.12080
48	6	11	13	1.61893
49	6	12	5	0.62267
50	6	13	8	0.99626
51	6	14	7	0.87173
52	6	15	16	1.99253
53	6	16	15	1.86800
54	6	17	3	0.37360
55	7	9	2	0.24907
56	7	10	7	0.87173
57	7	11	10	1.24533
58	7	12	13	1.61893
59	7	13	14	1.74346
60	7	14	7	0.87173
61	7	15	10	1.24533
62	7	16	9	1.12080
63	7	17	7	0.87173
64	8	9	2	0.24907
65	8	10	4	0.49813
66	8	11	12	1.49440
67	8	12	10	1.24533
68	8	13	11	1.36986
69	8	14	6	0.74720
70	8	15	14	1.74346
71	8	16	12	1.49440
72	8	17	4	0.49813
73	9	9	2	0.87173
52	6	15	16	1.99253
75	9	11	7	0.87173
76	9	12	7	0.87173
77	9	13	4	0.49813
78	9	14	5	0.62267
79	9	15	3	0.37360
80	9	16	10	1.24533
81	9	17	1	0.12453
82	10	9	2	0.24907
83	10	10	5	0.62267
84	10	11	5	0.62267
85	10	12	5	0.62267
86	10	13	3	0.37360
87	10	14	3	0.37360
88	10	15	3	0.37360
89	10	16	5	0.62267

Figure 11.10 (part 7)

Exercises

1. On the basis of the permanent SAS data set used in chapter 9, exercise 1 (REALEST.HOUSES) the following statistics are to be made. The relevant variables are: TYPE, ROOMS, FIREPL, PRICE.

   a. Calculate the lowest, the highest and the average price.

   b. Make a frequency table of the number of houses of each type of residence.

   c. Make a cross table of the number of rooms per house against type of residence. In each cell put only the percentage per type of residence; for example:

TYPE	NR. OF ROOMS			
	2	3	4	5
MANSION	8	21	28	43
PENTHOUSE	22	28	36	14

   d. Make a data set in which the average price per type of residence is further divided into those with and without fireplace and a data set for how many houses there are with and without fireplace. Merge the data sets and print the results.

   e. Try to extablish the number of houses and the average price per type of residence (as in exercise d) using a single PROC as kernel of the program and avoid using a DATA step and MERGE.

CHAPTER 12

PROC TABULATE

Introduction

PROC TABULATE is a versatile procedure for producing many kinds of tabular reports. It can make crosstabulations such as those made with PROC FREQ, but also more complex reports in which hierarchies of variables determine the rows and columns, and in which the cells could contain a variety of statistical calculations. As an example, figure 12.1 is a summary of the demographics developed for a number of cities.

	Demographic summary				
	age group 0-10	age group 11-20	age group 21-40	age group 41-60	age group 61+
	perc.	perc.	perc.	perc.	perc.
City					
New York	11	13	27	30	19
Boston	13	14	27	27	19
...	...	...	...	...	...

Figure 12.1: A table like this can be created easily with PROC TABULATE. You could expand it with absolute numbers of inhabitants or with an extra hierarchical level vertically: first countries, then the cities within the countries.

This table is easily expanded in the vertical direction with another level: e.g. country and then within the country each row representing a city (first cities in the US, then cities in Canada, in the UK, in the Netherlands and so on). In the horizontal direction, expansion could include the absolute number of inhabitants next to the percentage of the population for each age group.

The method that PROC TABULATE uses for generating a report is primarily determined by three statements: the CLASS statement to declare the variables which compose the rows and columns, the VAR statement to define the variables which determine the contents of the cells, and the TABLE statement to further define the layout. FORMAT, LABEL and KEYLABEL statements can be used to further define rows and columns and dress up the report.

There are so many possibilities with PROC TABULATE that a separate book is published by SAS Institute: *SAS Guide to TABULATE Processing, Second Edition*. This chapter covers only the basic principles, which, however, will enable you to make many different kinds of reports.

Description of the procedure

The PROC statement

The PROC statement has the classic form:

```
PROC TABULATE DATA=dataset <options>;
```

The options in the PROC statement are primarily options which influence the way the tables look. The most important are FORMAT, NOSEPS and ORDER.

FORMAT=.. specifies a standard cell format. Without this option the SAS System uses the BEST12.2 format. NOSEPS suppresses the horizontal dividing lines in the table. A second option can be used here, FORMCHAR, which specifies the characters for all lines and vertices. By specifying blank spaces, the line will be invisible. The difference from the NOSEPS option, however, is that with NOSEPS the table is more compact, because the lines are actually removed whereas with FORMCHAR they are filled with spaces. Refer to the Procedures Guide for the exact operation of FORMCHAR. The ORDER= option specifies the order of the table. Choices are INTERNAL, DATA, FORMATTED and FREQ. If the option is omitted, default is INTERNAL.

The CLASS statement

The CLASS statement declares which variables are to be used for the definition of rows and columns. The form is simple:

```
CLASS variable1 variable2 ...;
```

Each formatted value of a class variable generates 1 row or 1 column. Class variables are thus typically variables with a limited number of discrete values or are made to look that way by applying an appropriate format. A date (many different values), for example, can be consolidated to figures per month using a MONYY. format. Class variables can be both character and numeric variables. The order is not important in the CLASS statement; that is determined in the TABLE statement.

The VAR statement

The VAR has the form:

```
VAR analysisvariable1 analysisvariable2 ...;
```

The variables declared in the VAR statement determine the contents of the cells of the report. They are called the 'analysis variables '. These must be numeric variables. Often these variables have a continuous nature, thus all possible values can occur. Here too the order is not important.

The TABLE statement

The TABLE statement is the heart of the procedure. It specifies how the rows and columns are to be constructed and what the exact contents of each cell is. The form is:

```
TABLE <page definition,> <row definition,>
      column definition </options>;
```

The statement will be discussed in the next section.

You could specify multiple TABLE statements in a single PROC TABULATE. The other statements are valid for all TABLE statements. There are also, however, various setup specifications possible within the TABLE statement, which can give each table a unique layout.

Statements for further formatting

In the discussion of the CLASS statement it has already been stated that the SAS System generates a row or column for each formatted value of a class variable. FORMAT statements can be used to group class variables of the correct values into rows or columns. Standard formats can of course be used, but a format can be defined just as well with PROC FORMAT. The columns and rows are indicated with the corresponding variable name; if the variable has a label, that label is used. Since variables are usually marked with labels in the data set which are defined to explain the variable rather than to show up as category names in a report, the LABEL statement is frequently used in PROC TABULATE to give the variable a new label for the duration of the procedure. The KEYLABEL statement has a function similar to the LABEL statement, but can be used for the statistical keywords in PROC TABULATE, as in:

```
KEYLABEL MEAN='Average value';
```

The TABLE statement

Dimensions

For rows and columns, the SAS System works with so-called 'dimensions': the 'Page dimension', the 'Row dimension' and the 'Column dimension'. In the TABLE statement, the dimensions are separated by commas. If only one dimension is used (no comma in the TABLE statement), that will be the column dimension. In other words the report will consist of a single row with one column for each value of the class variable(s). With two dimensions (a single comma in the TABLE statement), the first dimension (before the comma) is the row dimension and the second (after the comma) the column dimension. The report takes the form of a matrix, such as the one sketched in figure 12.1. If a third dimension is declared, the first dimension is the page dimension, which generates a separate page of output for each value of the class variables in that dimension. In practice, the two-dimensional form is the most common, and will also become a push off point.

Nesting and concatenation

Multiple class variables can be declared in each of the dimensions. You can specify whether separate rows or columns are to be used for each value for any of these variables (concatenation) or that a second variable should be used as a subdivision of the first (nesting). Concatenation is specified by declaring the variables separated by a space and for nesting by placing an '*' between them. Combinations of these can occur, in which parentheses are used to declare the variables in clear groups. Figure 12.2 gives a number of 'skeletons' of TABLE statements showing this principle of nesting and concatenation. Figure 12.2 starts out with 3 class variables (the third only in a couple of cases): A, B and C. Each class variable has only a few different values. A can have values A1, A2 and A3, B can have values B1 and B2 and C can have values C1 and C2.

The first statement involves a concatenation and only one dimension. Successive columns are made for all values of A and all values of B. In the second example there is again only one dimension, now combined with nesting. For each value of A the column branches to the value of B. In the third example where the class variables are separated by a comma, we are now dealing with two dimensions: A forms the row dimension and B the column dimension. The fourth example also has two dimensions, in which a nesting occurs in the row dimension. Thus a row is set up for each combination of an A value with a C value. The last example shows how concatenation and nesting can be combined. More examples can be found in appendix C.

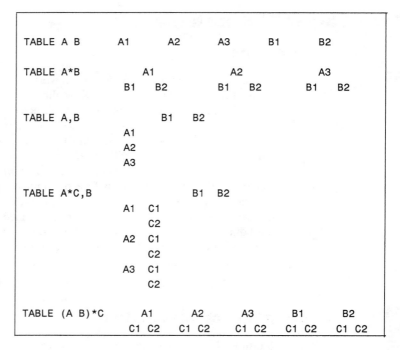

Figure 12.2: Some examples of nesting and concatenation and their effect on the layout of the produced table.

The 'Universal Class Variable'

If totals are required in a table, the 'Universal Class Variable' ALL can be applied to each required level. ALL stands for all values of the class variable on that level. ALL is applied to the variable by means of concatenation. You see an application of ALL in the sample program. ALL is not declared in the CLASS statement; it can always be used in the TABLE statement.

The cell definition

The cell definition is nested within the class variables. The analysis variable(s) are first and inside that is nested a statistic, for example SUM, N, MEAN and so on.

The whole thing now looks like this:

```
classvariable * analysisvariable * statistic
```

If there are multiple analysis variables, or if more statistics are required, these can be declared by concatenation and the use of parentheses:

```
class_v * (anal_v1 anal_v2) * statistic
```
or
```
class_v * anal_v1 * (statistic1 statistic2)
          anal_v2 * statistic3
```

In PROC TABULATE you can use the same statistics as in PROC MEANS and PROC SUMMARY (see table in figure 11.5), with a few exceptions: SKEWNESS, KURTOSIS, CLM, UCLM and LCLM are not available. Extra for PROC TABULATE are PCTN and PCTSUM. PCTN gives a percentage of a number (N) and PCTSUM gives a percentage of a sum. If nothing else is specified, this percentage will be based on the whole table. If something else should be used as 100% base, this should be declared in the 'denominator'. Usually this is a class variable. The percentages shall then add up to 100% for the values of this variable. The denominator is declared between < and > signs and placed after PCTN or PCTSUM. If an analysis variable rather than a class variable is used for the denominator, index numbers are calculated:

```
TABLE PRODUCT*(LAST_YR*SUM CURR_YR*(SUM PCTSUM<LAST_YR>));
```

More extensive denominator constructions are possible. For these, refer to the Guide.

An analysis variable is necessary for all analyses except N and PCTN. For N and PCTN without an analysis variable, it simply counted how often the relevant combinations of values of the class variables occur.

The TABLE statement in three simple questions

You can easily see the process of constructing a TABLE statement by answering the following three questions:

1. *Which variables determine the rows and columns?* These are the class variables. They come in the CLASS statement and form the basis of the TABLE statement.

2. *Which variables are to be reported on?* These are the analysis variables. They come in the VAR statement and are nested inside the class variables in the TABLE statement.

3. *What is to be reported about the variables?* The answer indicates the statistics which are in turn to be nested inside the analysis variables.

If more than one answer applies for a question, this leads to concatenation. At the moment you can formulate an answer with the words 'in which' or 'of which' or the like, you will do a nesting. Also the transfer to the next question involves nesting. In the sample program, CLASS, VAR and TABLE statements will be filled in with these questions in mind.

Layout

The table we have now defined can be dressed up in a variety of ways. In the general procedure description it became evident how the LABEL, KEYLABEL and FORMAT statements play key roles. The TABLE statement also offers many possibilities for dressing up the layout.

The SAS System normally identifies the rows and columns by the variable name or the variable label. It is possible to temporarily replace these by declaring a new label in the TABLE statement immediately after the name of the variable, for example DATE="date in service". If the temporary label is specified as a single space, no header is printed for that column.

The default cell format is BEST12.2. In the PROC statement it has already been shown how this can be changed for the whole table, but changes can be made at the individual cell level by including the format in the nesting structure in the table statement, nested within the specification of the statistic, for example ...*SUM*F=8.1.

Also the options you can add in the TABLE statement after a '/' are primarily intended for further layout specifications.

The RTS= option defines the 'Row Title Space'. The SAS System reserves about a third of the total row length for the row titles. This space can be lengthened or shortened using RTS=. The number of positions to be filled in is 'gross': the lines before and after the RTS count as well (see also the sample program).

At the top left of the table is an empty space, the 'BOX'. If we are talking about three dimensions, the value of the page dimension might be put there, but a chunk of text is also possible. This is done respectively be declaring BOX=_PAGE_ and BOX='This is the BOX text'.

Sample TABULATE program

The problem

This sample program is based on the turnover figures of a liquor wholesaler. Figure 12.3 shows the input data set.

We need to make a summary of the turnover per product category for the year, both in absolute figures and as portions of the total.

OBS	YEAR	CAT	TURNOVER
1	88/89	BEER	1413
2	88/89	COLA	440
3	88/89	ORANGE	334
4	88/89	M.WATER	260
5	89/90	BEER	1578
6	89/90	COLA	488
7	89/90	ORANGE	339
8	89/90	M.WATER	236
9	90/91	BEER	1614
10	90/91	COLA	492
11	90/91	ORANGE	339
12	90/91	M.WATER	236
13	91/92	BEER	1910
14	91/92	COLA	561
15	91/92	ORANGE	341
16	91/92	M.WATER	235
17	92/93	BEER	2205
18	92/93	COLA	686
19	92/93	ORANGE	345
20	92/93	M.WATER	260
21	93/94	BEER	2754
22	93/94	COLA	813
23	93/94	ORANGE	356
24	93/94	M.WATER	249

Figure 12.3: The data set that functions as the basis for the sample program. It contains turnover figures per fiscal year for each product category.

The program

In the program (see the SAS log in figure 12.4) two PROC TABULATEs are executed. Both TABULATEs have the same data set as input, also the basic structure is the same. The only differences are in the setup and layout. In general it is good practice to first make a skeletal TABULATE to make sure that the table and its contents are correct, and then flesh it out and dress it up.

We can develop the specification statements for PROC TABULATE from the questions on page 233.

What do we want to see as rows and columns? The years and products. The variables YEAR and CAT should thus be declared in the CLASS statement. We also see that YEAR and CAT are variables with a limited number of different values, characteristic of class variables.

What do we want to report on? The turnover, in the variable TURN-OVER. This is the analysis variable, to be declared in the VAR statement.

What do we want to know about the turnover? The total, the SUM statistic and a percentage of the total, the PCTSUM statistic.

In the TABLE statement the class variables are first declared, separated by a comma, so that YEAR forms the row dimension and CAT the column dimension. The analysis variable is nested inside CAT. Nested inside the analysis variable are the two statistic keywords, which produce the two analyses: SUM and PCTSUM.

In the output (figure 12.5 part 1) you can see that there is a column for each value of CAT and that there is a row for each year. The cells are formatted with BEST12.2. We also see that the percentage in PCTSUM is the percentage of the cell with respect to the total table and not per year, so that you get no clear insight into the portions for each product.

The shortcoming in this first summary is corrected in the second. The first change takes place in the PROC statement, where the standard format is replaced by 6., seeing that BEST12.2 is too broad. The other changes show up in and around the TABLE statement. The variable names are replaced by labels as are the statistical keywords. We simply include the variable labels in the TABLE statement. TURNOVER gets a label: ' ', so that it is effectively excluded from the printout. It is superfluous after labeling the statistics with the KEYLABEL statement. Secondly it is declared that the percentage should be calculated with respect to the turnover from all categories for one year. The denominator is thus <CAT>. The formatting of the percentage is changed into 6.1 (overruling the standard 6 from the PROC statement). Then the total turnovers are calculated, both per year and for all years together, by including the 'universal class variable' ALL both in the row and column dimensions.

Finally a title is put in at the top left of the table and the space for the row titles is shortened with the RTS= option.

```
1                        The SAS System (6.08)
                                    11:29 Thursday, June 9, 1994

NOTE: Copyright(c) 1989 by SAS Institute Inc., Cary, NC USA.
NOTE: SAS (r) Proprietary Software Release 6.08   TS405

NOTE: The initialization phase used 0.06 CPU seconds and 1092K.

NOTE: SAS job started on Thursday 09JUN94 11:29 (199406091129)

1              /*----------------------------------------------------*/
2              /* PROC TABULATE EXAMPLE                              */
3              /*----------------------------------------------------*/
4              LIBNAME IN '.GENERAL.SASLIB' DISP=SHR;
NOTE: Libref IN was successfully assigned as follows:
      Engine:        V608
      Physical Name: TILANE.GENERAL.SASLIB
5
6              TITLE2 'EXAMPLE PROC TABULATE';
7              PROC TABULATE DATA=IN.TURNOVE2;
8                 CLASS YEAR CAT;
9                 VAR TURNOVER;
10                TABLE YEAR,CAT*TURNOVER*(SUM PCTSUM);

NOTE: The PROCEDURE TABULATE printed pages 1-2.
NOTE: The PROCEDURE TABULATE used 0.02 CPU seconds and 1853K.

11             PROC TABULATE DATA=IN.TURNOVE2 FORMAT=6.;
12                CLASS YEAR CAT;
13                VAR TURNOVER;
14                TABLE YEAR ALL,CAT='PRODUCT CATEGORY'*TURNOVER=' '*
15                     (SUM PCTSUM<CAT>*F=6.1) ALL*TURNOVER*SUM/
16                     BOX='TURNOVER SUMMARY' RTS=7;
17                KEYLABEL SUM='TURN-OVER IN USD X 1000'
18                         PCTSUM='PERCENTAGE OF TURN-OVER';

NOTE: The PROCEDURE TABULATE printed page 3.
NOTE: The PROCEDURE TABULATE used 0.03 CPU seconds and 1865K.

NOTE: The SAS session used 0.30 CPU seconds and 1865K.
NOTE: SAS Institute BV, 1217 KR Hilversum, The Netherlands
```

Figure 12.4: Both TABULATEs are basically the same, but the extra options applied in the second make a big difference in the appearance of the result.

```
              The SAS System, Version 6.08                    1
                 EXAMPLE PROC TABULATE
                               11:29 Thursday, June 9, 1994
```

	CAT			
	BEER		COLA	
	TURNOVER		TURNOVER	
	SUM	PCTSUM	SUM	PCTSUM
YEAR				
88/89	1413.00	7.64	440.00	2.38
89/90	1578.00	8.54	488.00	2.64
90/91	1614.00	8.73	492.00	2.66
91/92	1910.00	10.33	561.00	3.04
92/93	2205.00	11.93	686.00	3.71
93/94	2754.00	14.90	813.00	4.40

```
              The SAS System, Version 6.08                    2
                 EXAMPLE PROC TABULATE
                               11:29 Thursday, June 9, 1994
```

	CAT			
	M.WATER		ORANGE	
	TURNOVER		TURNOVER	
	SUM	PCTSUM	SUM	PCTSUM
YEAR				
88/89	260.00	1.41	334.00	1.81
89/90	236.00	1.28	339.00	1.83
90/91	236.00	1.28	339.00	1.83
91/92	235.00	1.27	341.00	1.84
92/93	260.00	1.41	345.00	1.87
93/94	249.00	1.35	356.00	1.93

Figure 12.5 (part 1): The result of the "skeletal" PROC TABULATE. Note that the percentages are with respect to the whole table.

```
                The SAS System, Version 6.08                   3
                    EXAMPLE PROC TABULATE
                            11:29 Thursday, June 9, 1994
```

TURN- OVER SUMM- ARY	PRODUCT CATEGORY								ALL TURNO- VER
	BEER		COLA		M.WATER		ORANGE		
	TURN- OVER IN USD X 1000	PERCE- NTAGE OF TURN- OVER	TURN- OVER IN USD X 1000	PERCE- NTAGE OF TURN- OVER	TURN- OVER IN USD X 1000	PERCE- NTAGE OF TURN- OVER	TURN- OVER IN USD X 1000	PERCE- NTAGE OF TURN- OVER	TURN- OVER IN USD X 1000
YEAR									
88/89	1413	57.7	440	18.0	260	10.6	334	13.6	2447
89/90	1578	59.8	488	18.5	236	8.9	339	12.8	2641
90/91	1614	60.2	492	18.4	236	8.8	339	12.6	2681
91/92	1910	62.7	561	18.4	235	7.7	341	11.2	3047
92/93	2205	63.1	686	19.6	260	7.4	345	9.9	3496
93/94	2754	66.0	813	19.5	249	6.0	356	8.5	4172
ALL	11474	62.1	3480	18.8	1476	8.0	2054	11.1	18484

Figure 12.5 (part 2): With a few "bells and whistles" PROC TABULATE produces a complete well designed report. Note the omission of the intermediate column header level TURNOVER. This is done by temporarily assigning TURNOVER a label ' '.

Exercises

1. Make a table like the one sketched below, based on the same data
    set as the one used in exercise 1 of chapter 9.

		Fireplace		Garage	
		With	Without	With	Without
		Ave. price	Ave. price	Quantity	Quantity
TYPE	ROOMS				
MANSION	2				
	3				
	4				
	5				
	6				
APARTMENT	2				
	3				
	4				
	...				
...	...				

CHAPTER 13

Graphic Presentation

Introduction

Graphic presentation is an important component of management information. The SAS product SAS/GRAPH has a wealth of capabilities, from simple line diagrams and bar charts to facilities for drawing maps. But also base SAS software has several graphics capabilities, although more limited and primitive: the so-called printer graphics. With printer graphics you can make a number of simple graphics presentations on normal (non graphic) terminals and normal printers. It cannot do nearly as nice work as a true graphics workstation or plotter, but it is cheap, within the reach of everyone, and good for mass production. When you are ready to make the switch: it is simple to upgrade to SAS/GRAPH software. Chapter 20 helps you with an introduction to SAS/GRAPH.

Example, the situation

In this chapter we use the same data as in chapter 12 (see figure 12.3), the turnover data of a liquor wholesaler now filled out with profit figures and in another form. Figure 13.1 shows the data set in its new form. The form in figure 12.3 will also be used.

OBS	YEAR	PROFIT	BEER	COLA	ORANGE	WATER
1	88/89	77	1413	440	334	260
2	89/90	117	1578	488	339	236
3	90/91	82	1614	492	339	236
4	91/92	65	1910	561	341	235
5	92/93	111	2205	686	345	260
6	93/94	92	2754	813	356	249

Figure 13.1: The input data set for the examples in this chapter. The turnover and profit figures of a liquor wholesaler. The variables BEER, COLA, ORANGE and WATER contain the turnover figures of that product category (in USD x 1000).

PROC PLOT

The first of the two printer graphics procedures is PROC PLOT. PLOT produces simple X-Y graphs: two variables are plotted against each other with a plotting symbol for each combination of X and Y values.

The basic form of PROC PLOT is:

```
PROC PLOT DATA=dataset <options>;
 PLOT Yvariable*Xvariable<label><=plotting symbol>
     </options>;
```

Multiple PLOT statements can be included in a PROC PLOT and multiple graphs can also be specified in a PLOT statement.

Of the options which can be included in the PROC statement, the most interesting are HPERCENT and VPERCENT, which define vertically and horizontally which portions of the output page shall be used for the graph. Default is 100% (using the whole page), but if you enter, for example, HPERCENT=50 VPERCENT=50, four graphs will fit on a page. By entering numbers greater than 100, the graph can be spread over more than one page. By entering multiple numbers, various graphs can be made in different sizes. HPERCENT= 100 33 33 33 VPERCENT=50, for example, will make four graphs on one output page; the first will take up the entire top half and the other three will be fit next to each other on the bottom half.

The PLOT statement

A graph definition consists of at least two variables: first the Y variable (the vertical dimension) and the X variable (the horizontal dimension). The two variables are separated by a '*':

```
PLOT Yvariable * Xvariable;
```

With this specification the SAS System automatically sets the scale based on the lowest and highest values of the variables and uses letters as plotting symbols: an A if 1 observation is associated with the coordinates involved, B for 2 observations, C for 3 observations and so on.

The first extension is a user definition of the plotting symbol. These plotting symbols can be a character constant (for example ...='*') or a variable (for example ...=plot_var) in which case the first character of the (formatted) value of the variable is used as plotting symbol.

In Version 6 it is also possible to attach labels to a point in the graph. This is done by including a third variable between the y and x variables and the plotting symbol, preceded by a $ sign:

```
PLOT Yvariable*Xvariable $ labelvariable = plotting symbol;
```

If no plotting symbols are specified when using the labeling capability, then "arrowheads" are used to indicate to which point the label belongs. There are various possibilities for placing labels and for instructing the SAS System what to do if labels come on top of each other. You can use the PLACE= option to give the instructions. For details of this, refer to the Procedures Guide.

Finally you can include some options after a '/' in the PLOT statement, which control the appearance of the plot. The most important are listed in figure 13.2.

The HAXIS= and VAXIS= option, after which a series of values can be entered, define the horizontal and vertical axes. The series of values can be entered in a variety of ways:

```
HAXIS = 1 2 3 4 5
HAXIS = 100 TO 1000 BY 100
HAXIS = '01JAN93'D TO '01JAN94'D BY MONTH
HAXIS = 10 100 1000
HAXIS = BY n
```

The last three variants require some explanation. The third form shows how an axis can be defined with date intervals. Also the other interval specifications which can be used with the INTCK or INTNX functions, can be used here. In the fourth variant a logarithmic scale is defined and in the last variant only the interval is declared; the lowest and highest value will be inferred by the SAS System from the data.

The same forms (except the last) can also be used with the VAXIS, VREF and HREF options.

HAXIS=	defines the scale for the horzontal axis
VAXIS=	defines the scale for the vertical axis
HREF=	defines a reference line, perpendicular to the horizontal axis
VREF=	defines a reference line, perpendicular to the vertical axis
HZERO	forces the beginning of the horizontal axis to the origin (X=0)
VZERO	forces the beginning of the vertical axis to the origin (Y=0)
HREVERSE	reverses direction of the horizontal axis (highest value at left side)
VREVERSE	reverses direction of the vertical axis (highest value at the bottom)
OVERLAY	prints all plots on the same axes

Figure 13.2: Some of the options in the PLOT statement.

The OVERLAY option is applied if there are multiple graphs (thus multiple XY pairs) included in the PLOT statement and you want all graphs to be superimposed on the same set of axes. Multiple graphs can be specified in various ways:

```
PLOT y_var1*x_var1 y_var2*x_var2 ...;
PLOT (y_var1 y_var2)*(x_var1 x_var2) ...;
PLOT (y_var1 - y_var4):(x_var1 - x_var4) ...;
```

In the second variant graphs are made for all combinations: y_var1*x_var1 y_var2*x-var1 y_var1*x_var2 y_var2*x_var2; in the third variant only the corresponding pairs are plotted: y_var1*x_var1 y_var2*x_var2 y_var3*x_var3 y_var4*x_var4.

PROC PLOT sample program

Figure 13.3 has a printout of a program with three variants of PROC PLOT. The first variant makes a simple graph of the profits of the liquor wholesaler with a reference line to level 100 and in a second graph plots the turnover figures of the product categories. The OVERLAY option plots the graphs for all products on one set of axes. Along the vertical axis PROC PLOT will use the label of the first variable in the PLOT statement as label for the axis. Therefore WATER is relabeled with something more appropriate for the occasion. The second PROC PLOT shows the effects of VPERCENT and HPERCENT. Vertically there is room for two graphs on a page. The whole top half of the page is taken up by one graph, the bottom half by three small graphs side by side. Note that due to the reduction of the vertical space the label at the vertical axis does not fit anymore. In the third PROC PLOT the label option is demonstrated. There the variant of the data as displayed in figure 12.3 is used as input because you need the turnover figures in one variable and another variable to indicate the product.

```
1                        The SAS System (6.08)
                              20:46 Thursday, June 9, 1994

NOTE: Copyright(c) 1989 by SAS Institute Inc., Cary, NC USA.
NOTE: SAS (r) Proprietary Software Release 6.08   TS405

NOTE: The initialization phase used 0.06 CPU seconds and 1092K.

NOTE: SAS job started on Thursday 09JUN94 20:46 (199406092046)

1            /*-----------------------------------------------------*/
2            /* PROC PLOT EXAMPLES                                  */
3            /*-----------------------------------------------------*/
4            TITLE2 'EXAMPLES PROC PLOT';
5            LIBNAME F1 '.GENERAL.SASLIB' DISP=SHR;
NOTE: Libref F1 was successfully assigned as follows:
      Engine:        V608
      Physical Name: TILANE.GENERAL.SASLIB
6            PROC PLOT DATA=F1.TURNOVE1;
7               PLOT PROFIT*YEAR/VREF=100;
8               PLOT WATER*YEAR='M' ORANGE*YEAR='O' COLA*YEAR='C'
9                    BEER*YEAR='B' /OVERLAY;
10              LABEL WATER='TURNOVER IN USD X 1000';

NOTE: The PROCEDURE PLOT printed pages 1-2.
NOTE: The PROCEDURE PLOT used 0.03 CPU seconds and 1764K.

11           PROC PLOT DATA=F1.TURNOVE1 HPERCENT=100 33 33 33 VPERCENT=50;
12              PLOT PROFIT*YEAR/VREF=100;
13              PLOT WATER*YEAR='M' ORANGE*YEAR='O' COLA*YEAR='C';
14              LABEL WATER='TURNOVER IN USD X 1000';

WARNING: Label for variable WATER is too long for axis. Try increasing
         axis length or reducing label length.
         Variable name will be used instead.
NOTE: The PROCEDURE PLOT printed page 3.
NOTE: The PROCEDURE PLOT used 0.01 CPU seconds and 1764K.

15           PROC PLOT DATA=F1.TURNOVE2;
16              PLOT TURNOVER*YEAR $ CAT;
17           RUN;

NOTE: The PROCEDURE PLOT printed page 4.
NOTE: The PROCEDURE PLOT used 0.02 CPU seconds and 1764K.

NOTE: The SAS session used 0.28 CPU seconds and 1764K.
NOTE: SAS Institute BV, 1217 KR Hilversum, The Netherlands
```

Figure 13.3: Several variants of PROC PLOT. Compare the output (figure 13.4) with the PLOT statements and their options.

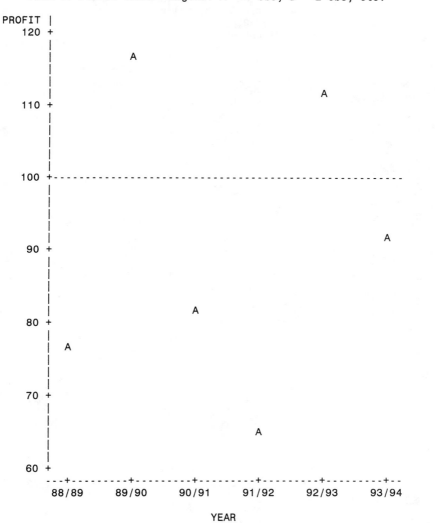

Figure 13.4 (part 1): A simple plot of the profit over the years. Note the reference line (VREF = 100).

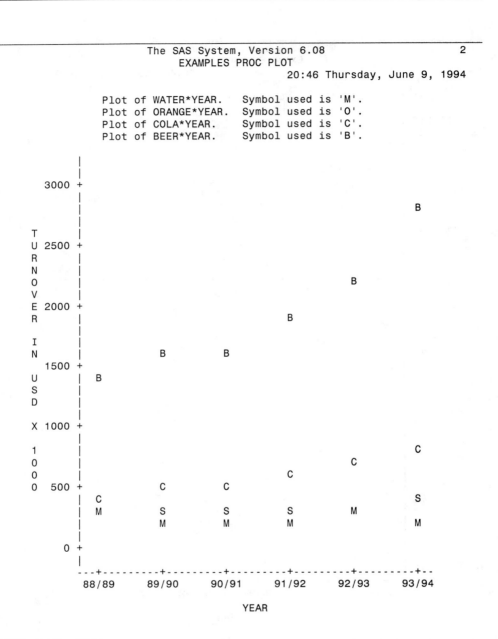

Figure 13.4 (part 2): With the OVERLAY option you can put the graphs for each product together in one pair of axes.

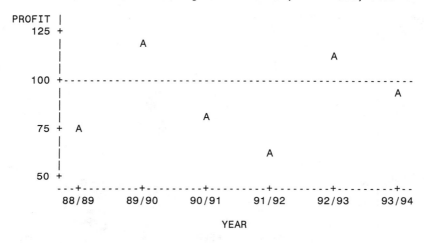

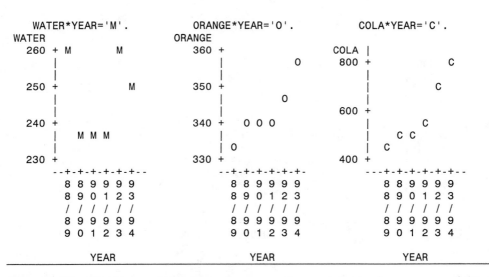

Figure 13.4 (part 3): More graphs on one page or one graph spanning several pages are possibilities that are controlled with the VPERCENT and HPERCENT options in the PROC PLOT statement.

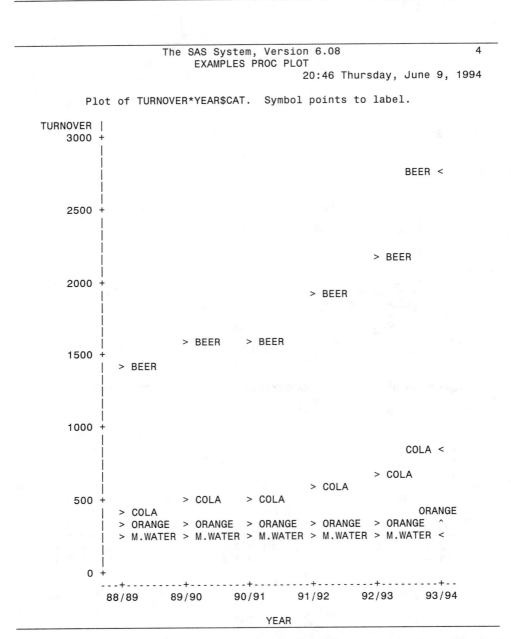

Figure 13.4 (part 4): The result of the label option. The arrowheads are at the plot position and point to the related label. Note that the label is normally to the right of the plot position. However if it does not fit there, PROC PLOT uses an "anti collision" algorithm to find a better place.

PROC CHART

PROC CHART makes vertical and horizontal bar charts, pie charts, star charts and '3-dimensional' charts. The basis for all these is in fact the histogram, which portrays graphically how often a particular value of the magnitude to be measured occurs. It also follows from this that PROC CHART in its basic form only works with one variable, in contrast to PROC PLOT which always involves an X and a Y variable. In this basic form, what you will see is a simple frequency count, graphically portrayed. The PROC statement is nothing new:

```
PROC CHART DATA=dataset <options>;
```

There is only one option of real importance, the LPI option. This is however only relevant with star and pie charts, and will be covered with those subjects.

CHART is typically a procedure in which, with the help of examples, you must decide which form you want and then from that, work out the required statements. This is why so much of the Procedures Guide is devoted to examples. Also in this chapter you will see many examples, and there are still more in appendix D.

Basis of PROC CHART: the VBAR and HBAR

Vertical and horizontal bar charts are defined respectively in a VBAR and HBAR statement:

```
VBAR chart variables </options>;
HBAR chart variables </options>;
```

The form indicates that multiple chart variables can be declared. For each variable a separate chart will be made. The chart variables can be both character and numeric. In principle, a bar is drawn for each value of the chart variable. For numeric chart variables the situation is somewhat more complicated. Numeric variables will be regarded as having a continuous nature, in other words any value can occur. The SAS System automatically fixes the number of bars and with that it determines which values of the chart variable will be grouped together in one bar, unless this process is controlled by setting various options (see figure 13.5). Regarding numeric variables as continuous is inconvenient if, for instance, you want to make a chart in which the chart variable is a date, for example the SAS date for the first of the month. Then you have to use the DISCRETE option to make the system generate a separate bar for each month.

Type of presentation

TYPE =	<u>FREQ</u>, CFREQ, PERCENT, CPERCENT indicate which type of frequency count is required.
SUMVAR=	Specifies a variable whose value will be used to calculate the bar height. To be combined with TYPE=<u>SUM</u> or TYPE=MEAN.
GROUP=	Specifies a variable which splits up the chart variable in groups. For each group a chart will be produced.
G100	In combination with the GROUP= option and TYPE=(C)PERCENT: adds up to 100% per group.
SUBGROUP=	Specifies a variable which is used to subdivide bars in proportion with the contribution of those observations to the bar.

Horizontal axis

DISCRETE	Indicates that the (numeric) chart variable has a discrete rather than a continuous nature.
MIDPOINTS=	Specifies the values of the chart variable for which a bar is to be drawn. Compare the HAXIS= option of PROC PLOT. The BY n specification as present in PROC PLOT is not valid here.
LEVELS=	Specifies the number of bars if no MIDPOINTS have been specified. If omitted PROC CHART will infer the number of bars automatically.

Vertical axis

AXIS=	Specifies the scale for the vertical (response) axis. This can only be linear, e.g. AXIS = 0 to 10 by 2.
REF=	Specifies values for reference lines on the vertical axis.

Figue 13.5: Some of the options of PROC CHART. Vertical and horizontal are referring to the VBAR chart: horizontal meaning the values of the chart variable, vertical the response. Underlined values are defaults.

In addition to simple frequency charting it is also possible to print frequencies as percentages and to render cumulative frequencies and percentages: each bar has its own value + the sum of all previous bars. The desired variant is specified in the TYPE option.

With SUMVAR a second variable can be brought into the process. The sum or the mean value of this variable determines the ultimate size of the bar. The sample program illustrates its use.

PIE and STAR charts

The processing of the PIE and STAR charts is analogous to the processing of the VBAR and HBAR.

```
PIE chart variables </options>;
STAR chart variables </options>;
```

Both these charts produce a circular chart. Naturally this causes a problem: there are many printers in circulation with many different fonts and line spacings. How do you prevent the circle from looking elliptical? For this, use the LPI= option in the PROC statement. The value for the LPI parameter can be calculated as follows: LPI=(lines per inch vertically) / (characters per inch horizontally) * 10. Without the LPI option, the default is LPI=6.

3-Dimensional diagrams (BLOCK charts)

The BLOCK statement produces a sort of 3-dimensional diagram. A base with fields for the midpoint values and the groups and on each field a kind of tower that indicates the response value.

This method of making diagrams takes a lot of space and can therefore only be used for a very small number of midpoints and groups. The Procedures Guide states what the exact limitations are for a given line length. Typically this is in the range of three to six midpoints by zero to four group levels.

If the line length or page size is insufficient for a BLOCK chart, PROC CHART will report that in the log and create an HBAR chart instead.

PROC CHART sample program

The majority of the sample program relates to the 2 data sets with figures from the liquor wholesaler. Data set TURNOVE1 is the layout according to figure 13.1 and TURNOVE2 is the layout according to figure 12.3. The log of the sample program is in figure 13.6.

The first PROC CHART produces two charts in which the years are noted as midpoints. Without other specifications, CHART makes a frequency count and since each year occurs once, we get the simple chart of figure 13.7 part 1.

By using the PROFIT as SUMVAR variable (line 8) we get a good impression of the profit (figure 13.7 part 2).

The following PROC CHART starts out from the data set as in figure 12.3 and shows the effect of GROUP and SUBGROUP. Because the data set contains too much information to make a BLOCK chart that will fit in the line length of this book, the amount of information is reduced by deleting older years and removing the beer turnover. The PIE chart follows the standard pattern. By leaving out the LPI option the circle is a bit off. In the last PROC CHART the circle is drawn better by including the LPI option.

The liquor wholesaler data sets do not lend themselves very well to a STAR chart. Therefore this is based on the ORDER data set presented in chapter 8 (figure 8.4). Now by using the LPI option a reasonable circle is achieved.

The output of the program (figure 13.7) needs no further explanation.

```
1                           The SAS System (6.08)
                                    21:07 Thursday, June 9, 1994

NOTE: Copyright(c) 1989 by SAS Institute Inc., Cary, NC USA.
NOTE: SAS (r) Proprietary Software Release 6.08  TS405

NOTE: The initialization phase used 0.06 CPU seconds and 1092K.

NOTE: SAS job started on Thursday 09JUN94 21:07 (199406092107)


1              /*----------------------------------------------------*/
2              /* PROC CHART EXAMPLES                                */
3              /*----------------------------------------------------*/
4              TITLE2 'EXAMPLES PROC CHART';
5              LIBNAME F1 '.GENERAL.SASLIB' DISP=SHR;
NOTE: Libref F1 was successfully assigned as follows:
      Engine:        V608
      Physical Name: TILANE.GENERAL.SASLIB
6              PROC CHART DATA=F1.TURNOVE1;
7                 VBAR YEAR;
8                 VBAR YEAR/SUMVAR=PROFIT;

NOTE: The PROCEDURE CHART printed pages 1-2.
NOTE: The PROCEDURE CHART used 0.02 CPU seconds and 1734K.

9              PROC CHART DATA=F1.TURNOVE2;
10                VBAR YEAR/SUBGROUP=CAT SUMVAR=TURNOVER;
11                VBAR YEAR/GROUP=CAT SUMVAR=TURNOVER;
12                HBAR YEAR/SUBGROUP=CAT SUMVAR=TURNOVER;
13             RUN;

NOTE: The PROCEDURE CHART printed pages 3-5.
NOTE: The PROCEDURE CHART used 0.01 CPU seconds and 1734K.

14             DATA A B;
15                SET F1.TURNOVE2;
16                IF YEAR GE '91/92';              * REMOVE OLD INFO;
17                IF CAT NE 'BEER' THEN OUTPUT A;
18                OUTPUT B;

NOTE: The data set WORK.A has 9 observations and 3 variables.
NOTE: The data set WORK.B has 12 observations and 3 variables.
NOTE: The DATA statement used 0.02 CPU seconds and 2065K.

19             PROC CHART DATA=A;
20                BLOCK YEAR/GROUP=CAT SUMVAR=TURNOVER;

NOTE: The PROCEDURE CHART printed page 6.
NOTE: The PROCEDURE CHART used 0.01 CPU seconds and 2065K.
```

Figure 13.6 (part 1): The easiest way to learn PROC CHART is by studying examples. Compare the output in figure 13.7 with the chart instructions in this log. The DATA step starting at line 14 reduces the amount of data for use with the BLOCK and the PIE chart.

```
2                          The SAS System (6.08)
                                    21:07 Thursday, June 9, 1994

19              PROC CHART DATA=B;
20                PIE CAT/SUMVAR=TURNOVER;

NOTE: The PROCEDURE CHART printed page 7.
NOTE: The PROCEDURE CHART used 0.01 CPU seconds and 2065K.

23              PROC CHART DATA=F1.ORDER  LPI=5.42;
24                STAR ART_CAT;

NOTE: The PROCEDURE CHART printed page 8.
NOTE: The PROCEDURE CHART used 0.01 CPU seconds and 2065K.

NOTE: The SAS session used 0.31 CPU seconds and 2065K.
NOTE: SAS Institute BV, 1217 KR Hilversum, The Netherlands
```

Figure 13.6 (part 2): The last PROC CHART in this program uses the DIY shop dataset from chapter 8. Note that by applying the LPI= option in the PROC statement the output is now a better circle.

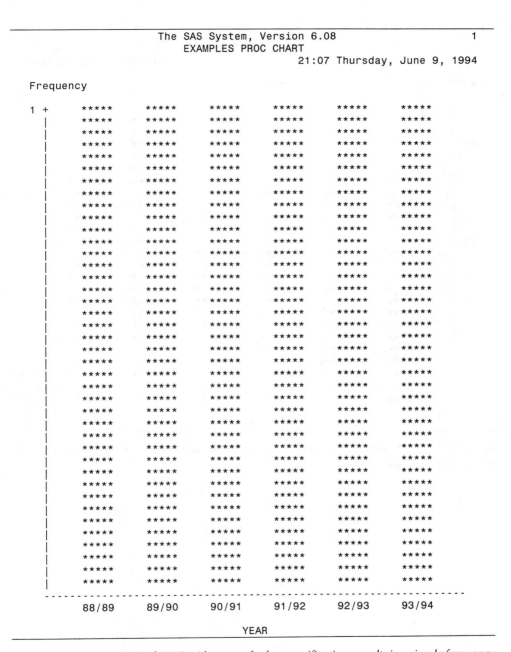

The SAS System, Version 6.08   1
EXAMPLES PROC CHART
                                 21:07 Thursday, June 9, 1994

Figure 13.7 (part 1): VBAR of YEAR without any further specifications results in a simple frequency count: how often does each year occur in the data set?

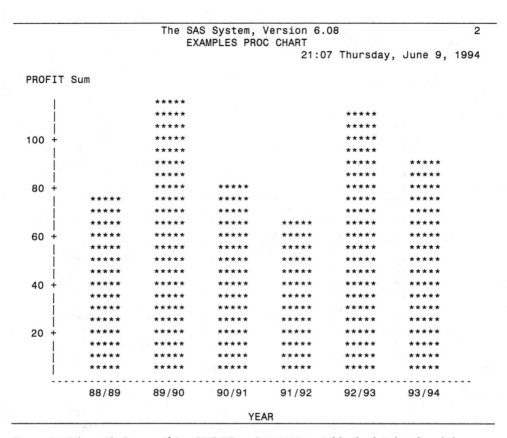

Figure 13.7 (part 2): By specifying PROFIT as SUMVAR variable the height of each bar now represents the profit of each year.

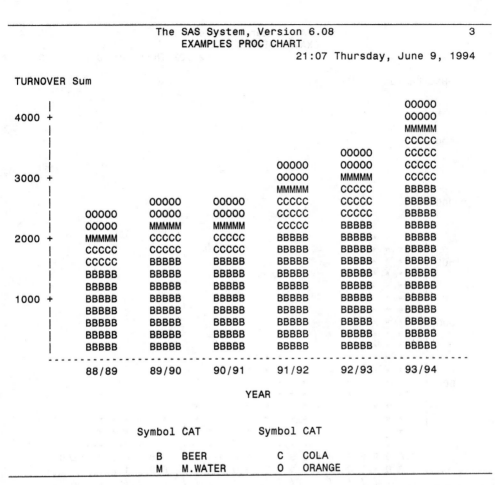

Figure 13.7 (part 3): The SUBGROUP option divides the bars per product category, showing the contribution of each product.

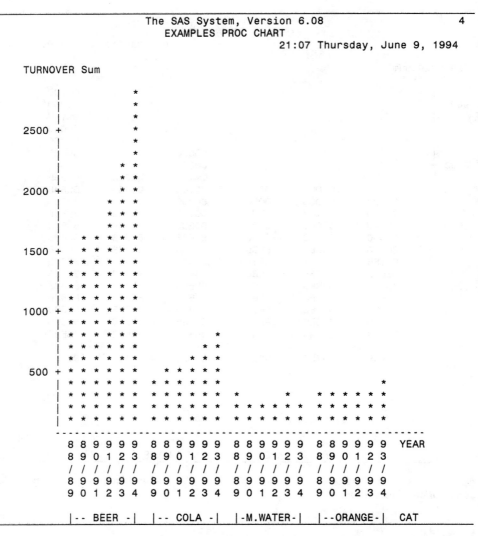

Figure 13.7 (part 4): The GROUP option creates bars next to each other for each value of the GROUP variable.

```
                        The SAS System, Version 6.08                    5
                           EXAMPLES PROC CHART
                                  21:07 Thursday, June 9, 1994

   YEAR                                                       TURNOVER
                                                  Freq            Sum
        |
  88/89 |BBBBBBBBBBBBBBBCCCCMMMOOO                  4        2447.000
        |
  89/90 |BBBBBBBBBBBBBBBBBCCCCCMMOOO                4        2641.000
        |
  90/91 |BBBBBBBBBBBBBBBBBCCCCCMMOOO                4        2681.000
        |
  91/92 |BBBBBBBBBBBBBBBBBBBCCCCCCMMOOO             4        3047.000
        |
  92/93 |BBBBBBBBBBBBBBBBBBBBBBCCCCCCCMMMOOO        4        3496.000
        |
  93/94 |BBBBBBBBBBBBBBBBBBBBBBBBBBBBBBCCCCCCCCMMOOOO  4     4172.000
        |
        ----+----+----+----+----+----+----+----+--
          500  1000 1500 2000 2500 3000 3500 4000

                        TURNOVER Sum


        Symbol CAT          Symbol CAT

          B    BEER           C     COLA
          M    M.WATER        O     ORANGE
```

Figure 13.7 (part 5): Same as part 3, this time as HBAR.

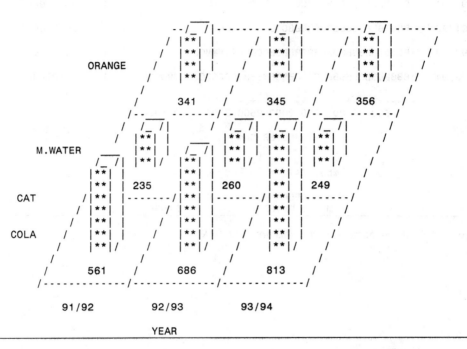

Figure 13.7 (part 6): The BLOCK chart. This is only possible with a limited number of midpoints and groups.

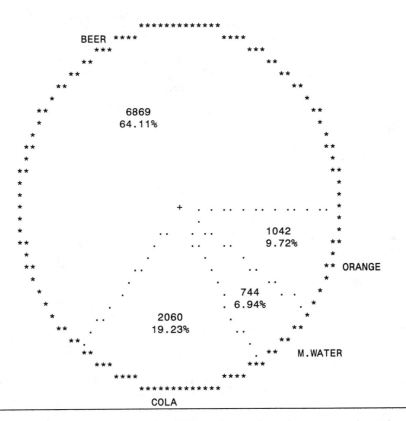

Figure 13.7 (part 7): The PIE chart. You should limit the number of segments to keep the result legible. Note the distortion of the circle. You could correct this with the LPI= option.

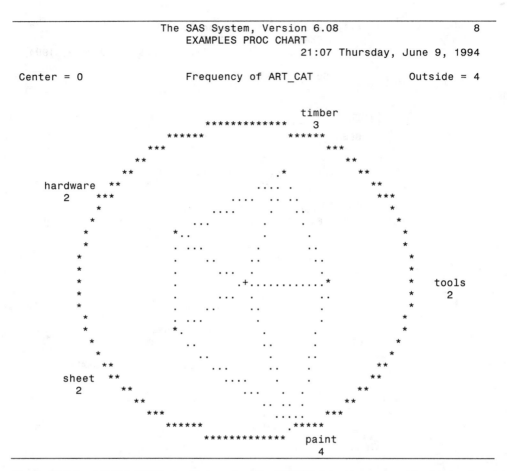

```
               The SAS System, Version 6.08                    8
               EXAMPLES PROC CHART
                                    21:07 Thursday, June 9, 1994

Center = 0              Frequency of ART_CAT              Outside = 4
```

Figure 13.7 (part 8) This STAR chart is based on the ORDER data set as created in chapter 8 and illustrates the number of different articles ordered per category.

Exercises

1   In exercise 1 of chapter 6 a SAS data set is created with data on the temperature per month per state. The relevant variables are STATE, MONTH, MAXTEMP, MINTEMP and CLIMATE. Make the graphs described below based on these data.

   a. Plot in one graph the minimum and maximum temperature. Use as plotting symbols '-' for minimum and '+' for maximum. Arrange the months horizontally. Make a separate graph for each state.

       Note: The readings in the data set are in random order. Think carefully about the horizontal axis!

   b. Make a vertical bar chart of the temperature distribution (CLIMATE).

   c. Make a pie chart of the temperature distribution. In it indicate the percentage of occurrence of each of the values.

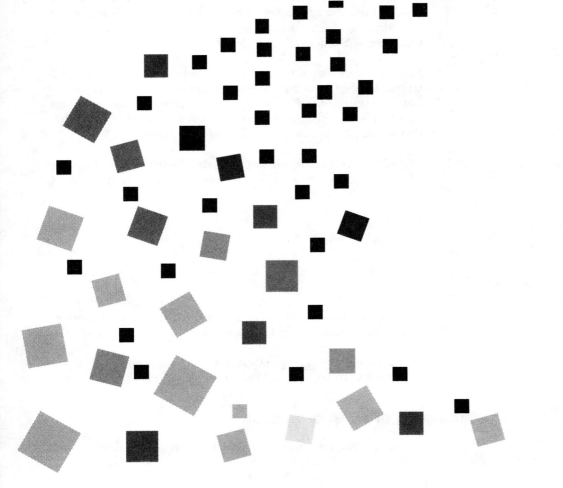

CHAPTER 14

The SAS® Macro Language

Introduction to the SAS macro language

The SAS macro language is a programming language within the SAS programming language. The macro language is intended to enable modification of a SAS program while it is running, based on conditions that arise. You can also use it to write routines that you use frequently in the form of a MACRO. These macros can then be called with one statement, the MACRO-call, and run as many times as needed. It is even possible to develop interactive menu driven applications, although this is a complex task. SAS/AF offers the same capability and is much simpler. The macro language plays, however, an important role in the use of SAS/AF.

In fact, the macro language preceeds the SAS program. When a macro is run, it generates (segments of) SAS statements, which are then compiled and can be executed. From this you can conclude that the macro language is a text manipulation language: it works with the source text of the SAS program.

For the most part the macro language follows the same syntax as the SAS language, except that it uses the & and % signs. All statement keywords and all function names begin with % and all references to variables begin with &. The output of macro can be as small as a single character, but also as extensive as multiple DATA and PROC steps.

To distinguish between the macro text and text which is to be sent to the SAS compiler, we will use different fonts in this chapter. In the macro definition:

```
%MACRO P;
    PROC PRINT;
    RUN;
%MEND P;
```

the difference in fonts can be clearly seen. %MACRO and %MEND are macro statements while PROC PRINT; and RUN; are text (SAS statements) which are to be sent to the compiler.

In this chapter we will frequently refer to the Macro Guide. By this we mean the *SAS Guide to Macro Processing, Version 6, Second Edition.*

Examples of simple macros

Just as with other programming languages, the quickest way to learn the SAS macro language is by example.

The previous example creates a macro P which generates a PROC PRINT. The macro definition begins with the %MACRO statement and ends with the %MEND statement. The contents of the definition is simply the text of the SAS statements PROC PRINT and RUN. After the macro has been created, it can be used in a SAS program by entering %P. Every place in the SAS program where the %P occurs, the SAS System replaces %P with:

```
PROC PRINT;
RUN;
```

before the program goes to the compiler.

We can expand the example a bit by specifying which data set is to be printed when calling the macro. If no data set were declared, the last data set created would be printed:

```
%MACRO P(DEST);
    %IF &DSET= %THEN %LET DSET=_LAST_;
    PROC PRINT DATA=&DSET;
    RUN;
%MEND P;
```

The data set to be printed gets a symbolic name: DSET. The IF statement tests whether or not DSET has a value; if not, DSET gets the value _LAST_ by means of the macro assignment statement %LET ...;. You see that whenever you refer to DSET meaning the value of DSET (thus the declared data set name), you put &DSET. When the macro is executed &DSET is replaced by the contents of DSET; thus in the first call (see below) by SASFILE and in the second by _LAST_, because DSET is empty prior to the IF statement.

With the call:

```
%P(SASFILE)
```

the SAS compiler receives the statements;

```
PROC PRINT DATA=SASFILE;
RUN;
```

and with the call:

```
%P
```

the SAS compiler sees:

```
PROC  PRINT  DATA=_LAST_;
RUN;
```

Macro structure

From the previous examples you can see that a macro must first be defined. The definition begins with the %MACRO statement and ends with the %MEND statement. The defined macro is stored in a macro library (a catalog!) and waits there until it is called. This is done by calling the name preceded by a % sign. At that moment the macro is executed and the resulting SAS statements are inserted in place of the call in the source code of the program (see figure 14.1).

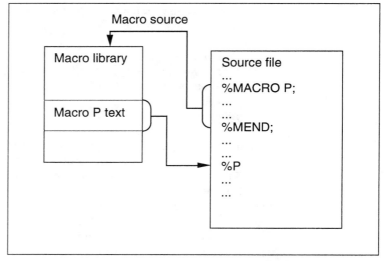

Figure 14.1 A macro has to defined before it can be used. The defined macro is stored in a macro library and executed at the time it is called. The resulting SAS code is inserted in the program and presented to the compiler.

Elements and syntax of the SAS macro language

From the examples it is also clear what the elements are that make up the macro language. The first group of elements are the macro statements, which control the execution of the macro, in a similar way that SAS statements control the execution of a SAS program. All macro statements and keywords begin with a % sign. To complement the statements there are also a number of macro functions available which correspond to the SAS functions, except that the macro functions begin with a % sign. The second group of elements are the macro variables, whose content are replaced during macro execution. And the last element is the text, which produces the output of the macro. This text is transmitted to the SAS compiler and thus consists normally of SAS statements or parts thereof.

In general the macro language follows the same syntax rules as the SAS programming language. Thus all names are 1 to 8 positions long and statements end with a semicolon. The macro call does not end with a semicolon. At first this may seem like a contradiction with respect to the SAS language, but it is not. If a macro is developed which generates only a piece of a statement, it is logical not to put a semicolon after it. If the macro generates complete statements, the semicolon would be inserted along with them and another one would be one semicolon too many.

Comparing macro and SAS languages

To help you understand macros better, figure 14.2 gives a number of characteristics of the normal SAS language and the macro language side-by-side. The most important thing to remember is that in the SAS System, as soon as it recognizes the end of a step, it compiles and executes that step. In the macro language compiling takes place whenever the macro is created and it is executed after being called into the SAS program.

	SAS language	Macro language
begin step	DATA statement, PROC statement	%MACRO statement
end step	next DATA or PROC statement, RUN statement	%MEND statement
variable	Numeric, Character, fixed length	Character, variable length
compilation	at step boundary (end of step)	at step boundary (%MEND)
execution	directly after compilation	when called, during SAS compilation phase

Figure 14.2: Some characteristic differences between the SAS language and the macro language.

Macro variables

The concept of macro variables

An important element of the macro language is the macro variable. From the previous section, it should be clear that this is a very different kind of variable from the SAS variable. The macro variable is a character variable, but with no fixed length. It is as long as the text stored in the variable. Reference to the variable brings its contents into play. The variable name is only a symbol for the contents of the variable. For this reason the macro variable is often referred to in SAS books as Symbolic Variable. There are two kinds of macro variables. The 'Local' macro variables, which can only be defined and used within a macro, and the 'Global' macro variables, which can be defined and used everywhere in a SAS program. To this last category also belong a number of macro variables which the system itself creates and maintains, the so-called 'Automatic macro variables'.

Definition of macro variables

In general, macro variables do not need to be explicitly declared, just as SAS variables do not need to be explicitly declared. At the moment they are used, they exist! At this moment the SAS System also determines whether a local or a global variable is involved. If a macro variable is created within a macro, it is by definition local, unless the definition takes place in a %GLOBAL statement:

```
%GLOBAL variables;
```

If the variable occurs outside a macro, it is by definition global. Should reference be made in a macro to a macro variable which already exists as a global variable, it will not be interpreted as a local variable. If you want to use a local variable with the same name, you can explicitly redeclare the variable as local:

```
%LOCAL variables;
```

This is a situation which should for the most part be strongly discouraged, because it is an invitation to misunderstanding.

A macro variable can be assigned a value with the %LET statement:

```
%LET variable = value ;
```

Here too, as in the SAS System, if the variable does not already exist, it will be created. If there is a %LET statement in a macro, a local variable will be created; if there is a %LET statement outside a macro, a global variable is involved.

Parameterizing constants

A parameter has once been defined as: 'a constant which has the tiresome quality of being variable'. An example is the percentage of VAT (Value added tax). At any moment it is constant, but over the long term the percentage varies. Such 'variable constants' often turn up in practice. The use of %LET statements and reference to macro variables is an ideal solution.

The required macro variables are defined at the beginning of a program and these can be used as constants throughout the entire program:

```
%LET VAT = .175;
...
PRICE_IN = PRICE_EX * (1 +&VAT);
```

Should the percentage of VAT change, it is sufficient to adjust the %LET statement and the whole program will incorporate the new value.

Reference of macro variables

In the situation as previously described, the macro processor will replace &VAT with the contents of it before sending the information to the SAS compiler. While compiling, .175 is used rather than &VAT.

The capabilities of macro variables go even further: they can be used to parameterize SAS variable names. Here too, after the macro variable has been replaced with its contents, the text (now the modified variable name) is sent to the SAS compiler.

If these constructions are made using macro variables for one part of a variable name (or another piece of text), uncertainties can arise over the end of the name of the macro variable. In that case a macro variable can be terminated with a period. If there needs to be a period present in the final result, then two periods should follow the macro variable:

```
%LET M=DEC;

&M85      → Apparent reference not resolved
&M.85     → results in text DEC85
&M..85    → results in text DEC.85
```

Here is another variant on the theme:

```
%LET FR=fileref;
%LET DS=dataset;

PROC PRINT DATA=&FR.&DS;   → Error!
PROC PRINT DATA=&FR..&DS;
   → PROC PRINT DATA=fileref.dataset;
```

Macro variables can also be used to fill in text strings. For this the strings should be placed in double quotation marks. No substitution will take place if single quotation marks are used. The statements:

```
%LET A=JAN;
TITLE1 'RESULTS OF &A';
TITLE2 "RESULTS OF &A";
...
IF MONTH='&A' OR MONTH="&A" THEN ...;
```

produce these results:

```
TITLE1 'RESULTS OF &A';
TITLE2 "RESULTS OF JAN";
...
IF MONTH='&A' OR MONTH="JAN" THEN ...;
```

Automatic macro variables

The SAS System also maintains many macro variables internally, with which the status of the SAS session and any important conditions and system information can be passed to the user.

Figure 14.3 lists a number of these 'Automatic macro variables'. Of the entries on this list, SYSDATE is the most important. It is all-in-all a better and faster alternative to the TODAY() function. SYSDATE contains the system date in DATE7. format. The constant "&SYSDATE"D produces the same value as TODAY(), with one difference: SYSDATE is set the moment the SAS program or session starts. Should the program run through midnight, "&SYSDATE"D remains on the old date, while TODAY() changes over.

Indirect reference

A macro variable can itself contain the name of a macro variable. With this kind of indirect reference the SAS System goes on evaluating the macro variables until all & signs are gone. In this the SAS System evaluates && down to a single & sign. With indirect references, we can end up with a long string of & signs. Take a look at the following example:

```
%LET DOG=POODLE;
%LET POODLE=BLACK;

&DOG → POODLE
&&DOG → &DOG → POODLE
&&&DOG → &POODLE → BLACK
```

&DOG is naturally a direct reference to the macro variable DOG and produces by substitution POODLE. In &&DOG, first the && is processed down to a single & leaving &DOG, which yields POODLE. &&&DOG works a bit differently: && becomes & again, but this time it is followed by &DOG, and &DOG yields POODLE. Now you have &POODLE which yields BLACK. Nice games can be played with this, but the legibility and comprehensibility of a program comes first. Therefore we strongly advise you to make minimal use of this sort of thing.

Date/time

SYSDATE	Date on which program or session is started (e.g. 15JUL92).
SYSTIME	Time at which program or session is started (e.g. 15:25).
SYSDAY	Weekday on which program or session is started (e.g. Monday).

System environment

SYSENV	FORE (foreground, interactief) or BACK (background).
SYSJOBID	Program name or user-ID.
SYSPARM	Contains the SYSPARM text.

SAS status

SYSVER	SAS version number
SYSRC	Return code of latest host system call (0=successful)
SYSFILRC	Return code of latest FILENAME statement (0=successful)
SYSLIBRC	Return code of latest LIBNAME statement (0=successful)
SYSMSG	Contains text of "message line" in windows
SYSPBUFF	Contains all parameters as specified with a macrocall.
SYSDSN	Libref and data set name of last created data set in 2 separate words, each 8 positions (padded with blanks).
SYSLAST	Libref and data set name of last created data set, in libref.datasetname notation

---

Figure 14.3: Some of the dozens of automatic macro variables.

Definition and use of MACROs

As we have already said, a macro definition begins with the %MACRO statement and ends with the %MEND statement. In this section we shall look at the whole process under the microscope.

The %MACRO statement

The form of the %MACRO statement is:

```
%MACRO macroname (parameters) </options>;
```

The macro name cannot be identical to one of the 'reserved names'. All statement keywords and standard elements which occur in the macro language are in the list of reserved names. How else can the SAS System recognize the difference between %IF as a macro reference and %IF as a macro statement?

The parameters are (local) macro variables, which are assigned a value when the macro is called. Reference can always be made to the macro variable in the macro, and during macro execution the references are replaced by the declared parameter values. The parameters go in parentheses.

There are two kinds of parameters: 'positional' parameters and 'keyword' parameters. With positional parameters the order in which they are specified is important: the same order must be maintained when calling the macro, in other words the position of the parameters in the macro call must correspond to those in the definition. All parameters must also be specified in the macro call. The keyword parameters have a clear advantage: they are freer (order is not important), produce more readable programs and can be given default values. We strongly recommend that you use them in preference to positional parameters.

Declaring parameters is in principle very simple. Positional parameters are always declared one after another. With keyword parameters the parameter name is followed by an = sign and then, if required, by the default value for the parameter. The choice of keywords is arbitrary, but it goes without saying that you should choose clear and memorable names, as in the following example:

```
%MACRO PRINT_IT(DATA=_LAST_,VAR=_ALL_);
    PROC PRINT DATA=&DATA;
        VAR &VAR;
%MEND;
```

Remembering the keywords in the above sample macro will not present problems to anyone.

If you are using both positional and keyword parameters, the positional parameters always come first, so that their position is definite.

Options in the %MACRO statement come after a '/'. With the STMT option you can make macros whose macro call has the same appearance as normal SAS statements. With the CMD option you can make commands to be used in the Display Manager and in SAS/AF.

The PARMBUFF option places the complete set of input parameters (including parentheses) as text in the automatic macro variable SYSPBUFF. You can use this to advantage with interactive macros (more on this later), because here the parameters are interpreted by the program rather then having to go through the system.

None of the three options is used very often. They are mentioned here for the sake of completeness. For details refer to the Macro Guide.

The %MEND statement

The %MEND statement ends a macro definition. For the sake of clarity, the macro name can be repeated in the statement. It is not necessary, however.

Use of macros

After they have been defined, macros can be called anywhere in the SAS program. This is done simply by stating the macro name, preceded by a % sign and followed by the parameters in parentheses. With positional parameters declare only the values (keep the order in mind!) and with keyword parameters declare first the keyword and then the value, for example DS_NAME=MY_DATA.

If commas occur in a parameter, for example to declare multiple options which will be sorted out within the macro, then give the value of the parameter in parentheses, as in:

```
%SEL_CNTR(CNTRCODE=("US","CA","NL","UK"))
```

We remind you that in general the macro call does not end with a semicolon. If the macro generates part of a statement, the comma would show up in the middle of the statement, signaling to the system that the statement had ended!

Macro statements

Macro statements are used to build a macro, just as SAS statements are used to build a DATA step. It is easy to see the parallel between macro statements and SAS statements. Just keep in mind that every element of a macro always begins with %.

Macro statements can be generally divided into four groups:

1. definition of macro variables (%GLOBAL, %LOCAL, %LET);

2. statements which control macro execution (%IF, %DO, %GOTO);

3. statements for interaction with the 'outside world' (%INPUT, %PUT, %WINDOW, %DISPLAY);

4. special statements (%SYSEXEC, %TSO).

Definition of macro variables

In dealing with the concept of macro variables, we have already covered the %GLOBAL, %LOCAL, and %LET statements. To recall: %GLO-BAL and %LOCAL declare macro variables, without any instructions about what to do with them. The %LET statement functions as an assignment statement: it assigns a value to a macro variable. If the macro variable does not exist, it will be created. If the %LET statement is used within a macro to define a variable, a local variable will be created. If you want to create a global variable within a macro, you must use the %GLOBAL statement.

The %IF statement

The %IF statement is virtually the same as the SAS IF statement

```
%IF condition %THEN statement;
                %ELSE statement;
```

The condition in the %IF statement is usually a comparison of a macro variable with a fixed value. But it can also be more complex, by first performing some kind of processing on either the macro variable or the value. Multiple conditions can also be combined using AND, OR and so on. Take note: not %AND or %OR. The mnemonics AND and OR are universal, as are the = and * signs. The statement in the %THEN or %ELSE branches can be either a macro statement or a piece of text.

In the introduction to this chapter we already stated that the macro language is a text manipulation language, with a few exceptions. One such exception concerns the evaluation of a condition. The SAS System will always try to evaluate the condition numerically; only when it runs into an obstacle, such as a character which could absolutely not be a number, will it do a character evaluation. You can also perform numerical evaluation with the %EVAL function, so one could say that normal evaluation of conditions implies the %EVAL function. If numerical evaluation should not take place, the argument of the condition may be placed in quotation marks to make it clear that it is to be a text evaluation. Figure 14.4 shows this effect clearly.

```
%MACRO COMPARE(X,Y);
%IF &X > &Y %THEN %PUT &X > &Y;
              %ELSE %PUT &X < &Y;
%IF "&X" > "&Y" %THEN %PUT &Y > &Y;
              %ELSE %PUT &X < &Y;
%MEND;

%COMPARE(12,2)
12 > 2
12 < 2
```

Figure 14.4: The macro processor evaluates conditions in the %IF statements in a numeric way if possible. By enclosing the macro variables in double quotes you force in the second %IF statement a character comparison.

In the following example, a special report is made in December, while for all other months only a PROC PRINT is produced:

```
. . .
%IF &MONTH = 12 %THEN %DO;
    %ANN_REPT
%END;
%ELSE %DO;
    PROC PRINT DATA=F.MASTER;
    TITLE "MONTHLY REPORT FOR MONTH &MONTH";
%END;
```

In this bit of program code you can see that macros can be called even within macros: if &MONTH equals 12, the macro %ANN_REPT is executed.

The %DO statement

The %DO statement is of course similar to the SAS DO statement. The three basic forms -- iterative, while, until -- are all available. Only the special form of the DO loop, in which a number of discrete values are declared, is not available. Be sure that in the iterative DO statement the index variable is a macro variable, but that it does not have the & in front of it. In this case you are not referring to the contents but to the variable itself!

```
%DO A=n %TO m <%BY o>;  (A is macro variable)
%DO %WHILE (condition);
%DO %UNTIL (condition);
```

Analogous to its SAS counterpart, a %DO loop is closed with a %END statement.

The %DO-%END combination can also be used in %IF statements, as DO-END can be used in an IF statement, to declare that multiple statements in %THEN or %ELSE branches are to be executed.

The following example shows a %DO-%WHILE construction, to generate a number of TITLE statements:

```
%MACRO TITLES;
    %LET A=1;
    %DO %WHILE (&A < 5);
        TITLE&A "This is a title on line &A";
    %LET A= %EVAL(&A+1);
    %END;
%MEND;
```

In this case, the %DO .. %TO form would have been easier, but this example also shows how %EVAL function is used to build in a counter. The %EVAL function is explained on page 289. Calling the macro, %TITLES, generates the following statements:

```
TITLE1 "This is a title on line 1";
TITLE2 "This is a title on line 2";
TITLE3 "This is a title on line 3";
TITLE4 "This is a title on line 4";
```

The %GOTO statement

Using the GOTO statement is considered by many to be a serious violation of the rules of decent programming and a curse. Certainly irresponsible use of GOTO statement has lead to many bad programs.

But responsible use of GOTO is not bad. An example of responsible use of GOTO is to exit a DO loop prematurely, where the GOTO statement functions as a kind of emergency brake. The GOTO statement then jumps to the statement directly after the END statement. This would be a responsible use of the DATA step GOTO statement (in V6 it is made superfluous by the LEAVE statement). The same applies in the macro language, but of course for the %GOTO statement.

The label reference must begin with a %, to distinguish between SAS text and macro label:

```
%GOTO label;
 . . .
%label:
 . . .
```

The label naturally can be a normal name, however it is also possible to put a macro there, so that during the execution of this macro a decision is made where to jump to. It can, but it brings forth the curse attached to GOTO. The following example is cleaner:

```
%DO %WHILE(&N GT 10);
    . . .
   %IF &A LT &N %THEN %GOTO OUT;
    . . .
%END;
%OUT:
```

The %INPUT statement

There are different provisions for interfacing between the macro environment and a terminal. The statements for this all have their counterparts in SAS statements. We only have to be aware that we are always dealing with macro variables instead of SAS variables.

An %INPUT statement can be used to input data from a terminal. The form is:

```
%INPUT macrovar1 macrovar2 ... ;
```

When it receives an %INPUT statement, the SAS System pauses and waits for input from the terminal. This will then be stored in the specified macro variables. The first word of the input in the first variable, the second word in the second variable and so on. If there is more input than expected (more input than variables), the system will put the remainder in the macro variable SYSBUFFR.

Special characters in the input are often a source of confusion and error, as is shown in figure 14.5. In this example a name and an address are requested. As long as a single name and a single address are typed in, there is no problem. When a double name is entered, things get out of control. The situation gets even worse if special characters are thrown in, such as the quote in Stevens' Place. To get better control of input, it can be useful to not put any macro variables in the %INPUT statement and let everything go into SYSBUFFR. The input can be interpreted and processed under program control. Processing SYSBUFFR with 'quoting' functions can even handle Stevens' place. Quoting is one of the most troublesome components of the macro language. We will deal with its principles later.

```
%INPUT NAME  CITY;
%PUT *&NAME* *&CITY* **&SYSBUFFR**;

input:  john   boston
result %PUT:    *john* *boston* ****

input:  paul john toronto
result %PUT:    *paul* *john* **toronto**

input:  'paul john' toronto
result %PUT:    *'paul john'* *toronto* ****

input:      john   stevens' place
ERROR: Expected closing quote for %INPUT item not
found.

input:      john   stevens%' place
ERROR: Literal contains unmatched quote.

remedy:
%INPUT;
%PUT **%BQUOTE(&SYSBUFFR)**;
```

Figure 14.5: While working interactively you can use the %INPUT statement for entering data. The information is stored in macro variables. Note that if more words are entered than there are macro variables in the %INPUT statement, the remainder is stored in the automatic macro variable SYSBUFFR. Special characters may cause a lot of trouble in %INPUT.

The %INPUT statement cannot be used in batch mode. It is therefore sensible to first test whether interactive processing is possible. This can be determined from the automatic macro variable SYSENV. This must have the value FORE.

The use of the %INPUT statement is not limited to macros; it can also be used in other parts of a SAS program. It still works the same way. In the Display Manager the line submitted after the %INPUT statement is regarded as the reply to the %INPUT.

The %PUT statement

%PUT writes text or the contents of macro variables to the terminal. It can be used in combination with %INPUT statements to write instructions on the screen and after the %INPUT to display any responses.

In contrast to the %INPUT statement, the %PUT statement can also be used in background processing. Then the output of the %PUT statement goes to the SAS log. The form of the %PUT statement is:

```
%PUT text;
```

in which the text can either be actual text (without quotation marks!) or references to macro variables.

%PUT is important not only for dialog with the terminal; %PUT is also one of the most helpful tools for debugging macros. By putting %PUTs in strategic locations in a macro or in a program, you can take a quick look at the value of macro variables, or (in macros) inspect the flow through %IF statements.

The %WINDOW and %DISPLAY statements

With the %WINDOW statement you define a window on the screen which can be displayed with the %DISPLAY statement. %WINDOW and %DISPLAY statements can be used within or outside of macros. The structure is parallel to the structure of the DATA step WINDOW and DISPLAY statements, which will be covered in the next chapter. An application of these statements is shown in figure 14.7: before the actual program comes a %WINDOW and %DISPLAY statement to load a macro variable with a selection criterion which can be used later in the DATA step.

The %WINDOW statement is very comprehensive. It begins with:

```
%WINDOW windowname <options>
```

for which the most important options are: IROW=n, in which n indicates the row on the screen which will be the top row of the window; ICOLUMN= o, in which o indicates the column position on the screen for the left side of the window; ROWS=p and COLUMNS=q, in which p and q indicate respectively the number of rows and column positions of the window. Without these four options the window will fill the whole screen. Other options are available for, among other things, setting the color of the window.

After this segment of the statement comes the definition of the contents of the window. This consists of group definitions and definitions of fields within the group. If there is only one group, the group can be omitted. The group definition is simple:

```
GROUP=groupname
```

The field definitions consist of a position indication, consisting of a row and column pointer such as those used with the SAS INPUT and PUT statements, followed by the macro variable name and the length of the field or the text (within quotation marks) which is to go in that place. Then come any options for controlling the appearance of the field:

```
#line @pos macrovariable length <options>
#line @pos "fixed text" <options>
```

The line pointer counts the 'net' space in the window. Within the frame, just as in the Display Manager windows, there is a command line and a message line. #1 is the line under the message line. Watch out for the apparently inconsistent syntax of the field specification: the reference to the macro variable contains no & and the length contains no point. But this is not at all illogical: &macrovariable would refer to the contents; in other words, the contents of the variable would be used in the definition of the window, which is not the intention. A point after the length would make it into a format, but here it only indicates a length and is definitely not a format.

The length is essential because macro variables have no fixed length. If the length is not declared, then the length of the field equals the length of the macro variable at that moment. If that variable is only just defined, then the variable is still empty and the length of the field is 0! Options for the fields in the %WINDOW statement are the same as those in the SAS WINDOW statement. They are listed in figure 14.6.

AUTOSKIP=	YES I <u>NO</u>: if YES then the cursor will move to the next field when the end of this field is reached
DISPLAY=	<u>YES</u> I NO: displays or suppresses the contents of this field (e.g. when entering passwords).
PROTECT=	YES I <u>NO</u>: locks the field, i.e no input possible.
REQUIRED=	YES I <u>NO</u>: defines whether input in this field is mandatory.
ATTR=	BLINK I HIGHLIGHT I REV_VIDEO I UNDERLINE: determines appearance of the field (for displays with extended attributes)
COLOR=	Color definition when working with a color screen.

Figure 14.6: The options which can be used when defining %WINDOW or WINDOW statements. Default values are underlined.

Each time that %WINDOW is executed, the window is redefined. It is therefore sensible not to put %WINDOW in a macro which will be called many times.

%WINDOW before a macro and %DISPLAY within a macro is the most efficient method.

Figure 14.7 shows a simple example of the use of windows. The example is based on the articles data set of the do-it-yourself shop, as used in chapter 8.

First of all the window (with the name SELECT) is defined using the %WINDOW statement. This writes a prompt on line 2 and requests input on line 4. The input field is defined as 8 long and that is made visible by ATTR=UNDERLINE which underlines the field. The %DIS-PLAY statement displays the window; after filling the input field and keying Enter, the contents become available to the following DATA step in a macro variable.

Macro functions

The functions in the macro language have the same purpose as the functions in the DATA step: making complex processes simple. The most important group functions are the text manipulation functions, which all have their counterparts in the DATA step.

There is only one arithmetic function. This underscores again that the macro language is primarily a text manipulation language.

```
%WINDOW select
    ICOLUMN=10 COLUMNS=60 IROW=5 ROWS=12
    #2 @5 "Select article category"
    #4 @5 art_grp 8 ATTR=UNDERLINE;
%DISPLAY select;

DATA SELECT;
    SET DB.COMBINED;
    IF ART_CAT = "&ART_GRP";
RUN;
PROC PRINT;
RUN;
```

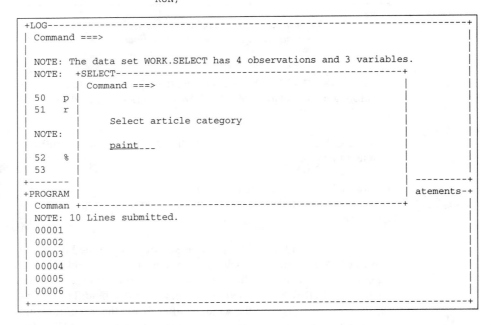

```
+LOG----------------------------------------------------------------+
| Command ===>                                                      |
|                                                                   |
| NOTE: The data set WORK.SELECT has 4 observations and 3 variables.|
| NOTE:    +SELECT----------------------------------------------+   |
|          | Command ===>                                       |   |
| 50    p  |                                                    |   |
| 51    r  |                                                    |   |
|          |       Select article category                      |   |
| NOTE:    |                                                    |   |
|          |       paint___                                     |   |
| 52    %  |                                                    |   |
| 53       |                                                    |   |
+-------   |                                                    |----------+
+PROGRAM   |                                                    | atements-+
| Comman   +----------------------------------------------------+   |
| NOTE: 10 Lines submitted.                                         |
| 00001                                                             |
| 00002                                                             |
| 00003                                                             |
| 00004                                                             |
| 00005                                                             |
| 00006                                                             |
+-------------------------------------------------------------------+
```

```
            The SAS System, Version 6.08
                            22:44 Thursday, June 9, 1994

        OBS     ART_CAT     ART_NBR     QUANTITY

         1       paint       20060         17
         2       paint       20100          8
         3       paint       21090          9
         4       paint       22001          3
```

Figure 14.7: The use of the %WINDOW and %DISPLAY statement.

Finally there is an important group of functions which have no DATA step equivalent, namely the quoting functions. Quoting functions are designed to mask pieces of text, which otherwise would be interpreted through the macro language, and preserve them as explicit text.

The arguments for the macro functions are always macro expressions: references to macro variables, other macro functions or macro calls themselves.

The %LENGTH function

The %LENGTH function is comparable to the DATA step function LENGTH, although it works a bit differently. In the DATA step function text length is declared through the last non-blank position. %LENGTH includes any blank positions at the end. Seeing that macro variables have no fixed length, this is understandable. The form is simple:

```
%LENGTH(argument)
```

The following example shows the use of the %LENGTH function in a %LET statement:

```
%LET A=THIS IS 25 POSITIONS LONG;
%LET B=%LENGTH(&A);                    → B=25
```

As we have said, the function argument can also be a macro. To illustrate this, the macro STARS is defined:

```
%MACRO STARS(N);
    %DO M=1 %TO &N;%STR(*)%END;
%MEND;
```

%LET A=%LENGTH(%STARS(12));   → A=12

The macro %STARS(..) makes a series of stars, using a simple %DO loop. %STARS(12) produces a series of 12 stars. The %STR function used in the example belongs to the family of quoting functions and prevents the SAS System from interpreting the stars as multiplication signs or commentaries.

The %SUBSTR, %INDEX, and %UPCASE functions

There is not much more to say about the %SUBSTR, %INDEX and %UPCASE functions than that they function the same way as their DATA step counterparts. Thus %SUBSTR isolates a piece of the input argument, from a start position (second parameter) and a certain number of positions long (third parameter):

```
%SUBSTR(argument,start,length)
```

%INDEX looks to see if the text of the second argument occurs in the first argument. If so, then %INDEX gives its position number; if not, it returns 0:

```
%INDEX(argument,searchtext)
```

%UPCASE is often used by interactive macros in particular for validating terminal input.

```
%UPCASE(argument)
```

With %UPCASE the program no longer has to deal with the question of whether lowercase letters were used as input or not.

The %SCAN function

The %SCAN function can be used to dissect a text into separate words. The arguments include the input text, the word number and any separators between words:

```
%SCAN(argument,word_nbr,separator)
```

If the separators parameter is left out, all standard punctuation marks are used as separators. In the following example only spaces serve as separators:

```
%LET A=SIOUX APACHE CHEYENNE ARAPAHO COMANCHE;
%LET N=3;
%LET B=%SCAN(&A,&N,%STR( ));  → B=CHEYENNE
```

Because the SAS System normally does not react to spaces, The %STR function explicitly denotes the spaces as separators.

If a higher word number is requested than the number of words in the input, the result will be empty. All words of a text can be easily picked up one-for-one by the %DO %UNTIL group: always pick the following word up until an empty word is picked up.

Special manipulations

Not all text manipulation functions of the DATA step have an equivalent macro function. The equivalents of the TRIM, CMPRES and LEFT functions are regretably absent. As compensation, a few macros which perform these functions have been included with the SAS System. These macros can be used as if they were functions, and might be implemented as functions in a future release. They are now located in the so-called Autocall library: a library of macros which are always available for every program, without having to be first defined. The %TRIM macro removes any spaces at the end of the argument; the %LEFT macro removes any spaces at the beginning and the %CMPRES macro removes spaces at both beginning and end and compresses multiple spaces in between to a single space. The use of the Autocall libraries will be covered later in this chapter.

Removing spaces before and after a macro variable can also be done simply by using a %LET statement to attach a variable to itself as a value:

```
%LET macrovariable = &macrovariable;
```

The %EVAL function

The only arithmetic function in the macro language is %EVAL:

```
%EVAL(expression)
```

It is used for elementary calculating with exclusively whole numbers (integers). Without %EVAL everything is text for the SAS System, even digits and algebraic operators, as you can clearly see in the first half of the following example:

```
%LET A=1;
%LET B=2;
%LET C=&A+&B;
%PUT C=&C;              → C=1+2
%LET C=%EVAL(&A+&B);
%PUT C=&C;              → C=3
```

As mentioned when discussing the %IF statement the SAS System performs the evaluation of %IF conditions or conditional %DO groups with implicit use of %EVAL. Only if the text cannot be interpreted as numerical is it evaluated as a character.

The quoting principle and the quoting functions

The concept of quoting has already been casually mentioned a few times in the preceding pages. Let us lay out the basic principle of quoting with the help of an example. A report for Procter & Gamble (P&G) must give market share in various months. A title stating the month goes at the top of the report. In order to be able to change the month easily, it is put in a macro variable. Thus for the macro variable MONTH to be interpreted, the title string should be in double quotation marks:

```
%LET MONTH=JUN90;
...
TITLE "Market share P&G in &MONTH";
```

But now the SAS System also tries to interpret the &G from the name P&G, which is not the intention! We must mask the & in P&G to hide it from the SAS System. That is the purpose of quoting: to include text as text and prevent any special signs which might form a part of that text being interpreted. The problem can arise in two situations: in defining macros and setting up macro variables, as in the above example, and in executing macros as when substituting a macro variable by its value. In the first case we speak of 'compile time quoting', because the masking takes place during macro compilation, and in the second case we speak of 'execution time quoting', because the masking takes place during macro execution.

Quoting is the most complex part of the SAS macro language. Here we cover only the principle, with a few examples of the most used quoting functions, so that in four out of five cases a solution can be found for quoting problems.

Compile time quoting

Compile time quoting is the simplest form of quoting. There are two functions for it, the %STR and the %NRSTR functions:

```
%STR(argument)
%NRSTR(argument)
```

For the most part the functions do the same thing. The difference lies in the blocking or not blocking of the % and & signs. The %STR function permits the interpretation of the % and & signs, thus any references to macros or macro variables will be processed. The %NRSTR ('Non-Rescan String' function) blocks the interpretation of % and & and thus temporarily switches the macroprocessor off. (The name refers to the fact that the quoted text does not have to be rescanned to assess the effect of symbolic resolution and macro execution. This normally happens because still more references may be included.)

In the introduction on quoting, &G needed to be masked. To mask the significance of the & sign, %NRSTR is used:

```
TITLE "Market share %NRSTR(P&G) in &MONTH";
```

One of the applications of %STR is to explicitly insert spaces or add semicolons after the text to be generated, without closing the macro statement.

```
%LET BLANK= ;
%PUT *&BLANK*;  →  **
%LET BLANK = %STR( );
%PUT *&BLANK*;  →  * *
%IF ... %THEN PROC PRINT %STR(;) ;
```

The last example signals a common error made in using the macro language. If the statement were written:

```
%IF ... %THEN PROC PRINT;
```

the %IF statement would be closed, but in the execution PROC PRINT would be generated, without the semicolon! %STR(;) makes the semicolon invisible to the macro compiler and shows up when the PROC PRINT gets executed.

Special characters

In the quoting function arguments special characters, such as ( ) ' " and %, can occur. These can be neutralized in the function argument if they are preceded by a % sign.

Look at the following constructions:

```
%LET A = %LENGTH(ABC)DEF);
%PUT &A=;                            →  A=3DEF)
%LET A = %LENGTH(ABC%STR(%))DEF);
%PUT &A=;                            →  A=7
```

In the first case the closing parenthesis in the text is regarded as the end of the function; in the second case, %STR(%)) makes it clear that)DEF also belongs to the function argument.

Execution time quoting

Execution time quoting is more difficult than compile time quoting, because you never know beforehand which values will be entered for the macro parameters. Different functions are available for different situations. The basic execution time quoting functions are:

```
%QUOTE(argument)
%NRQUOTE(argument)
```

%QUOTE and %NRQUOTE serve as simple text masks, where %NRQUOTE masks both % and & and %QUOTE does not. The masking means that the macro processor does not attach any special significance to the words or signs in the quoted text. However if loose quotation marks or parentheses occur in the text, this form of quoting is inappropriate. Then you must use heavier means, the 'Blind quote' functions:

```
%BQUOTE(argument)
%NRBQUOTE(argument)
```

In general you can say that BQUOTE is 'safer' than %QUOTE, unless parentheses and the like are significant.

The biggest gun in this series is the %SUPERQ function. This is used to mask a whole piece of text: the SAS System interprets nothing which is in the text.

Often a text is built up of multiple parts through quoting, any of those parts could be significant to the SAS System, but the SAS System should not look into it before the construction is complete. This means that the quoting must be undone when the construction is ready. For this you use the %UNQUOTE function

```
%UNQUOTE(argument)
```

All the pieces are quoted together, and afterwards by means of %UNQUOTE the whole thing is sent at one time to the macro processor. When text is built up by quoting, which is not relevant for the macro processor anymore but where the SAS compiler has to keep going, no explicit %UNQUOTE need take place: at the moment text is transferred from the macro processor to the compiler unquoting takes place automatically.

Quoting versions of standard macro functions

The previously covered macro functions all produce unquoted results, even if the input argument was quoted. To balance that, most functions also have a quoting counterpart. These have the same names, but are preceded by a Q, as in %QSUBSTR.

Examples of quoting

To get any feel for the use of quoting functions, let us take a close look at two practical situations.

The first situation involves working with a macro variable STATE, which contains the code for some American state (such as CA for California; you can find a complete list in the Procedures Guide under PROC FORMAT). STATE is tested for the value OR (Oregon). OR is however not only the code for the state of Oregon, it is also a boolean operator, which will certainly cause problems if processing does not include quoting. The pieces of program code shown are only those parts of the macro in which the situation develops.

```
%LET STATE=XX;
%IF &STATE=OR
    %THEN %PUT THEN BRANCH;
    %ELSE %PUT ELSE BRANCH;

ERROR: A character operand was found in the %EVAL func-
tion or %IF condition where a numeric operand is re-
quired. The condition was: &state = OR
ERROR: The macro will stop executing.
```

Here OR is seen as a boolean operator, however one side is missing from the OR relation and thus an error is returned. By putting OR in a %STR statement the significance is masked and the equation can be correctly processed. OR becomes a piece of text, which makes compile time quoting the indicated method:

```
%LET STATE=XX;
%IF &STATE=%STR(OR)
    %THEN %PUT THEN BRANCH;
    %ELSE %PUT ELSE BRANCH;  → ELSE BRANCH
```

If now, however, the value of the macro variable STATE is also OR, we are again caught in the problem. This time through the reference to STATE.

```
%LET STATE=OR;
%IF &STATE=%STR(OR)
    %THEN %PUT THEN BRANCH;
    %ELSE %PUT ELSE BRANCH;
```

```
ERROR: A character operand was found in the %EVAL func-
tion or %IF condition where a numeric operand is re-
quired. The condition was: &state = OR
ERROR: The macro will stop executing.
```

The solution here is execution time quoting, because this time things go wrong during the execution of the macro:

```
%LET STATE=OR;
%IF %QUOTE(&STATE)=%STR(OR)
    %THEN %PUT THEN BRANCH;
    %ELSE %PUT ELSE BRANCH; → THEN BRANCH
```

A second series of examples shows a struggle to determine whether the first position of a macro variable is a parenthesis. Here too only the relevant statements are shown.

A simple soul might formulate the following:

```
%LET PARENTH=(XX;
%IF %SUBSTR(&PARENTH,1,1) = (
    %THEN %PUT THEN BRANCH;
    %ELSE %PUT ELSE BRANCH;
```

```
ERROR: Macro keyword PUT appears as text.  A semicolon
or other delimiter may be missing.
```

Because of the parenthesis in the right hand term of the equation, %THEN becomes invisible to the macro processor. The SAS System no longer knows where the condition ends, and gives an error message as a result. The parenthesis should be regarded as regular text. Therefore compile time quoting is used

```
%LET PARENTH=(XX;
%IF %SUBSTR(&PARENTH,1,1) = %STR(%()
    %THEN %PUT THEN BRANCH;
    %ELSE %PUT ELSE BRANCH;
```

```
NOTE: One or more missing close parentheses have been
supplied for the %SUBSTR function.
ERROR: Macro function %SUBSTR has too few arguments.
```

```
ERROR: %EVAL function has no expression to evaluate, or
%IF-statement has no condition.
ERROR: The macro will stop executing.
```

Now that the parenthesis is masked, the SAS System can evaluate the condition. This produces another error, however, because now the substitution of PARENTH in the %SUBSTR function leads to an extra parenthesis, with the result that the segment ",1,1)" is seen as part of the first parameter for the %SUBSTR function. Thus the second and third parameters and the closing parenthesis are missing. To sort this problem out &PARENTH must also be quoted. This time, however, with execution time quoting, because things go wrong during the execution of the macro. The %BQUOTE function is the indicated means, because PARENTH only has an opening parenthesis and is thus unbalanced:

```
%LET PARENTH=(XX;
%IF %SUBSTR(%BQUOTE(&PARENTH),1,1) =
  %STR(%()
    %THEN %PUT THEN BRANCH;
    %ELSE %PUT ELSE BRANCH; → ELSE BRANCH
```

The error message is gone, but it still is not good. This is because the %SUBSTR produces an unquoted result, which will however be compared with a quoted result. Thus %QSUBSTR should be used, not %SUBSTR:

```
%LET PARENTH=(XX;
%IF %QSUBSTR(%BQUOTE(&PARENTH),1,1) =
  %STR(%()
    %THEN %PUT THEN BRANCH;
    %ELSE %PUT ELSE BRANCH; → THEN BRANCH
```

Position of macro actions on the timeline

How the macro processor fits into the process

Figure 14.8 depicts a simplified flow chart of the operation of a SAS program involving the macro processor. Input statements go first to the so-called Tokenizer and Wordscanner. There the statements are 'dissected'.

If no % or & sign occurs, the statement is sent on to the SAS compiler where it is held until the end of the step is reached. Then it is compiled and executed.

As soon as a % or & sign is signaled, the macro processor comes into action. If the % sign is followed by the keyword MACRO, the definition of a new macro begins and the macro processor takes over the job of the tokenizer completely: all statements, regardless of contents, go to the macro processor to be used in defining the macro.

If %MEND comes along, the macro is compiled and is sent to the work library. Then normal program execution is resumed. If a % reference is signaled, and no macro is being defined, then the program looks to see if the % reference is a macro call or if it might be one of the macro functions or macro statements which can also be used outside a macro. In the last case, the relevant routine is executed. In the first case the macro processor looks for the macro in the table of defined macros and if it finds it, it executes it; that is, the references to macro variables will be processed, the %IFs will be executed and so on.

The SAS statements which ultimately come out of this process will be sent back to the tokenizer for processing by the SAS compiler.

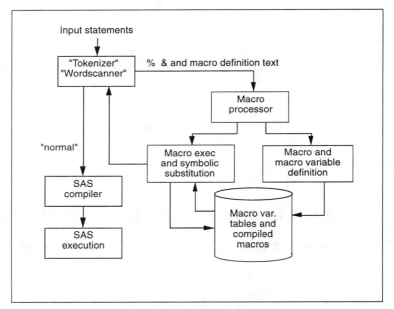

Figure 14.8: A simplified schematic drawing of the place of the macro facility in the total context of SAS processing. The execution of macros takes place before the SAS compiler becomes active.

Something similar happens with & signs: first the system looks to see if it refers to an existing macro variable; if not, it will be created if possible or a warning will be given that a reference to a macro variable cannot be resolved.

All this activity takes place before the SAS compiler can function and before the DATA or PROC step can be compiled and executed. There are, however, many imaginable situations in which you might want to have an exchange of data between the macro processor and the DATA step while the step is in execution. The way to do this is covered in the next section.

The CALL SYMPUT routine

With the CALL SYMPUT routine it is possible to assign values to macro variables during the execution of a DATA step. CALL SYMPUT belongs to a family of so-called CALL routines. In general these are routines which are separate from normal SAS System operation. CALL LABEL is also such a routine, for example. This is used to assign the label of one variable as the value of another variable. For more information on CALL routines, refer to the Language Guide.

CALL SYMPUT has two arguments: the first argument states, directly or indirectly, the macro variable whose value is to be replaced, and the second argument contains, also directly or indirectly, the new value:

```
CALL SYMPUT(macrovariable,value)
```

If the first argument is a word in quotation marks, this word is the name of the (global!) macro variable which is getting a new value. If a variable is declared as the first argument, it must be a character variable and the value of this variable is the name of the macro variable. In this way it is possible to update another macro variable with each successive observation processed in the DATA step. And also for CALL SYMPUT is true, that if the macro variable does not already exist, it will be created.

The same framework applies in principle for the second argument. If it is a text string, that is the value which will be assigned to the macro variable. If a character variable is declared, then the value of the variable is the value of the macro variable. If a numeric value is declared, either as a fixed value or via a numeric variable, this will first be converted into text with the BEST12. format. BEST 12. produces a text of 12 positions, of which the SAS System itself determines how many decimal places it can have (depending on the number of positions before the decimal) or which, in the case of extremely large numbers, is converted to exponential (scientific) notation. A consequence of using BEST12. is that often unneeded and unwanted spaces appear in the macro variable, such as those shown below:

```
DATA ...;
   X=1;
   CALL SYMPUT('SWITCH',X);
   ...
RUN;
%PUT SWITCH=*&SWITCH*;              → SWITCH=*         1*
```

This problem can be solved by using a LEFT function, even though it is not such an elegant solution; it produces the warning 'Numeric value converted to character...', because the LEFT function expects a character argument:

```
CALL SYMPUT('SWITCH',LEFT(X));
```

A neater solution is to convert the numerical value to text with a PUT function:

```
CALL SYMPUT('SWITCH',PUT(X,1.));
```

The SYMGET function

SYMGET is the complement of CALL SYMPUT: it retrieves the value of a macro variable. SYMGET is a normal DATA step function:

```
SYMGET(macrovariable)
```

The argument of the function is the name of the macro variable, either directly as a word in quotation marks, or indirectly through the use of a character variable in which the value of the variable is the name of the macro variable.

Figure 14.9 is a piece of a program that shows the difference between a normal DATA step reference to a macro variable and the retrieval of the macro variable with SYMGET. The example also clearly shows the time relationships among the macro processor, SAS compiler and execution.

```
%LET MVAR=XYZ;

DATA TEST;
    LENGTH A B C D $3;
    A="&MVAR";
    B=SYMGET('MVAR');
    CALL SYMPUT('MVAR','ABC');
    C="&MVAR";
    D=SYMGET('MVAR');
PROC PRINT DATA=TEST;


OBS     A       B       C       D
 1      XYZ     XYZ     XYZ     ABC
```

Figure 14.9: Direct references to macro variables are resolved at compilation time. CALL SYMPUT has no influence on that. SYMGET retrieves the current information of a macro variable.

The reference &MVAR is evaluated during DATA step compilation, thus the value of variables A and C is XYZ, the value of MVAR before the execution of the DATA step, at the time of compiling. When the SYMGET is executed for variable B, MVAR will not yet have been changed, and B will also have the value XYZ. Immediately afterwards CALL SYMPUT will change the value of MVAR and the changed value will be retrieved by the last SYMGET.

The RESOLVE function

The RESOLVE function goes a step further than SYMGET. SYMGET just returns the value of the declared macro variable as function result. RESOLVE calls the macro processor to process the function argument completely. That argument can be a macro as well as a simple macro variable. The difference becomes clear quickly in an example (figure 14.10). The macro variable contains a reference to another macro variable. SYMGET does not resolve this; RESOLVE does. Be careful to put the RESOLVE argument in single quotation marks, to prevent the macro processor from processing the argument prematurely.

```
%LET MSG=WELCOME TO &CITY;
DATA _NULL_;
   CALL SYMPUT('CITY','AMSTERDAM');
   LENGTH X Y $25;
   X=SYMGET('MSG');
   Y=RESOLVE('&MSG');
   PUT X= Y=;


X=WELCOME TO &CITY
Y=WELCOME TO AMSTERDAM
```

Figure 14.10: The difference between the SYMGET function and the RESOLVE function is that the RESOLVE function activates the macro processor to work out all references. If the argument of RESOLVE would be a macro, that macro is executed and the resulting text is the function result. SYMGET just returns the text of the macro variable.

The CALL EXECUTE routine

A fourth interactive DATA step routine is CALL EXECUTE. CALL EXECUTE causes the DATA step to pause; the macro processor executes the macro declared in the CALL EXECUTE argument and inserts any resulting statements after the end of the DATA step. CALL EXECUTE can be useful for tracking down errors in DATA steps in the way shown in figure 14.11.

```
%MACRO TPRINT;
    PROC PRINT;
%MEND TPRINT;

DATA ANALYSIS;
   SET ...;
   . . .
   IF ERROR THEN CALL EXECUTE('%TPRINT');
   . . .
RUN;
        ← This is where PROC PRINT is inserted when an error occurred.

DATA ANALYSI2;
   . . .
```

Figure 14.11: The PROC PRINT will be inserted and executed only when an error occurs. Otherwise the next step is started.

If the DATA step has run correctly, CALL EXECUTE will not be executed and the program proceeds normally. If however an error condition occurred, then PROC PRINT will be inserted so you can inspect what is going wrong.

Another example is shown in figure 14.12. There is a file with airline reservations data per flight (FLTDATA). Data from a select number of flights are to be output to external files: a separate file for each flight. The flight numbers involved are in the data set FLTEXEC. The main program reads the FLTEXEC data set and executes a CALL EXECUTE which has as argument the macro DOALLOC, which in turn has the combination of airline code and flight number as argument. Note that the macro does not yet process during the compiling of the DATA step as a result of the single quotation marks. The execution of the macro produces a FILENAME statement to create the output file for the flight and a DATA step to fill the file. Thus exactly as many DATA steps get generated as there are flights listed in FLTEXEC. The displayed options in the FILENAME statement are for creating files under the IBM MVS operating system. In other system environments it will be somewhat different.

Macros in programs

Direct inclusion or %INCLUDE statement

The simplest method of including a macro in a program is naturally to place the definition directly into the source code of the program. For a macro specifically written for a particular program, this is of course the best solution. There will be, however, many macros written which have a more general character. In this case central storage is preferable. The indicated method is to set up a separate library of macro definitions, in which each member of the library is a macro or a group of macros which belong together. With the help of the %INCLUDE statement the source code of the macro can be included in the program. In practice this statement is used not only to include macros, but for all occasions where a program consists of multiple source code components. The form of the %INCLUDE statement is:

```
%INCLUDE fileref(membername) </options>;
```

The library must be allocated beforehand with a FILENAME statement or a host system allocation command. If an allocation at the member level has already been made in the FILENAME statement, then the fileref in the %INCLUDE statement is sufficient; otherwise follow the fileref with the member name.

```
1                            The SAS System (6.08)
                                          22:04 Friday, June 10, 1994

NOTE: Copyright(c) 1989 by SAS Institute Inc., Cary, NC USA.
NOTE: SAS (r) Proprietary Software Release 6.08  TS405

NOTE: The initialization phase used 0.06 CPU seconds and 1092K.

NOTE: SAS job started on Friday 10JUN94 22:04 (199406102204)

1              /*-----------------------------------------------------*/
2              /* CALL EXECUTE IN ACTION                              */
3              /*-----------------------------------------------------*/
4          %MACRO DOALLOC(FLIGHT);
5             FILENAME &FLIGHT "TILANE.&FLIGHT..DATA" DISP=NEW
6                       SPACE=(TRK,(1,1));
7             DATA _NULL_;
8                SET FLT.FLTDATA;
9                IF AIRLINE||FLTNBR="&FLIGHT" THEN
10                  DO;
11                     FILE &FLIGHT NOPRINT;
12                     PUT AIRLINE FLTNBR +1 FLDTE DATE7. +1 CAP PAX;
13                  END;
14             RUN;
15          %MEND;
16
17          LIBNAME FLT 'FLIB.FLTDATA.SASLIB';
NOTE: Libref FLT was successfully assigned as follows:
      Engine:        V608
      Physical Name: FLIB.FLTDATA.SASLIB
18          LIBNAME EXC 'FLIB.FLTEXEC.SASLIB';
NOTE: Libref EXC was successfully assigned as follows:
      Engine:        V608
      Physical Name: FLIB.FLTEXEC.SASLIB
19
20          DATA _NULL_;
21             SET EXC.FLTEXEC;
22             CALL EXECUTE('%DOALLOC('||AIRLINE||FLTNBR||')');
23          RUN;

NOTE: The DATA statement used 0.03 CPU seconds and 1515K.

NOTE: CALL EXECUTE generated line.
NOTE:  TILANE.KL0641.DATA has been created.
1          FILENAME KL0641 "TILANE.KL0641.DATA" DISP=NEW
      SPACE=(TRK,(1,1));
1          DATA _NULL_; SET FLT.FLTDATA; IF AIRLINE||FLTNBR=
NOTE: CALL EXECUTE generated line.
2          "KL0641" THEN DO; FILE KL0641 NOPRINT;
NOTE: CALL EXECUTE generated line.
3          PUT AIRLINE FLTNBR +1 FLDTE DATE7. +1 CAP PAX; END;
NOTE: CALL EXECUTE generated line.
4          RUN;
```

Figure 14.12 (part 1): The macro DoAlloc creates and allocates a new file and writes information into it. Note the 2 periods in the FILENAME statement: the first to terminate the macro variable FLIGHT, the second as separator in the file name. Reminder: +1 in the PUT statement advances the pointer one position before writing the next variable. The main program consists only of lines 20-23.

```
2                        The SAS System (6.08)
                                    22:04 Friday, June 10, 1994

NOTE: The file KL0641 is:
      Dsname=TILANE.KL0641.DATA,
      Unit=3390,Volume=VPB019,Disp=NEW,Blksize=27920,
      Lrecl=80,Recfm=FB

NOTE: 343 records were written to the file KL0641.
NOTE: The DATA statement used 0.08 CPU seconds and 1709K.

NOTE: CALL EXECUTE generated line.
NOTE:  TILANE.KL0642.DATA has been created.
5           FILENAME KL0642 "TILANE.KL0642.DATA" DISP=NEW
      SPACE=(TRK,(1,1));
5           DATA _NULL_; SET FLT.FLTDATA; IF AIRLINE||FLTNBR=
NOTE: CALL EXECUTE generated line.
6           "KL0642" THEN DO; FILE KL0642 NOPRINT;
NOTE: CALL EXECUTE generated line.
7           PUT AIRLINE FLTNBR +1 FLDTE +DATE7. +1 CAP PAX; END;
NOTE: CALL EXECUTE generated line.
8           RUN;

NOTE: The file KL0642 is:
      Dsname=TILANE.KL0642.DATA,
      Unit=3390,Volume=VPB025,Disp=NEW,Blksize=27920,
      Lrecl=80,Recfm=FB

NOTE: 342 records were written to the file KL0642.
NOTE: The DATA statement used 0.07 CPU seconds and 1709K.

NOTE: The SAS session used 0.47 CPU seconds and 1709K.
NOTE: SAS Institute BV, 1217 KR Hilversum, The Netherlands
```

Figure 14.12 (part 2): For each observation in data set FLTEXEC the CALL EXECUTE routine is called, resulting in a new output file.

Alternatively you can specify the name of the file directly in the %INCLUDE statement, enclosed in quotes. The options are used relatively rarely. In the IBM mainframe environment the JCLEXCL option is useful, to keep any JCL statement out of the include file.

The %INCLUDE statement replaces %INCLUDE in the program with lines from the indicated file. The SAS compiler sees no difference between statements brought in with %INCLUDE and statements which have been written directly in the program.

Autocall facility

Another method to include macros in a program is to set up an 'Autocall library'. Such an Autocall library is also a library whose members are macro source code, just as previously described. The name of the member must be the same as the macro which it contains. When the SAS System during program compilation encounters a macro, it first looks into the WORK data library to see if the macro is identified and has been defined. If so, the macro is executed; if not the system checks to see if there is an Autocall library and if the macro source code is in it. If that is the case, the macro is immediately compiled and then the call can be processed. You identify this Autocall library to the SAS System with the option SASAUTOS.

```
FILENAME MYMACS 'macro library';
OPTIONS SASAUTOS=MYMACS;
```

A condition for using Autocall libraries is that the system option MAUTOSOURCE is turned on. This is normally the case.

SAS Institute has produced a starter Autocall library: a number of utility macros are produced as a matter of course, such as %TRIM and %CMPRES. This SAS Autocall library will generally be allocated with fileref SASAUTOS. To use your own library alongside this one, both must be declared in the OPTIONS statement:

```
OPTIONS SASAUTOS=(SASAUTOS,MYMACS);
```

The order of the declaration of the libraries is important, since this is the order in which the SAS System searches the libraries to find the macro. It will be clear that an Autocall library is first and foremost a good storage location for general purpose macros.

Development and testing of macros

Macros in general produce a piece of executable SAS source code, exceptions like macros which only produce components of statements or constants left aside. It is therefore sensible to first develop and test the desired SAS source code outside a macro, so that when developing the macro itself, you can give your full attention to macro source code and macro errors.

Errors in the use of the macro language in general fall into three categories: errors in creating macros and defining macro variables, errors in executing macros and referencing macro variables and errors in the resulting SAS statements. By using the above procedure, the last category rarely occurs; moreover they are not actually macro errors so we will not go into them any further here.

The first category has the consequence that the macro does not get defined. The error message will indicate what the error is.

The second category, errors in macro execution, is the most troublesome.

The first tip is to place %PUT statements in strategic locations in the macro, so that you can follow the value of various macro variables. With the %PUTs it is useful to print an asterisk before and after the macro variable, to see if any blanks occur as these might cause trouble when making comparisons.

If %PUTs do not solve the problem, there are a few system options with which extra information can be written into the SAS log to make it easier to look for errors.

MPRINT is the first hope: all SAS statements which the macro sends to the SAS compiler are printed in the SAS log. SYMBOLGEN shows how the substitution of macro variables during execution takes place and what results are yielded.

MLOGIC finally gives a detailed survey of the macro run, for example evaluation of conditions of %IF or %DO %WHILE. The maximum of information is obtained when all options are switched on. This is done in the OPTIONS statement:

```
OPTIONS MPRINT MLOGIC SYMBOLGEN;
```

Switching off the options after the test is done simply by putting NO before the option involved, for example NOMLOGIC.

To illustrate, a macro is printed in figure 14.13 (this example is covered in the section on quoting functions) and then called, where you can see the MLOGIC and SYMBOLGEN. In this case MPRINT makes little sense, because no SAS code has been generated.

```
%MACRO PARENTH(PARENTH);
%LET PARENTH = %SUBSTR(&PARENTH,1,3);
%IF %SUBSTR(%BQUOTE(&PARENTH),1,1)=%STR(%()
    %THEN %PUT THEN BRANCH;
    %ELSE %PUT ELSE BRANCH;
%MEND;


OPTIONS    MLOGIC SYMBOLGEN;

%PARENTH((XX))
MLOGIC(PARENTH):  Beginning execution.
MLOGIC(PARENTH):  Parameter PARENTH has value (XX)
MLOGIC(PARENTH):  %LET (variable name is PARENTH)
SYMBOLGEN:  Macro variable PARENTH resolves to (XX)
SYMBOLGEN:  Macro variable PARENTH resolves to (XX
MLOGIC(PARENTH):  %IF condition %SUBSTR(%BQUOTE(&PARENTH),1,1) = ... is
    FALSE
MLOGIC(PARENTH):  %PUT ELSE BRANCH
ELSE BRANCH
MLOGIC(PARENTH):  Ending execution.
```

Figure 14.13: By switching on the options SYMBOLGEN and MLOGIC you can have good insight into the macro execution.

Exercises

Relating to the section 'Macro variables' (page 272):

1. State which (parts of) statements the SAS compiler sees as a result of the following statements:

   %LET VAR=DATE;

   a. `DROP &VAR1-&VAR3;`

   b. `DROP &VAR.1-&VAR.3;`

2. The following macro variables have been defined:

   ```
   %LET A=DATE;
   %LET B=7;
   ```

These macro variables are used in PUT statements:

a. `PUT X &A&B.;`

b. `PUT X &A&B..;`

c. `PUT X &A.&B..;`

What result is produced by the three PUT statements?

Answer the same questions if macro variable B is defined with: %LET B=7.;

3. If the most recently created data set is to be used in a SAS DATA step or PROC step, it does not normally need to be specified. If data set options are to be used, however, the data set name must be explicitly declared.

    Write a PROC PRINT for the most recently created data set, of which only the observations 100-200 are to be printed.

4. The following definitions are made:

    ```
    %LET T=GRAND;
    %LET &T=TOTAL;
    ```

    a. How does the second statement get evaluated?

    b. What does the reference &T &GRAND produce?

Relating to the section 'Definition and use of macros' (page 276):

5. Study the following macro definition:

    ```
    %MACRO INPUT(IN,FROM,VAR1,VAR2,VAR3,OUT=RESULT);
        %LET VARS=&VAR1 &VAR2 &VAR3;
        DATA &IN;
            INFILE &FROM;
            INPUT &VARS;
        PROC SORT DATA=&IN OUT=&OUT;
            BY &VAR3 &VAR1 &VAR2;
    %MEND;
    ```

    a. Is this definition correct? If not, correct it!

b. Write a call to this macro, inventing your own variable names and so on, and write the statements which the SAS compiler should see.

Relating to the section 'Macro statements' (page 278):

6. Write a macro which executes a procedure (PROC PRINT is the default) on a given SAS data set. The macro call should have the following form:

    ```
    %PROCED(DS)
    ```

    to print data set DS,

    ```
    %PROCED(DS, PROC=MEANS)
    ```

    to determine averages and the like.

7. Expand the macro of exercise 6 with a specification of the variables which should be processed for the PROC. In case no variables are declared, PROC should work for all variables.

Relating to the section 'Macro functions' (page 285):

8. Develop a macro with one parameter. The macro counts how many words (separated with spaces) are contained in the input parameter text. Put all the words in separate macro variables while counting the words. When the whole text has been analyzed print the number of words found.

Relating to the section 'Position of macro actions on the timeline' (page 295):

9. Create a macro which produces reference lines in a PROC PLOT on the vertical (Y) axis at the level of the mean value of the Y variable at one standard deviation above and below the mean value.

    Hint: Run a PROC MEANS on the input data set to establish MEAN and STD, read these in a DATA step, store these in macro variables and use those in the PROC PLOT.

CHAPTER 15

Advanced DATA Step Features

The DATA step operation

The SAS compiler - Program Data Vector

Figure 15.1 is a schematic of the steps a SAS program goes through during execution. SAS statements are read by the system from the beginning to the end of a step. A step begins with the DATA or the PROC statement and ends with either another DATA or PROC statement or a RUN statement. Some procedures remain active after a RUN statement and only end with a QUIT statement or when a next DATA or PROC statement is encountered. This is the case with PROC DATASETS, PROC CATALOG, PROC PLOT, PROC CHART and procedures in SAS/GRAPH software. With these procedures you can, after the RUN statement, declare another group of specification statements for execution, without starting the procedure over again. In the DATA step, the CARDS statement also marks the end of a step (and indicates that input lines follow). If the step is a PROC step, the specification statements are transferred to the relevant 'procedure parser' which processes the specification statements and then executes the procedure; if a DATA step is involved, then the DATA step compiler is invoked.

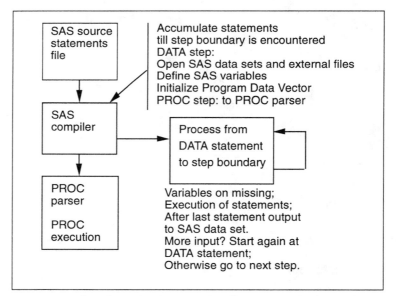

Figure 15.1: The relationship between the phases in the execution of a SAS program.

This compiles the SAS statements into machine code and in the process opens SAS and external data sets to inspect what is in them. In the case of external files the SAS System examines also how they are organized, so that the correct read/write routines can be used. With external output files this can have the consequence that they are emptied without there being any certainty at that moment that the program will work correctly and will create a new version of the data set.

During compilation the so-called 'Program Data Vector' (PDV) is initialized; this is a buffer where the SAS System stores all variables during DATA step execution. The PDV has room for each variable from input data sets and all variables defined in the DATA step via assignments. In addition the PDV contains a number of 'Automatic SAS variables', variables which the SAS System automatically defines and retains, for example _N_: the number of iterations through the DATA step, _ERROR_ which gets the value 1 if an error is detected and which otherwise has the value 0. In V5 the capacity of the PDV is limited to 32K, that is to say room for 4096 variables of 8 positions (the internal length of a numeric variable). In V6, the capacity is no longer limited. During compiling, the descriptive section of a SAS data set is examined to determine which variables are present in the data set. Based on that information the SAS System determines how the data set should be recorded in the PDV (taking into account the length and type of variables and possible DROP/KEEP and RENAME options). In addition the number of observations is determined at that moment.

In the execution phase of a DATA step, in a kind of loop, all statements (except for the effects of IF statements or DO statements) are executed from the beginning of the DATA step to the end. This loop runs until a stop signal is given. The stop signal can be an End-of-File signal from an input data set, but it can also be an ABORT or a STOP statement. These statements are covered on page 314. With each pass through the DATA step, all variables in the PDV are first initialized to a missing value, except if the variables are 'retained'. To this category belong all variables which have been read from a SAS data set. Only by transition to another BY group (if there is a BY statement) or by transition to another data set (for example if more than one data set has been declared in a SET statement) does the SAS System reset those variables to missing.

The values of all variables are maintained in the PDV and from them an observation is constructed which will be output to the output data set.

Referring to variables - 'Variable lists'

In many places in a SAS program, variables are referred to. Often individual variables, as well as whole series of variables, must be specified. In the latter case, much writing can be saved by specifying 'variable lists'. A variable list is none other than a short notation for a whole series of variables; you only have to give the first and last variable name and the SAS System will determine which others come in between. There are several possibilities for entering variables in a list. If they all have the same name with a serial number, such as VAR1 - VAR20, then the SAS System will put all variables with this name and a serial number in the range into the list. In this example, it means VAR1, VAR2, VAR3, ..., VAR18, VAR19, VAR20. You can also make use of any knowledge you have of the PDV. By declaring two variables with two dashes in between, the SAS System regards all variables which are physically located between declared variables in the PDV to be part of the list. Bear in mind that the order in the PDV is determined by the first reference to the variable. For variables from a SAS data set this makes the order in the data set important as well (check it with PROC CONTENTS).

The SAS System also recognizes some special lists which include all variables of a particular type: _CHARACTER_, _NUMERIC_ and _ALL_. Take note that the variables must already be declared in the PDV before they can be referred this way. Watch out for SET statements: the variables are present in the PDV just after the SET statement.

Length of variables - LENGTH statement

The length of SAS variables is fixed in each step. With character variables this happens the moment the variable is added to the PDV. The length of a numeric variable in the PDV is always 8 positions; the length in a data set is fixed the moment the variable is written to it. As a consequence, the length of a variable can also be changed per step. This is done with the LENGTH statement:

```
LENGTH variable <more variables> <$> length;
LENGTH DEFAULT = n;
```

The $ sign as always indicates that a character variable is involved. The second form of the LENGTH statement is only to be used with numberic variables. It indicates that all new variables shall have the given length (2-8 positions, in some system environments 3-8) in the output data sets, unless they are given another length with the first form of the LENGTH statement.

To change the length of a character variable, the new length must be declared at first reference to the variable, thus before the variable is put into the PDV by INPUT or SET statements. For numeric variables the LENGTH statement can be placed anywhere in the DATA step, because it has effect only when writing out to the data set.

Character-numeric conversions

The SAS System is very tolerant of the intermixing use of character and numeric variables. If a character variable is used where the SAS System expects a numeric value, the system will try to convert that variable into a numeric value. If that does not work, the variable will be processed with a missing value. Likewise, if a numeric value or numeric variable is used where the SAS System expects a character value, this numeric value gets converted. If a number gets assigned to a character variable, it will be converted with the BESTn. format, where n is the length of the character variable. This situation has already been illustrated in the section on CALL SYMPUT.

In every case the SAS System puts a warning in the log that a conversion has taken place. It is good to check these warnings as a precaution against untidy or faulty programming.

Character comparison

If the SAS System needs to make a character comparison, it is done routinely on the basis of the longest character string. The shorter string gets extended with spaces to the length of the longer. Thus:

```
IF 'AA' = 'AAAA' ...→  IF 'AA  ' = 'AAAA' ...
```

If the short string must not be extended for some reaason, a colon can be placed after the = sign. This could be read as 'begins with', because the comparison only judges the beginning of the longest string:

```
IF 'AA' =: 'AAAA' ...→  IF 'AA' = 'AA' ...
```

In the above example, two character constants are used. The same also holds true for character variables. The two IF statements below thus test the same condition:

```
A='ABCDE';
IF  SUBSTR(A,1,2)  =  'AB'  ...
IF A =: 'AB' ...
```

The second form is more efficient, however, because no function needs
to be called.

Termination of the DATA step

In general the SAS System terminates the DATA step when the end of
the input file of the data set is reached. However there are situations in
which either the SAS System can not determine that the end of the input
has been reached, or that the DATA step must be ended sooner, for
example because of errors. For termination of the DATA step under
program control, two statements are available, the STOP statement and
the ABORT statement. The STOP statement has the simple syntax:

```
STOP;
```

Executing the STOP statement immediately halts the DATA step. The
observation which was being processed at that moment will not be
output to the output data set. If you do want to output the last observation,
you need to use the OUTPUT statement before you issue the STOP
statement.

The second method of terminating the DATA step is with the ABORT
statement:

```
ABORT   <ABEND|RETURN>   <returncode>;
```

In batch mode it ends the entire SAS program. The manner in which
termination takes place depends on the options used. Without options,
only OBS=0 gets set and the SAS System goes on with syntax checking.
With ABEND the computer's operating system is notified of an abnor-
mal termination with some specified return code, and RETURN notifies
the system of a normal termination.

In interactive processing (for example in the Display Manager) the
ABEND and RETURN options lead to terminaton of the session and
return to the host environment. Without any options, the DATA step is
just terminated and the system goes on to the next step as if nothing had
happened.

In all cases an appropriate message is written in the log and no existing
data set will be replaced by a data set under construction.

Stored Program facility

The SAS System is a compiled language, but until Version 6 there was no advantage to be gained: each time the program was executed, a new compiling took place. With the introduction of Version 6 it is possible to store a compiled DATA step and execute it again later, without having to recompile it.

The compiled step gets saved as a member of the type PROGRAM in a SAS data library.

To just compile a DATA step and not execute it, use an option in the DATA statement: /PGM=. In the PGM= option the libref and member name for the compiled step are given in the usual way:

```
DATA CREATE / PGM=libref.progname;
...
(DATA step source)
...
RUN;
```

If you want to execute the DATA step later on, you specify the compiled step in the DATA statement:

```
DAT  PGM=libref.progname;
    REDIRECT...;
RUN;
```

Now PGM= is no longer just an option after a slash, but an essential component of the DATA statement.

At the time of execution it is still possible to change input or output data sets. This is done with the REDIRECT statement:

```
REDIRECT INPUT oldname = newname ...;
REDIRECT OUTPUT oldname = newname ...;
```

The old and new names are given in the usual manner, libref.dataset. A condition for input data sets is of course that the variables in the original data set and the new data set are identical. A redirect of a data library can also take place using LIBNAME or job control statements, and that has priority because it does not have to be taken into the program.

Be careful when using macros and macro variables. These get processed during the compile phase and are then fixed, also in the compiled program. For macro variables the solution is simple: do not use a straight reference to a macro variable. Instead, get the value by means of the SYMGET function, for example X=SYMGET("Y"); instead of X=&Y. Also the other DATA step routines of the macro language (such as CALL SYMPUT and CALL EXECUTE) can be used.

The WINDOW and DISPLAY statement

The more the SAS System is used interactively, the more direct interaction is needed between DATA step and user. One of these interactive possibilities is provided by the combination of the WINDOW and the DISPLAY statement. The WINDOW statement defines a window and the DISPLAY statement displays it on the screen.

Both the operation and the syntax are analogous to the %WINDOW and %DISPLAY statement covered earlier.

The WINDOW statement

The WINDOW statement begins with the definition of the window itself: name, screen location and dimensions and, when applicable, color. Location is determined by declaring the coordinates of the top left corner in IROW and ICOLUMN. The default value for both is 1, referring to the very top left of the screen. The size is declared in the number of rows and columns. The default value for these is determined by the size of the screen. If the terminal supports it, color can also be declared:

```
WINDOW windowname
     <IROW=.. ICOLUMN=.. ROWS=.. COLUMNS=..>
     <COLOR= BLUE|BLACK|BROWN|CYAN|GRAY|GREEN|MAGENTA|
             ORANGE|PINK|RED|WHITE|YELLOW>
```

The dimensions of the window (the values in ROWS= and COLUMNS=) include space for the border of the window. In many cases the border consumes four positions of the usable space; take this into account. In addition to the above options, it is possible to define function keys specially for the window or for eventual 'pull-down' menus (such as with Apple Macintosh or MS Windows). This, however, is done outside the WINDOW statement; in the WINDOW statement you only put a reference to the KEYS catalog or the MENU catalog. (Function keys and pull down menus are defined with PROC PMENU. For a description of this, refer to the Procedures Guide.)

After the definition of the window is the specification of its contents. This consists of one or more groups of field definitions. Such a group begins with the GROUP name followed by the definition of each field belonging to the group:

```
GROUP =groupname
#line @pos variable <format.> <options>
#line @pos "text" <options>
```

The group indicator can be left out if there is only one group. The groups enable the user to specify multiple layouts for the same window and, with the DISPLAY statement, establish which group applies.

The field definitions are more or less analogous to the manner used in the PUT statement: a line (#) and a position pointer (@) are to be specified, followed by what is to go on the screen, text or a variable. The + pointer is also available for blending fixed text with a variable (+1 leaves one space in between). The line pointer counts from the beginning of the net space in the window: line 1 is the line under the message line. Positions are reserved on the screen for variables corresponding to their formats. An informat to be used must be the same as the format, or declared separately in an INFORMAT statement. The options determine the use of the field: input or no input, color, underlining and the like. These options amount to the same thing as the field options in the %WINDOW statement; see the table in figure 14.6.

The DISPLAY statement

The DISPLAY statement displays the window on the screen. Once a window is on the screen, it stays until the end of the DATA step. The form is:

```
DISPLAY windowname<.groupname> <options>;
```

Each time the DISPLAY statement is executed, the window is refreshed. When using groups with different layouts, it is often desirable to first clear the window, before displaying the next group. This can be done with the BLANK option. The NOINPUT option blocks any input into the window during this display action and the BELL option activates the terminal's sound signal, if available. The DISPLAY statement causes the DATA step to pause until you press Enter to indicate that the filling of the fields is finished, or until you give an END command (PF3). In the first case the DATA step continues its execution. When the end of the DATA step is reached, an observation is output and the next iteration of the DATA step begins. If the window is vacated by using an END command, a STOP statement is executed: the DATA step stops and the contents of the window will not be processed.

The 'automatic variable' _MSG_

In the window display, a message can be placed on the message line. This is declared before the execution of the DISPLAY statement in the automatic variable _MSG_. After the DISPLAY statement, _MSG_ is again empty. _MSG_ is a character variable with a length of 80 positions.

WINDOW and DISPLAY in combination with an input data set

If the WINDOW and DISPLAY statements are used in combination with an existing SAS data set (so probably there is a SET statement present), the SAS System ends the DATA step after the last observation, or as soon as the window is vacated via PF3 (END command). In the latter case, further observations from the input data set will no longer be present in the output.

Should the SET statement be executed before the DISPLAY statement, the values of the variables will be displayed in the window, insofar as the variables in the window have been defined.

Sample WINDOW and DISPLAY statements

After the section on Arrays, a combined sample program is discussed for the WINDOW and DISPLAY statement and for arrays.

Arrays

It regularly happens that a particular operation on multiple variables has to be executed. This can of course be written in the usual way, as in:

```
IF VAR1 = . THEN VAR1 = 0;
IF VAR2 = . THEN VAR2 = 0;
IF VAR3 = . THEN VAR3 = 0;
IF VAR4 = . THEN VAR4 = 0;
IF VAR5 = . THEN VAR5 = 0;
IF VAR6 = . THEN VAR6 = 0;
```

but it would be easier if you could use a shorter notation, with a kind of DO-END group whose IF statement would process all variables. This is what arrays are for. An array is nothing other than a collection of variables, in which each variable can be identified by referring to the array and, by means of an index, to the location of the variable within the array. The previous example can be formulated using an array as follows:

```
ARRAY VAR{*} VAR1 - VAR6;

DO X=1 TO 6;
   IF VAR{X} = . THEN VAR{X} = 0;
END;
```

By means of the ARRAY statement, the array VAR is defined, consisting of the variables VAR1 through VAR6. In the subsequent DO loop all individual variables are tested and eventually set to 0, by referring to them with the array name plus (between braces) the element number (the index) within the array.

Sometimes it is not just one simple list of variables which must go into the array, but groups might need to be distinguished within the list. Think, for example, of variables which contain monthly figures of some kind, but over a period of several years. Each variable is now marked with year and month number. For this kind of situation, a 2-dimensional array should be defined, in which each element is entered with a year index and a month index, as in:

```
FIGURE  =MNTH_FIG{year,month};
```

This concept can be translated into more dimensions, but in practice 1- and 2-dimensional arrays occur most often. The best way to understand a 2-dimensional array is to regard it as a large matrix or a spreadsheet, in which the first dimension represents the rows of the matrix and the second dimension the columns.

ARRAY definition

The definition of an array needs to be done before the first reference and it should be repeated in each DATA step, because an array is not something which is stored in a data set; only the variables (the elements of the array) get output. There are different variants of the ARRAY statement. The basis is always the same: specifying an array name, declaring the number of elements (the dimension, possibly multiple), naming the elements and eventually specifying the initial values for the elements.

```
ARRAY arrayname {*}        <type> variables
                           <(initial values)>;
ARRAY arrayname {n<,m,...>} <type>;
ARRAY arrayname {n<,m,...>} <type> _TEMPORARY_
                           <(initial values)>;
```

The array name must always be declared. This must conform to the same rules as a variable. Names of SAS functions should be avoided, to prevent confusion. If an array has the same name as a function, that function will no longer be available in the DATA step.

Either the dimension(s) or the elements can be left out, if the SAS System can automatically infer them from the information given.

In the first form, the variables are explicitly declared (possibly in a variable list). The dimension can then be indicated with an asterisk (*). The SAS System can calculate the number of elements from the number of declared variables. This method always defines a 1-dimensional array.

If the dimension is explicitly declared, in multiple dimensions when appropriate, and no variables have been declared (the second variant), the SAS System automatically defines the variables by assigning the array name with a serial number, presuming that the total variable name fits into 8 positions. Dimensions can also be explicitly declared in combination with explicitly declared variables. This occurs most of all when 2- or more-dimensional arrays need to be defined.

The array MNTH_FIG, mentioned in the introduction to this section, could thus be created as follows:

```
ARRAY MNTH_FIG {10,12} M_FIG1 - M_FIG120;
```

In this array monthly figures for 10 years can be declared. The relation between the array elements and the variables is by rows. Thus M_FIG1 is element MNTH_FIG{1,1}, M_FIG2 is MDTH_FIG{1,2} and M_FIG13 is MNTH_FIG{2,1}.

In V6 an array can also be created with temporary variables, which are neither declared nor output to an output data set. Such an array with temporary variables is defined with elements marked _TEMPORARY_.

If the variables that compose the array are not yet known to the SAS System you might need to specify their type and length. This is done between the dimension specification and the list of elements, similar to the description of the variables in a LENGTH statement. Thus $5 means that the array elements are character variables 5 positions long. Should an array be created with new variables, or with _TEMPORARY_ and the type description is left out, then the elements are numeric. If the array consists of pre-existing variables, then the type indicators naturally do not have to be included.

Any initial values for the array elements are given in parentheses, at the end of the ARRAY statement. The values correspond 1:1 with the array elements. If there are fewer values declared than there are elements, the extra elements are initialized with a missing value.

As an example, figure 15.2 shows a number of array definitions and an example of how the elements should be used in a DATA step.

In the last two examples in figure 15.2, be sure that all variables to be included in the array definition have already been identified in the PDV. If there are variables involved which will be read from a data set, then the ARRAY statement comes after the SET or MERGE statement.

```
ARRAY RAIN {12} JAN FEB MAR … NOV DEC;
IF RAIN{8} < 5 THEN COMMENT='DRY MONTH';


ARRAY RAIN {*} JAN FEB MAR … NOV DEC;


ARRAY RAIN {4,3}  JAN FEB MAR … NOV DEC;
QTR = 3;
MONTH = 2;
IF RAIN{QTR,MONTH} < 5 THEN
    COMMENT='DRY MONTH';


ARRAY RAIN {12};


ARRAY RAIN {*} RAIN1-RAIN12;


ARRAY ALLCHAR {*} $25 _CHARACTER_;


ARRAY ALLNUM {*} _NUMERIC_;
```

Figure 15.2: A number of ARRAY definitions and illustrations of their use. In the third definition the quarter is the first dimension, so RAIN{2,1} refers to APR. The last two definitions create an array of all variables of the indicated type, as far as they are known at the time the array statement is compiled.

The DIM function

In figure 15.2 the last two ARRAY statements do not say directly how
many elements are in the array and therefore what the maximum value
for the index might be. This can be obtained from the SAS System by
means of the DIM function. With a 1-dimensional array this is simple:

```
DIM(arrayname)
```

but with multi-dimensional arrays you must also state for which dimension the size is being requested. This can be done in two ways:

```
DIM2(arrayname)              DIM(arrayname,dimension)
DIM3(arrayname)
 . . .
```

The second form has more flexibility, because the dimension can be
determined during the execution of the program. The DIM function can
be used to advantage in DO loops by which an array is to be processed;
changing the array dimension does not require that the DO loop be
adapted:

```
DO X=1 TO DIM(array);
 . . .
END;
```

Sample program WINDOW and ARRAY

Mastermind is a popular game for young and old. The computer
generates a code which must then be guessed by the player. The code
consists of four randomly chosen digits. Each time a code is typed in, the
computer responds with a hint indicating how many of the digits are
correct and whether or not they are in their correct positions. Figure 15.3
shows how Mastermind would look in the SAS System and figure 15.4
shows a printout of the program used for it. (Neither the author nor the
publisher is responsible for game playing during working hours.)

The program begins with the definition of a format for printing the hints.

The DATA step which follows contains the actual game. It begins with
the definition of a few arrays. The array ANSWER contains lines for the
last five answers. The first will contain the answer most recently typed
in. The digits get stored in the first four elements of each line and the
evaluation (digit correct/incorrect, in/not in correct position) in the last
four elements. The array SCORE contains the translation of the evalu-

ation into '=' and '!' signs, according to the format. The array CODE contains the generated code. Then the UNIFORM function generates the four digits for the code. The DO UNTIL condition makes sure that all the digits are different. After that follows the WINDOW statement. It contains two groups: GUESS and SCORE. In GUESS the input fields and the history fields are defined; in SCORE there is only a message that displays if the code is guessed. The following DO UNTIL loop executes the DISPLAY statement for the group GUESS and analyzes the typed code. Be aware of the BLANK option in the DISPLAY statement. This makes sure that the text of the SCORE group does not remain on the screen for a second game. The evaluation is put in the second half of the array line: 1 for a correct digit in the wrong position and 2 for a correct digit in the right position. This is then translated into a string in the SCORE array. If an evaluaton of 2 is given for all typed digits, the loop ends and the group SCORE is displayed.

```
+M_MIND-----------------------------------------------------------------+
| Command ===>                                                          |
| GUESS THE CODE. GOOD LUCK! - PF3 FOR EXIT                             |
|                                                                       |
|    THIS IS ATTEMPT    1                                               |
|                                                                       |
|    TYPE YOUR GUESS:         .   .   .   .                             |
|                                                                       |
|    THESE WERE YOUR LAST 4 GUESSES:                                    |
|                                                                       |
|                            .   .   .   .                             |
|                            .   .   .   .                             |
|                            .   .   .   .                             |
|                            .   .   .   .                             |
|                                                                       |
|                                                                       |
|                                                                       |
|                                                                       |
|                                                                       |
|                                                                       |
|                                                                       |
+-----------------------------------------------------------------------+
```

Figure 15.3 (part1): The opening window of the Mastermind game...

```
+M_MIND---------------------------------------------------------------------+
| Command ===>                                                              |
|                                                                           |
|                                                                           |
|   THIS IS ATTEMPT     8                                                    |
|                                                                           |
|   TYPE YOUR GUESS:         6   7   4   9                                   |
|                                                                           |
|   THESE WERE YOUR LAST 4 GUESSES:                                         |
|                                                                           |
|                            6   7   4   8      !!!                          |
|                            6   7   3   4      !!=                          |
|                            6   4   7   3      !==                          |
|                            6   3   2   4      !=                           |
|                                                                           |
|                                                                           |
|   GUESSED IN   8 ATTEMPTS                                                  |
|                                                                           |
|                                                                           |
|                                                                           |
|                                                                           |
|                                                                           |
+---------------------------------------------------------------------------+
```

Figure 15.3 (part2): ...and the window when the code is found.

```
PROC FORMAT ;
VALUE CODEFMT 1='=' 2='!' OTHER=' ';
RUN;
DATA _NULL_;
ARRAY ANSWER {5,8};
ARRAY SCORE {5} $5;
ARRAY CODE {4};
RETAIN TRY 0 POINT;
*----------------------------------------------------;
* Generate the random digits                         ;
*----------------------------------------------------;
DO N=1 TO 4;
   DO UNTIL (M NE CODE{1} AND M NE CODE{2}
      AND M NE CODE{3} AND M NE CODE{4} AND M LT 10);
      M=INT(UNIFORM(0)*10);
   END;
   CODE{N} = M;
END;
WINDOW M_MIND
   GROUP=GUESS
   #2 @3 "THIS IS ATTEMPT" +1 TRY 3. PROTECT=YES
   #4 @3 "TYPE YOUR GUESS:"
      @25 ANSWER{1,1} 1. REQUIRED=YES
      @28 ANSWER{1,2} 1. REQUIRED=YES
      @31 ANSWER{1,3} 1. REQUIRED=YES
      @34 ANSWER{1,4} 1. REQUIRED=YES
   #6 @3 "THESE WERE YOUR LAST 4 GUESSES:"
   #8 @25 ANSWER{2,1} 1. PROTECT=YES
      @28 ANSWER{2,2} 1. PROTECT=YES
      @31 ANSWER{2,3} 1. PROTECT=YES
      @34 ANSWER{2,4} 1. PROTECT=YES
      @40 SCORE {2} PROTECT=YES
   #9 @25 ANSWER{3,1} 1. PROTECT=YES
      @28 ANSWER{3,2} 1. PROTECT=YES
      @31 ANSWER{3,3} 1. PROTECT=YES
      @34 ANSWER{3,4} 1. PROTECT=YES
      @40 SCORE {3} PROTECT=YES
  #10 @25 ANSWER{4,1} 1. PROTECT=YES
      @28 ANSWER{4,2} 1. PROTECT=YES
      @31 ANSWER{4,3} 1. PROTECT=YES
      @34 ANSWER{4,4} 1. PROTECT=YES
      @40 SCORE {4} PROTECT=YES
  #11 @25 ANSWER{5,1} 1. PROTECT=YES
      @28 ANSWER{5,2} 1. PROTECT=YES
      @31 ANSWER{5,3} 1. PROTECT=YES
      @34 ANSWER{5,4} 1. PROTECT=YES
      @40 SCORE {5} PROTECT=YES
   GROUP=SCORE
  #14 @3 "GUESSED IN " TRY 2. PROTECT=YES
         +1 "ATTEMPTS"
```

Figure 15.4 (part 1): The program for Mastermind. This part contains the preparations: the array and window definitions and the generation of the random digits.

```
TRY=0;
POINT=0;
_MSG_="GUESS THE CODE. GOOD LUCK! - PF3 FOR EXIT";
DO UNTIL (POINT = 8);
   *---------------------------------------------------;
   * Shift the answers and the score down one line    ;
   *---------------------------------------------------;
   DO N=5 TO 2 BY -1;
      DO M=1 TO 8;
         ANSWER{N,M} = ANSWER{N-1,M};
         SCORE{N} = SCORE{N-1};
      END;
   END;
   *---------------------------------------------------;
   * Clear the first line of the array's              ;
   *---------------------------------------------------;
   DO M=1 TO 8;
      ANSWER{1,M} = .;
   END;
   SCORE{1} =' ';
   TRY + 1;
   DISPLAY M_MIND.GUESS BLANK;
   DO N=1 TO 4;
     DO M=1 TO 4;
       IF CODE{N} = ANSWER{1,M} THEN
          IF M=N THEN ANSWER{1,M+4} = 2;
          ELSE ANSWER{1,M+4} = 1;
     END;
   END;
   POINT = SUM(OF ANSWER5 -- ANSWER8);
   DO N=5 TO 8;
      SCORE{1}=TRIM(SCORE{1})||PUT(ANSWER{1,N},CODEFMT.);
   END;
END;
DISPLAY M_MIND.SCORE            ;
RUN;
```

Figure 15.4 (part 2): The actual game part is contained in a DO UNTIL loop. After some housekeeping it starts with the display of the game window, then validates the response and stores it. If the code has been found, the DO UNTIL loop is left and the second group of the window is displayed. Note the variable list construction in the SUM statement: you cannot use array notations here.

The IF statement trauma

Many programs are written in which there are endless series of IF statements. Figure 15.5 shows an example. In most cases such series of IF statements can be avoided through the use of the SELECT statement or the use of formats! The SELECT statement is pre-eminently suitable when, on the basis of the built in condition there are more than two possible courses in the program. Formats are especially suitable for consulting tables. In fact, that is what happens in figure 15.5.

```
DATA REGION;
    SET CUSTDATA;
    LENGTH REGION $ 12;
    REGION = 'UNKNOWN';
    IF POSTCDE GE '1000AA' AND POSTCDE LE '1199ZZ'
        OR POSTCDE GE '1420AA' AND POSTCDE LE
        '2159ZZ' THEN REGION = 'NORTH-WEST';
    IF POSTCDE GE '1200AA' AND POSTCDE LE '1419ZZ'
        OR POSTCDE GE '3400AA' AND POSTCDE LE
        '4299ZZ' THEN REGION = 'MIDDLE';
    IF POSTCDE GE '2160AA' AND POSTCDE LE '3399ZZ'
        THEN REGION = 'WEST';
    IF POSTCDE GE '4300AA' AND POSTCDE LE '4799ZZ'
        THEN REGION = 'SOUTH-WEST';
    IF POSTCDE GE '4800AA' AND POSTCDE LE '5699ZZ'
        THEN REGION = 'SOUTH';
    IF POSTCDE GE '5700AA' AND POSTCDE LE '6499ZZ'
        THEN REGION = 'SOUTH-EAST';
    IF POSTCDE GE '6500AA' AND POSTCDE LE '7699ZZ'
        OR POSTCDE GE '8000AA' AND POSTCDE LE
        '8299ZZ' THEN REGION = 'EAST';
    IF POSTCDE GE '7700AA' AND POSTCDE LE '7999ZZ'
        OR POSTCDE GE '8300AA' AND POSTCDE LE
        '9999ZZ' THEN REGION = 'NORTH_EAST';
    RUN;
```

Figure 15.5: A gruesome collection of IF statements. The program is not easily legible and therefore difficult to maintain.

The SELECT statement

The SELECT statement is ideal when a simple IF/THEN/ELSE combination offers few choices. In a single SELECT statement you can include a whole series of alternative choices. The SELECT statement occurs in two variants. The first is:

```
SELECT (expression);
    WHEN (expression1) statement;
    WHEN (expression2) statement;
    . . .
    WHEN (expressionn) statement;
    OTHERWISE statement;
END;
```

The expressions in the SELECT and WHEN statements are evaluated and the values which emerge are then compared. If the value in the SELECT statement equals the value of the expression in a WHEN statement, then the statement after WHEN gets executed. If no WHEN expression equals the SELECT expression, then the OTHERWISE statement gets executed. There is always a 1:1 relation between the value of the SELECT expression and the WHEN expression. To execute the same statement with multiple values of the WHEN expression, more WHEN statements can of course be declared, but multiple expressions can also be declared in a single WHEN statement. They are separated by commas:

```
WHEN (expression1,expression2,...) statement;
```

The second variant of the SELECT statement is:

```
SELECT;
    WHEN (condition) statement;
    WHEN (condition) statement;
    . . .
    WHEN (condition) statement;
    OTHERWISE statement;
END;
```

Now the conditions in any WHEN statement are evaluated separately as TRUE or FALSE, until a TRUE condition is found, or until the OTHERWISE statement is reached. Here too multiple conditions can be declared in a single WHEN statement, as stated above.

```
DATA REGION;
   SET CUSTDATA;
   LENGTH REGION $ 12;
   SELECT;
      WHEN (
          POSTCDE GE '1000AA' AND  POSTCDE LE
          '1199ZZ'  OR  POSTCDE GE '1420AA' AND
          POSTCDE LE '2159ZZ')
          REGION = 'NORTH-WEST';
      WHEN (
          POSTCDE GE '1200AA' AND POSTCDE LE
          '1419ZZ' OR POSTCDE GE '3400AA' AND
          POSTCDE LE '4299ZZ')
          REGION = 'MIDDLE';
      WHEN (
          POSTCDE GE '2160AA' AND POSTCDE LE
          '3399ZZ')
          REGION = 'WEST';
      WHEN (
          POSTCDE GE '4300AA' AND POSTCDE LE
          '4799ZZ')
          REGION = 'SOUTH-WEST';
      WHEN (
          POSTCDE GE '4800AA' AND POSTCDE LE
          '5699ZZ')
          REGION = 'SOUTH';
      WHEN (
          POSTCDE GE '5700AA' AND POSTCDE LE
          '6499ZZ')
          REGION = 'SOUTH-EAST';
      WHEN (
          POSTCDE GE '6500AA' AND POSTCDE LE
          '7699ZZ'  OR POSTCDE GE '8000AA' AND
          POSTCDE LE  '8299ZZ')
          REGION = 'EAST';
      WHEN (
          POSTCDE GE '7700AA' AND POSTCDE LE
          '7999ZZ' OR POSTCDE GE '8300AA' AND
         POSTCDE LE '9999ZZ')
          REGION = 'NORTH-EAST';
      OTHERWISE REGION = 'UNKNOWN';
   END;
RUN;
```

Figure 15.6: The same program as in figure 15.5, but this time with a SELECT statement.

For both statements, as soon as an acceptable WHEN statement is found, no other statements are examined. Just as with the IF statement, the statement after WHEN or OTHERWISE may be replaced by a DO-END group. The OTHERWISE statement is not required, but strongly recommended, since the SAS System gives an error message whenever no WHEN statement applies and there is no OTHERWISE statement present.

Figure 15.6 shows an alternative to the program of figure 15.5, but this time it uses a SELECT statement. Because the conditions are not 1:1, the second variant of the SELECT statement is used.

Formats as IF busters

Figure 15.7 presents a third variant of the same program as in figure 15.5, but this time using a format. This program is more legible, therefore better maintainable and faster! To begin, the table of postal codes is constructed as a format by means of PROC FORMAT. In the following DATA step the REGION variable is filled using the PUT function.

```
PROC FORMAT;
   VALUE $REGION
   '1000AA' - '1199ZZ',
   '1420AA' - '2159ZZ' = 'NORTH-WEST'
   '1200AA' - '1419ZZ',
   '3400AA' - '4299ZZ' = 'MIDDLE'
   '2160AA' - '3399ZZ' = 'WEST'
   '4300AA' - '4799ZZ' = 'SOUTH-WEST'
   '4800AA' - '5699ZZ' = 'SOUTH'
   '5700AA' - '6499ZZ' = 'SOUTH-EAST'
   '6500AA' - '7699ZZ',
   '8000AA' - '8299ZZ' = 'EAST'
   '7700AA' - '7999ZZ',
   '8300AA' - '9999ZZ' = 'NORTH-EAST'
                OTHER   = 'UNKNOWN';
DATA REGION;
   SET CUSTDATA;
   LENGTH REGION $ 12;
   REGION = PUT(POSTCDE,$REGION.);
RUN;
```

Figure 15.7: Functionally the same program as in figure 15.5 and 15.6, but this time with the table in a format. The format can be stored in a separate library and can be used in any program.

Note that in figure 15.5 the variable REGION first gets assigned the value 'UNKNOWN' and only after that are the IF statements executed to determine whether another value is needed. This is not necessary when using the SELECT statement variant (figure 15.6) and the PROC FORMAT variant (figure 15.7): the test is built into the OTHERWISE statement and the OTHER option of the format.

Input validations

The preceding example also gives an indication of how data validations can be processed with formats: the OTHER specification gets a very recognizable label and with the PUT function you can check for errors:

```
IF PUT(POSTCDE,$REGION.) = 'UNKNOWN' THEN ...;
```

A good alternative is of course to define your own informats. For this possibility refer to PROC FORMAT in the Procedures Guide.

LINK and RETURN statements

Subroutines in the DATA step can be defined using combinations of LINK and RETURN statements. In the LINK statement a program label is declared, to which the SAS System will jump during the execution of the LINK statement. After that the statements following the label are executed, until a RETURN statement or the end of the DATA step is reached. At that moment the program jumps back to the statement after the LINK statement. This is shown schematically in figure 15.8.

Should a subsequent LINK statement be present in the subroutine, then the following RETURN statement will not return directly to the main program, but to the statement after the LINK statement in the subroutine. This 'nesting' of subroutines can take place up to a maximum of 10 levels deep.

If a RETURN statement appears without a LINK statement first having been executed, then the SAS System regards this as the last statement of the run through the DATA step. Eventually, the SAS System outputs an observation and starts the next DATA step iteration from the DATA statement.

```
DATA ...;
   * main program;

   ...

   LINK SUBRTN1;
   * continuation main program;

   ...

RETURN; * termination main program, return to begin;
SUBRTN1:
   * first subroutine;

   ...

   LINK SUBRTN2;
   * continuation first subroutine;
 ...

RETURN; * jump back to continuation main program;
SUBRTN2:

   ...

RETURN; * jump back to continuation first subroutine;
```

Figure 15.8: With LINK and RETURN statements you can construct sub-routines in your program.

Exercises

1. In an analysis with many measurement variables and a corresponding number of readings there are a lot of missing values. These should all be set to 0. Write a routine to do that. The data have already been stored in a SAS data set. The measurement variables are all numerical. There is also a number of identification variables, which are all character variables.

2. In an on-screen form (next page) the user can make a choice from a number of economical statistics and call up these statistics for various countries. To process the query further, a data set has to be constructed in which an observation appears for each choice made. It is of course not guaranteed that everyone who fills in the form will list the countries one after the other: they could be spread anywhere over the ten input fields. The program should however push them to the first positions. Write a program to create the window and the required data set.

```
+CHOICE----------------------------------------------------------------------+
| Command ===>                                                                |
|                                                                             |
|                                                                             |
|   _ POPULATION        _ AREA            x CURRENCY         _ NAT. PRODUCT    |
|   x GOVERN.BUDGET     x OFF. INTEREST %  _ TAX %           _ NAT. INCOME     |
|                                                                             |
|      NL      __      BE      __      __                                      |
|      __      GB      __      __      __                                      |
|                                                                             |
|                                                                             |
|                                                                             |
|                                                                             |
+-----------------------------------------------------------------------------+
```

3. In part D of exercise 3 in chapter 6 you were asked to characterize the weather in various months on the basis of the temperature. Write this program using a SELECT statement instead of a number of IF statements.

CHAPTER 16

Accessing SAS® Data Sets

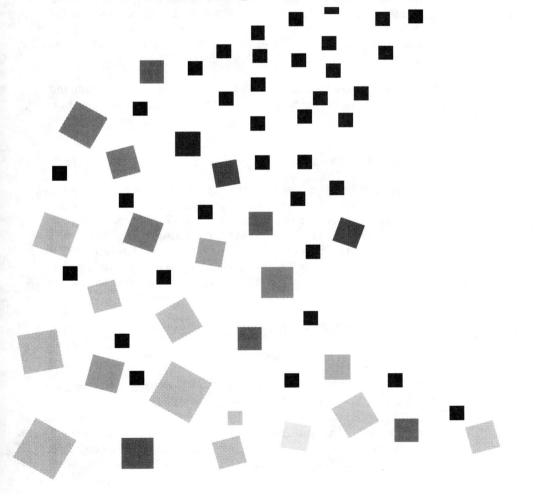

The SET statement

In chapter 8 we already became acquainted with the SET statement as a means to read observations from a SAS data set. In this section we shall examine a number of options and a few details of the SET statement.

Compiler actions with the SET statement

During DATA step compilation, the data sets which were declared in the SET statements are opened . The SAS System determines from the data set description what variables there are and how many observations there are. The variables are subsequently (taking into account DROP, KEEP and RENAME data set options) declared in the PDV. The number of observations is recorded in an internal variable and if the NOBS=variable option is specified it will also be recorded in the declared variable. Finally a pointer is initialized which, during the execution phase, keeps track of how far the reading of the data set has progressed.

The variable declared in the NOBS option will not be included in the output data set, but can be used in the DATA step as a normal numeric variable.

The execution phase

In principle the SAS System reads sequentially through the data set declared in a SET statement; each subsequent execution of the SET statement (normally the next iteration of the DATA step) reads the next observation until an End-of-File (EOF) indicator is reached. Since each SET statement has its own pointer, a data set can be read by several SET statements at the same time, with each SET statement reading at a different point. With the following construction, the opposite of the LAG function can be achieved, namely a 'look ahead':

```
SET dataset(FIRSTOBS=2 RENAME=(variable=nextvar));
SET dataset;
step = nextvar - variable;
```

Because both SET statements are always executed, the first statement stays ahead one observation all of the time. Watch out at the end: the first SET statement shall also first switch on an EOF indicator, which means that the last observation in the data set will not be read in the second SET statement, unless you take special measures (execute the second SET statement twice if the first signals EOF through the END= option). With the POINT option in the first SET, you could also prevent the EOF indication.

The POINT option

Up to now the data set has always been read sequentially by the SET statement. In many cases a SAS data set can also be read in random order. This cannot be done with compressed data sets or data sets on tape, but with SAS data sets on disk it is possible. The first possiblity is using the POINT option:

```
SET dataset POINT=pointer;
```

in which the pointer is a numeric variable. The value of the pointer variable is the observation number which will be read. This makes the order random; the reading of the last observation no longer automatically means the end of the operation. You have to stop the DATA step manually with a STOP statement.

The KEY option

If an index to a SAS data set has been constructed (by means of the INDEX=data set option or with an INDEX CREATE statement in PROC DATASETS), the index variable can also be used as a basis for random access to the data set, with the KEY option:

```
SET dataset KEY=index;
```

in which index is the name of the index variable or the 'composite key'. The index variable(s) is(are) provided with the key values to be found before the SET statement. The first execution of a SET statement with a fixed key value yields the first observation meeting the criterion. Each subsequent execution of the SET statement with the same key value automatically gives the next observation. If all observations of the key value have been read, the SAS System signals an End-of-File error in the _IORC_ variable (see ahead) while returning again the last observation in the group. The next time the SAS System starts over at the beginning of the group. If another key value is requested and then you revert back to the former, then the system restarts at the beginning of the group. You can change this behavior by adding the option /UNIQUE to the SET statement. In that case each execution of the SET statement will reset the pointer and come up with the first observation. This method of consulting data sets is very suitable for consulting tables; refer to the section 'Table look-up', later in this chapter.

It is important to test the automatic variable _IORC_ when using the KEY option. This has the value 0 if the execution of the SET statement has been successful. At the End-of-File indicator the value is -1. Other values of _IORC_ indicate an unsuccessful execution of the SET statement and here the value of the variables is unpredictable. We will go further into this in our discussion of the MODIFY statement later in this chapter.

Binary Search

In Version 5 many users developed their own methods for quickly accessing large SAS data sets. These techniques have become obsolete as standard indexing capabilities have been introduced for SAS data sets. One technique, the binary search technique, remains attractive however. With this technique no index needs to be constructed, thus eliminating considerable use of computer resources. The binary search requires only that the data set be sorted according to the key variable. The principle is simple (figure 16.1).

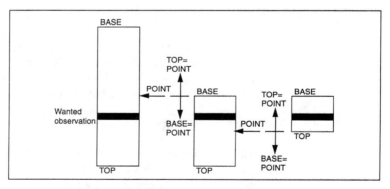

Figure 16.1: The principle of a binary search. The data set is cut into halves. Then it is inspected to determine which half contains the required observation. Then that half is again divided into halves and so on.

A first SET statement is executed halfway through the data set: the NOBS= option tells how many observations there are and then the halfway point of the data set is marked and used in the POINT option. Then a check is made to see if the desired observation lies in the first or second half of the data set. Then that part is halved, and so on. In just a few steps the choice is brought down to three observations in which the desired value must be found. In figure 16.2 this technique is applied to a file of 800,000 observations. With the PUT statement it is easy to follow how the SAS System jumps through the file to find the desired

observation. The DATA step first initializes the variables BASE and
TOP. Then a first POINT position is calculated. Then the SET statement
in the DO loop is executed, after which it can be determined whether the
desired observation lies in the first half or the second half of the data set.
Based on this determination, either TOP or BASE is adjusted for the next
try. It can happen that a 'lucky shot' occurs, in which case the loop is
exited.

```
1                         The SAS System (6.08)
                                     21:06 Tuesday, June 14, 1994
NOTE: Copyright(c) 1989 by SAS Institute Inc., Cary, NC USA.
NOTE: SAS (r) Proprietary Software Release 6.08   TS405

NOTE: The initialization phase used 0.06 CPU seconds and 1092K.

NOTE: SAS job started on Tuesday 14JUN94 21:06 (199406142106)

1          /*-------------------------------------------------*/
2          /* BINARY SEARCH ROUTINE                           */
3          /*-------------------------------------------------*/
4          LIBNAME LIBR 'TILANE.LIBRARY.SASLIB' DISP=SHR;
NOTE: Libref LIBR was successfully assigned as follows:
      Engine:        V608
      Physical Name: TILANE.LIBRARY.SASLIB
5          %LET ISBN = 155544381-8;
6          DATA SELECT;
7          BASE=1;
8          TOP=NOBS;
9          POINT=INT((TOP+BASE)/2);
10         DO WHILE (TOP-BASE > 2);
11            SET LIBR.ISBNINDX POINT=POINT NOBS=NOBS;
12            PUT BASE= TOP= POINT=;
13            IF ISBN = "&ISBN" THEN LEAVE;
14            IF ISBN < "&ISBN" THEN BASE = POINT +1;
15            IF ISBN > "&ISBN" THEN TOP  = POINT -1;
16            POINT=INT((TOP+BASE)/2);
17         END;
18         PUT BASE= TOP= POINT=;
19         DO N=MAX(1,POINT-1) TO MIN(NOBS,POINT+1);
20            SET LIBR.ISBNINDX POINT=N;
21            IF ISBN NE "&ISBN" THEN CONTINUE;
22            OUTPUT;
23            LEAVE;
24         END;
25         STOP;
26         RUN;
```

Figure 16.2: An example of a binary search. Note the STOP statement, to stop the DATA step when the required observation is found. This is a necessity when using the POINT option.

```
2                              The SAS System (6.08)
                                      21:06 Tuesday, June 14, 1994

BASE=1 TOP=784800 POINT=392400
BASE=1 TOP=392399 POINT=196200
BASE=196201 TOP=392399 POINT=294300
BASE=294301 TOP=392399 POINT=343350
BASE=343351 TOP=392399 POINT=367875
BASE=367876 TOP=392399 POINT=380137
BASE=380138 TOP=392399 POINT=386268
BASE=386269 TOP=392399 POINT=389334
BASE=386269 TOP=389333 POINT=387801
BASE=387802 TOP=389333 POINT=388567
BASE=388568 TOP=389333 POINT=388950
BASE=388568 TOP=388949 POINT=388758
BASE=388568 TOP=388757 POINT=388662
BASE=388568 TOP=388661 POINT=388614
BASE=388568 TOP=388613 POINT=388590
BASE=388568 TOP=388589 POINT=388578
BASE=388568 TOP=388577 POINT=388572
BASE=388573 TOP=388577 POINT=388575
BASE=388576 TOP=388577 POINT=388576
NOTE: The data set WORK.SELECT has 1 observations and 12 variables.
NOTE: The DATA statement used 0.11 CPU seconds and 1233K.

NOTE: The SAS session used 0.53 CPU seconds and 1284K.
NOTE: SAS Institute BV, 1217 KR Hilversum, The Netherlands
```

Figure 16.2 (part 2): Through the inclusion of the PUT statement in the search routine you can follow how the program jumps through the data set to reach its target. Going sequentially through some 800,000 observations would require considerably more processing resources.

If no 'lucky shot' forces an exit from the loop, then the loop ends when BASE and TOP have come so close together that no further calculating is possible. The observation you are looking for will lie at most one observation before or after the POINT value, if it exists at all. Now a second DO loop is run to see if an observation is found. The program in figure 16.2 does not look to see if there are multiple observations with the same key value.

Appendix E has a Binary Search routine written in the form of a macro, in which multiple variables together can form the key and in which multiple observations with the same key value are selected.

The MODIFY statement

The MODIFY statement reads and modifies a data set 'in place'. That is, a new data set is not created as output as with SET, MERGE, or UPDATE; the observation is modified directly in the data set. One or two data sets can be declared in the MODIFY statement. If one data set is declared, the MODIFY statement works similarly to the SET statement, and otherwise more like the UPDATE statement. The options available are like those for the SET statement: POINT=.., NOBS=.., KEY=.., END=... The syntax can be summarized as:

```
MODIFY  dataset1 <dataset2> <options>;
```

MODIFY as SET statement

Without any special options and with only one data set declared, the MODIFY statement reads the data set sequentially; each iteration of the DATA step reads a following observation, as with the SET statement. Because the MODIFY statement does not create a new data set, the same data set must be declared in the DATA statement as in the MODIFY statement and no new variables can be entered. Should observations drop out because of the programming of the DATA step, they continue to exist physically, but they get marked 'deleted' and can no longer be called. The next time the data set is reconstructed (for example in a DATA step with a SET statement, or a PROC SORT), the 'deleted' observations are also physically removed. The two DATA steps below perform the same function, but the execution of the MODIFY statement is faster because the unmarked observations do not have to be written out again.

```
DATA IN_OUT;                          DATA IN_OUT;
   MODIFY IN_OUT;                        SET IN_OUT;
   IF COUNT = . THEN                     IF COUNT = . THEN
      COUNT = 0;                            COUNT = 0;
RUN;                                  RUN;
```

The OUTPUT, REPLACE and REMOVE statements

In the above routines all observations were read from the data set and modified if so desired. Just as with an INPUT or a SET statement an observation is automatically output at the end of the DATA step, which means in this case that the observation is updated with the new values for the variables. In combination with INPUT and SET statements you can force output to the data set before the end of the DATA step is reached by using the OUTPUT statement. When using the MODIFY statement you have similar facilities, but with a choice of three statements. The OUTPUT statement adds a new observation to the end of the data set, the REPLACE statement replaces the value of the most recently read observation and the REMOVE statement removes the most recently read observation. Be careful that REMOVE is used here, not the DELETE statement. The DELETE statement interrupts the processing of an observation and outputs nothing. Thus the observation remains unchanged!

Updating a master file using MODIFY

In the second form of the MODIFY statement two data sets and a BY statement are declared :

```
MODIFY masterdataset transactiondataset;
BY keyvariable;
```

The processing is now more or less similar to the UPDATE statement, although there are clear differences:

1. The data sets do not have to be sorted according to BY variable. The master data set does have to be indexed to the BY variable.

2. Multiple observations with the same BY value may be present in the master data set.

3. Any variables which appear in the transaction data set but not in the master data set are not transferred.

4. New observations must be explicitly transferred to the master data set and are added at the end.

The MODIFY statement reads the transaction data set sequentially and looks for the observation related to it in the master data set. If this is found, then the non-missing values will be transferred from the transaction data set. If the master data set has multiple observations with the same BY values, then only the first is updated. Test the _IORC_ variable: by doing so you can find out if the BY value you are looking for was present in the master data set. If not, the new value must be explicitly added using an OUTPUT statement. But using the OUTPUT statement has the additional consequence that the existing observations also must be explicitly updated with a REPLACE statement.

Because the transaction data set is read sequentially, the modifications affect the master data set cumulatively.

The _IORC_ variable

When using the MODIFY statement or the SET statement with the KEY option, the SAS System defines a new automatic variable: _IORC_. This has the value 0 after a successful SET or MODIFY statement execution and the value -1 if an End-of-File condition occurred. All other values of _IORC_ indicate an error condition. The autocall macro %SYSRC(...) can be used to test which error condition occurred. The error condition you want to test is declared as argument to %SYSRC. %SYSRC returns the corresponding value for _IORC_. In the following sample program you can see how to use this. The most important conditions are listed in figure 16.3. In the source code of %SYSRC you can see the value of _IORC_ with various error codes. You should not hard code these values into your program. They could change in a later SAS release. %SYSRC would then change along with it. It is very important to test _IORC_, because the results of an unsuccessful SET or MODIFY are unpredictable.

_DSENMR	BY-value of observation in transaction data set not in master dataset.
_DSENOM	No corresponding observation found in the master dataset.
_SENODEL	Observations may not be deleted from the dataset.
_SERECRD	No observation read from the input file.
_SWDLREC	Observation deleted.

Figure 16.3: Some of the error conditions that can be tested using %SYSRC.

Example of MODIFY

In this program (see the log printed in figure 16.4), the ART_DES data set (as used in chapter 8) is updated with the same transaction data set which has been used to demonstrate the operation of the UPDATE statement. Since ART_DES had not been indexed, that gets done first. Normally of course, the indexed data set is permanently stored. The second DATA step shows how the MODIFY runs. With 'Dynamic WHERE processing' the SAS System uses the index to search for the correct observation in the master data set. Note the testing of _IORC_ and the use of the OUTPUT and REPLACE statements.

```
1                        The SAS System (6.08)
                                    16:29 Saturday, June 11, 1994

NOTE: Copyright(c) 1989 by SAS Institute Inc., Cary, NC USA.
NOTE: SAS (r) Proprietary Software Release 6.08  TS405

NOTE: The initialization phase used 0.06 CPU seconds and 1092K.

NOTE: SAS job started on Saturday 11JUN94 16:29 (199406111629)

1           /*-----------------------------------------------------*/
2           /* USE OF MODIFY STATEMENT                             */
3           /*-----------------------------------------------------*/
4           LIBNAME GEN '.GENERAL.SASLIB';
NOTE: Libref GEN was successfully assigned as follows:
      Engine:        V608
      Physical Name: TILANE.GENERAL.SASLIB
5           DATA ART_DES(INDEX=(ART_NBR));
6              SET GEN.ART_DES;
7           RUN;

NOTE: The data set WORK.ART_DES has 13 observations and 3 variables.
INFO: Single index ART_NBR defined.
NOTE: The DATA statement used 0.03 CPU seconds and 1939K.

8           DATA ART_DES;
9              MODIFY ART_DES GEN.ART_UPD;
10             BY ART_NBR;
11             IF _IORC_=%SYSRC(_DSENMR) THEN OUTPUT;
12             IF _IORC_=0 THEN REPLACE;
13          RUN;

INFO: Index ART_NBR selected for WHERE clause optimization.
INFO: Use of index ART_NBR for WHERE clause optimization cancelled.
INFO: Index ART_NBR selected for WHERE clause optimization.
ART_NBR=11060 DESCRIPT=plywood 12 PRICE=48.5 FIRST.ART_NBR=1
LAST.ART_NBR=1 _ERROR_=1 _IORC_=1230013 _N_=2
INFO: Use of index ART_NBR for WHERE clause optimization cancelled.
INFO: Index ART_NBR selected for WHERE clause optimization.
INFO: Use of index ART_NBR for WHERE clause optimization cancelled.
INFO: Index ART_NBR selected for WHERE clause optimization.
ART_NBR=20105 DESCRIPT=acrylyello PRICE=12.7 FIRST.ART_NBR=1
LAST.ART_NBR=1 _ERROR_=1 _IORC_=1230013 _N_=4
INFO: Use of index ART_NBR for WHERE clause optimization cancelled.
INFO: Index ART_NBR selected for WHERE clause optimization.
INFO: Use of index ART_NBR for WHERE clause optimization cancelled.
INFO: Index ART_NBR selected for WHERE clause optimization.
NOTE: The data set WORK.ART_DES has been updated.  There were 4
      observations rewritten, 2 observations added and 0 observations
      deleted.
NOTE: The DATA statement used 0.12 CPU seconds and 1939K.

NOTE: The SAS session used 0.39 CPU seconds and 1993K.
NOTE: SAS Institute BV, 1217 KR Hilversum, The Netherlands
```

Figure 16.4: The modify statement as an alternative for the update statement. Note the test of
IORC and the use of %SYSRC.

Table look-up

Table look-up is a frequently occurring task: a file contains some code and using that code you can access a table with more information on the code. A familiar example is in personnel administration: there is a file with personnel numbers, name, address and any other personal information; all other files (salary administration, among others) only contain the personnel number as a reference.

If, for example, a salary statement has to be made, the personnel file is consulted to attach the name and address to the given personnel number. The data set with just the code will be referred to in this section with the base data set or file. The file with the explanation of the code will be referred to as the table.

Summary of available techniques

The SAS System has various techniques available for consulting tables. Each of these techniques has its advantages and disadvantages. The techniques can be split into two groups: the table is stored in a format or the table is stored in a SAS data set. Storing the table in a format is the best method when an 'N:1' consulting is desired: multiple values in the base file can lead to a single value in the table. In case of a '1:1' consulting, where each value in the base file leads to a unique value in the table, both formats and data sets are useful. Table capacity with formats is, in practice, limited to about 10,000 lines; the exact limit depends on the system environment. The amount of information which can be retrieved from the table is limited to 200 positions (in V5 only 40 positions) in one string of characters. With data sets the size is practically unlimited. Tables of over a million lines create no special problem. The amount of information to be retrieved is also virtually unlimited: every variable in the table data set is available.

Table look-up with formats

The first group is in fact the situation covered on page 330 in chapter 15 and shown in figure 15.7. An important consideration when using formats as a table is that neither the base file nor the table has to be sorted. They can always be consulted with a PUT function.

Table look-up with MERGE

If both the base file and the table are in a SAS data set and both are sorted according to the 'linking pin' (the code, the personnel number in the situation described above), then a simple MERGE between the two data sets can be executed to add table information to the base data set. This technique has already been shown in figures 8.9 and 8.10. There is a SORT_TOT data set with article numbers, quantities and categories and an ART_DES data set with descriptions and prices. These can be combined using the article number (ART_NBR) as linking pin.

Table look-up with SET

If the base file is not sorted or has not even been declared in a SAS data set, then you must consult the table with a SET statement, because random access to the table data set is required. If the table is sorted, then a Binary Search routine can be used to find the correct observation, as shown in figure 16.2. If the table is indexed, it can be consulted with the KEY option in the SET statement. In this case you must use the UNIQUE option in the SET statement to prevent problems in the use of the index. To bring about the same situation as in figures 8.9 and 8.10, two things have to be done; first, index the ART_DES data set (the table):

```
DATA ART_DESX(INDEX=(ART_NR));
   SET ART_DES;
RUN;
```

and then a description can be sought for each line in the order list (data sets DEPT1, DEPT2 and DEPT3, see also figure 8.2):

```
DATA ORDER;
   SET DEPT1 DEPT2 DEPT3;
   SET ART_DESX KEY=ART_NBR/UNIQUE;
   IF _IORC_ NE 0 AND _IORC_ NE -1 THEN DO;
      DESCRIPT = 'XXXXXXXX';
      PRICE = .;
   END;
RUN;
```

After the first SET statement is executed, the variable ART_NBR will contain the current article number, which is then sought in the ART_DESX data set. Note the test on the automatic variable _IORC_. Only if this variable has the value 0 or -1 has an observation with the desired index value been found. The test is necessary, since as has been mentioned before, the result of the second SET statement is unpredictable, if no fitting observation is found.

Exercises

1. Write a program that counts the number of observations in a SAS data set and puts that number in a macro variable without reading the data set!

2. A large publisher and books importer has listed every book in a SAS data set. This dataset (BOOKS) contains the variables:

   AUTHOR
   TITLE
   ISBN (International Standard Book Number)
   CATEGORY (for example novel, sci-fi, detective)
   PRICE
   DATE_FE (date of first edition)
   DATE_LP (date of latest printing)
   CIRCUL (circulation)

   a. Most often this data is accessed by author name. So they want to create an index on author name. Write a program that creates this index.

   b. Write a routine to find the books by the authors Mailer and Vidal using the index you have just created. Hint: use a WHERE statement.

   c. Because the ISBN is the standard international book reference, you want a quick access to ISBN. However, you do not want to use the extra processing needed to create an index. How then can you search ISBN?

   d. Find the book number 0-917382-65-X using Binary Search.

3. SAS data sets A and B have a common variable ID. The data sets are sorted by ID. In both data sets multiple observations can appear with the same value of this variable.

   Create a new data set in which each observation of A is combined with each observation of B with the same ID value. This is sometimes referred to as an N x M merge.

Hint: First create a data set based on data set B, containing one observation for each value of ID. In these observations, in addition to the ID variable, there are two other variables which contain the observation number of the first and last observation in B with that ID value. Combine this data set with A and use the observation pointers to B in a SET statement with a POINT option.

CHAPTER 17

PROC REPORT

Introduction

PROC REPORT is a new facility in Version 6 of the SAS System. It is a supplement to the reporting capabilities that already exist through procedures such as PROC PRINT and PROC TABULATE. In PROC REPORT you can use pieces of DATA step programming to perform calculations, such as calculating extra columns or subtotals.

In its simplest form the whole procedure consists of a single statement:

```
PROC REPORT DATA=inputdataset;
```

The outcome depends on the contents of the input data set. If there are only numeric variables, the PROC REPORT output is just one line: the total of each variable. The output below would result if PROC REPORT were used on the data set which formed the basis for the examples in chapter 11 (Descriptive Statistics): the logging of customers at a supermarket check-out. The variable TIME is the time (in HHMM) customers arrive at the check-outs, DURATION is the number of minutes and seconds the transaction takes and CHECKOUT the number of the check-out. Because the totals of TIME and DURATION are beyond the limit of their standard format, TIME is in hours only and DURATION in minutes only.

```
      TIME      DURATION       CHECKOUT
     10478          1560           3850
```

Should there be one or more character variables, then the output is similar to that of PROC PRINT.

Here is a PROC REPORT which has been applied to the ORDER data set from the SET/MERGE chapter (chapter 8):

```
ART_CAT    ART_NBR   QUANTITY   DESCRIPT       PRICE
timber      10020          4    plank 3x5       10.6
timber      10030          9    plank 2x3       4.95
timber      10050         12    profile pl       7.8
sheet       11030          8    chipwood 8     12.95
sheet       11070         16    plywood 18      64.5
paint       20060         17    glos white       8.4
paint       20100          8    acrylwhite      12.7
paint       21090          9    brush 2x1        4.5
paint       22001          3    abbr p 180       0.9
tools       40090          4    el drill         149
tools       45030          9    handsaw         29.9
hardware    50010         15    screw 1x5       21.5
hardware    50030         17    nail 1.75       12.6
```

Starting from these two basic forms, you can now develop more advanced reports. It is possible to write a report completely with SAS statements, but it can also be developed in an interactive manner, through 'Report by example'. In this last case PROC REPORT is called up in a window environment, such as the Display Manager. The construction can be done with the help of prompts from the SAS System.

Interactive report definition

Since the interactive method of defining reports is the easiest, because you can always see what the effect of a modification is, we first deal with this method, creating two examples.

The ORDER data set

The first example contains a report based on the ORDER data set printed above. PROC REPORT is called in the following way:

```
PROC REPORT DATA=GEN.ORDER PROMPT;
RUN;
```

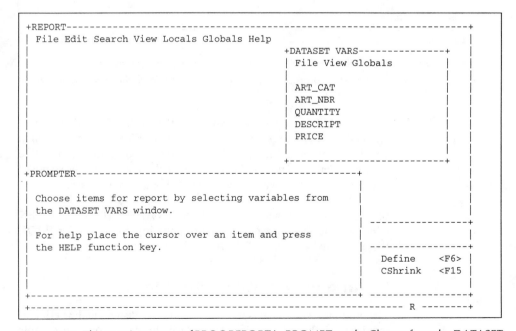

*Figure 17.1: The opening screen of PROC REPORT in PROMPT mode. Choose from the DATASET VARS window those variables that are needed for the report. The selected variables are marked with an * and will move to the top of the list in the order in which they are selected.*

As you can see from these statements we assume that the ORDER data set is in a datalibrary with libname GEN. The PROMPT option instructs the SAS System to guide us through the process of defining the report. After submitting the above statements, you see a screen as in figure 17.1.

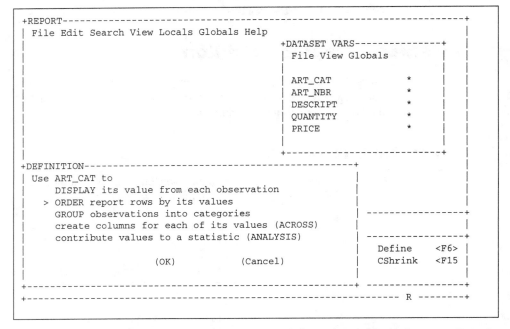

```
+REPORT-----------------------------------------------------------------+
| File Edit Search View Locals Globals Help                              |
|                                              +DATASET VARS-------------+  |
|                                              | File View Globals        |  |
|                                              |                          |  |
|                                              | ART_CAT          *       |  |
|                                              | ART_NBR          *       |  |
|                                              | DESCRIPT         *       |  |
|                                              | QUANTITY         *       |  |
|                                              | PRICE            *       |  |
|                                              |                          |  |
|                                              +--------------------------+  |
+DEFINITION----------------------------------------------+                  |
| Use ART_CAT to                                         |                  |
|     DISPLAY its value from each observation            |                  |
|   > ORDER report rows by its values                    |                  |
|     GROUP observations into categories                 | ---------------+ |
|     create columns for each of its values (ACROSS)     | ---------------+ |
|     contribute values to a statistic (ANALYSIS)        | --------------+  |
|                                                        | Define   <F6> |  |
|              (OK)              (Cancel)                 | CShrink  <F15> |  |
|                                                        |               |  |
+--------------------------------------------------------+ --------------+  |
+------------------------------------------------------------- R -------+  |
```

Figure 17.2: After selecting, you are prompted to specify for each variable the function of it in the report.

The two windows in the background are the REPORT window, where the report is about to be displayed, and the RKEYS window, in which you declare the key functions. This function key definition is not alike in all installations. The keys in the figures in this chapter are the standard keys for MVS/TSO, with a few of the author's own adaptations.

In the foreground are shown the DATASET VARS and the PROMPTER window. The variables which occur in the input data set for PROC REPORT are listed in the DATASET VARS window.

Selecting and designating variables

The prompter window tells that it is now time to designate the variables required for the report. You must place the cursor on the variable concerned, which you then select by keying Enter (or clicking the mouse, if appropriate). The variables will move to the top of the list in the order they are selected and are marked with an asterisk.

In our situation the order of the variables is not changed much: only DESCRIPT and QUANTITY change sequence. Once all relevant variables have been assigned, quit the DATASET VARS window by choosing END from the File pull down menu. You can also use PF3, of course.

Next, for each variable you have declared, the SAS System will ask questions about the function of that variable in the report; the choice is among five possibilities (see figure 17.5). Here again you choose the option you want by placing the cursor on its line and keying Enter. An arrow (>) then appears at the head of the line. Your choice is confirmed by moving the cursor to OK and keying Enter.

For ART_CAT we choose the option ORDER to get a report sorted by article category. We also choose ORDER for ART_NBR. For DESCRIPT, QUANTITY and PRICE it is not important for us at this moment to opt for DISPLAY or ORDER, since each line is already unique.

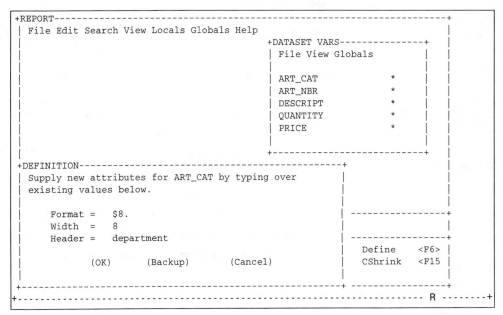

Figure 17.3: The formatting of the ART_CAT column is specified. Default values are derived from the variable attributes. For character variables the format is $--. (length of the variable), for numeric variables BEST9. unless another format had been specified for the variable in the data set. Width is set equal to the length of the format. Header contains the variable label or the name, if no label is provided.

After declaring ART_CAT as ORDER variable, you will be asked to declare the attributes of ART_CAT; that is the format, the heading above the column (default the variable name or label) and the column width (figure 17.3). With ORDER variables you also are asked whether a subtotal needs to be calculated, by transferring to another value of the ORDER variable (figure 17.4). In our example there are not yet any variables which fulfill that criterion, but we still go ahead and choose YES for an immediate subtotal.

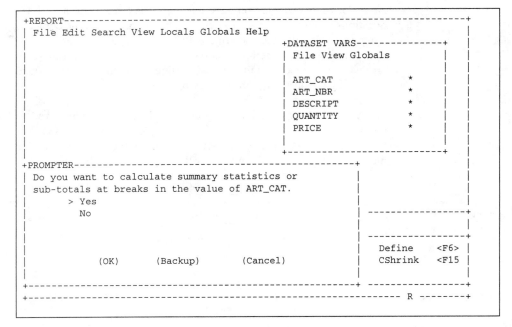

```
+REPORT------------------------------------------------------------------+
| File Edit Search View Locals Globals Help                              |
|                                         +DATASET VARS--------------+   |
|                                         | File View Globals        |   |
|                                         |                          |   |
|                                         | ART_CAT              *   |   |
|                                         | ART_NBR              *   |   |
|                                         | DESCRIPT             *   |   |
|                                         | QUANTITY             *   |   |
|                                         | PRICE                *   |   |
|                                         |                          |   |
|                                         +--------------------------+   |
+PROMPTER------------------------------------------------+               |
| Do you want to calculate summary statistics or         |               |
| sub-totals at breaks in the value of ART_CAT.          |               |
|        > Yes                                           |               |
|          No                                            | ----------------+
|                                                        |                 |
|                                                        | ----------------+
|                                                        | Define    <F6>  |
|           (OK)       (Backup)       (Cancel)           | CShrink   <F15> |
|                                                        |                 |
+--------------------------------------------------------+ ----------------+
+---------------------------------------------------------------- R -------+
```

Figure 17.4: When an order variable changes to a new value you can compute subtotals in PROC REPORT in a so-called "break section".

DISPLAY	For each observation a line will be produced in the report.
ORDER	The report will be sorted according to this variable.
GROUP	Defines groups in the report. Only a summary line will be produced per group.
ACROSS	For each (possibly formatted value) of this variable a separate column is created.
ANALYSIS	The variable is basis for analysis, e.g. calculation of a sum, mean, et cetera.

Figure 17.5: The functions that a variable can have in a report.

When you opt for a subtotal, there are several possibilities: a simple subtotal, but also possibly an average value. Then you are asked how the subtotal line (the 'break line') should be marked in the report. The marking can consist of a single or double line above and/or below the line. You can also declare whether lines should be allowed to run over or whether a new page should begin (figure 17.6).

Once all the columns have been set up, the report becomes visible. This does not mean that the report is finished and can no longer be changed. But the SAS System now has enough information to make and display a preliminary version of the report (figure 17.7). From this point on, columns can be added, calculations made, break lines changed and so on. The results of the changes will always be visible on the screen.

Adding a column of calculated values

First we are going to add a few columns: namely columns for a price per article including VAT, a total order amount excluding VAT and a total order amount including VAT. We do this by means of the ADD RIGHT command. First we place the cursor on the column 'Price ex VAT' and key Enter. This selects the price column. The ADD RIGHT command is then issued to define a new column to the right of Price ex VAT. The SAS System then asks what should go to the right of Price: a data set variable, a calculated variable or some statistic (figure 17.8). In our case, we choose 'Computed', because we are going to calculate the price including VAT. After the OK signal, the COMPUTE window is opened (figure 17.9) and the calculation line can now be entered as a normal SAS assignment statement. To round out the definition, the attributes such as format and header need to be declared (figure 17.10).

The variables PRICE and PR_INCL up to this moment have been formatted with the BEST9. format. Because they are prices and because adding two more columns will cramp the space, we will change the format to 6.2. To do this, we place the cursor on the column PRICE and opt for DEFINE (figure 17.11). We do the same for amount excluding VAT and amount including VAT.

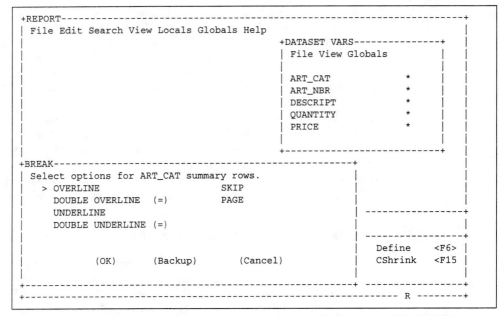

```
+REPORT------------------------------------------------------------------+
| File Edit Search View Locals Globals Help                              |
|                                        +DATASET VARS---------------+    |
|                                        | File View Globals          |   |
|                                        |                            |   |
|                                        | ART_CAT            *       |   |
|                                        | ART_NBR            *       |   |
|                                        | DESCRIPT           *       |   |
|                                        | QUANTITY           *       |   |
|                                        | PRICE              *       |   |
|                                        |                            |   |
|                                        +----------------------------+   |
|                                                                        |
+BREAK----------------------------------------------------+              |
| Select options for ART_CAT summary rows.                |              |
|    > OVERLINE                   SKIP                     |              |
|      DOUBLE OVERLINE   (=)       PAGE                    |              |
|      UNDERLINE                                           | -----------------+
|      DOUBLE UNDERLINE (=)                                |                 |
|                                                          | -----------------+
|                                                          | Define    <F6> |
|          (OK)         (Backup)         (Cancel)          | CShrink   <F15> |
|                                                          |                 |
+---------------------------------------------------------+ -----------------+
+------------------------------------------------------------- R --------+
```

Figure 17.6: Break sections can be marked in several ways. OVERLINE and UNDERLINE can be specified independently.

```
+REPORT------------------------------------------------------------------+
| File Edit Search View Locals Globals Help                              |
|                                                                        |
|                    The SAS System, Version 6.08                   1    |
|                                 20:26 Saturday, June 11, 1994          |
|                                                                        |
|                                               Price ex                 |
|         Departm.    ART_NBR  Descript.   QUANTITY      VAT             |
|         hardware     50010   screw 1x5       15       21.5             |
|                      50030   nail 1.75       17       12.6             |
|         --------                                                       |
|         hardware                                                       |
+PROMPTER-----------------------------------------------+    8.4         |
| You can now modify the report directly or             |   12.7         |
| continue to add items with prompting.                 |    4.5         |
| Do you want to add more items?                        |    0.9         |
|                                                       | -----------------+
|        Yes                                            |                 |
|      > No                                             | -----------------+
|                                                       | Define    <F6> |
|               (OK)          (Cancel)                  | CShrink   <F15> |
|                                                       |                 |
+-------------------------------------------------------+ -----------------+
+------------------------------------------------------------- R --------+
```

Figure 17.7: The initial version of the report is ready and is shown in the report window.

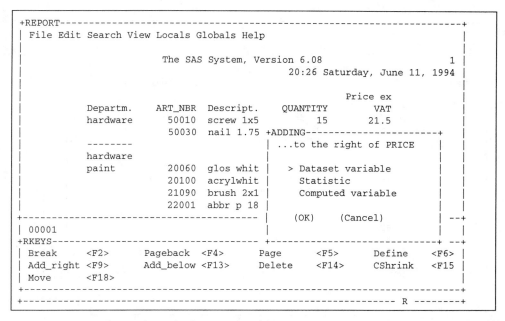

```
+REPORT----------------------------------------------------------------------+
| File Edit Search View Locals Globals Help                                   |
|                                                                             |
|                        The SAS System, Version 6.08                    1 |
|                                        20:26 Saturday, June 11, 1994 |
|                                                                             |
|                                                  Price ex                   |
|            Departm.    ART_NBR  Descript.    QUANTITY       VAT             |
|            hardware     50010   screw 1x5        15        21.5             |
|                         50030   nail 1.75 +ADDING----------------------+     |
|            --------              |  ...to the right of PRICE           |   |
|            hardware              |                                     |   |
|            paint        20060   glos whit |   > Dataset variable        |   |
|                         20100   acrylwhit |     Statistic               |   |
|                         21090   brush 2x1 |     Computed variable       |   |
|                         22001   abbr p 18 |                             |   |
+-----------------------------------------  |   (OK)     (Cancel)         | --+
| 00001                                     |                             |   |
+RKEYS------------------------------------  +-----------------------------+ --+
| Break      <F2>      Pageback  <F4>     Page      <F5>     Define    <F6> |
| Add_right  <F9>      Add_below <F13>    Delete    <F14>    CShrink   <F15> |
| Move       <F18>                                                           |
+----------------------------------------------------------------------------+
+------------------------------------------------------------- R --------+
```

Figure 17.8: Now that we have the first version of the report, we can start changing. First we add a column with the price including VAT, to the right of the existing column for price excl. VAT.

```
+REPORT----------------------------------------------------------------------+
| File Edit Search View Locals Globals Help                                   |
|                        The SAS System, Version 6.08                    1 |
|                                        20:26 Saturday, June 11, 1994 |
|                                                                             |
|                                                  Price ex                   |
+COMPUTE---------------------------------------------------------------------+
| File View Globals                                                           |
|                                                                             |
| 00001 PR_INC = ROUND(PRICE * 1.175,0.01);                                   |
| 00002                                                                       |
| 00003                                                                       |
| 00004                                                                       |
| 00005                                                                       |
| 00006                                                                       |
| 00007                                                                       |
| 00008                                                                       |
| 00009                                                                       |
| 00010                                                                       |
| 00011                                                                       |
| 00012                                                                       |
| 00013                                                                       |
+------------------------------------------------------------- R --------+
```

Figure 17.9: The extra column is for a computed variable: the price incl. VAT. Therefore the COMPUTE window is opened to write the formula.

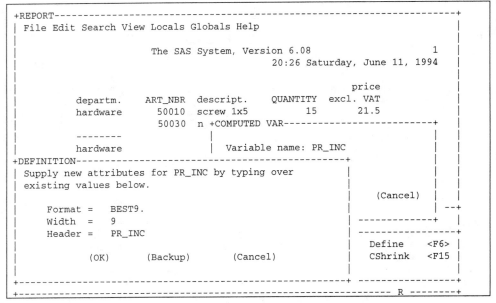

```
+REPORT------------------------------------------------------------------------+
| File Edit Search View Locals Globals Help                                    |
|                                                                              |
|                     The SAS System, Version 6.08                      1      |
|                                       20:26 Saturday, June 11, 1994          |
|                                                                              |
|                                                      price                   |
|          departm.   ART_NBR  descript.    QUANTITY  excl. VAT                |
|          hardware     50010  screw 1x5         15     21.5                   |
|                       50030  n +COMPUTED VAR-------------------------+        |
|          --------            |                                      |        |
|          hardware            | Variable name: PR_INC                |        |
|+DEFINITION----------------------------------------------------+     |        |
| Supply new attributes for PR_INC by typing over             |     |        |
| existing values below.                                      |     |        |
|                                               |  (Cancel)    |     |        |
|    Format  =   BEST9.                          |             |    --+      |
|    Width   =   9                               | ------------+     |        |
|    Header  =   PR_INC                          | ----------------+        |
|                                               | Define    <F6> |        |
|       (OK)       (Backup)       (Cancel)       | CShrink   <F15> |        |
|                                               |                 |        |
+---------------------------------------------------------------+ ----------------+
+------------------------------------------------------------------- R --------+
```

Figure 17.10: Also for the new column you have to specify the attributes.

```
+REPORT------------------------------------------------------------------------+
| File Edit Search View Locals Globals Help                                    |
|                                                                              |
|    +DEFINITION----------------------------------------------------------+ 1 |
|    |                    Definition of PRICE                             | 4 |
|    |    Usage    Attributes                   Options       Color       |   |
|    |  > DISPLAY  Format    = 6.2              NOPRINT     BLUE          |   |
|    |    ORDER    Spacing   = 2                NOZERO      RED           |   |
|    |    GROUP    Width     = 6                DESCENDING  PINK          |   |
|    |    ACROSS   Item help =                  PAGE        GREEN         |   |
|    |    ANALYSIS Statistic =                  FLOW        CYAN          |   |
|    |    COMPUTED Order     = FORMATTED                    YELLOW        |   |
|    |             Justify   = RIGHT                        WHITE    *    |   |
|    |             Data type= NUMERIC                       ORANGE        |   |
|    |                                                      BLACK         |   |
|    |                                                      MAGENTA       |   |
+----  |                                                     GRAY         --+ |
| 000 | Header = Price ex VAT                                 BROWN        |   |
+RKEY |                                                                   --+ |
| Bre |        (Edit Program)     (OK)       (Cancel)                     | > |
| Add +-------------------------------------------------------------------+ 5 |
| Mov +-------------------------------------------------------------------+   |
+------------------------------------------------------------------------------+
+------------------------------------------------------------------- R --------+
```

Figure 17.11: If you want to change the function, formatting or programming of a column you choose the DEFINE command which opens the DEFINE window. In this case we change the format of PRICE into 6.2 and the column width to 6.

The calculation rules are of course simple: QUANTITY x PRICE and QUANTITY x PR_INCL. Figure 17.12 shows how the report looks at this point. The break line is still empty, apart from the departments column and the missing values in the three columns of figures. These missing values occur because PROC REPORT constructs the report by lines. Since QUANTITY and PRICE have not been defined as ANALY-SIS variables but as a DISPLAY variable, there is no subtotal for these columns, which leads to the missing values in the columns of figures.

```
+REPORT---------------------------------------------------------------+
| File Edit Search View Locals Globals Help                           |
|                                                                     |
|                  The SAS System, Version 6.08                  1 |
|                                     20:26 Saturday, June 11, 1994 |
|                                                                     |
|                                    Price    Price   Amount   Amount |
| Departm.   ART_NBR  Descript.  Quant.  ex VAT  inc VAT  ex VAT  inc VAT |
| hardware    50010   screw 1x5     15   21.50   25.26   322.50   378.90 |
|             50030   nail 1.75     17   12.60   14.81   214.20   251.77 |
| --------                                                            |
| hardware                                       .        .        . |
|                                                                     |
| paint       20060   glos white    17    8.40    9.87   142.80   167.79 |
|             20100   acrylwhite     8   12.70   14.92   101.60   119.36 |
|             21090   brush 2x1      9    4.50    5.29    40.50    47.61 |
+---------------------------------------------------------------------+
| 00001                                                               |
+RKEYS----------------------------------------------------------------+
| Break      <F2>      Pageback  <F4>      Page     <F5>      Define    <F6> |
| Add_right  <F9>      Add_below <F13>     Delete   <F14>     CShrink   <F15 |
| Move       <F18>                                                    |
+---------------------------------------------------------------------+
+------------------------------------------------------- R --------+
```

Figure 17.12: After adding the price including VAT, the total amount excluding and including VAT and changing the formatting a little bit the report looks as shown here.

Subtotals

In a first attempt to create subtotals, we convert the PRICE variable from a DISPLAY variable to an ANALYSIS variable, with the analysis type SUM (figure 17.13). By doing this we also have to change the calculation rules referring to PRICE since now we have to refer to PRICE.SUM instead, because PRICE no longer exists as a reference (figure 17.14). This is done by going again to the DEFINE window for the columns 'PRICE including VAT' and 'AMOUNT excluding/including VAT' and from there to the COMPUTE window. Now the calculation rule for the price including VAT has become: PR_INC=PRICE.SUM*1.75; the reference for other columns follows suit.

This change is still not satisfactory since, as figure 17.15 now shows, the columns PRICE excluding VAT and PRICE including VAT are also totaled, although that doesn't make sense at all. To make matters worse the subtotals for the amount columns are still missing. The latter problem can be eliminated also by changing QUANTITY into an ANALYSIS variable, but this is to jump from the frying pan into the fire: now QUANTITY will be totaled as well and the subtotals of the amount columns appear to be the product of the subtotals of QUANTITY and PRICE (figure 17.16)!

These disasters arise from the previously mentioned property of PROC REPORT to construct a report exclusively by line, combined with the habit of regarding all ANALYSIS and calculated variables as legible for a subtotal. Although we would intuitively calculate all subtotals through column addition, PROC REPORT only does that for the ANALYSIS variables. The subtotals for the calculated variables will still be calculated at the row level, on the total row with what is there in the QUANTITY and PRICE columns.

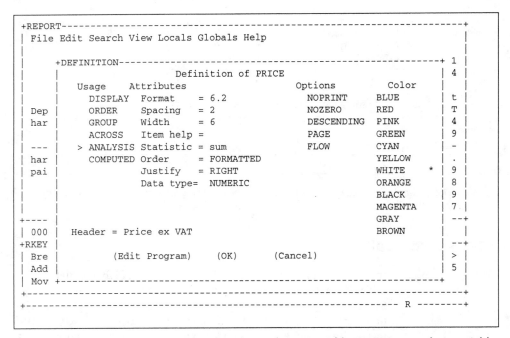

```
+REPORT--------------------------------------------------------------------+
| File Edit Search View Locals Globals Help                                |
|                                                                          |
|     +DEFINITION-------------------------------------------------------+ 1 |
|     |                    Definition of PRICE                          | 4 |
|     | Usage    Attributes                   Options        Color      |   |
|     | DISPLAY  Format    = 6.2                NOPRINT       BLUE       | t |
| Dep |   ORDER  Spacing   = 2                  NOZERO        RED        | T |
| har |   GROUP  Width     = 6                  DESCENDING    PINK       | 4 |
|     |  ACROSS  Item help =                    PAGE          GREEN      | 9 |
| --- | > ANALYSIS Statistic = sum              FLOW          CYAN       | - |
| har |  COMPUTED Order    = FORMATTED                        YELLOW     | . |
| pai |          Justify   = RIGHT                            WHITE   *  | 9 |
|     |          Data type=  NUMERIC                          ORANGE     | 8 |
|     |                                                      BLACK      | 9 |
|     |                                                      MAGENTA    | 7 |
+---- |                                                      GRAY       | --+
| 000 | Header = Price ex VAT                                BROWN      |   |
+RKEY |                                                                 | --+
| Bre |        (Edit Program)     (OK)      (Cancel)                    | > |
| Add |                                                                 | 5 |
| Mov +-------------------------------------------------------------+   |   |
+--------------------------------------------------------------------------+
+------------------------------------------------------------ R -------+
```

Figure 17.13: In a first attempt to get subtotals we change variable PRICE into analysis variable, with statistic: SUM.

```
+MESSAGES---------------------------------------------------------------+
| File View Globals                                                     |
|                                                                       |
|   NOTE: Variable PRICE is uninitialized.                              |
|   NOTE: Missing values were generated as a result of performing an    |
|         operation on missing values.                                  |
|         Each place is given by: (Number of times) at (Line):(Column). |
|         12 at 1:16    12 at 1:20    12 at 1:20                         |
+-----------------------------------------------------------------------+
|                  50030   nail 1.75       17    12.60       .       .       . |
|      --------                                 ------   -------   -------   ------- |
|   hardware                                    34.10       .       .       . |
|                                                                       |
|   paint          20060   glos white      17     8.40       .       .       . |
|                  20100   acrylwhite       8    12.70       .       .       . |
|                  21090   brush 2x1        9     4.50       .       .       . |
+-----------------------------------------------------------------------+
|   00001                                                               |
+RKEYS------------------------------------------------------------------+
|   Break     <F2>        Pageback  <F4>      Page      <F5>      Define     <F6> |
|   Add_right <F9>        Add_below <F13>     Delete    <F14>     CShrink    <F15 |
|   Move      <F18>                                                      |
+-----------------------------------------------------------------------+
+----------------------------------------------------------- R --------+
```

Figure 17.14: By changing PRICE into an analysis variable, PRICE is no longer available for computations. Now you should refer to PRICE.SUM. Note that there is now a subtotal for PRICE, which is of course absurd.

```
+REPORT-----------------------------------------------------------------+
| File Edit Search View Locals Globals Help                             |
|                                                                       |
|              The SAS System, Version 6.08                    1        |
|                              20:26 Saturday, June 11, 1994            |
|                                                                       |
|                                      Price   Price   Amount   Amount  |
|   Departm.  ART_NBR  Descript.  Quant.  ex VAT  inc VAT  ex VAT  inc VAT |
|   hardware   50010   screw 1x5      15   21.50   25.26   322.50  378.90 |
|              50030   nail 1.75      17   12.60   14.81   214.20  251.77 |
|      --------                            ------  -------  -------  ------- |
|   hardware                               34.10   40.07       .       . |
|                                                                       |
|   paint      20060   glos white     17    8.40    9.87   142.80  167.79 |
|              20100   acrylwhite      8   12.70   14.92   101.60  119.36 |
|              21090   brush 2x1       9    4.50    5.29    40.50   47.61 |
+-----------------------------------------------------------------------+
|   00001                                                               |
+RKEYS------------------------------------------------------------------+
|   Break     <F2>        Pageback  <F4>      Page      <F5>      Define     <F6> |
|   Add_right <F9>        Add_below <F13>     Delete    <F14>     CShrink    <F15 |
|   Move      <F18>                                                      |
+-----------------------------------------------------------------------+
+----------------------------------------------------------- R --------+
```

Figure 17.15: By changing PRICE into an analysis variable we get a subtotal on both price columns, but there are still no subtotals in the amount columns, because QUANTITY is no analysis variable and therefore has no subtotal.

Cumulative variables

Nevertheless, it is still possible to calculate subtotals. For this we are going to add up the amount variables ourselves in a couple of new computed variables, which however will not be displayed on the screen. To do so we expand the calculation rules for the amount variables with a SUM statement (figure 17.17).

If you are going to calculate the subtotals in this manner, you must also initialize the computed (total) variables at the beginning of each group. For this you give the BREAK command on the Department column (ART_CAT variable): cursor on the appropriate column and press the BREAK function key, or first key Enter and then go to the EDIT pull down menu.

To initialize the total variables 'Break Before' is selected. Choose "Suppress" for the break before section since it should not be visible in the report. In the compute window however TOT_EX and TOT_IN are set to 0. By way of a second BREAK command and a 'Break After', we come back to the definition of the break line after each department for printing the subtotals. This we can do by making, at this moment, AMNT_EX equal to TOT_EX and AMNT_IN equal to TOT_IN. This copying of the totals back to the original amount variables also has to do with the fact that REPORT processes by line. AMNT_EX and AMNT_IN will be printed in the totals lines.

At this moment the report is as shown in figure 17.18. We came to the point where the subtotals are correctly printed, but a few 'cosmetic errors' still cling to the report: first, warnings are given during execution for missing values and, second, there is still a line under PRICE INCL. VAT, as if there should be a total there.

```
+REPORT----------------------------------------------------------------------+
| File Edit Search View Locals Globals Help                                  |
|                                                                            |
|                     The SAS System, Version 6.08                    1 |
|                                           20:26 Saturday, June 11, 1994 |
|                                                                            |
|                                   Price    Price    Amount   Amount |
| Departm.    ART_NBR  Descript.   Quant.  ex VAT  inc VAT   ex VAT  inc VAT |
| hardware     50010   screw 1x5      15   21.50    25.26   322.50       . |
|              50030   nail 1.75      17   12.60    14.81   214.20       . |
|                                                                            |
| --------                         ------  ------  -------  -------  ------- |
| hardware                            32   34.10    40.07  1091.20       . |
|                                                                            |
| paint        20060   glos white     17    8.40     9.87   142.80       . |
|              20100   acrylwhite      8   12.70    14.92   101.60       . |
|              21090   brush 2x1       9    4.50     5.29    40.50       . |
+----------------------------------------------------------------------------+
| 00001                                                                      |
+RKEYS-----------------------------------------------------------------------+
| Break       <F2>       Pageback  <F4>       Page     <F5>      Define   <F6> |
| Add_right <F9>         Add_below <F13>      Delete   <F14>     CShrink  <F15 |
| Move        <F18>                                                           |
+-------------------------------------------------------- R  -------+
```

*Figure 17.16: By changing QUANTITY and PRICE into analysis variables, subtotals do appear. For the QUANTITY and PRICE columns they are meaningless, although they are mathematically correct. The subtotal of amount excl. VAT is created by a row calculation: total quantity * total price. So this is apparently not the right way to do it!*

```
+REPORT----------------------------------------------------------------------+
| File Edit Search View Locals Globals Help                                  |
|                                                                            |
|     +DEFINITION-------------------------------------------------------+ 1 |
|     |                  Definition of AMNT_IN                          | 4 |
|     |  Usage    Attributes                  Options        Color      |   |
|     |  DISPLAY  Format    = 7.2             NOPRINT        BLUE        |   |
+COMPUTE---------------------------------------------------------------------+
| File View Globals                                                          |
|                                                                            |
| 00001 AMNT_IN = QUANTITY * PR_INC;                                         |
| 00002 TOT_IN = SUM(TOT_IN,AMNT_IN);                                        |
| 00003                                                                      |
| 00004                                                                      |
| 00005                                                                      |
| 00006                                                                      |
| 00007                                                                      |
| 00008                                                                      |
| 00009                                                                      |
| 00010                                                                      |
| 00011                                                                      |
| 00012                                                                      |
+-------------------------------------------------------- R  -------+
```

Figure 17.17: In our case we have to do the calculation of the subtotals ourself. With each detail line we sum the amount in the variable TOT_IN (similar also TOT_EX). Of course we have to reset these variables back to 0 at the beginning of each department.

```
+REPORT--------------------------------------------------------------------+
| File Edit Search View Locals Globals Help                                 |
|                                                                           |
|                    The SAS System, Version 6.08                    1 |
|                                      20:26 Saturday, June 11, 1994 |
|                                                                           |
|                                                                           |
|                                  Price    Price   Amount   Amount |
|  Departm.    ART_NBR  Descript.   Quant.  ex VAT  inc VAT  ex VAT  inc VAT |
|  hardware     50010   screw 1x5      15   21.50    25.26   322.50   378.90 |
|               50030   nail 1.75      17   12.60    14.81   214.20   251.77 |
|  --------                                        -------  -------  ------- |
|  hardware                                             .    536.70   630.67 |
|                                                                           |
|  paint        20060   glos white     17    8.40     9.87   142.80   167.79 |
|               20100   acrylwhite      8   12.70    14.92   101.60   119.36 |
+---------------------------------------------------------------------------+
| 00001                                                                     |
+RKEYS----------------------------------------------------------------------+
|  Break      <F2>       Pageback   <F4>      Page     <F5>      Define   <F6>  |
|  Add_right  <F9>       Add_below  <F13>     Delete   <F14>     CShrink  <F15> |
|  Move       <F18>                                                         |
+---------------------------------------------------------------------------+
+-------------------------------------------------------------- R --------+
```

Figure 17.18: It's there! The correct subtotals for the amount columns. But still the result is not satisfying: There are warnings for missing values and in the column "Price inc VAT" you find a line as if that should be added as well.

Do-it-yourself break lines

To solve these last problems, you might choose to set up all the break lines yourself. First, again give the BREAK command on ART_CAT and deselect making summaries and overline. Then open the compute window for the break line (figure 17.20) and create the break line using LINE statements.

The LINE statement is best compared to the PUT statement of the DATA step; you can put fixed segments of text or variables in break sections with it. The first LINE statement creates the dividing line, however only in the places where they should go. For this use the 'multiply modifier': 8*'-' gives the instruction 'print a dash 8 times', thus: '--------'. Then in the second LINE statement the variables are printed which go in the break lines. This is done in pointer notation, as is familiar from the PUT statement: 'pointer-variable-format'.

By constructing break lines in this manner, we have the totals the way we wanted them. Now only the missing values have to be worked out, as we were warned in figure 17.21. These arise because PROC REPORT' executes the calculation in the compute blocks for each report line, thus also for the break lines where there are no values for QUANTITY and PRICE. The solution is simple: go back to the DEFINE window for the calculation variables and from there to the COMPUTE window and place the calculation in an IF statement, for example:

```
IF PRICE NE . THEN PR_INCL=PRICE*1.175;.
```

With that, this phase of the report construction is complete.

```
+REPORT-------------------------------------------------------------------------+
| File Edit Search View Locals Globals Help                                      |
|                                                                                |
+BREAK-----------------------------------+ ersion 6.08                       1  |
|      Breaking AFTER   ART_CAT           |       20:26 Saturday, June 11, 1994  |
|  Options                    Color       |                                      |
|     OVERLINE                BLUE        |                                      |
|     DOUBLE OVERLINE  (=)     RED        |   Price     Price    Amount   Amount |
|     UNDERLINE               PINK        |  ex VAT   inc VAT    ex VAT  inc VAT |
|     DOUBLE UNDERLINE (=)    GREEN        |   21.50     25.26    322.50   378.90 |
|                            CYAN         |   12.60     14.81    214.20   251.77 |
|   > SKIP                    YELLOW      |           -------   -------  ------- |
|     PAGE                    WHITE    *  |              .      536.70   630.67 |
|                            ORANGE       |                                      |
|     SUMMARIZE               BLACK       |    8.40      9.87    142.80   167.79 |
|     SUPPRESS                MAGENTA      |   12.70     14.92    101.60   119.36 |
|                            GRAY         |  -----------------------------------+
|                            BROWN        |                                      |
|                                         |  -----------------------------------+
|   (Edit Program)    (OK)    (Cancel)    |  Page      <F5>      Define    <F6>  |
|                                         |  Delete    <F14>     CShrink   <F15> |
+-----------------------------------------+                                      |
+-------------------------------------------------------------------------------+
+------------------------------------------------------------- R --------+
```

Figure 17.19: To limit the subtotals to only the amount columns we have to follow a different strategy. First of all we turn off the SUMMARIZE and OVERLINE option.

```
+REPORT---------------------------------------------------------------------+
| File Edit Search View Locals Globals Help                                 |
|                                                                           |
+BREAK----------------------------------+ ersion 6.08                    1 |
|       Breaking AFTER  ART_CAT          |       20:26 Saturday, June 11, 1994 |
| Options                      Color     |                                   |
|     OVERLINE                 BLUE      |                                   |
+COMPUTE--------------------------------------------------------------------+
| File View Globals                                                         |
|                                                                           |
| 00001 LINE @1 8*'-' 50*' ' 7*'-' '  ' 7*'-';                              |
| 00002 LINE @1 ART_CAT $8. @59 TOT_EX 7.2 @68 TOT_IN 7.2;                  |
| 00003                                                                     |
| 00004                                                                     |
| 00005                                                                     |
| 00006                                                                     |
| 00007                                                                     |
| 00008                                                                     |
| 00009                                                                     |
| 00010                                                                     |
| 00011                                                                     |
| 00012                                                                    |
+---------------------------------------------------------- R --------+
```

Figure 17.20: The LINE statement is a PROC REPORT specification statement. It functions similarly to the PUT statement of the DATA step. You can use it to print text or variables in the report at break sections.

```
+MESSAGES-------------------------------------------------------------------+
| File View Globals                                                         |
|                                                                           |
| NOTE: Missing values were generated as a result of performing an          |
|       operation on missing values.                                        |
|       Each place is given by: (Number of times) at (Line):(Column).       |
|       5 at 1:10    5 at 1:21    5 at 1:20    1 at 2:10    5 at 1:20        |
|       1 at 2:10                                                           |
+---------------------------------------------------------------------------+
| hardware      50010   screw 1x5      15   21.50   25.26   322.50   378.90 |
|               50030   nail 1.75      17   12.60   14.81   214.20   251.77 |
| --------                                              -------   ------- |
| hardware                                                536.70   630.67 |
|                                                                           |
| paint         20060   glos white     17    8.40    9.87   142.80   167.79 |
|               20100   acrylwhite      8   12.70   14.92   101.60   119.36 |
+---------------------------------------------------------------------------+
| 00001                                                                     |
+RKEYS----------------------------------------------------------------------+
| Break      <F2>      Pageback  <F4>     Page      <F5>     Define   <F6>  |
| Add_right <F9>       Add_below <F13>    Delete    <F14>    CShrink  <F15> |
| Move      <F18>                                                           |
+---------------------------------------------------------- R --------+
```

Figure 17.21: Now the subtotals are in the right columns and nowhere else. This only thing that is still required is to get rid of those "missing value" warnings.

Adding end lines

To fully complete the report, you want to add a total amount including VAT at the bottom and a count of the number of items in the orders list.

For this an RBREAK command must be given. This is not normally on a function key, so you have to do it with the EDIT pull down menu (figure 17.22). Setting up the lines is analogous to the earlier break lines (figure 17.23). Also the calculation lines in the AMOUNT including VAT compute window should be adjusted. You must declare a new variable N, in which the number of items is counted, and a variable ORD_AMNT, in which the total invoice amount is accumulated. The result is shown in figure 17.24.

```
+REPORT-----------------------------------------------------------------+
| File Edit Search View Locals Globals Help                             |
|     +------------+                                                    |
|     | Add_above  |       The SAS System, Version 6.08              1 |
|     | Add_below  |                        20:26 Saturday, June 11, 1994 |
|     | Add_left   |                                                    |
|     | Add_right  |                                                    |
|     | Break      |                      Price   Price   Amount  Amount |
| De  | CGrow      | R  Descript.   Quant. ex VAT  inc VAT ex VAT  inc VAT |
| ha  | CShrink    | 0  screw 1x5      15   21.50   25.26   322.50  378.90 |
|     | Define     | 0  nail 1.75      17   12.60   14.81   214.20  251.77 |
| --  | Delete     |                                       -------  ------- |
| ha  | Move       |                                       536.70  630.67 |
|     | RBreak     |                                                    |
| pa  | Refresh    | 0  glos white     17    8.40    9.87   142.80  167.79 |
|     | Span       | 0  acrylwhite      8   12.70   14.92   101.60  119.36 |
+--- +------------+ --------------------------------------------------+
| 00001                                                               |
+RKEYS------------------------------------------------------------------+
| Break       <F2>      Pageback  <F4>     Page     <F5>    Define   <F6> |
| Add_right <F9>      Add_below <F13>    Delete   <F14>   CShrink  <F15 |
| Move        <F18>                                                    |
+----------------------------------------------------------------------+
+-------------------------------------------------------- R -------+
```

Figure 17.22: To add something at the top or the bottom of the report, you choose the RBREAK command from the EDIT pull down menu.

```
+REPORT-------------------------------------------------------------------+
| File Edit Search View Locals Globals Help                               |
|                                                                         |
|         +BREAK--------------------------------+                     1  |
|         |          At bottom of report        | Saturday, June 11, 1994 |
|         | Options                   Color      |                         |
|         |    OVERLINE               BLUE       |                         |
+COMPUTE--+-------------------------------------+-------------------------+
| File View Globals                                                       |
|                                                                         |
| 00001 LINE 72*'=';                                                      |
| 00002 LINE 'Number of items ordered:' +1 N 3.;                         |
| 00003 LINE 'Total order amount incl. VAT:' +1 ORD_AMNT 7.2;            |
| 00004 LINE 72*'=';                                                      |
| 00005                                                                   |
| 00006                                                                   |
| 00007                                                                   |
| 00008                                                                   |
| 00009                                                                   |
| 00010                                                                   |
| 00011                                                                   |
| 00012                                                                   |
+------------------------------------------------------------- R -------+
```

Figure 17.23: Also lines in the title or at the bottom of the report can be created with LINE statements. Unless otherwise specified PROC REPORT centers the output of LINE statements.

```
+REPORT-------------------------------------------------------------------+
| File Edit Search View Locals Globals Help                               |
|                                                                         |
|                    The SAS System, Version 6.08                 3      |
|                                        20:26 Saturday, June 11, 1994   |
|                                                                         |
|                                                                         |
|                                    Price    Price   Amount   Amount    |
| Departm.    ART_NBR  Descript.  Quant.  ex VAT  inc VAT  ex VAT  inc VAT |
| ======================================================================= |
|                     Number of items ordered:  13                        |
|                 Total order amount incl. VAT: 3531.72                   |
| ======================================================================= |
|                                                                         |
|                                                                         |
|                                                                         |
+-------------------------------------------------------------------------+
| 00001                                                                   |
+RKEYS--------------------------------------------------------------------+
| Break       <F2>      Pageback  <F4>      Page      <F5>    Define   <F6> |
| Add_right <F9>      Add_below <F13>      Delete    <F14>    CShrink  <F15 |
| Move        <F18>                                                        |
+------------------------------------------------------------- R -------+
```

Figure 17.24: Underneath the total report we add the total number of items ordered and the total amount including VAT.

Saving and reusing the report definition

The report is now ready. The definition can now be stored for later use. You can do this in two ways: put the complete definition in a catalog in an SAS data library or write the SAS statements generated by PROC REPORT to an external file.

The first is done using the FILE pull down menu with the RSTORE option. When the option is selected, a new window becomes visible in which you can declare which data library and catalog you want the report definition to go into, and under what name.

The second possibility, writing out the source code is done via the LOCAL pull-down menu and the LIST option. The LIST option brings up the SOURCE window (figure 17.25). From this window the statements generated by PROC REPORT during the construction of the report are sent to an external file.

A stored report definition can be reused by declaring it in the PROC REPORT call. Say that the report outlined above has been stored in the catalog REPORTS of the data library with libref GEN, the same which contains the input data set, with the entry name DIY_REPT. With the following call of PROC REPORT, this report will be reloaded:

```
PROC REPORT DATA=GEN.ORDER REPORT=GEN.REPORTS.DIY_REPT;
```

The report can also be recalled after PROC REPORT is started, by using the RLOAD option under the FILE menu. You can add the NOWINDOWS option to the PROC statement if you don't want to execute in the interactive environment of PROC REPORT. It causes the procedure to be executed like every other procedure. In the Display Manager it means that the output of PROC REPORT appears in the standard output window, otherwise it will be sent to the SAS list file. Figure 17.26 shows the report once again, but this time not in an interactive environment. If you declare a new line size or page size in the PROC REPORT call, these will be used instead of those set out in the report definition. Be very careful of line statements: a different line size can confuse the pointer.

Another way of reusing the definition is to use the generated source code. Figure 17.25 shows how the source code which was developed during the interactive definition can be output to a separate file. This file can be brought back into programs with an %INCLUDE statement.

To leave PROC REPORT, use the QUIT option under the FILE menu.

```
+SOURCE-------------------------------------------------------------------+
| File View Globals                                                       |
|                                                                         |
| 00001 PROC REPORT LS=75  PS=20  SPLIT="/" CENTER ;                      |
| 00002 COLUMN  ART_CAT ART_NBR DESCRIPT QUANTITY PRICE PR_INC AMNT_EX AMNT_ |
| 00003                                                                   |
| 00004 DEFINE  ART_CAT / ORDER FORMAT= $8. WIDTH=8   SPACING=2   LEFT "Depa |
| 00005 ;                                                                 |
| 00006 DEFINE  ART_NBR / ORDER FORMAT= BEST9. WIDTH=9   SPACING=2   RIGHT |
| 00007 "ART_NBR" ;                                                       |
| 00008 DEFINE  DESCRIPT / DISPLAY FORMAT= $10. WIDTH=10  SPACING=2   LEFT |
| 00009 "Descript." ;                                                    |
| 00010 DEFINE  QUANTITY / DISPLAY FORMAT= BEST6. WIDTH=6   SPACING=2   RIGH |
| 00011 "Quant." ;                                                       |
| 00012 DEFINE  PRICE / DISPLAY FORMAT= 6.2 WIDTH=6   SPACING=2   RIGHT   |
| 00013 "Price ex VAT" ;                                                 |
| 00014 DEFINE  PR_INC / COMPUTED FORMAT= 7.2 WIDTH=7   SPACING=2   RIGHT |
+-------------------------------------------------------------------------+
+RKEYS--------------------------------------------------------------------+
| Break      <F2>       Pageback <F4>     Page      <F5>     Define   <F6> |
| Add_right <F9>       Add_below <F13>    Delete    <F14>    CShrink  <F15 |
| Move       <F18>                                                        |
+-------------------------------------------------------------------------+
+------------------------------------------------------------- R -------+
```

Figure 17.25: Via the LOCAL pull down menu in the Report window you can open the SOURCE window (option LIST). There you can see which statements PROC REPORT has generated during the construction of the report. The FILE menu enables you to save the source statements to an external file.

Report on the checkout time log

The second example comes from the data set used in chapter 11 (log of the check-out activities of a supermarket) and shows some other possiblities of PROC REPORT. In figure 11.1 you find a printout of a piece of this data set.

Because all variables in this data set are numeric, PROC REPORT assumes when nothing else is specified that all variables are ANALYSIS variables of type SUM. The result is one line:

```
        TIME     DURATION     CHECKOUT
       10478         1560         3850
```

We start PROC REPORT interactively and from this first version we make a report which shows the activity per check-out per hour in number of minutes and seconds that the check-out was actually used. This example will not be handled in as great detail as the previous one. It is assumed that the basic principles of PROC REPORT are now well understood.

```
                      The SAS System, Version 6.08                          1
                                      22:04 Saturday, June 11, 1994

                                       Price    Price    Amount    Amount
Departm.    ART_NBR  Descript.  Quant.  ex VAT   inc VAT  ex VAT    inc VAT
hardware     50010   screw 1x5      15   21.50    25.26   322.50    378.90
             50030   nail 1.75      17   12.60    14.81   214.20    251.77
--------                                          -------   -------
hardware                                          536.70    630.67

paint        20060   glos white     17    8.40     9.87   142.80    167.79
             20100   acrylwhite      8   12.70    14.92   101.60    119.36
             21090   brush 2x1       9    4.50     5.29    40.50     47.61
             22001   abbr p 180      3    0.90     1.06     2.70      3.18
--------                                          -------   -------
paint                                             287.60    337.94

sheet        11030   chipwood 8      8   12.95    15.22   103.60    121.76
             11070   plywood 18     16   64.50    75.79  1032.00   1212.64
--------                                          -------   -------
sheet                                            1135.60   1334.40

timber       10020   plank 3x5       4   10.60    12.46    42.40     49.84
             10030   plank 2x3       9    4.95     5.82    44.55     52.38
             10050   profile pl     12    7.80     9.17    93.60    110.04
--------                                          -------   -------
timber                                            180.55    212.26

tools        40090   el drill        4  149.00   175.07   596.00    700.28
             45030   handsaw         9   29.90    35.13   269.10    316.17
--------                                          -------   -------
tools                                             865.10   1016.45

================================================================================
                       Total items ordered:  13
                Total order amount incl. VAT: 3531.72
================================================================================
```

Figure 17.26: The same report definition, this time used non-interactively. The result is then written in the SAS list (or the Output window in the Display Manager).

Grouping observations

First we change the role of the TIME variable from ANALYSIS variable to GROUP variable.

With this we indicate that all observations with the same (formatted) value in the data set should be combined into a single line in the report.

```
+REPORT------------------------------------------------------------------+
| File Edit Search View Locals Globals Help                              |
|                                                                        |
|                   The SAS System, Version 6.08                    1 |
|                                       21:54 Saturday, June 11, 1994 |
|                                                                        |
|                 TIME  DURATION   CHECKOUT                              |
|                   9    59:33         190                               |
|                  10      168         437                               |
|                  11      212         585                               |
|                  12      154         481                               |
|                  13      120         468                               |
|                  14      124         353                               |
|                  15      173         522                               |
|                  16      195         628                               |
|                  17    85:01         186                               |
|                                                                        |
|                                                                        |
+------------------------------------------------------------------------+
+RKEYS-------------------------------------------------------------------+
| Break      <F2>       Pageback  <F4>     Page    <F5>    Define  <F6> |
| Add_right <F9>        Add_below <F13>    Delete  <F14>   CShrink <F15 |
| Move       <F18>                                                       |
+------------------------------------------------------- R --------+
```

Figure 17.27: By specifying TIME as a group variable, combined with the specification of the HOUR. format for TIME, we get a line per hour. DURATION still has the MMSS5. format, but for most hours the value is too high to be formatted correctly.

```
+REPORT------------------------------------------------------------------+
| File Edit Search View Locals Globals Help                              |
|                                                                        |
|                   The SAS System, Version 6.08                    1 |
|                                       21:54 Saturday, June 11, 1994 |
|                                                                        |
|                                CHECKOUT                                |
| TIME    1     2     3     4     5     6     7     8     9    10 |
|    9    6     4     6     9     6     4     2     2     2     2 |
|   10    9    14    14    11    15     9     7     4     6     5 |
|   11   19    13    12    13    19    13    10    12     7     5 |
|   12    7    13    16     9    10     5    13    10     7     5 |
|   13   12     6    16     9    12     8    14    11     4     3 |
|   14   10    13    12     8     7     7     7     6     5     3 |
|   15   13    15    14    13    10    16    10    14     3     3 |
|   16   10    12    18    19    15    15     9    12    10     5 |
|   17    5     3     3     7     6     3     7     4     1     0 |
|                                                                        |
+------------------------------------------------------------------------+
+RKEYS-------------------------------------------------------------------+
| Break      <F2>       Pageback  <F4>     Page    <F5>    Define  <F6> |
| Add_right <F9>        Add_below <F13>    Delete  <F14>   CShrink <F15 |
| Move       <F18>                                                       |
+------------------------------------------------------- R --------+
```

Figure 17.28: DURATION is temporarily removed from the report with the DELETE command. CHECKOUT is changed from analysis variable to across variable.

```
+REPORT------------------------------------------------------------------+
| File Edit Search View Locals Globals Help                              |
|                                                                        |
|                   The SAS System, Version 6.08                    1 |
|                                      21:54 Saturday, June 11, 1994 |
|                                                                        |
|                             CHECKOUT                                   |
|   TIME     1      2      3      4      +ADDING---------------------+  10 |
|     9      6      4      6      9      | ...below CHECKOUT         |   2 |
|    10      9     14     14     11      |                          |   5 |
|    11     19     13     12     13      |   > Dataset variable      |   5 |
|    12      7     13     16      9      |     Statistic             |   5 |
|    13     12      6     16      9      |     Header line           |   3 |
|    14     10     13     12      8      |                          |   3 |
|    15     13     15     14     13      |   (OK)      (Cancel)      |   3 |
|    16     10     12     18     19      |                          |   5 |
|    17      5      3      3      7      +--------------------------+   0 |
|                                                                        |
+------------------------------------------------------------------------+
+RKEYS-------------------------------------------------------------------+
| Break      <F2>       Pageback  <F4>      Page      <F5>     Define   <F6> |
| Add_right  <F9>       Add_below <F13>     Delete    <F14>    CShrink  <F15 |
| Move       <F18>                                                       |
+---------------------------------------------------------------- R -------+
```

Figure 17.29: With the ADD_BELOW command we can nest another variable underneath CHECKOUT. We bring DURATION back into the report this way.

At the same time we change the format from HHMM5., which is the format of the variable in the data set, to HOUR3. You see the result in figure 17.27. Also from figure 17.27 it is apparent that DURATION is still printed in MMSS., but in many cases only the minutes are displayed because of the magnitude of the values is too big.

ACROSS variables

As a second step, DURATION is temporarily removed from the report with the DELETE command and CHECKOUT is converted from an ANALYSIS variable to an ACROSS variable. What this accomplishes is that for each value of CHECKOUT a separate column is created. By adjusting the format and the column width, there is just enough room for all the check-outs (figure 17.28). The numbers under check-out now form a frequency count: how often the check-out has been visited during a particular hour.

If we now want to replace this frequency count with what we originally wanted - the calculation of the number of minutes per hour that the check-out was busy - we must bring the variable DURATION back into

the report. We do this with an ADD_BELOW command, after selecting
CHECKOUT (figure 17.29). We decide to add a data set variable and we
subsequently indicate DURATION in the DATASET VARS window.
Because DURATION is numeric, it will have already been marked as a
possible ANALYSIS variable, with SUM as statistic. We confirm this
choice and the report is ready. The result is shown in figure 17.30.

```
+REPORT-----------------------------------------------------------------+
| File Edit Search View Locals Globals Help                             |
|                                                                       |
|                     The SAS System, Version 6.08                    1 |
|                                      21:54 Saturday, June 11, 1994    |
|                                                                       |
|                              CHECKOUT                                 |
|             1       2       3       4       5       6       7       8       9      10 |
| TIME    Durat   Durat   Durat   Durat   Durat   Durat   Durat   Durat   Durat   Durat |
|    9     7:28    4:36   12:29   11:26    7:23    4:32    2:21    3:47    2:46    2:44 |
|   10    17:12   22:12   23:11   21:14   38:21   11:47   12:22    4:14   10:26    7:17 |
|   11    29:29   25:37   20:15   15:20   38:19   15:23   19:47   17:06   20:19   10:53 |
|   12     7:32   32:44   17:01   14:31   14:52    5:19   33:54   12:14   10:02    6:32 |
|   13    16:08    5:19   28:35   12:25   12:29    8:36   15:52   13:13    3:48    4:10 |
|   14    17:00   15:43   17:12   10:41   12:45   10:05   17:58   13:43    6:48    3:02 |
|   15    18:35   24:53   22:07   16:34   21:04   24:50   11:09   28:00    2:24    3:56 |
|   16     8:44   26:18   31:12   23:14   22:46   22:51   17:38   19:36   15:45    7:32 |
|   17     7:32    5:28   11:12   26:58    8:55    8:26   11:06    3:57    1:27    0:00 |
+-----------------------------------------------------------------------+
+RKEYS------------------------------------------------------------------+
| Break      <F2>        Pageback <F4>       Page        <F5>    Define    <F6> |
| Add_right  <F9>        Add_below <F13>     Delete      <F14>   CShrink   <F15 |
| Move       <F18>                                                      |
+------------------------------------------------------- R --------+
```

*Figure 17.30: DURATION has been added as analysis variable with a SUM statistic. This report
results, where it is easy to see for each hour how many minutes the check-outs were really active.
(To fit everything on the screen we assigned a label "Durat" to the variable DURATION.)*

PROC REPORT programming statements

PROC REPORT can also be used without the window environment, in
which case the report definition must be given in the form of SAS
statements. It is also possible to develop interactively and then to save
the source statements, as stated earlier. You can change them later on,
if necessary. In figure 17.31 and 17.32 the source code is printed which
was developed by the SAS System during the definition process of the
two examples in the first half of this chapter.

```
PROC REPORT LS=75  PS=20  SPLIT="/" CENTER ;
COLUMN  ART_CAT ART_NBR DESCRIPT QUANTITY PRICE
    PR_INC AMNT_EX AMNT_IN;

DEFINE  ART_CAT / ORDER FORMAT= $8. WIDTH=8
    SPACING=2 LEFT "Departm." ;
DEFINE  ART_NBR / ORDER FORMAT= 6. WIDTH=6
    SPACING=2 RIGHT "ART_NBR" ;
DEFINE  DESCRIPT / ORDER FORMAT= $10. WIDTH=12
    SPACING=2 LEFT "Descript." ;
DEFINE  QUANTITY / ORDER FORMAT= 6. WIDTH=6
    SPACING=2 RIGHT "Quant." ;
DEFINE  PRICE / DISPLAY FORMAT= 6.2 WIDTH=6
    SPACING=2 RIGHT "Price ex VAT" ;
DEFINE  PR_INC / COMPUTED FORMAT= 7.2 WIDTH=7
    SPACING=2 RIGHT "Price inc VAT" ;
DEFINE  AMNT_EX / COMPUTED FORMAT= 7.2 WIDTH=7
    SPACING=2 RIGHT "Amount ex VAT" ;
DEFINE  AMNT_IN / COMPUTED FORMAT= 7.2 WIDTH=7
    SPACING=2 RIGHT "Amount inc VAT" ;

COMPUTE  PR_INC;
    IF PRICE NE . THEN PR_INC = ROUND(PRICE*1.175,0.01);
ENDCOMP;

COMPUTE  AMNT_EX;
 IF QUANTITY NE . THEN DO;
     AMNT_EX = QUANTITY*PRICE;
     TOT_EX = SUM(TOT_EX,AMNT_EX);
 END;
ENDCOMP;

COMPUTE  AMNT_IN;
 IF QUANTITY NE . THEN DO;
     AMNT_IN = QUANTITY*PR_INC;
     TOT_IN = SUM(TOT_IN,AMNT_IN);
     ORD_AMNT = SUM(ORD_AMNT,AMNT_IN)
     N +1;
 END;
ENDCOMP;
```

Figure 17.31 (part 1): The source that has been generated by PROC REPORT during the definition of the first sample report. Note the sequence in build up: first the definition of the columns and their variables. Then the related compute blocks and finally the break sections and their compute blocks.

```
BREAK BEFORE ART_CAT / SUPPRESS ;
BREAK AFTER ART_CAT / SKIP ;
COMPUTE BEFORE ART_CAT ;
 TOT_IN=0;
 TOT_EX=0;
ENDCOMP;
COMPUTE AFTER ART_CAT ;
 LINE @2 8*'-' 49*' ' 7*'-' '  ' 7*'-';
 LINE @2 ART_CAT $8. @59 TOT_EX 7.2 @68 TOT_IN 7.2;
ENDCOMP;

RBREAK AFTER  / ;

COMPUTE AFTER ;
 LINE 72*'=';
 LINE 'Number of items ordered:' +1 N 3.;
 LINE 'Total order amount incl. VAT:' +1 ORD_AMNT 7.2;
 LINE 72*'=';
ENDCOMP;
```

Fig 17.31 (part 2)

```
PROC REPORT LS=76  PS=24  SPLIT="/" CENTER ;
COLUMN  TIME ( CHECKOUT,( DURATION ) );

DEFINE  TIME / GROUP FORMAT= hour3. WIDTH=3
 SPACING=0 RIGHT "TIME" ;
DEFINE  CHECKOUT / ACROSS FORMAT= BEST5. WIDTH=5
 SPACING=1 RIGHT "CHECKOUT" ;
DEFINE  DURATION / SUM FORMAT= MMSS5. WIDTH=5
 SPACING=2 RIGHT "Durat" ;
```

Figure 17.32: The source code of the second example. Note the nesting of CHECKOUT and DURATION in the COLUMN statement.

The PROC REPORT statement

PROC REPORT begins of course with the PROC statement. In this PROC statement the general attributes for the use of PROC REPORT are given. The most important options in the PROC statement are listed in figure 17.33. There are more options available for special situations, for which you can refer to the REPORT Guide.

DATA = libref.dataset	Name of input data set.
REPORT = libref.catalog.entry	Name of input report definition
OUTREPT = libref.catalog.entry	Name of output report definition
PANELS=n	Number of report columns per page (compare phone book, don't confuse with columns in the report)
PROMPT	Activates PROMPT mode during interactive report creation
WINDOWSI NOWINDOWS	Specifies whether or not PROC REPORT will function in a window environment and thus enabling interactive creation.
LS=	Linesize (from 64 to 256)
PS=	Pagesize (from 15 to 32767)
SPLIT='character'	Character on which titles are split over more lines. The split character is not printed in the title. Default: '/'.
CENTER/ NOCENTER	Specifies whether the report will be centered on the output page. It overrules settings in the report definition or system option.

Figure 17.33: The most important options of the PROC REPORT statement.

The COLUMN statement

After the PROC REPORT statement comes the definition of the columns. In our case this is a simple summing up of the variables which are to be used. In this phase it is not yet necessary to distinguish between GROUP, ORDER, COMPUTED and so on. COMPUTED variables must be declared insofar as they appear in columns. Computed variables for 'internal use' need not be declared. Nesting is declared by separating the variables with a comma. Eventually parentheses are used to make it clear what belongs to what. Nesting of a variable with a statistic can also occur; BUDGET,MEAN, for example, means that PROC REPORT must give the average for the budget for each line which appears in the report.

In the COLUMN statement also headers which will be spanned over several columns are declared. For this the header and the variables for the columns concerned are put in parentheses, for example ("Overview per &SYSDATE" PRICE QUANTITY) puts the header "Overview per date" above the columns for PRICE and QUANTITY. In case the header is shorter than the width of the columns it has to span, the header can be 'filled out' with a repetition sign. These repetition signs are -, =, _, *, +, or the pairs <> and ><. The repetition signs must be entered at the beginning and end of the header.

The DEFINE statement

Next comes the DEFINE statement, in which the role of each column variable and its format are declared. The form is:

```
DEFINE variable / specifications;
```

in which the variable indicates the column variable. The first specification concerns the role of the variable, as given in figure 17.34.

After the indication of the role of the variable, the display attributes are given, beginning with FORMAT= followed by the format to be used, WIDTH= with the number of positions to be used for the column and SPACING= to give the space between this column and the previous column. Here too comes the statistic keyword which indicates which statistic is to be calculated for an ANALYSIS variable.

ACROSS	Each (formatted) value creates a separate column in the report. Typically used in periodic reports, e.g. a column for first quarter results, a column for second quarter results etc. while quarter is derived from a plain date variable, formatted with QTR format.
ANALYSIS	Specifies that the variable is an analysis variable. You should also specify a statistic keyword to indicate which analysis to perform.
COMPUTED	The variable is not coming from the input data set, but is computed within PROC REPORT.
DISPLAY	Produces a row in the report for each observation in the data set.
GROUP	Defines groups of observations with a unique value of the group variable and tries to consolidate all observations of a group into one row. Cannot be combined with ORDER.
ORDER	Sorts the report according to this variable. The sort sequence can be: INTERNAL, FORMATTED (default value), DATA (sequence in the data set) and FREQ (descending order of frequency of values), e.g. ORDER=INTERNAL.

Figure 17.34: The role of a variable in the report is defined in the DEFINE statement. This table defines the possibilities.

After the column format come any options needed, including also the ORDER= option as described earlier (refer also to figure 71.34). In addition you can specify, among others: DESCENDING or PAGE (which forces a 'vertical page break' before the column involved).

The last three items which appear are the specification for justifying (LEFT, RIGHT, CENTER), the header and the color, insofar as these apply.

Compute blocks

After the DEFINE comes the COMPUTE statements which set up the COMPUTE blocks for the calculation of the COMPUTED variables. Each calculation goes in a separate COMPUTE block, that begins with the COMPUTE statement and ends with the ENDCOMP statement. In the COMPUTE statement goes the name of the variable to be computed. The statements in the COMPUTE block need no further explanation; they are normal DATA step statements.

BREAK statement

If BREAKs are defined in the report, BREAK statements now follow to set up the BREAK section. Any calculations which must take place during the break sections come after the BREAK statements and refer to them.

The BREAK statement declares when the BREAK is to take place and how it should be indicated in the report. In this case we have a BREAK BEFORE ART_CAT, which produces no visible output and a BREAK AFTER ART_CAT, which declares that a line is to be skipped (SKIP). No OL or UL is declared and also no SUMMARIZE, because in this report the structure of the BREAK line is totally controlled by the LINE statements in the COMPUTE blocks which belong to the BREAKs. The options in the BREAK statements are listed in figure 17.35.

After the BREAK statements follow their COMPUTE blocks. In the COMPUTE statement you declare if the block involved is to be executed at the beginning or the end of a section, just by declaring BEFORE or AFTER in the BREAK statement. The COMPUTE block is executed only once in combination with the BREAK.

PAGE	Start a new page after the break section.
SKIP	Skip a line after the break section.
OL, DOL	Draws a separator line above the break section. OL single (-), DOL double (=).
UL, DUL	Same as OL and DOL, but after the break section.
SUMMARIZE	Specifies that summary statistics have to be computed and printed in a break section.
SUPPRESS	Suppresses output of the break section.
COLOR =	Specifies the color to be used in case of a color screen.

Figure 17.35: Options for the creation of break sections.

A COMPUTE BEFORE or a COMPUTE AFTER without the declaration of a BREAK variable sets up a COMPUTE block which is to be executed once at the beginning or the end of a report. These blocks are preceded by an RBREAK statement, which is equivalent to the BREAK statement, only no variable is declared here.

With BREAK lines it is important to be very aware of the processing order: first of all the overline (OL, DOL), then the summary line (SUMMARIZE), then UL/DUL specifications, then lines created with LINE statements in the COMPUTE block and finally the SKIP or PAGE.

LINE statement

In the COMPUTE block a statement can be used which does not appear in the DATA step: the LINE statement. The LINE statement is best compared to the PUT statement. The LINE statement prints a line in the report. It is used like the PUT statement in pointer mode, thus an item to be printed (a variable or a piece of text) is always preceded by a pointer (both the @ and the + pointer can be used) and followed by a format, insofar as it applies. COMPUTED variables where no format is specified are printed according to the default format in the PROC statement, in general BEST9. An extra possibility is printing text with a repeat factor; for example 5*'=' prints =====. Multiple specifications can appear one after the other in the LINE statement.

Each subsequent LINE statement will print on the following line. The 'trailing @', familiar from the PUT statement, is not supported by the LINE statement.

Examples:

```
LINE ' ';               Prints an empty line
LINE 80*'_';            Prints an underlining
LINE @25 MY_VAR 10.2;   Prints the variable MY_VAR from position
                        25 with format 10.2
```

'Traffic lighting'

When PROC REPORT is used on a color screen, the color of a field can be controlled from a COMPUTE block, by means of the CALL DEFINE statement. The form is:

```
CALL DEFINE(column, attribute, value);
```

in which the column specification consists of the name of the column, the attribute specification indicates the type of attribute (e.g. 'COLOR' or 'HIGHLIGHT') and the value specification tells the setting for the attribute. It could be used as follows:

```
IF PROFIT > 0 THEN
    CALL DEFINE('PROFIT','COLOR','GREEN');
    ELSE CALL DEFINE('PROFIT','COLOR','RED');
```

The attributes which can be declared are: COLOR, FORMAT, BLINK, HIGHLIGHT, RVSVIDEO. For the last three the value is 0 for off and 1 for on. With CALL DEFINE you can also execute command line commands. With this you can realize so-called 'Drill Down': Select a particular report item and then give an EXECUTE command. This generates a RLOAD command to pull up a detail report. In the foregoing example a detail report of the profit components could be pulled up with:

```
CALL DEFINE('PROFIT','COMMAND',
                    'RLOAD libref.catalog.report');
```

This line goes in the COMPUTE block with the PROFIT variable.

Exercises

1. On the basis of the climatic data that was used in chapter 6, exercise 3, make a report in which the maximum and minimun temperature per month is mentioned and an average for the states, as in the example below:

```
       >>>>>>>>>>>>>>>>>>>>>>>>>>>>month<<<<<<<<<<<<<<<<<<<<<<<<<<<<<<
            JAN         FEB         MAR         APR         MAY         JUN
        min. max.   min. max.   min. max.   min. max.   min. max.   min. max.
State   temp temp   temp temp   temp temp   temp temp   temp temp   temp temp
NJ      -0.3  8.7   -9.4  3.8    7.1 16.3    6.9 13.5    8.9 19.6   12.7 24.8
OR       0.2  9.3   -8.9  5.1    6.6 15.1    9.5 14.5   11.5 17.9   17.8   26
        ==== ====   ==== ====   ==== ====   ==== ====   ==== ====   ==== ====
        -.05    9   -9.2 4.45   6.85 15.7    8.2   14   10.2 18.7   15.3 25.4
```

CHAPTER 18

Support Routines

Introduction

Program development and management often involve activities of a universal supporting nature, such as page numbering, data set sorting and so on. Support routines and procedures have already been covered in several sections of this book, such as PROC DATASETS and PROC CATALOG (chapter 10) and PROC SORT (chapter 4). In this chapter we shall bring together a number of others, both procedures and other routines.

SAS options

SAS options define the SAS processing environment. Installing the SAS System involves setting hundreds of parameters related to the host environment. Fortunately, few of these are of direct concern to the user. The majority is set up by the responsible software consultant or simply copied from the default settings which SAS Institute provides with the installation material. A limited number are of interest and will be covered here.

The options split into two main groups: options to be set at SAS session startup and options that can be changed during the session. The latter can be done with the OPTIONS statement or with the OPTIONS command in the Display Manager.

PROC OPTIONS

To see which options have been set in the system, you can use PROC OPTIONS. This procedure recognizes no specification statements. The most common form is simple:

```
PROC OPTIONS;
```

PROC OPTIONS then produces a complete list of all options, grouped into three categories: SESSION, CONFIGURATION and HOST. The first group consists of those options which can be set during a session or the execution of a SAS program, the second group contains options which have to be specified at SAS System startup and the third group contains options dedicated to a specific system environment and could be part of both the first and second group as well. Many options have only a yes/no choice. This is usually given by specifying NO before the option name, for example MPRINT and NOMPRINT.

The list of options does not get printed in the SAS list, but in the log.

In the PROC OPTIONS statement the option SHORT can be given, which returns only the current settings without any description of the option.

AUTOEXEC= fileref	Fileref for file with SAS statements which will be executed at the start-up of a SAS session.
CENTER	Centers the placement of output.
DATE	Prints date and time at the top of log and output pages.
FMTSEARCH= libref	Specifies the libref (or librefs) of permanent format libraries.
LINESIZE=n	Specifies line length for log and output. Value: 64 - 256.
MAUTOSOURCE	Activates Autocall facility.
MISSING= "character"	Determines character used when printing numeric missing values. Default is a period.
MLOGIC	Writes debugging information to the log for testing macros.
MPRINT	Prints SAS source which results from macro execution.
NOTES	Prints NOTE lines in the log.
NUMBER	Prints page numbers in output.
OBS=n | MAX	Indicates maximum number of observations to be processed. Use, for example, OBS=100 during development, MAX during production.
PAGENO=n	Resets the page number for the next output page.
PAGESIZE=n	Number of output lines per page, between 15 and 32767.
SASAUTOS= fileref	Specifies the fileref (or filerefs) for Autocall libraries.
SOURCE	Writes the SAS source statements to the log.
SOURCE2	Writes the lines that are included in the program via a %INCLUDE statement to the log.
SYMBOLGEN	Prints the results of symbolic resolution (resolution of macro variables) to the log.
USER= libref	Defines the library reference for the default data library. Data sets in this library need not be preceded by a libref indication.

Figure 18.1: Some of the hundreds of system options of the SAS System. Most options are primarily for system management tasks, the above are likely to be changed by users occasionally. The AUTOEXEC option is to be used during start-up of a SAS session; the others can be changed during a SAS session with the OPTIONS statement. The opposite of the options without a parameter can be reached by putting NO in front of it, e.g. NOCENTER.

The OPTIONS statement

Most options can be declared in the OPTIONS statement and can be changed as needed during the session or the program run. A small number must be declared at SAS system startup. The specification goes like this:

```
OPTIONS NODATE
        PAGENUMBER=125
        SASAUTOS=(SASAUTOS,MYMACLIB);
```

All options have a default value. In most cases this is such that no other value is needed. The options which will be most often changed or set by the user are listed in figure 18.1. For the dozens of other options, refer to the Language Guide.

FORMATs

Permanent formats

In chapter 9 the concept 'format' was already introduced together with PROC FORMAT which can be used to create them. Formats created with PROC FORMAT are stored in catalogs. Default is the catalog FORMATS in the data library WORK. They will then be lost at the end of the program or session. It is also possible to save formats in a permanent library. For this, declare it in the PROC FORMAT statement:

```
PROC FORMAT LIBRARY=libref;
```

However these formats are not automatically available in SAS programs. To make them available, two solutions are imaginable:

1. With PROC CATALOG copy the desired formats to the WORK.FORMATS catalog.

2. Enter the libref for the permanent format library in the FMTSEARCH option:

```
OPTIONS FMTSEARCH= (libref1 libref2 ...)
```

In an environment where multiple users can use the permanent formats at the same time, the first variant is preferred. With that you prevent one user from holding the format library for a longer time, making it difficult to bring in modifications:

```
LIBNAME MYFMTS 'datalibrary' ACCESS=READONLY;
PROC CATALOG CAT=MYFMTS.FORMATS;
COPY OUT=WORK.FORMATS;
SELECT numeric formats/ENTRYTYPE=FORMAT;
SELECT character formats/ENTRYTYPE=FORMATC;
RUN;
LIBNAME MYFMTS CLEAR;
```

Be careful not to declare formats with the $ sign in SELECT statements. From the entry type the SAS System knows whether a character or numeric format is to be copied. Should no SELECT statements follow the COPY statement, all members of the catalog are copied.

In the second variant formats are sought in the order in which the data libraries have been declared. That is, if multiple versions of the same format are available, only the first one found is applied. In contrast with the first method, the format library is now retained for the whole program or session.

The WORK library does not have to be specified: this is always sought first. If you however declare WORK in the list, then the WORK.FORMATS catalog will be referenced 'in turn' following the FMTSEARCH list.

The FMTLIB option

To get a summary of the definition of a (permanent) format, the FMTLIB option can be declared in the PROC FORMAT statement. The formats to be presented can be subsequently given in SELECT or EXCLUDE statements:

```
PROC FORMAT LIBRARY=libref FMTLIB;
  SELECT formats;
```
or:
```
  EXCLUDE formats;
```

If SELECT or EXCLUDE statements are not present, then all formats in the library are printed.

The formats which were created in chapter 9 in connection with demonstrating PROC FORMAT are recorded in a permanent catalog. Figure 18.2 shows a printout of the result of FMTLIB on this catalog.

```
                  The SAS System, Version 6.08                          1
                                          12:15 Monday, June 13, 1994

-----------------------------------------------------------------------
|       FORMAT NAME: AGEGRP    LENGTH:    8   NUMBER OF VALUES:    6   |
|   MIN LENGTH:   1  MAX LENGTH:  40  DEFAULT LENGTH   8  FUZZ: STD   |
|--------------------------------------------------------------------|
|START            |END              |LABEL  (VER. 6.08    13JUN94:12:03:57)  |
|-----------------+-----------------+------------------------------------|
|               0|                1|Baby                                 |
|               2|                3|Infant                               |
|               4|                5|Toddler                              |
|               6|               12|Child                                |
|              13|               19|Teenager                             |
|              20|HIGH             |Adult                                |
-----------------------------------------------------------------------


-----------------------------------------------------------------------
|       FORMAT NAME: CREDIT    LENGTH:   11   NUMBER OF VALUES:    2   |
|   MIN LENGTH:   1  MAX LENGTH:  40  DEFAULT LENGTH  11  FUZZ: STD   |
|--------------------------------------------------------------------|
|START            |END              |LABEL  (VER. 6.08    20OCT92:22:54:40)  |
|-----------------+-----------------+------------------------------------|
|LOW              |                 |0<00.009,99 D        P    F   M100   |
|                 |0|HIGH            |00.009,99           P    F   M100   |
-----------------------------------------------------------------------


-----------------------------------------------------------------------
|       FORMAT NAME: EXCEPT    LENGTH:    5   NUMBER OF VALUES:    5   |
|   MIN LENGTH:   1  MAX LENGTH:  40  DEFAULT LENGTH   5  FUZZ: STD   |
|--------------------------------------------------------------------|
|START            |END              |LABEL  (VER. 6.08    20OCT92:22:54:40)  |
|-----------------+-----------------+------------------------------------|
|               1|                5|*                                    |
|               5<|              10|**                                   |
|              10<|              20|***                                  |
|              20<|              50|****                                 |
|              50<HIGH            |*****                                |
-----------------------------------------------------------------------
```

Figure 18.2 (part 1): The formats as created in chapter 9 as they are printed with the FMTLIB option of PROC FORMAT. Note the boundary specifications when value ranges are adjacent.

```
1                        The SAS System, Version 6.08                         2
                                              12:15 Monday, June 13, 1994

-----------------------------------------------------------------------------
|        FORMAT NAME: FEVER     LENGTH:     6    NUMBER OF VALUES:    1       |
|   MIN LENGTH:    1 MAX LENGTH:  40   DEFAULT LENGTH   6   FUZZ: STD         |
|---------------------------------------------------------------------------|
|START                |END                |LABEL   (VER. 6.08    13JUN94:12:03:57) |
|-----------------+-----------------+-----------------------------------------|
|            36.5|            37.5|Normal                                      |
-----------------------------------------------------------------------------


-----------------------------------------------------------------------------
|        FORMAT NAME: PHONE     LENGTH:    14    NUMBER OF VALUES:    1       |
|   MIN LENGTH:    1 MAX LENGTH:  40   DEFAULT LENGTH  14   FUZZ: STD         |
|---------------------------------------------------------------------------|
|START                |END                |LABEL   (VER. 6.08    13JUN94:12:03:57) |
|-----------------+-----------------+-----------------------------------------|
|               0|HIGH            | 999) 999 9999        P(  F   M1           |
-----------------------------------------------------------------------------
```

Figure 18.2 (part 2)

Generating formats

It quite often happens in practice that the information which is to be
recorded in a format exists already in a SAS data set or in an external file.
In that case there is no need to type in data as input for PROC FORMAT.
If the information is already in a SAS data set, then it can often be
processed using the CNTLIN option in PROC FORMAT:

```
PROC FORMAT CNTLIN=libref.dataset;
```

The SAS System expects certain variables in such a data set. At the least,
the following variables must be present:

FMTNAME: the name of the format to be created, preceded by a $ sign
for a character format.

START: the start value of the value range.

LABEL: the appropriate label.

If the format only recognizes value ranges of a single discrete value, then
no end value for the range needs to be given. Otherwise an END variable
must also be declared. This should then have a proper value in each
observation. In case use is made of the special value ranges OTHER,

LOW or HIGH in START or END, then the variable HLO must also be present: this normally has a missing value, but for observations where one of the special ranges occurs, this variable has the value O (OTHER), L (LOW), H (HIGH) or LH (LOW to HIGH).

To get a better feel for the structure of a CNTLIN data set, one can be created from an existing format by means of the CNTLOUT option:

```
PROC FORMAT CNTLOUT=libref.dataset;
    SELECT formatname;
```
or:
```
    EXCLUDE formatname;
```

The CNTLOUT data set contains more variables than the minimum for a CNTLIN data set. These extra variables can also be needed in CNTLIN data set, depending on the type of format to be made. As an example, figure 18.3 shows a printout of the CNTLOUT data set which goes with the format AGEGRP.

The variables START and END are both defined as $16. The values are in BEST16., thus right justified, except for the special value HIGH. This makes the START and END columns look different in the printout.

In case the input for a format is not yet in a SAS data set, a data set following CNTLIN specifications can, of course, be created in a DATA step using INFILE and INPUT statements.

OBS	FMTNAME	START	END	LABEL	MIN	MAX	DEFAULT	LENGTH	FUZZ	PREFIX	MULT	FILL	NOEDIT	TYPE	SEXCL	EEXCL	HLO
1	AGEGRP	0	1	Baby	1	40	8	8	1E-12	0			O	N	N	N	
2	AGEGRP	2	3	Infant	1	40	8	8	1E-12	0			O	N	N	N	
3	AGEGRP	4	5	Toddler	1	40	8	8	1E-12	0			O	N	N	N	
4	AGEGRP	6	12	Child	1	40	8	8	1E-12	0			O	N	N	N	
5	AGEGRP	13	19	Teenager	1	40	8	8	1E-12	0			O	N	N	N	
6	AGEGRP	20	HIGH	Adult	1	40	8	8	1E-12	0			O	N	N	N	H

Figure 18.3: The CNTLOUT data set as created from the format AGEGRP. The variables are the same as in the CNTLIN data set. Minimal requirements for the CNTLIN data set are the variables: FMTNAME, START and LABEL. In most cases you will also need END.

```
FILENAME TEMP 'temporary file';
DATA _NULL_;
   INFILE .... END=EOF;
   INPUT ....;
   FILE TEMP;
   IF _N_=1 THEN DO;
      PUT "PROC FORMAT;";
      PUT "VALUE formatname";
   END;
   PUT " ' " START " '-' " EIND " '=' " LABEL " ' ";
   IF EOF THEN DO;
      * put possible OTHER value ;
      PUT ";" ;
   END;
RUN;
%INCLUDE TEMP;
RUN;
FILENAME TEMP CLEAR;
```

Figure 18.4: This program generates a SAS format based on information in an external file. It assumes the start and end values of the value ranges to be in the variables START and END, and the label information in LABEL. The spaces in the PUT statement are added primarily for readibility, but are normally unwanted in practice, because they also lead to spaces in value ranges and labels.

Alternatively the source code for **PROC FORMAT** can be created directly. The kernel of a program to do this is printed in figure 18.4. In this program the source code for the **PROC FORMAT** is sent to the file TEMP. This file is afterwards retrieved with a %INCLUDE and with this the generated **PROC FORMAT** is executed.

PROC PRINTTO

PROC PRINTTO changes the default destination of the SAS log or the SAS list (procedure) output. In PROC PRINTTO the file is designated to which the SAS System should send the output concerned. The file designated in PROC PRINTTO to receive SAS output can be used for many purposes, for example:

1. store output permanently in a file for later print actions or microfiche creation;

2. sending output from different steps in a program to separate files for separate forwarding or postprocessing;

3.   reading output back in with INFILE and INPUT for further process-
     ing.

This last area of application is the least known, but it constitutes one of
the most powerful applications of PROC PRINTTO. Various procedures produce output on paper but not in a SAS data set, or they cannot
output all the information which appears on paper to a data set, or they
produce output in a layout other than the one desired. Then PROC
PRINTTO can be used to send the procedure output to a temporary file
so that it can be reread and processed in a later DATA step. An example
of this will be given in chapter 19 when discussing PROC FSBROWSE.

Designating destination of log and list.

There are three forms of PROC PRINTTO for getting output to a
destination other than the standard one:

```
PROC PRINTTO LOG=fileref;
PROC PRINTTO PRINT=fileref;
PROC PRINTTO UNIT=nn;
```

The first form sends the SAS log to the declared file; the other two forms
send the procedure output (SAS list) to the declared file. The form
UNIT=nn tells the SAS System that the output file has been allocated
with a fileref in the form FTnnF001. nn can in principle have a value
from 01 - 99. In V5 and in some implementations of Version 6 however,
several numbers have already been used by the SAS System. Therefore
we only recommend the use of numbers from 20 on.

In principle the SAS System always writes at the end of information
already present in the file. Should the file have to be emptied first, then
the option NEW comes after the fileref.

Be careful that the SAS System does not reset the page number to 1 when
it starts writing output to a new file. To do that, you must use the
OPTIONS statement:

```
OPTIONS PAGENO=1;
```

Resetting destination

The log file and list file can each be reset independently to its standard
destination:

```
PROC PRINTTO LOG=LOG;
PROC PRINTTO PRINT=PRINT;
```

By using PROC PRINTTO without any other options, both the log and the list file are reset to their standard destinations.

PROC TRANSPOSE

PROC TRANSPOSE "rotates" a SAS data set, which is to say that TRANSPOSE turns variables into observations and observations into variables. With TRANSPOSE you can create a certain level of independence between program and data. Now processing and presentation can be optimized separately from defining the data set for optimal efficiency. Figure 18.5 shows an example.

Dataset layout:

OBS	SALESREP	REGION	TURNOVER
1	X	A	7
2	Y	C	8
3	Y	D	5
4	Z	B	6

Transposition:

```
PROC TRANSPOSE DATA=... OUT=..;
    ID REGION;
    VAR TURNOVER;
    BY SALESREP;
```

Presentation form:

OBS	SALESREP	A	B	C	D
1	X	7	.	.	.
2	Y	.	.	8	5
3	Z	.	6	.	.

Figure 18.5: The data set has a compact vertical form, which makes it easy to add salesreps and regions. If you would store the data set in the layout as used for presentation you would have a lot of wasted space and adding regions would be problematic.

Specification statements

The three statements on which everything in PROC TRANSPOSE hinges are the ID statement, the VAR statement and the BY statement. The variables to be declared in these statements can be determined with the help of a few simple questions:

1.   *Which variable in the input data set contains (after formatting!) the variable names of the output data set?*

This variable is declared in the ID statement. From the question it is clear that this variable must have a unique value in each observation (per BY group) after formatting, since this becomes the name of the transposed variable. If the contents of the variable do not comply with the rules for variable names, the SAS System will adapt it by, among other things, replacing unacceptable characters with underscores. If the ID variable is numeric it is necessary to attach a prefix to its value, to change for example the value 3 into SCORE3 or the value 12 into SCORE12. Such a prefix is declared in the PROC statement with the PREFIX= option.

If the value of one of the variables can be used as a label for the new variable, then this can be declared in the IDLABEL statement:

```
IDLABEL variable;
```

2.   *Which variable(s) in the input data set contain(s) the value of the variable to be transposed?*

These variables are declared in the VAR statement. Now, in order to find out from which original variable the value originates, the SAS System adds the variable _NAME_ in the output data set. Should another variable name be desired here, the name must be given in the option NAME= in the PROC statement. If the VAR statement is left out, then all numeric variables which do not as yet have any other task (declared in an ID or BY statement) will be transposed.

3.   *For which group of observation is the value of the ID variable unique (forms the 'block' to be transposed)?*

This group of observations is designated in the BY statement. The BY statement means that the data set will not be transposed as a whole, but transposing will be by BY group.

Double transposition

There are situations where a data set cannot to be transposed at once into the desired form. An example of this follows.

Say that there are two groups of variables in a data set: X1 - X20 and Y1 - Y20. Of this data set, a vertical structure is to be made with 2 variables: X and Y. A simple transposition will not lead to the desired result. If X1 - X20 and Y1 - Y20 were declared in the VAR statement, all 40 variables would end up in a single variable. However by executing a PROC

TRANSPOSE twice, the first time for X1 - X20 and the second for Y1 - Y20, you create two data sets, which can then be combined in a one-to-one merge with the desired result.

Example: distance table

A distance table for a road map often contains city names both in the columns and the rows, so that a distance can always be determined in both directions. By means of PROC TRANSPOSE, this can be realized very simply from a straight distance data set. Figure 18.7 shows the input data set and the resulting distance table, and figure 18.6 the log of the program that produced this result.

The data has been read in a simple DATA step with CARDS input. Subsequently extra observations are generated. First for the return journey by exchanging FROM and TO. Then observations where FROM = TO and vice versa with MILE missing. These observations are used to construct the diagonal of the table. It is done for both FROM = TO and TO = FROM to be sure that every city is present. In our case Washington to Washington would be absent if we did not add these extra observations. This can result in double observations. These will be removed with the PROC SORT NODUPLICATES.

With the help of the questions listed on page 394, the PROC TRANSPOSE is constructed: which variable contains the names of the output variables? TO. So TO is specified in the ID statement. The city name, however, might be longer than 8 positions and will in that case be truncated by the SAS System. That is why we declare this variable also in an IDLABEL statement. Which variable contains the values to be transposed? MILE. Thus the VAR statement will be: VAR MILE;. Which variable marks the groups which will form the blocks to be transposed? FROM. And that then produces the BY statement.

The rest of the program will hardly require any explaining.

```
1                          The SAS System (6.08)
                                    12:44 Monday, June 13, 1994

NOTE: Copyright(c) 1989 by SAS Institute Inc., Cary, NC USA.
NOTE: SAS (r) Proprietary Software Release 6.08   TS405

NOTE: The initialization phase used 0.06 CPU seconds and 1092K.

NOTE: SAS job started on Monday 13JUN94 12:44 (199406131244)

1            /*-------------------------------------------------------*/
2            /*  DISTANCE TABLE USING PROC TRANSPOSE                   */
3            /*-------------------------------------------------------*/
4            DATA DISTANCE;
5            INPUT FROM $15. TO  $15. MILE;
6            CARDS;

NOTE: The data set WORK.DISTANCE has 6 observations and 3 variables.
NOTE: The DATA statement used 0.02 CPU seconds and 1759K.

13           RUN;
14           PROC PRINT;
15           TITLE 'INPUT DISTANCE TABLE';
16           RUN;

NOTE: The PROCEDURE PRINT printed page 1.
NOTE: The PROCEDURE PRINT used 0.01 CPU seconds and 1813K.

17           DATA EXPAND(DROP=TEMP);
18              SET DISTANCE;
19              * FIRST WRITE THE ORIGINAL OBSERVATION;
20              OUTPUT;
21              * EXCHANGE FROM AND TO, USING A TEMPORARY VARIABLE;
22              TEMP = FROM;
23              FROM = TO;
24              TO = TEMP;
25              OUTPUT;
26              * GENERATE OBSERVATION TO ITSELF;
27              TO = FROM;
28              MILE=.;
29              OUTPUT;
30              FROM = TEMP;
31              TO = TEMP;
32              OUTPUT;
33           RUN;

NOTE: The data set WORK.EXPAND has 24 observations and 3 variables.
NOTE: The DATA statement used 0.02 CPU seconds and 1909K.
```

Figure 18.6 (part 1): The first step reads in the distances. The second step generates additional observations for the return journey. Note the use of the TEMP variable.

```
2                          The SAS System (6.08)
                                   12:44 Monday, June 13, 1994

34          PROC PRINT;
35          TITLE 'INTERMEDIATE RESULT AFTER EXPANSION';
36          RUN;

NOTE: The PROCEDURE PRINT printed page 2.
NOTE: The PROCEDURE PRINT used 0.01 CPU seconds and 1909K.

37          PROC SORT NODUPLICATES;
38          BY FROM TO;

NOTE: SAS sort was used.
NOTE: 8 duplicate observations were deleted.
NOTE: The data set WORK.EXPAND has 16 observations and 3 variables.
NOTE: The PROCEDURE SORT used 0.01 CPU seconds and 2036K.

39          PROC TRANSPOSE OUT=TABLE(DROP=_NAME_);
40             ID TO;
41             IDLABEL TO;
42             VAR MILE;
43             BY FROM;
44          RUN;

NOTE: The data set WORK.TABLE has 4 observations and 5 variables.
NOTE: The PROCEDURE TRANSPOSE used 0.02 CPU seconds and 1984K.

45          PROC PRINT LABEL NOOBS;
46          TITLE 'FINAL RESULT';
47          RUN;

NOTE: The PROCEDURE PRINT printed page 3.
NOTE: The PROCEDURE PRINT used 0.01 CPU seconds and 1984K.

NOTE: The SAS session used 0.31 CPU seconds and 2060K.
NOTE: SAS Institute BV, 1217 KR Hilversum, The Netherlands
```

Figure 18.6: Duplicate observations are removed with PROC SORT. PROC TRANSPOSE does the rest.

```
                    INPUT DISTANCE TABLE                              1
                                       12:44 Monday, June 13, 1994

        OBS     FROM            TO          MILE

         1      NEW YORK        TORONTO      495
         2      NEW YORK        BOSTON       215
         3      BOSTON          TORONTO      582
         4      WASHINGTON      NEW YORK     236
         5      WASHINGTON      BOSTON       443
         6      WASHINGTON      TORONTO      494


              INTERMEDIATE RESULT AFTER EXPANSION                     2
                                       12:44 Monday, June 13, 1994

        OBS     FROM            TO           MILE

         1      NEW YORK        TORONTO       495
         2      TORONTO         NEW YORK      495
         3      TORONTO         TORONTO        .
         4      NEW YORK        NEW YORK       .
         5      NEW YORK        BOSTON        215
         6      BOSTON          NEW YORK      215
         7      BOSTON          BOSTON         .
         8      NEW YORK        NEW YORK       .
         9      BOSTON          TORONTO       582
        10      TORONTO         BOSTON        582
        11      TORONTO         TORONTO        .
        12      BOSTON          BOSTON         .
        13      WASHINGTON      NEW YORK      236
        14      NEW YORK        WASHINGTON    236
        15      NEW YORK        NEW YORK       .
        16      WASHINGTON      WASHINGTON     .
        17      WASHINGTON      BOSTON        443
        18      BOSTON          WASHINGTON    443
        19      BOSTON          BOSTON         .
        20      WASHINGTON      WASHINGTON     .
        21      WASHINGTON      TORONTO       494
        22      TORONTO         WASHINGTON    494
        23      TORONTO         TORONTO        .
        24      WASHINGTON      WASHINGTON     .
```

Figure 18.7 (part 1): From a simple table of cities and distances it is easy to generate a complete distance table. You start with generating extra observations and after that remove any duplicates. PROC TRANSPOSE creates the data set in the right shape which can be printed with PROC PRINT.

```
                        FINAL RESULT                              3
                                      12:44 Monday, June 13, 1994

                              NEW
        FROM          BOSTON   YORK   TORONTO   WASHINGTON

        BOSTON           .      215     582        443
        NEW YORK        215      .      495        236
        TORONTO         582     495      .         494
        WASHINGTON      443     236     494          .
```

Figure 18.7 (part 2)

PROC COMPARE

PROC COMPARE compares the contents of two SAS data sets and produces a report on the differences between the data sets and, ultimately, also produces an output data set. The comparison can go very far, particularly with number variables, in which a complete statistical analysis can take place with respect to the differences.

In its simplest form, it goes like this:

```
PROC COMPARE DATA=libref.dataset COMPARE=libref.dataset;
    ID variable(s);
```

If you want to write the information about the differences to an output data set, you should add the option OUT=libref.dataset to the PROC statement.

The ID and BY statements

The ID statement contains the variables which PROC COMPARE must use to compare the observations of the two data sets. Should there be no ID statement, PROC COMPARE compares the two data sets 1:1. That has the consequence that if a single observation from either of the two data sets is added or left out, none of the rest can be equated.

Also a BY statement is regularly used with PROC COMPARE, particularly if the data set is large. The comparison is then carried out by BY group, making it easier to survey.

The VAR and the WITH statement

By using a VAR statement, the comparison is limited to the variables which are declared in the statement; otherwise all variables not appearing in the ID statement will be compared.

If the corresponding variables in the two datasets do not have identical names, you can link them using the WITH statement. The VAR and WITH statement have identical form:

```
VAR variable1 variable2 ...;
WITH variable1 variable2 ...;
```

The lists of variables in these statements are linked 1:1, this means that the first variable in the VAR statement is linked to the first variable in the WITH statement, and so on. Should the list of variables in the WITH statement be shorter that the list in the VAR statement, then the extra variables will be considered to have the same name.

PROC COMPARE example

As an example, PROC COMPARE in its basic form will be applied to the ART_DES and NART_DES data set from chapter 8. We also make an output data set:

```
PROC COMPARE DATA=GEN.ART_DES COMPARE=GEN.NART_DES
             OUT=DIFFER;
     ID ART_NBR;
```

Figure 18.8 shows a printout of the output of this PROC COMPARE. It begins with a summary on the data set level. Then a summary of the differences on the variable level and the observation level. Finally comes a detail section where all differences are given on the observation level.

Figure 18.9 contains a printout of the standard data set which can be made by PROC COMPARE. Each compared observation is present, which is troublesome with a much larger data set. By using the option OUTNOEQUAL, the contents of the data set are limited to the observations which show differences.

There are many other options possible with PROC COMPARE to get more information about diagnosed differences. These options are used relatively little in practice. However if you have found differences between two data sets which are not so easy to explain, then the extra options would perhaps provide the extra information you need to track

down the causes of the differences. For these options, refer to the
Procedures Guide.

```
1                        The SAS System, Version 6.08                        1
                                         13:14 Monday, June 13, 1994

                              COMPARE Procedure
                 Comparison of GEN.ART_DES with GEN.NART_DES
                              (Method=EXACT)

                             Data Set Summary

     Dataset               Created          Modified   NVar    NObs

     GEN.ART_DES    06JUN94:13:03:15  06JUN94:13:14:21     3      13
     GEN.NART_DES   13JUN94:13:12:49  13JUN94:13:12:49     3      15


                           Variables Summary

              Number of Variables in Common: 3.
              Number of ID Variables: 1.


                          Observation Summary

         Observation        Base  Compare  ID

         First Obs             1        1   ART_NBR=10020
         First Unequal         3        3   ART_NBR=10050
         Last  Unequal        13       15   ART_NBR=50030
         Last  Obs            13       15   ART_NBR=50030

     Number of Observations in Common: 13.
     Number of Observations in GEN.NART_DEE but not in GEN.ART_DESE: 2.
     Total Number of Observations Read from GEN.ART_DESE: 13.
     Total Number of Observations Read from GEN.NART_DEE: 15.

     Number of Observations with Some Compared Variables Unequal: 4.
     Number of Observations with All Compared Variables Equal: 9.


                        Values Comparison Summary

      Number of Variables Compared with All Observations Equal: 0.
      Number of Variables Compared with Some Observations Unequal: 2.
      Total Number of Values which Compare Unequal: 4.
      Maximum Difference: 5.
```

Figure 18.8 (part 1): The standard output of PROC COMPARE starts with a comparison on the data set level, followed by a comparison on the variable level.

```
                    The SAS System, Version 6.08                    2
                                        13:14 Monday, June 13, 1994

                         COMPARE Procedure
              Comparison of GEN.ART_DES with GEN.NART_DES
                          (Method=EXACT)

              All Variables Compared have Unequal Values

                  Variable   Type  Len  Ndif   MaxDif

                  DESCRIPT   CHAR   10    1
                  PRICE      NUM     8    3     5.000



              Value Comparison Results for Variables
```

ART_NBR	||	Base Value DESCRIPT	Compare Value DESCRIPT
	||		
	||		
50030	||	nail 1.75	nail sp 2

ART_NBR	||	Base PRICE	Compare PRICE	Diff.	% Diff
	||				
	||				
10050	||	7.8000	8.1500	0.3500	4.4872
20060	||	8.4000	8.9500	0.5500	6.5476
45030	||	29.9000	24.9000	-5.0000	-16.7224

Figure 18.8 (part 2): After the summaries follow detailed comparisons.

```
                 The SAS System, Version 6.08                  3
                                       13:14 Monday, June 13, 1994

   OBS    _TYPE_    _OBS_    ART_NBR    DESCRIPT    PRICE

    1     DIF        1       10020     ..........    0.00
    2     DIF        2       10030     ..........    0.00
    3     DIF        3       10050     ..........    0.35
    4     DIF        4       11030     ..........    0.00
    5     DIF        5       11070     ..........    0.00
    6     DIF        6       20060     ..........    0.55
    7     DIF        7       20100     ..........    0.00
    8     DIF        8       21090     ..........    0.00
    9     DIF        9       22001     ..........    0.00
   10     DIF       10       40090     ..........    0.00
   11     DIF       11       45030     ..........   -5.00
   12     DIF       12       50010     ..........    0.00
   13     DIF       13       50030     .....XXXX.    0.00
```

Figure 18.9: The standard output data set of PROC COMPARE. For each compared variable the differences are indicated.

Autoexec routines

The SAS System can, if required, directly execute a program or a number of commands at startup. In this way you could execute a number of LIBNAME and FILENAME statements at the startup of the Display Manager, to make often-used libraries and files directly available.

To accomplish this, the program (or commands) are stored in a file. This file must be allocated before the startup of the SAS System. The fileref in this allocation will be included in the AUTOEXEC option at startup and through it the program will be executed as soon as the SAS System starts.

For each system environment there are a few differences in the way an AUTOEXEC file can be allocated. The system appendices in this book contain more information about this.

DATA step views

In chapter 10, the concept VIEW is defined as a special type of SAS data set: a VIEW contains the description of the data and a reference to the data, but not the data itself. One of the implementations of views is the DATA step view. The view describes the data set which results from a DATA step. You can use it for example as input for a PROC step, as if it were a normal data set.

Possible applications of DATA step views

SAS procedures normally use only one data set as input. Should the input be spread over multiple data sets, then a DATA step must first be inserted to 'glue' the parts together. Then the combined data sets can serve as input for the next step. Instead of the DATA step, a DATA step view can be created here. By using the view as input for the procedures, it appears as if only one data set is used, whereas in reality the input for the procedure will be constructed 'on the fly' by executing the view.

Many PC programs can export data in the form of a 'Tab Separated Values' file (TSV file) or another structure which can be read with INFILE and INPUT statements. Mainframes too have various file structures which can be converted into SAS data sets in this way. If the only purpose of this conversion is to make a summary of the contents of such a file, you could of course run the DATA step and then run for example PROC SUMMARY to create the summary. However you can also create a DATA step view here, through which the external data can be directly accessed by the procedure.

A completely different application lies in data security. Say that a department must have access to certain data sets to do its job, but that in these data sets there is also confidential information which must not be accessed. A DATA step view in which only the permitted variables appear (the rest will be suppressed with a DROP) takes care of the security. Instead of granting access to the data set, you grant access to the view.

Creation and use of DATA step views

The creation and testing of DATA step views is not difficult. First of all the DATA step which will produce the desired output data set is written in the normal way. Here use can be made as needed of INFILE and INPUT if the data is not in a SAS file, or of SET or MERGE if data must be combined from multiple data sets. If the output data set tests OK, then the DATA step is reconstructed to create a DATA step view by changing the DATA statement:

```
DATA dataset / VIEW=dataset;
```

by which 'dataset' designates the libref and the data set name in the normal way. Be careful that these are declared twice: in the DATA statement and in the VIEW option. The DATA step view will be stored under this name (with MEMTYPE=VIEW) in the designated data library. No ordinary data set with the same name can appear in the library.

Consider that the DATA step view contains a compiled DATA step, thus no statements can be included which have a global character, such as LIBNAME, TITLE and so on. The warning with respect to the use of macro variables which has already been brought up regarding the Stored Program Facility also applies here: the macro variable gets processed during the creation of the view, not during the use of the view.

The use of the DATA step view is simple: where normally you would specify a data set, for example in a SET statement or a DATA= option of a PROC statement, the libref and name of the view is specified. Functionally there is no longer any difference between a data set and a view. In reality the SAS System will execute the DATA step view to create an observation each time a subsequent observation has to be processed.

Example of the creation and use of a DATA step view

This example is based on a spreadsheet in which sales objectives are recorded. The spreadsheet is available as a TSV file to be read into the SAS System. Figure 18.10 shows a piece of the spreadsheet. Spreadsheets often have the 'horizontal structure' shown here, while a 'vertical structure' is usually easier to work with in the SAS System.

```
product.land.apr92.may92.jun92.jul92.aug92.sep92.oct92
CDplayer.BE.315.345.343.379.373.348.386
CDplayer.DE.1278.1120.1114.1539.1513.1413.1565
CDplayer.GB.468.513.510.564.554.518.573
CDplayer.IT.50.30.50.300.307.100.227
CDplayer.NL.1383.1515.1168.1354.1313.866.1514
Tuner.BE.116.110.89.106.95.91.113
Tuner.DE.1160.883.717.1064.952.916.1132
Tuner.GB.900.900.1179.1400.1252.1204.1489
Tuner.IT.50.50.60.104.118.60.110
Tuner.NL.1124.1069.868.1031.923.887.1097
```

Figure 18.10: A TSV file created by some spreadsheet program should be stored in a SAS data set. The periods represent the tab-characters.

The DATA step with which the conversion to the vertical structure is achieved is set up as a DATA step view (figure 18.11). For the purposes of the program, the view created will be used as the input data set to PROC PRINT.

The DATA step contains some techniques which require further explanation. In such a TSV file, fields do not have a fixed position, and cannot therefore be processed with pointer input. List input would be appropriate, but the SAS System normally expects spaces between the fields instead of tabs. This, however, can be changed with the DELIMITER= option in the INFILE statement. In this case DELIMITER='05'X on IBM mainframes or DELIMITER='09'X on other systems (PCs and VAXs). The first line contains the periods for which the targets apply. The related INPUT statement is oversized: up to 24 periods can be read, so that a growth of the spreadsheet will not immediately require a modification of the program. The MISSOVER option is used to prevent the SAS System from searching in subsequent input records for unfilled-in periods.

The subsequent input lines are read column by column. Because of the 'trailing @' in the INPUT statement, the SAS System will read the next target each time the INPUT statement is executed.

There is still a problem with this program. If there are missing values in the spreadsheet, there will be two (or more) tabs after each other. However the SAS System regards repeated delimiters as one, so that the sales figures would turn up in the wrong months. To solve this, use the DSD option in the INFILE statement. In the current release of the SAS System, however, DSD and MISSOVER do not go together. Should there be a risk of missing values in the spreadsheet, then you have to give up the oversizing and read exactly as many columns as are present in the spreadsheet.

At the creation of the view, no FILENAME statement has yet been used to link an actual file to the fileref of the INFILE statement. This is done when we want to use the view: just before the PROC PRINT.

Finally, figure 18.12 shows a small piece of the PROC PRINT output.

```
1                          The SAS System (6.08)
                                          13:30 Monday, June 13, 1994

NOTE: Copyright(c) 1989 by SAS Institute Inc., Cary, NC USA.
NOTE: SAS (r) Proprietary Software Release 6.08  TS405

NOTE: The initialization phase used 0.06 CPU seconds and 1092K.

NOTE: SAS job started on Monday 13JUN94 13:30 (199406131330)

1              /*------------------------------------------------------*/
2              /* CREATION OF A DATA STEP VIEW                         */
3              /*------------------------------------------------------*/
4              DATA VERTICAL(KEEP=PRODUCT COUNTRY MONTH TARGET)/VIEW=VERTICAL;
5              * Define some variables and attributes;
6              LENGTH PRODUCT $8 COUNTRY $2;
7              ARRAY PERIOD {24} _TEMPORARY_;
8              RETAIN PERIOD;
9              FORMAT MONTH MONYY.;
10             * TAB separated file, therefore delimiter option;
11             INFILE EXCEL DELIMITER='05'x MISSOVER;
12             * First line contains the periods;
13             IF _N_ = 1 THEN
14                INPUT DUMMY1 $ DUMMY2 $
15                      PERIOD{ 1}:MONYY. PERIOD{ 2}:MONYY. PERIOD{3}:MONYY.
16                      PERIOD{ 4}:MONYY. PERIOD{ 5}:MONYY. PERIOD{6}:MONYY.
17                      PERIOD{ 7}:MONYY. PERIOD{ 8}:MONYY. PERIOD{9}:MONYY.
18                      PERIOD{10}:MONYY. PERIOD{11}:MONYY. PERIOD{12}:MONYY.
19                      PERIOD{13}:MONYY. PERIOD{14}:MONYY. PERIOD{15}:MONYY.
20                      PERIOD{16}:MONYY. PERIOD{17}:MONYY. PERIOD{18}:MONYY.
21                      PERIOD{19}:MONYY. PERIOD{20}:MONYY. PERIOD{21}:MONYY.
22                      PERIOD{22}:MONYY. PERIOD{23}:MONYY. PERIOD{24}:MONYY.
23                      ;
24             * Next lines contain the product country and target;
25             ELSE DO;
26                INPUT PRODUCT COUNTRY @;
27                DO N=3 TO 26;
28                   IF PERIOD {N-2} NE . THEN DO;
29                     MONTH = PERIOD{N-2};
30                     INPUT TARGET @ ;
31                     OUTPUT;
32                   END;
33                   ELSE LEAVE;
34                END;
35             END;
36             RUN;
```

Figure 18.11 (part 1): The DATA step view is defined and stored as WORK.VERTICAL. WORK.VERTICAL can now be used as if it were an ordinary SAS data set.

2   The SAS System (6.08)
                                        13:30 Monday, June 13, 1994

NOTE: DATA STEP view saved on file WORK.VERTICAL.
NOTE: The original source statements cannot be retrieved from a stored
      DATA STEP view nor will a stored DATA STEP view run under a
      different release of the SAS system or under a different
      operating system.
      Please be sure to save the source statements for this DATA STEP
      view.
NOTE: The DATA statement used 0.04 CPU seconds and 1709K.

37
38   FILENAME EXCEL '.TILANE.UPLOAD.DATA';
39   PROC PRINT DATA=VERTICAL;
40   run;

NOTE: The infile EXCEL is:
      Dsname=TILANE.UPLOAD.DATA,
      Unit=3390,Volume=VPB804,Disp=SHR,Blksize=6160,
      Lrecl=80,Recfm=FB

NOTE: 12 records were read from the infile EXCEL.
NOTE: The view WORK.VERTICAL.VIEW used 0.03 CPU seconds and 2046K.
NOTE: The PROCEDURE PRINT printed pages 1-2.
NOTE: The PROCEDURE PRINT used 0.03 CPU seconds and 2046K.

NOTE: The SAS session used 0.32 CPU seconds and 2046K.
NOTE: SAS Institute BV, 1217 KR Hilversum, The Netherlands

Figure 18.11 (part 2): In this part the defined view is used as the input data set for PROC PRINT.

                    The SAS System, Version 6.08   1
                                        13:30 Monday, June 13, 1994

       OBS   PRODUCT   COUNTRY   MONTH   TARGET

        1   CDplayer   BE   APR92   315
        2   CDplayer   BE   MAY92   345
        3   CDplayer   BE   JUN92   343
        4   CDplayer   BE   JUL92   379
        5   CDplayer   BE   AUG92   373
        6   CDplayer   BE   SEP92   348
        7   CDplayer   BE   OCT92   386
        8   CDplayer   DE   APR92   1278
        9   CDplayer   DE   MAY92   1120
       10   CDplayer   DE   JUN92   1114
       11   CDplayer   DE   JUL92   1539
       12   CDplayer   DE   AUG92   1513
       13   CDplayer   DE   SEP92   1413
       14   CDplayer   DE   OCT92   1565
       . .   . .

Figure 18.12: A part of the PROC PRINT output.

Exercises

1. In a file you have amounts in foreign currency, with a specification of the type of currency. The amounts must be converted into US dollars. There is also a file with the exchange rates of various currencies with respect to the dollar (dollar value of one unit of the foreign currency):

   ```
   position:   000000000111111111122222222223
               123456789012345678901234567890

   record:     BFR 0.0299
               DMK 0.614
               FFR 0.180
               LIT 0.000707
               UKL 1.48
               NLG 0.543
   ```

   a. Generate a (permanent) FORMAT with the help of this file.

   b. Write the statement with which the foreign currency can be converted to dollars.

2. A file with projects, project budgets and the departments concerned looks like this:

OBS	DEPT	PROJ	WEEKS
1	A	X	6
2	A	Y	4
3	B	X	2
4	B	Z	1
5	C	Y	3
6	C	Z	7
7	D	Z	1

   For progress reporting however, another presentation is desired:

OBS	PROJ	A	B	C	D	TOT
1	X	6	2	.	.	8
2	Y	4	.	3	.	7
3	Z	.	1	7	1	9

   This presentation shows clearly per project which departments are involved and how much time the whole project takes.

It is also easy to see which project each department is working on.

Write a program to create the desired progress report from the project data set. Hint: first calculate the total number of work weeks per project and then use PROC TRANSPOSE for the presentation.

3.   In chapter 8 the three department data sets were first combined with a SET statement before they could be processed further. Write a DATA step view which would result in the same data and use this as input for the MERGE with the ART_DES data set.

CHAPTER 19

Introduction to SAS/FSP® Software

SAS/FSP Software

SAS/FSP software (originally called Full Screen Product) is an interactive environment for browsing and updating the contents of SAS data sets. In addition SAS/FSP software also contains facilities for computerized mailings and for on-line browsing of non-SAS files. In Version 6 SAS/FSP has been substantially expanded, particularly with the addition of the 'Screen Control Language' (SCL). By means of SCL you can set up relations between fields in a data entry screen, you can calculate fields and so on. We will not go into SCL in this introduction. For this, refer to the relevant SAS documentation.

SAS/FSP is a separate SAS product. It is not present in every installation. However it is available on the majority of SAS installations.

In this chapter you will become acquainted with the basic principles of some of the more popular SAS/FSP procedures.

PROC FSEDIT

Standard screen layout

PROC FSEDIT displays an observation of a SAS data set on the screen and permits the user to alter this observation. Observations can also be added or removed.

PROC FSEDIT starts up like any other procedure:

```
PROC FSEDIT DATA=libref.dataset;
```

PROC FSEDIT then constructs a standard screen layout, based on the variables in the designated data set. PROC FSEDIT is also available as a command rather than a procedure in the Display Manager. Simply typing FSEDIT and the data set name on the command line of any window or typing 'E' in front of the name of the data set in the DIR window also executes PROC FSEDIT.

Figure 19.1 shows how the standard screen looks for the data set HOUSES, which was used in chapter 9.

With the LABEL option:

```
PROC FSEDIT DATA=libref.dataset LABEL;
```

the SAS System will not use the variable name as field designator but will use the variable label, as in figure 19.2.

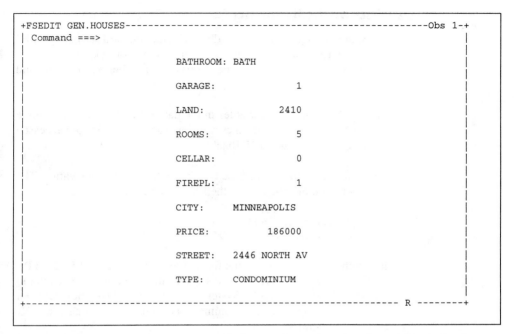

```
+FSEDIT GEN.HOUSES---------------------------------------------------------Obs 1-+
| Command ===>                                                                  |
|                                                                               |
|                         BATHROOM: BATH                                        |
|                                                                               |
|                         GARAGE:            1                                  |
|                                                                               |
|                         LAND:           2410                                  |
|                                                                               |
|                         ROOMS:             5                                  |
|                                                                               |
|                         CELLAR:            0                                  |
|                                                                               |
|                         FIREPL:            1                                  |
|                                                                               |
|                         CITY:      MINNEAPOLIS                                 |
|                                                                               |
|                         PRICE:        186000                                  |
|                                                                               |
|                         STREET:    2446 NORTH AV                              |
|                                                                               |
|                         TYPE:      CONDOMINIUM                                 |
|                                                                               |
+----------------------------------------------------------------- R --------+
```

Figure19.1: PROC FSEDIT generates a standard screen layout, based on the variables in the data set.

```
+FSEDIT GEN.HOUSES---------------------------------------------------------Obs 1-+
| Command ===>                                                                  |
|                                                                               |
|                 Type of bathroom          BATH                                |
|                                                                               |
|                 Garage present (1=yes)          1                             |
|                                                                               |
|                 Area (sq. feet)              2410                             |
|                                                                               |
|                 Number of rooms                 5                             |
|                                                                               |
|                 Cellar present (1=yes)          0                             |
|                                                                               |
|                 Fireplace present (1=yes)       1                             |
|                                                                               |
|                 City/town                 MINNEAPOLIS                          |
|                                                                               |
|                 Price                       186000                            |
|                                                                               |
|                 Street address            2446 NORTH AV                       |
|                                                                               |
|                 Type of house             CONDOMINIUM                         |
|                                                                               |
+----------------------------------------------------------------- R --------+
```

Figure 19.2: With the LABEL option PROC FSEDIT will use the labels of the variables as field descriptions.

Searching and changing

Scrolling through the data set is done with the standard scroll keys: PF8 ahead and PF7 back. If the number of an observation is known, you can jump directly to it by typing the observation number on the command line.

Should the number of variables in the data set be too big for a single screen, the SAS System defines additional screens, which are accessed via PF11 (ahead) and PF10 (back).

Searching can also be done based on the contents of an observation. The most common method is with the FIND command:

```
FIND criterion1 <criterion2 ...>
F@ criterion1 <criterion2 ...>
```

in which the criterion takes the form of an equation, as in FIND TYPE = DETACHED, or FIND ROOMS > 4. If multiple criteria are declared one after the other, the SAS System assumes an AND relation between the criteria, unless the F@ command is used, in which case an OR relation is assumed.

The combination of the STRING and the SEARCH (and S@) command searches for observations on the basis of substrings in character variables. First of all the variables to be sought are declared with a STRING command:

```
STRING variable1 <variable2 ...>;
```

Then the search text is specified in a SEARCH command:

```
SEARCH argument1 <argument2 ...>;
```

If multiple search arguments are declared, an AND relation is assumed between the arguments in the SEARCH command, or an OR relation if the S@ command is given.

The third possibility for tracking down observations is by means of the combination of NAME and LOCATE commands. The name of a variable is declared in the NAME command.

Next comes a LOCATE command (usually shortened to L) with the value being sought.

A colon after the LOCATE command makes the argument a 'begins with' condition.

All search commands search from the currently displayed observation to the end of the data set. The search is repeated by means of the REPEAT command (PF5).

If the desired observation is found, then the variables can simply be changed by typing over the new value. If informats are linked to the variables, then a validation is executed immediately after Enter is pressed. The changes are temporarily put in a buffer and are applied to the data set after a SAVE command, after 25 changes or when you quit the procedure. You can set the frequency of transferring data from the buffer to the data set with the AUTOSAVE command. For example the command AUTOSAVE=1 causes every altered observation to be output immediately.

New observations can be added by means of the ADD command (PF9) or the DUP command (PF6). ADD sets up an empty observation on the screen; DUP duplicates the displayed observation. The latter of course takes a lot less time if the new observation is only a partial modification of an existing observation.

Observations are removed by means of the DELETE command. This command does not physically remove observations from the data set, but marks them as DELETED. Physical removal happens the next time the data set is rebuilt, for example in a DATA step or in a PROC SORT.

Adapting screen layout

The MODIFY command leads you to the 'Screen modification' facilities of PROC FSEDIT. Access is through the menu shown in figure 19.3. For layout and presentation options, 2 and 4 are important. Options 3 and 6 are for SCL. The SAS System stores screen layouts as catalog entries of the type SCREEN. To use a screen catalog, declare it in the PROC statement.

```
PROC FSEDIT DATA=fileref.dataset
            SCREEN=fileref.catalog.member;
```

Option 2 (Screen modification and Field Identification) opens the screen in edit mode: using the same commands as in the PROG screen of the Display Manager, you can set up the entire screen the way you want (figure 19.4). The places where the variables will be displayed are indicated by underscores. Be careful to leave at least one space free before and after a field. Also, not all variables in the data set have to be present in the layout you create. When you have completed your layout, key PF3 to leave the screen. Now the SAS System will ask whether calculated fields are present; if not, it asks where the different fields have been put (figure 19.5). Variables that you left out are marked as UNWANTED. Should you want to call them up later, you do it with the DEFINE command:

```
DEFINE variable
```

Put the cursor on the desired variable and confirm by pressing Enter.

If the SAS System can successfully locate all the variables, you go back via the END command to the Screen Modification menu. You can then choose to leave Screen Modification (once again via an END command) after which the observations will become visible in the new layout (figure 19.6), or you can choose option 4 where, among others, initial values, permitted values and so forth can be adapted. You can also adjust field colors or make some of them protected (no input) in this menu option.

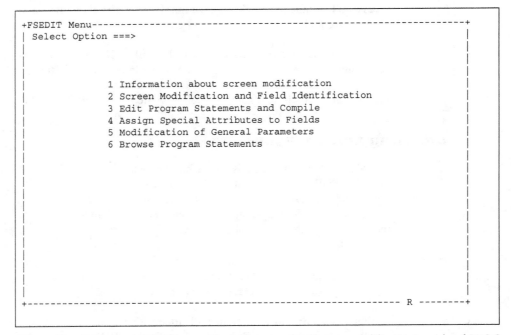

Figure 19.3: With the MODIFY command you enter the "Screen modification" mode of PROC FSEDIT. Option 2 leads you to the screens that let you design your own screen layout.

```
+FSEDIT Modify-----------------------------------------------------------------+
| Command ===>                                                                  |
|                                                                               |
|   Type of house:          _____        City:       _____    |
|                                               Street:     _____    |
|                                                                               |
|                                                                               |
|   Description:                                                                |
|                                               Facilities present (1=yes)       |
|                                                                               |
|   Area (sq. feet):     _____                 Cellar:     _                   |
|                                                                               |
|   Number of rooms:     _____                 Fireplace:  _                   |
|                                                                               |
|   Type of bathroom:    _____                 Garage:     _                   |
|                                                                               |
|                                                                               |
|                                                                               |
|           Price:   USD _____                                              |
|                                                                               |
|                                                                               |
|                                                                               |
+------------------------------------------------------------- R -------+
```

Figure 19.4: You are completely free in the design of the screen.

```
+FSEDIT Identify---------------------------------------------------------------+
| Command ===>                                                                  |
| Please put cursor on field: BATHROOM and press ENTER ... or UNWANTED           |
|   Type of house:          _____        City:       _____    |
|                                               Street:     _____    |
|                                                                               |
|                                                                               |
|   Description:                                                                |
|                                               Facilities present (1=yes)       |
|                                                                               |
|   Area (sq. feet):     _____                 Cellar:     _                   |
|                                                                               |
|   Number of rooms:     _____                 Fireplace:  _                   |
|                                                                               |
|   Type of bathroom:    _____                 Garage:     _                   |
|                                                                               |
|                                                                               |
|                                                                               |
|           Price:   USD _____                                              |
|                                                                               |
|                                                                               |
+------------------------------------------------------------- R -------+
```

Figure 19.5: After completion of the design you will be asked where all variables have gone.

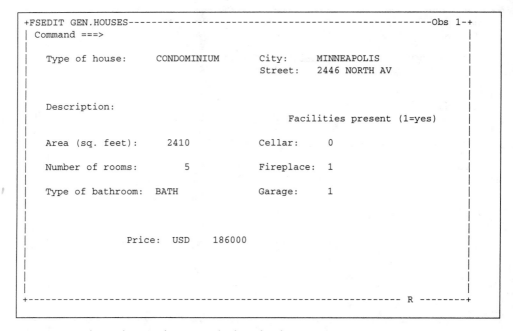

Figure 19.6: This is the new layout applied on the data set.

Creating a new data set

A data set does not have to exist already to be processed with **PROC FSEDIT**. By writing NEW=libref.dataset in place of the option DATA=libref.dataset in the PROC statement, the new data set will be created and a definition screen will be displayed, on which all variables, their length, (in)format and label can be entered (figure 19.7).

PROC FSBROWSE

Online use

Everything written so far about PROC FSEDIT is also valid for PROC FSBROWSE. In fact they are the same procedures. The only difference is that in PROC FSBROWSE the data set cannot be updated.

```
+FSEDIT: NEW WORK.TEST (E)-------------------------------------------------+
| Command ===>                                                             |
|                                                                          |
|   Name   Type  Length                  Label                  Format     |
|                                                                          |
|   _____  _   ___  _____  _____  |
|   _____  _   ___  _____  _____  |
|   _____  _   ___  _____  _____  |
|   _____  _   ___  _____  _____  |
|   _____  _   ___  _____  _____  |
|   _____  _   ___  _____  _____  |
|   _____  _   ___  _____  _____  |
|   _____  _   ___  _____  _____  |
|   _____  _   ___  _____  _____  |
|   _____  _   ___  _____  _____  |
|   _____  _   ___  _____  _____  |
|   _____  _   ___  _____  _____  |
|   _____  _   ___  _____  _____  |
|   _____  _   ___  _____  _____  |
|   _____  _   ___  _____  _____  |
|   _____  _   ___  _____  _____  |
|   _____  _   ___  _____  _____  |
|   _____  _   ___  _____  _____  |
+--------------------------------------------------------------- R --------+
```

Figure 19.7: On this screen you can specify the variables and their attributes for a new data set. PROC FSVIEW also uses this screen when you want to create a data set.

PROC FSBROWSE, non-interactive use

PROC FSBROWSE can also be used outside of a window environment. For this, the option PRINTALL should be added to the PROC statement:

```
PROC FSBROWSE DATA=... SCREEN=... PRINTALL;
```

In this case PROC FSBROWSE produces an output page in the SAS list for each observation, according to the layout as defined in the screen option.

Since the screens are usually smaller that the standard output pages, it is often desirable to put multiple screens on one page. FSBROWSE cannot do this, but playing intelligently with PROC PRINTTO will do the trick. The basis of a program to print four screens side by side on one page is shown in figure 19.8. With PROC PRINTTO, you send the FSBROWSE output to a temporary file. This file is then used as input in a DATA step.

You recognize the beginning of a new page by the ANSI print control sign '1' (Top-of-form) in the first position of a line. If the top-of-form sign is not present in your environment, then the beginning of a new page must be detected in another way, for example with the help of the title line. Because the SAS System writes print lines with variable length, we read them in with the $VARYING format. For this to work well, the length of the line must first be established. The SAS System puts the length of the line into the variable which is declared in the LENGTH option of the INFILE statement. However that happens only after the execution of an INPUT statement. Hence the 'dummy' INPUT statement (INPUT@;). The FSBROWSE information starts in this case (because of the top-of-form sign) on position 2 and that segment is thus L-1 positions long.

```
* Allocate library and temporary file;
* The form '&TEMP' is an IBM/MVS form;
LIBNAME GEN '.GENERAL.SASLIB';
FILENAME TEMP '&TEMP';
* Send output to the temporary file;
PROC PRINTTO PRINT=TEMP;
RUN;
* Print the screens left aligned in the file;
OPTIONS NOCENTER;
PROC FSBROWSE DATA=GEN.HOUSES
              SCREEN=GEN.SCREEN.HOUSES
              PRINTALL;
RUN;
* Reset output routing;
PROC PRINTTO;
RUN;
 * Reset pagenumber to 1;
OPTIONS PAGENO=1;
* Read the temporary file back in and print;
DATA  _NULL_;
 INFILE TEMP LENGTH=L;
 FILE   PRINT N=PS;
 * First a dummy INPUT statement to determine;
 * the length of the record;
```

Figure 19.8 (part 1): With a program like this you could bring several output pages (e.g. from PROC FSBROWSE) together on one page.

```
INPUT @;
* Position 1 contains the printer control character;
* The actual line starts at position 2 and is L-1 long;
L = L-1;
INPUT @1 N_PAGE 1. @2 LINE $VARYING65. L;
* With ANSI printer control a 1 in the first;
* position of a line means start of a new page;
IF N_PAGE THEN DO;
     PAGENBR + 1;
     N=0;
     * The 5th output page will initiate a new page;
     IF PAGENBR = 5 THEN DO;
         PUT _PAGE_;
         PAGENBR=1;
     END;
     RETURN;
END;
N+1;
* Page 1 and 3 are in the top half;
* Page 2 and 4 are in the lower half.
* The MOD function shifts the row pointer 25 lines;
ROW = MOD(PAGENBR+1,2)*25 + N;
* For page 3 and 4 the column pointer should shift;
* to position 65;
COLUMN = (PAGENBR GE 3)*65 + 1;
PUT #ROW @COLUMN LINE $CHAR65. @;
RUN;
```

Figure 19.8 (part 2)

PROC FSVIEW

Examining a data set with PROC FSVIEW

PROC FSVIEW shows a SAS data set in a form which is similar to
PROC PRINT. In SAS Version 5 this procedure was known as PROC
FSPRINT. FSPRINT however had no update capability for a data set.
For compatibility FSPRINT is still known to the system and in fact
invokes FSVIEW. The call to PROC FSVIEW is also similar to PROC
PRINT:

```
PROC FSVIEW DATA=libref.dataset;
   VAR variable(s);
   ID variable(s);
```

Figure 19.9 shows the same HOUSES data set in FSVIEW form. Not all variables from this data set are displayed on the screen at the same time. By means of the horizontal scroll commands or keys the variables which were originally left undisplayed can be looked up. The variables which are in the ID statement remain permanently on the screen while these other variables are coming and going.

Data set modification with PROC FSVIEW

The data set can also be modified with PROC FSVIEW. For this, type the command

```
MODIFY
```
or
```
MODIFY MEMBER
```

on the command line. With MODIFY, the SAS System opens the data set for modifications, at the 'record level locking' (figure 19.10). If the SAS/SHARE product has been installed, then the data set remains available to other users both for browsing or modification, because only the record to be modified is closed to the outside world. When using record locking the SAS System must always be told which observation is to be modified. To do this, place the cursor on the appropriate line and key Enter. The line will then be highlighted, if this is supported by the terminal, and the tab key can then be used to jump from variable to variable for entering new values.

MODIFY MEMBER opens the whole data set for modifications and nobody can access the data set until the modification is completed. In this case you no longer need to designate which observations you wish to modify: all observations are open for modification.

```
+FSVIEW:    GEN.HOUSES  (B)----------------------------------------------------+
| Command ===>                                                                 |
|                                                                              |
|   OBS      BATHROOM        GARAGE          LAND         ROOMS        CELLAR   |
|                                                                              |
|    1       BATH              1             2410           5            0      |
|    2       BATH              0             2545           6            1      |
|    3       SHOWER            1             1943           5            0      |
|    4       SHOWER            1             3146           4            0      |
|    5       BATH              1             5420           6            1      |
|    6       TUB               0             3893           6            0      |
|    7       SHOWER            0             1566           4            0      |
|    8       SHOWER            1             2370           5            0      |
|    9       BATH              1             2708           3            0      |
|   10       SHOWER            0             1850           5            0      |
|                                                                              |
|                                                                              |
|                                                                              |
|                                                                              |
+--------------------------------------------------------------- R --------+
```

Figure 19.9: The same HOUSES data set, opened with PROC FSVIEW. The variables that are not displayed can be reached with the horizontal scroll commands: LEFT/RIGHT.

```
+FSVIEW:    GEN.HOUSES  (E)----------------------------------------------------+
| Command ===>                                                                 |
| NOTE: The data set has been opened with RECORD level locking.                |
|   OBS      BATHROOM        GARAGE          LAND         ROOMS        CELLAR   |
|                                                                              |
|    1       BATH              1             2410           5            0      |
|    2       BATH              0             2545           6            1      |
|    3       SHOWER            1             1943           5            0      |
|    4       SHOWER            1             3146           4            0      |
|    5       BATH              1             5420           6            1      |
|    6       TUB               0             3893           6            0      |
|    7       SHOWER            0             1566           4            0      |
|    8       SHOWER            1             2370           5            0      |
|    9       BATH              1             2708           3            0      |
|   10       SHOWER            0             1850           5            0      |
|                                                                              |
|                                                                              |
|                                                                              |
|                                                                              |
+--------------------------------------------------------------- R --------+
```

Figure 19.10: By typing MODIFY on the command line, you open the data set for updates. By default the SAS System will choose "Record locking". To change an observation you have to select it first. Position the cursor on the observation and press ENTER. The observation will be highlighted (if the terminal supports this) and is open for modifications. The command MODIFY MEMBER will open all observations at once for update.

Adding and removing observations

The ADD command displays an extra line after the last observation of the data set with the tag NEW (figure 19.11). A new observation can be entered on this line. As soon as that is done, a next NEW line is displayed. To remove observations type DELETE on the command line and place the cursor on the observation to be removed before pressing ENTER. If the DELETE command must be used frequently, it can be assigned to a function key via the KEYS window. Then you put the cursor on the right line and hit the DELETE function key.

```
+FSVIEW:    GEN.HOUSES  (E)------------------------------------------------------------+
| Command ===>                                                                         |
| NOTE: The AUTOADD option has been turned on.                                         |
|   OBS        BATHROOM        GARAGE          LAND         ROOMS          CELLAR       |
|                                                                                      |
|    2         BATH             0             2545           6               1         |
|    3         SHOWER           1             1943           5               0         |
|    4         SHOWER           1             3146           4               0         |
|    5         BATH             1             5420           6               1         |
|    6         TUB              0             3893           6               0         |
|    7         SHOWER           0             1566           4               0         |
|    8         SHOWER           1             2370           5               0         |
|    9         BATH             1             2708           3               0         |
|   10         SHOWER           0             1850           5               0         |
|  NEW                          .               .             .               .        |
|                                                                                      |
|                                                                                      |
|                                                                                      |
|                                                                                      |
|                                                                                      |
|                                                                                      |
|                                                                                      |
+---------------------------------------------------------------------- R --------+
```

Figure 19.11: The ADD command will add a new observation to the data set. As soon as data has been entered for this observation a next NEW line will be added.

Creating a new data set

PROC FSVIEW can also be used to create a new data set. For this, just as in PROC FSEDIT, give the option NEW= in place of DATA= in the PROC statement. The screen for defining new data sets is similar to that of PROC FSEDIT (see figure 19.7).

Opening a data set directly for modification

In the previous section the data set was first opened in browse mode and then transferred to edit mode via the MODIFY command. However by putting MODIFY in the PROC statement, edit mode is immediately activated at the start of PROC FSVIEW. The record locking mode will be used, unless you specify the data set option CNTLLEV=MEMBER. The following statements will open the HOUSES data set for update at startup and all observations will be directly accessible:

```
PROC FSVIEW DATA=libref.HOUSES(CNTLLEV=MEMBER) MODIFY;
```

The FSVIEW command

PROC FSVIEW can also be activated by giving the command FSVIEW on the command line of any SAS window:

```
FSVIEW libref.dataset
```

There is no difference whether it is activated by the command or by the PROC statement. It is also possible with the FSVIEW command to examine multiple data sets simultaneously; the FSVIEW window has a command line, so the FSVIEW command can be given.

PROC FSLIST

PROC FSLIST is used to display a non-SAS file on the screen. The form is:

```
PROC FSLIST FILEREF=fileref;
```

in which 'fileref' is the fileref in the FILENAME statement with which the external file is allocated, or the actual name of the file between quotes. PROC FSLIST is especially useful to test SAS programs in which external files are created. In the program of figure 19.8, for example, a PROC FSLIST could be inserted after the PROC FSBROWSE:

```
PROC FSLIST FILEREF=TEMP;
```

to check whether the FSBROWSE output has been placed in the TEMP file correctly.

Standard FIND commands can be used to search for the occurrence of particular text in the list.

Exercises

1. Create the HOUSES data set as in figure 19.4, and construct a layout which corresponds to this figure.

CHAPTER 20

Introduction to
SAS/GRAPH® Software

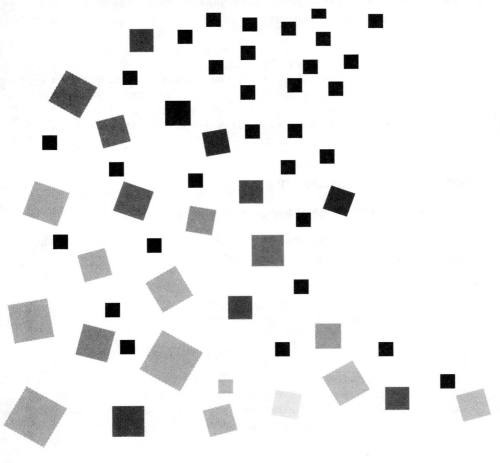

Introduction

SAS/GRAPH software is an all-purpose flexible graphics package, integrated into the general SAS environment. The package does much more than produce simple graphs: for example, you can also draw maps in various projections and make slides for presentations. To be able to work with SAS/GRAPH software, you will need access to a graphics output medium, such as a graphics terminal, a graphics printer or a plotter. In this the SAS System is not very fussy. Virtually all available terminals and printers can be driven by SAS/GRAPH software, by means of so-called 'device drivers'. And for that rare apparatus for which no standard device driver exists, you can write your own driver.

The environment in which SAS/GRAPH software is to function is defined in a GOPTIONS statement. In addition to declaring the apparatus to be used, this definition includes the available colors (to the extent these deviate from the standard colors of the device), the dimensions of the image to be produced and so on. Figure 20.1 lists the most frequently used options.

SAS/GRAPH Software: Reference, Version 6, First Edition counts over 1300 pages, divided into two volumes. Obviously we cannot cover all this here in a few pages. In this chapter we will limit ourselves to the conversion from printer graphics, as covered in chapter 13, with a short explanation of a number of additional capabilities and an introduction to the DATA step interfaces.

General statements

The GOPTIONS statement

The GOPTIONS statement is directly comparable to the usual OPTIONS statement, as in the form:

```
GOPTIONS <options>;
```

The options are simply strung out one after the other, as in;

```
GOPTIONS DEVICE=HPGL VSIZE=4 HSIZE=6 BORDER;
```

Default settings exist for almost all options. Particularly for the terminal, printer or plotter, the options seldom have to be modified, once the DEVICE= option has told the system which graphics device (type terminal, printer, plotter, etc.) is used.

The TITLE and FOOTNOTE statements

The TITLE and FOOTNOTE statements operate in SAS/GRAPH software just as in base SAS software. However because you are now working in a graphics environment, there are a number of additional features to deal with such as font, size, color and rotation of text. You always specify these additional functions with the keyword for the text concerned. Figure 20.2 gives an example of a few TITLE and FOOTNOTE possibilities.

What you see in figure 20.2 is accomplished with the following statements:

```
TITLE1 F=ITALIC H=2 A=30 'Going up'
       F=SWISS A=-30 R=30 'and down';
TITLE2 F=SWISSE A=90 H=2 'A special case ...';
TITLE3 F=COMPLEX A=-90 '... and this too!';
FOOTNOTE F=CARTOG BOX=2 'PLMNOONMLP';
PROC GSLIDE;
```

The letter size you choose depends on the device you are using. By not specifying any unit for height, the 'character cel' dimension is used as the unit and this is determined by the number of rows and columns defined for the device in character rather than graphics use. It is defined in the device driver; however, it can be overruled with GOPTIONS settings. Refer to the SAS/GRAPH manual for details.

The role of PROC GSLIDE in the above example is only for setting up an empty graphics screen.

A listing of the additional specifications such as font and letter size is given in figure 20.3. By comparing the table in figure 20.3 with the statements and the output in figure 20.2, you can easily figure out how it works. These keywords and codes apply everywhere when text formatting is required.

The options A= and R= calculate rotation angles to the left, in other words a positive angle of rotation turns the output counterclockwise. Rotating a text line rotates the letters along with it: they remain perpendicular to the base line. With the option R=, letters can be rotated with respect to the base line. This is shown in the second half of the TITLE1 statement: the base line has been turned -30°, thus to the right. However the letters have been turned back +30° with respect to the base line, so that they are straight up again.

Options	Description
Apparatus	
DEVICE=	Specifies the "device driver", e.g. IBM3179, VT240 (DEC), PS (PostScript), HPLJS3 (HP Laserjet-III), TEK4115 (Tektronix). Refer to the complete list in the SASHELP.DEVICES catalog.
GSFNAME=	Fileref for Graphics Stream File: Plot commands will be written to this file.
GSFMODE=	Determines how data are written to the GSF file: APPEND or REPLACE.
DISPLAY I NODISPLAY	Displays or suppresses output on the screen (NODISPLAY is often used in combination with PROC GREPLAY).
Presentation	
BORDER I NOBORDER	Border Line around picture.
VSIZE=n	Vertical size of picture in inch (unless CM is specified).
HSIZE=n	Horizontal size of picture in inches (unless CM is specified).
ROTATE I NOROTATE	Rotates picture 90°, especially for plotters or printers.
GUNIT= CELLS I CM I IN I PCT	Unit height for text, measured in cells, centimeters, inches or percentage of the picture size.
FBY= charactertype	The character type used to print BY lines (if a BY statement is used).
CBY = color	BY line color.
HBY = n	Height of characters in the BY line. HBY=0 suppresses the BY line.

Figure 20.1: Some of the commonly used options of the GOPTIONS statement. There are dozens of other options. Refer to the SAS/GRAPH manuals for more details.

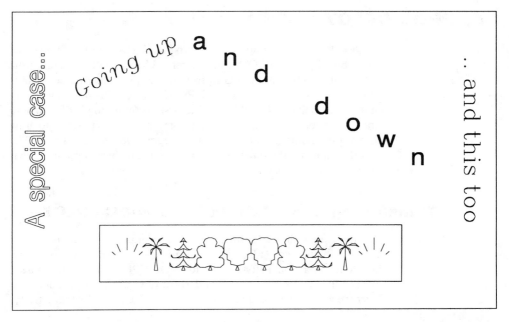

Figure 20.2: The TITLE and FOOTNOTE statements function in SAS/GRAPH software just as in base SAS, but due to the graphics environment there are additional features.

Options	Description
ANGLE= or A=	Rotation of the base line of text. In TITLE statements 90° and -90° will be printed on the side of the picture.
BOX= 1...4	Draws a box around text, with varying line thickness.
BC= color	Background color inside a BOX area.
C= color	Color of the text.
FONT= or F=	Character type to be used. F=NONE applies a hardware font available on the device Other standard SAS character types are: SIMPLEX, COMPLEX, SWISS, ITALIC, CARTOG (cartografic symbols), MARKER (diverse symbols), MATH (mathematic symbols), KANJI (Japanese text).
HEIGHT=n or H=n	Height of characters in units.
JUSTIFY= L I C I R or J= L I C I R	Justification of text (Left, Center, Right).
ROTATE= or R=	Rotation of characters relative to the base line. (default=0).
U= 0...4	Underlining of text (with thickness of the line specified).

Figure 20.3: The text formatting options which can be used in TITLE, NOTE (not discussed) and FOOTNOTE statements. These instructions are used anywhere in the SAS/GRAPH environment to format text.

PROC GPLOT

PROC GPLOT is the graphics counterpart of PROC PLOT. If you make a graph with PROC PLOT, you can get a SAS/GRAPH version of the output simply by putting a G in front of the procedure name. This is illustrated in figure 20.4 and 20.5. PROC GPLOT however has many more options than PROC PLOT. The first useful option is of course to draw a line connecting the points of the graph. It is also possible to draw through the points a smoothed line, a regression line and so on. The specifications for the line to be drawn through the graph points appear in the SYMBOL statement.

Transferring from PROC PLOT to PROC GPLOT

The data set with the log of the supermarket check-out activity (see example in chapter 11: Descriptive Statistics) can be used to illustrate how to transfer from PROC PLOT to PROC GPLOT. From the data set as used in chapter 11 it has been derived how many check-outs were busy at each moment in time (data set BUSY). Next we plot this activity.

```
PROC PLOT DATA=libref.BUSY;
    PLOT BUSY*TIME/HAXIS='09:00'T TO '17:00'T BY HOUR;
TITLE 'Output from PROC PLOT';
```

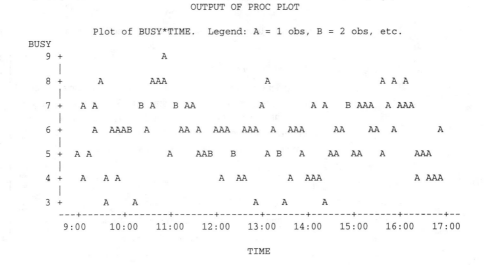

```
                          OUTPUT OF PROC PLOT

             Plot of BUSY*TIME.  Legend: A = 1 obs, B = 2 obs, etc.
    BUSY
       9 +                   A
         |
       8 +     A          AAA              A              A A A
         |
       7 +   A A       B A   B AA          A        A A   B AAA  A AAA
         |
       6 +     A  AAAB  A     AA A  AAA  AAA  A  AAA     AA    AA  A        A
         |
       5 +   A A             A     AAB   B     A B   A    AA  AA   A     AAA
         |
       4 +   A    A A              A  AA      A  AAA               A AAA
         |
       3 +        A    A                A    A     A
         ---+-------+-------+-------+-------+-------+-------+-------+-------+--
          9:00    10:00   11:00   12:00   13:00   14:00   15:00   16:00   17:00


                                      TIME
```

Figure 20.4: PROC PLOT output. Plotted is the number of check-outs busy at any time.

Figure 20.4 shows the resulting graph as PROC PLOT would produce it. Figure 20.5 then shows how the resulting graph would look using PROC GPLOT.

Starting from this basic transfer it is possible to enhance the graph in many directions. These three statements play an important role: the SYMBOL statement, the AXIS statement and the LEGEND statement.

The SYMBOL statement determines the appearance of the graph points: colors, symbols, connecting lines between the points and so on. The AXIS statement defines the format of the axes and the LEGEND statement defines the format of any legend which might ultimately be included. In the SAS/GRAPH manual, these statements are described as GLOBAL statements. The information remains in force as long as it is not replaced by new information, and is therefore beyond a single procedure. For the sake of clarity, here the statements will be handled directly in relation to procedures.

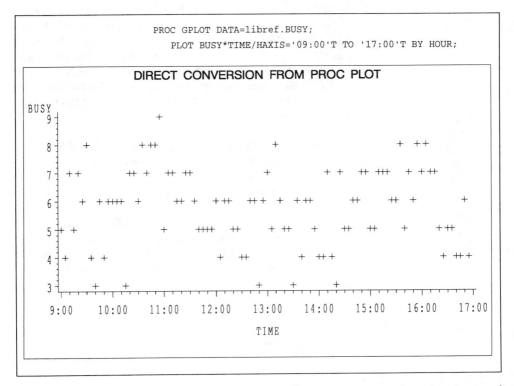

Figure 20.5: As figure 20.4. By placing a G in front of the procedure name, the output is created by SAS/GRAPH. At the same moment many new options are available to enhance the appearance of the graph. The title is created with the SWISS font.

The PLOT and PLOT2 statement

The PLOT statement is in principle similar to the PLOT statement of
PROC PLOT:

```
PLOT Y_variable * X_variable <=plot instruction>
                             </options>;
```

However the plot instruction deviates from the plot symbol specification
of PROC PLOT. In GPLOT the plot instruction can be a variable or a
number. If it is a variable, then this variable is used as a classification
variable and PROC GPLOT creates a graph line for each value of this
variable. If it is a number, it refers to a SYMBOL statement and the
design definition of the graph is then derived from that SYMBOL
statement. If no graph instruction is given, the SAS System will use any
previously defined SYMBOL statement.

The options in the PLOT statement are also comparable to those of
PROC PLOT. Here too there is an OVERLAY option to combine several
graphs (Y_var*X_var combinations) on one set of axes, and a VAXIS=
and HAXIS= option. These provide two capabilities: specify the desired
axis (as in PROC PLOT) or refer to an AXIS statement. Thus an option
HAXIS=AXIS4 refers to an AXIS4 statement. Multiple AXIS, SYM-
BOL and LEGEND statements can occur, up to 99 of each. These are
referred to by their rank number in the statement; thus AXIS4 refers to
an AXIS4 statement.

In a similar manner the LEGEND= option refers to a LEGEND statement, which determines the layout of a possible legend.

For other options refer to chapter 13, or the SAS/GRAPH manual.

In addition to the PLOT statement there is also a PLOT2 statement. This
PLOT2 statement functions precisely the same as the PLOT statement,
but defines a second vertical axis on the right side of the graph. The
PLOT2 statement can only be used in combination with the PLOT
statement.

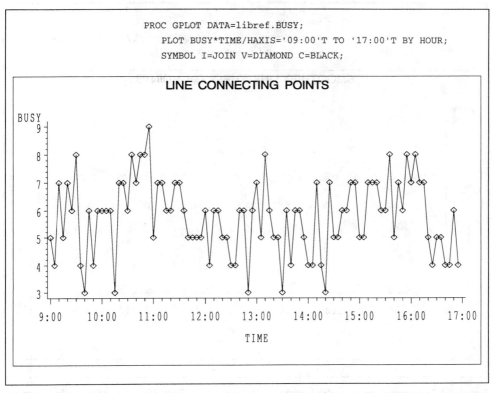

```
           PROC GPLOT DATA=libref.BUSY;
              PLOT BUSY*TIME/HAXIS='09:00'T TO '17:00'T BY HOUR;
              SYMBOL I=JOIN V=DIAMOND C=BLACK;
```

Figure 20.6: By adding a SYMBOL statement it is possible to change the appearance of the graph considerably. In this case by drawing a line through the graph points and by changing the points into a diamond.

The SYMBOL statement

The SYMBOL statement determines to a large extent the design of the graph you want to make. For graphs with multiple lines you can use multiple SYMBOL statements. You number these:
SYMBOL1-SYMBOL99.

In the PLOT statement these sequential numbers are referred to as 'plot instruction' as in:

```
PLOT Y_variable * X_variable = 4;
```

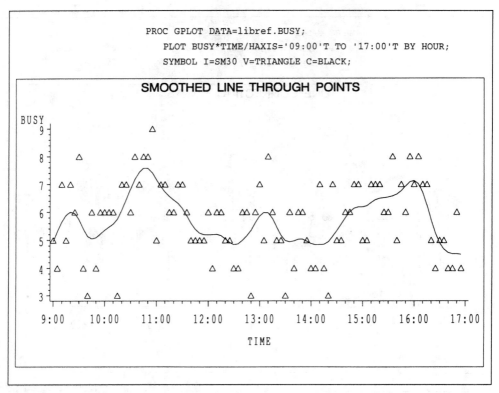

Figure 20.7: A smoothed line which reduces the effect of outliers. The level of smoothing can be adjusted.

which refers to the SYMBOL4 statement. (This is not true in every circumstance. If no color has been specified in the SYMBOL statement, the SAS System can automatically generate additional SYMBOL statements. Then the numbering goes out of whack. In this book, for clarity, a color will always be given.) In the SYMBOL statement the various options are declared one after the other as shown in the examples in figures 20.6 through 20.8. Figure 20.9 lists the most important options.

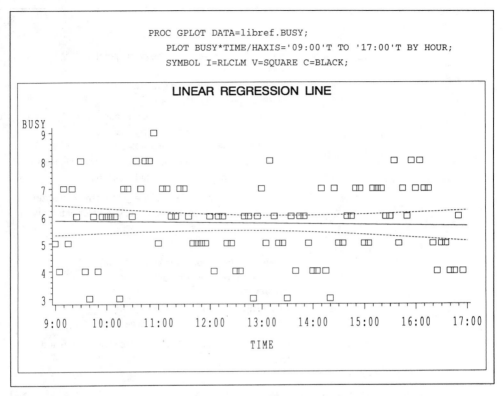

```
                    PROC GPLOT DATA=libref.BUSY;
                        PLOT BUSY*TIME/HAXIS='09:00'T TO '17:00'T BY HOUR;
                        SYMBOL I=RLCLM V=SQUARE C=BLACK;
```

Figure 20.8: To draw a regression line you don't need to go to one of the regression procedures (like PROC REG) first. PROC GPLOT can draw linear, quadratic and cubic regression lines through the graph points, including confidence intervals.

The AXIS statement

The AXIS statement sets up the axes. The COLOR= option declares the color of the axis and the WIDTH= option the thickness. The scale marks on the axis are set up with the ORDER= option, in the same manner as in the HAXIS= or VAXIS= option. These marks are in linear scale unless the option LOGBASE= specifies a logarithmic scale, in which case you have choice of LOGBASE=10 or LOGBASE=E.

Axes are labeled by means of the LABEL= option. The label specification consists of two parts: the design and the text. In the design part, attributes such as font and size are given, as you can do in the TITLE statement. With LABEL=NONE, the axis remains unlabeled, although the scale is printed. If the specification for an option consists of multiple components, the whole specification goes in parentheses, as shown in figure 20.10.

Options	Description
INTERPOL= or I=	Description of line through the graph points: NONE: no line JOIN: connect points with straight line STEP: stepwise line ("stairs") SM0-SM99: smoothed line through points. The higher the value, the stronger the smoothing. NEEDLE: Vertical lines from the X-axis. RL, RQ, RC: linear, quadratic and cubic regression lines. To be combined with CLM: confidence limits.
COLOR= or C=	Basic color definition. Parts of the graph can be colored separately, e.g. CI=color of the line, CV=color of the graph points.
VALUE=	plot sign NONE: no plotting of graph points; PLUS: + as plot sign (default); DIAMOND: ◇; TRIANGLE: △ ; SQUARE: □; STAR: *; HASH: #; DOT: • ; · CIRCLE: ° and many other options
LINE= or L=	Line type. 1=solid line, 2..46 different styles of dashed lines (default = 1)
WIDTH= or W=	Thickness of the line

Figure 20.9: Options in the SYMBOL statement with some of their possible values. The list is not exhaustive. For more details refer to the SAS/GRAPH manual.

The LEGEND statement

The LEGEND statement specifies the layout for any legends you might want to include. The presence of a LEGEND statement does not mean that a legend is being created; it is merely the layout definition should a legend be created. The SAS System creates a legend with PROC GPLOT if a classification variable is present in the PLOT statement, that is if the PLOT statement has the form Y_var*X_var=Z_var, in which Z_var represents the classification variable.

The most important components of the LEGEND statements are: LABEL=(text formatting instructions followed by label text), ACROSS=n: the number of legend elements across, DOWN=n: the number of legend components down, and FRAME to draw a border around the legend. The text formatting in the LABEL= option follows the same rules as the definition in the TITLE statement (see figure 20.3). If the label text has to be split over two lines, these have to be declared in two separate parts and the option J= (JUSTIFY=) must be repeated between the text segments. (Figure 20.10 and 20.11).

Theme for the examples of SAS/GRAPH procedures

The theme in the remainder of this chapter is the banknote circulation in the Netherlands. The currency unit is the Guilder (NLG), which has an exchange value of approximately US$ 0.50. There exist banknotes with face values of 5 (phased out), 10, 25, 50 (added in 1982), 100, 250 (added in 1986) and 1000 guilders. In the data set BANKNOTE there are the variables YEAR, BILL (face value), AMOUNT (value in millions of guilders) and QUANTITY (the number of bills of this type).

Example for PROC GPLOT

In the following example a number of elements from the previous sections have been applied. The graph in figure 20.11 shows the numbers of banknotes for each value over the course of the years. The PROC GPLOT definition to accomplish this is in figure 20.10.

The type of banknote (BILL) is entered as a classification variable. Thus a line is drawn for each value of BILL and a legend is created. The definition of the lines is given in the seven SYMBOL statements. For each subsequent banknote a subsequent SYMBOL definition is used.

In the AXIS1 statement the horizontal axis is defined. The year is rotated 45° with the A= option.

The LEGEND statement contains a label specification split over two lines. Whether or not these fit depends on the terminal. If there is insufficient space for the legend, the SAS System will indicate it in the log and create a default layout.

```
PROC GPLOT DATA=libref.BANKNOTE;
    PLOT QUANTITY*YEAR=BILL/
        HAXIS=AXIS1 LEGEND=LEGEND1;
    SYMBOL1 I=JOIN V=NONE L=2 C=BLACK;
    SYMBOL2 I=JOIN V=NONE L=14 C=BLACK;
    SYMBOL3 I=JOIN V=NONE L=33 C=BLACK;
    SYMBOL4 I=JOIN V=NONE L=8 C=BLACK;
    SYMBOL5 I=JOIN V=NONE L=43 C=BLACK;
    SYMBOL6 I=JOIN V=NONE L=3 C=BLACK;
    SYMBOL7 I=JOIN V=NONE L=1 C=BLACK;
    AXIS1 VALUE=(A=45 F=SIMPLEX H=.8) LABEL=NONE
        ORDER=(1976 TO 1992 BY 2);
    LEGEND1 LABEL=(F=SCRIPT H=1.3 J=C "Quantity"
        J=C "in millions") ACROSS=4 DOWN=2 FRAME;
    TITLE F=SCRIPT H=1.5
        "Banknote circulation in the Netherlands";
```

Figure 20.10: PROC GPLOT with a number of the described options. The resulting graph is printed in figure 20.11. Note the different line patterns. These have been chosen in such a way that adjacent lines can still be distinguished easily.

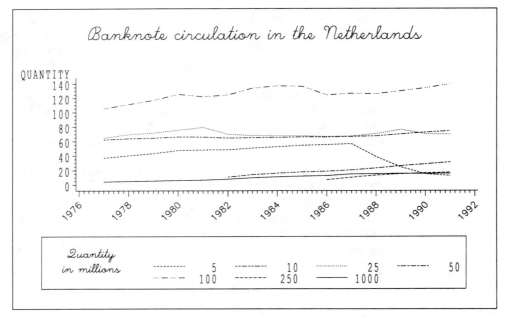

Figure 20.11: The banknote circulation in the Netherlands (source: De Nederlandse Bank N.V.). Analyze this result in relation to the statements in figure 20.10. The title is created with the SCRIPT font.

PROC GCHART

The operation of PROC GCHART is completely analogous to that of PROC CHART, except that you have many more options for formatting your results. So you get results just by adding the G to the procedure name.

The PATTERN statement

The pattern for bars in vertical or horizontal bar charts and segments of pie charts is set up in the PATTERN statement. The PATTERN definition has two options: the COLOR= (C=) option to specify the color and the VALUE= (V=) option to specify the pattern. The pattern definition in the VALUE= option is independent of how the pattern is used. Figure 20.12 summarizes the various possibilities.

Just as with the SYMBOL statement there can be multiple PATTERN statements, numbered from PATTERN1 to PATTERN99. There is however no direct linking of bar or segment to a PATTERN statement.

If no PATTERN definition is present, the SAS System automatically designates patterns. For VBAR and HBAR charts this is the X pattern (crosshatch), for PIE and STAR charts EMPTY.

VALUE=EMPTY	Empty bar or segment.
VALUE=SOLID	Solid colored bar or segment.
For HBAR and VBAR	
VALUE=Rn	Line pattern pointing to top right (n=thickness, default 1).
VALUE=Ln	Line pattern pointing to top left (n=thickness, default 1).
VALUE=Xn	Crosshatch lines (n=thickness, default 1).
For PIE and STAR	
VALUE=PnNa	Line pattern with thickness n and angle a relative to the radius of the segment. Defaults: n=1 a=0 (perpendicular).
VALUE=PnXa	Crosshatch lines with thickness n and angle a relative to the radius of the segment. Defaults: n=1 a=0 (perpendicular).

Figure 20.12: The PATTERN definitions which can be used in PROC GCHART to define patterns for segments of the chart.

Example of PROC GCHART VBAR

Figure 20.14 shows the value of the banknote circulation in the Netherlands. The chart makes use of different patterns to reveal the share for each type of banknote. The definition of this output is in figure 20.13.

```
PROC GCHART DATA=libref.BANKNOTE(WHERE=(YEAR > 1980));
    VBAR YEAR / SUMVAR = AMOUNT
        SUBGROUP=BILL DISCRETE;
    PATTERN1 C=BLACK V=EMPTY;
    PATTERN2 C=BLACK V=SOLID;
    PATTERN3 C=BLACK V=L1;
    PATTERN4 C=BLACK V=R3;
    PATTERN5 C=BLACK V=X3;
    PATTERN6 C=BLACK V=R5;
    PATTERN7 C=BLACK V=L4;
```

Figure 20.13: The PROC GCHART used to create the output in figure 20.14. The figures in the V= options define the thickness of the pattern lines. The DISCRETE option is needed to indicate that YEAR only has discrete values and that no interpolation should take place.

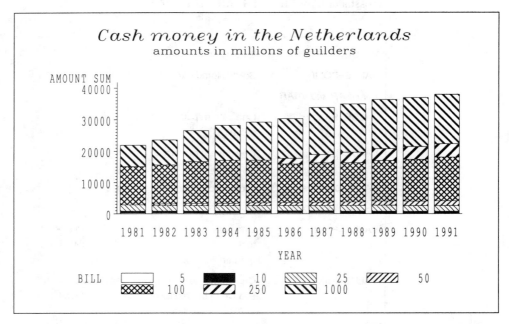

Figure 20.14: The VBAR output, resulting from the definition in figure 20.13. The first title line is created with the TITALIC font, the second line with the COMPLEX font.

Additional features of the PIE statement

In the SAS/GRAPH version, you can do much more with the PIE chart than in the printer graphics of chapter 13. Here we will go into three of the additional options.

With the EXPLODE= option one or more of the pie segments can be pulled out of the circle for emphasis. For this the relevant value of the chart variable is declared in EXPLODE=.

OTHER=.. determines the minimum percentage a segment must represent to be shown as a separate segment. Any segments of a percentage less than this are collected into an OTHER segment.

The SLICE= parameter determines how the legend is placed around the PIE. It can have the value ARROW (legend outside the segment with a reference line), INSIDE (legend inside the segment, if it fits), OUTSIDE (legend outside the segment) or NONE. In a similar manner values can be put on each segment with a VALUE= option.

Example of PIE chart

This example shows the composition (in value) of the banknote circulation for 1991. The share of the phased out bills (NLG 5) and the newest bills (NLG 250) are accented using the EXPLODE option.

Since in this chart all bills must be visible, OTHER=0 is declared.

Figure 20.15 shows the code used and figure 20.16 the results. The selection of the observations for 1991 takes place by means of the WHERE clause. This is easier than first running a DATA step to create a new data set with only the observations for 1991. Be sure to use the DISCRETE option. This is necessary because the values of BILL have a discrete character.

Annotate facility

The Annotate facility is a graphics environment controlled from the DATA step. The basis is a SAS data set containing a number of prescribed variables: the Annotate data set. By assigning the proper value to the variable, each point of the SAS/GRAPH output can be individually controlled.

```
PROC GCHART DATA=libref.BANKNOTE(WHERE=(YEAR=1991));
    PIE BILL/SUMVAR=AMOUNT DISCRETE
        OTHER=0 EXPLODE=5 250 SLICE=ARROW
        NOHEADING VALUE=NONE;
    PATTERN1 C=BLACK V=SOLID;
    PATTERN2 C=BLACK V=EMPTY;
    PATTERN3 C=BLACK V=P1N0;
    PATTERN4 C=BLACK V=P3N30;
    PATTERN5 C=BLACK V=P3X0;
    PATTERN6 C=BLACK V=P5N90;
    PATTERN7 C=BLACK V=P4N150;
```

Figure 20.15: The code used to create the PIE chart in figure 20.16.

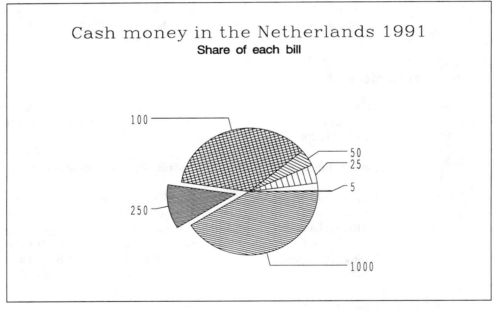

Figure 20.16: The PIE chart according to the specification in figure 20.15. TITLE1 is in the COMPLEX font, TITLE2 in SWISS.

The Annotate facility can be used in combination with the standard SAS/GRAPH procedures, such as GPLOT and GCHART, but it can also be used completely independently. In the first case, elements can be added to the output which cannot be realized with the standard options; in the second case graphics presentations can be made to your own design specifications.

If the Annotate data set created is for use in combination with a standard SAS/GRAPH procedure, then this should be declared in the ANNO= option with the procedure; for example:

```
PROC GPLOT DATA=libref.dataset ANNO=libref.dataset;
```

If the Annotate data set is intended to produce an autonomous graphics output, use PROC GANNO:

```
PROC GANNO ANNO=libref.dataset;
```

In addition to the Annotate facility, SAS Version 6 contains a second DATA step interface with SAS/GRAPH software: the DATA step Graphics Interface (DSGI). This second interface was inspired by the 'Graphics Kernel System' (GKS) standard. In principle the DSGI is more powerful than the Annotate facility, but the price which has to be paid is a less 'SAS like' way of working. Therefore we have chosen here only to describe the Annotate facility.

Annotate data sets

The Annotate data set contains a number of prescribed variables. These can be divided into three groups: group 1: *what* is to be done; group 2: *where* it should take place and group 3: *how* it should be done. The variables of each group with their descriptions are listed in figure 20.17. In addition to the variables listed, there are a few which are only used for special applications. Group 1 consists of a single variable: FUNCTION. In this variable you declare which graphics activity is to take place. This activity always takes place on or starting from the 'hot spot': the coordinates where the previous activity ended. A number of the possible functions and the required variables are listed in figure 20.18.

In group 2 the coordinates for the activity and the coordinate system are specified. Various coordinate systems are possible in the Annotate facility. It is even possible to have different systems horizontally and vertically! The most common systems are: system 3 and 5 for completely self-created presentations and 2 for additions to standard procedure output. Figure 20.19 illustrates the relation between the coordinates and position in the output for these three systems.

Besides the variables in the Annotate data set, four automatic SAS variables play an important role: XLAST, YLAST, XLSTT and YLSTT. XLAST and YLAST contain the most recently used coordinates and thus form the 'hot spot' coordinates. XLSTT and YLSTT contain the end coordinates of the most recent text placement.

Naturally the complete operation of Annotate is not clear from this summary. Two examples might be of some practical help.

Group 1: What

FUNCTION ($8) Name of the required graphics function

Group 2 Where

XSYS ($1)   Coordinate system in the X dimension

YSYS ($1)   Coordinate system in the Y dimension

HSYS ($1)   Measuring system for the SIZE-variabele
                   default 4: cel positions.

X (num.)   X coordinate

Y (num.)   Y coordinate

Group 3: How

COLOR ($8)   Color to be used

STYLE ($8)   Purpose varies with value of FUNCTION, e.g. patterns

LINE (num.)   Purpose varies with value of FUNCTION, e.g. line styles
                   (as in SYMBOL statement)

ANGLE (num.)   Rotation of base line of text;
                   Starting angle for circle segments.

ROTATE (num.)   Rotation of text relative to the base line;

TEXT ($..)   Text string (maximum 200 characters long)

POSITION ($1)   Positioning of text relative to the hot spot:
                   1, 2, 3: 1 position above hot spot, respectively justified as
                   R (Right), C (Centered) or L (Left).
                   4, 5, 6: on the hot spot, respectively R, C, L
                   7, 8, 9: 1 position below the hot spot, respectively R, C, L

Figure 20.17: The prime variables in the Annotate data set with their attributes.

MOVE	Positions the hot spot (XLAST, YLAST) at X, Y
DRAW	Draws a line from XLAST,YLAST to X,Y. The line type is in LINE
PIE	Draws a circle segment, with X,Y as center, SIZE as radius ANGLE as starting angle and ROTATE is rotation angle. LINE contains a drawing instruction: 0: only the arc;1: radius at the start + arc; 2: radius at the end + arc; 3 radius at both sides + arc.
POINT	Places a single point at X,Y
LABEL	Places the text in the TEXT variable from position X,Y. The font to be used is in STYLE, the positioning of the text relative to X,Y is specified in POSITION (refer to figure 20.17)

Figure 20.18: Some of the Annotate functions (= values for the FUNCTION variable) and the related parameters (= values for the other variables).

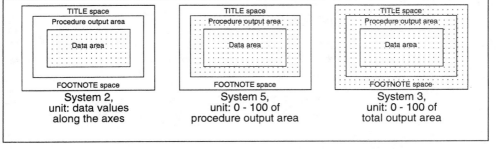

Figure 20.19: The three mostly used coordinate systems of the Annotate facility. System 2 in combination with output from other SAS/GRAPH procedures, system 5 or 3 for autonomous definition of graphs.

Independent use of the Annotate facility

The first example shows how the Annotate facility is used as an independent graphics environment. The assignment reads: draw a circle with a rectangle through it. The center of the circle must be in the center of the output area. Put text in the circle.

In this assignment we shall make a green circle, a red rectangle and blue text. These colors appear as black-and-white in this book, of course. Figure 20.20 shows the DATA step for creating the Annotate data set. The result is shown in figure 20.21.

```
DATA ANNOSET;
     * define the environment;
     LENGTH FUNCTION COLOR $8;
     LENGTH XSYS YSYS HSYS $1;
     XSYS='3';               * coördinates in % of screen;
     YSYS='3';               * 0,0 (bottomleft) - 100,100;
     HSYS='3';               * al other measures also on ;
                             * this scale;

     FUNCTION='MOVE';        * move hot spot ;
     X=50;Y=50;              * centre of circle;
     OUTPUT;

     FUNCTION='PIE';         * draw circle segment;
     ANGLE=0;                * start angle;
     ROTATE=360;             * rotation angle - whole circle;
     SIZE=40;                * radius;
     LINE=0;                 * draw arc only;
     COLOR='GREEN';
     OUTPUT;

     FUNCTION='MOVE';        * move hot spot;
     X=25;Y=25;              * bottomleft corner of rectangle;
     OUTPUT;

     FUNCTION='DRAW';        * draw line to next X,Y;
     SIZE=1;                 * line size;
     LINE=1;                 * straight line;
     COLOR='RED';
     X=75;                   * Y remains unchanged (25);
     OUTPUT;                 * bottom;
     Y=75;                   * X remains unchanged (75);
     OUTPUT;                 * right side;
     X=25;                   * Y remains unchanged (75);
     OUTPUT;                 * top;
     Y=25;                   * back to where we started;
     OUTPUT;                 * rectangle complete;

     FUNCTION='LABEL';       * write the text;
     X=50;Y=50;              * start coordinates;
     STYLE='TITALIC';        * font;
     SIZE=8;                 * character size;
     TEXT='Label text';      * on default position centered;
     COLOR='BLUE';           * at "hot spot";
     OUTPUT;
RUN;
PROC GANNO ANNO=ANNOSET;
RUN;
```

Figure 20.20: The creation of an ANNOTATE data set. Compare the used variables and their values to the tables in figures 20.17 and 20.18.

Another example of the independent use of the Annotate facility is given in Appendix G: creating the so-called 'Ternary diagram' which is often used to depict blendings of three components.

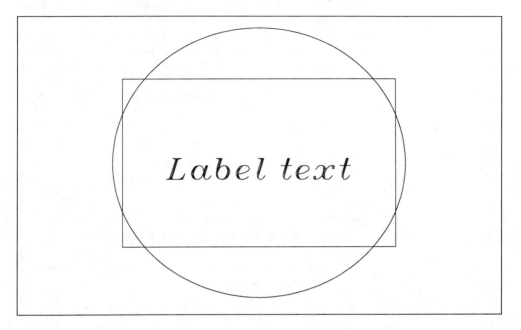

Figure 20.21: Graphical output created with the Annotate facility. The program used to create this result is in figure 20.20.

Annotate macros

From the simple example in the previous section it becomes clear that using the Annotate facility involves a lot of programming. To restrict this a bit and to simplify the use of the Annotate facility, SAS Institute has developed a number of macros. These will often be present in the Autocall library, but can also be stored in a separate file. In the first case they are directly available to your program, in the second case they can be included in the program via an %INCLUDE. Consult your system manager or your installation instructions to determine where the Annotate macros are stored. The macro %HELPANO(ALL) prints a description of these Annotate macros in the SAS log.

If need be, all Annotate macros can be compiled in advance. For this you must execute the macro %ANNOMAC.

The use of the macros begins with %DCLANNO: it defines all necessary variables and their attributes. Normally %SYSTEM would be called next to define the coordinate systems. Then the real work can begin. Figure 20.22 describes the macros which correspond to the functions listed in figure 20.18. The macros work with positional parameters, therefore the order in which the parameters are declared is important. The numeric parameters can be declared as numerical constants or as numeric variables. The character parameters however contain text without quotation marks and cannot be declared via variables. The label text is an exception to this rule: it can either go in quotation marks or in a character variable.

```
%DCLANNO
%SYSTEM(X_sys, Y_sys, H_sys)
%MOVE(X, Y)
%DRAW(X, Y, color, line type, thickness)
%LINE(X1, Y1, X2, Y2, color, line type, thickness)
%SLICE(X, Y, start angle, rotation angle, radius, color, pattern,
          NONE | LEAD | TRAIL | BOTH)
%LABEL(X, Y, 'text', color, rotation base line, rotation relative to base line,
          font size, font, positioning)
```

Figure 20.22: The Annotate macros. You start with %DCLANNO and %SYSTEM to define the environment. %LINE combines %MOVE and %DRAW. The last parameter of %SLICE determines the printing of the radius.

Expanding standard graphics with Annotate

The graph printed in figure 20.11 has been changed with the help of the Annotate macros. The legend is suppressed and at the end of each line the value of the banknote is printed.

Figure 20.23 shows the graph and figures 20.24 and 20.25 show the creation of the Annotate data set and PROC PRINT output of this data set.

Since some lines end very close to each other, the values for these lines would "collide" with each other. Therefore the positioning parameter is used to separate them. The desired positions have been determined by experimentation. Refer to figure 20.17 for the possible values of the positioning parameter.

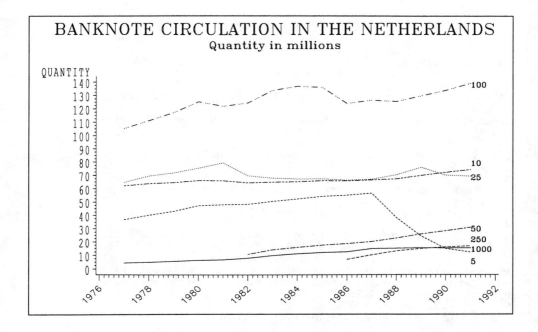

Figure 20.23: SAS/GRAPH procedure output combined with the Annotate facility. Instead of the standard legend (refer to figure 20.11) the value of the banknote is printed next to the line.

```
1                            The SAS System (6.08)
                                            21:20 Thursday, July 7, 1994

NOTE: Copyright(c) 1989 by SAS Institute Inc., Cary, NC USA.
NOTE: SAS (r) Proprietary Software Release 6.08   TS405

NOTE: The initialization phase used 0.06 CPU seconds and 1092K.

NOTE: SAS job started on Thursday 07JUL94 21:20 (199407072120)

1                 /*----------------------------------------------*/
2                 /* PROC GPLOT WITH ANNOTATE ENHANCEMENT         */
3                 /*----------------------------------------------*/
4               LIBNAME GEN '.GENERAL.SASLIB'          ;
NOTE: Libref GEN was successfully assigned as follows:
      Engine:        V608
      Physical Name: TILANE.GENERAL.SASLIB
4
5               GOPTIONS DEVICE=APLPLUS GSFNAME=DOWN GSFMODE=REPLACE
6                        GPROTOCOL=SASGPASC TRANTAB=GTABCMS   ROTATE BORDER
7                        HSIZE=10 VSIZE=6.7 GSFLEN=80;
NOTE: No units specified for the HSIZE option.   INCHES will be used.
NOTE: No units specified for the VSIZE option.   INCHES will be used.
8               DATA BANKNOTE;
9               SET GEN.BANKNOTE;
10              QUANTITY=QUANTITY/1000000; * COUNT IN MILLIONS;
11              RUN;

NOTE: The data set WORK.BANKNOTE has 91 observations and 4 variables.
NOTE: The DATA statement used 0.03 CPU seconds and 1991K.

12              DATA ANNO;
13              SET BANKNOTE;
14              BY BILL NOTSORTED;
15              IF _N_=1 THEN DO;
16                 %DCLANNO
17                 %SYSTEM(2,2,4)
18              END;
19              IF LAST.BILL THEN DO;
20                  SELECT (BILL);
21                    WHEN (5) DO;
22
%LABEL(YEAR,QUANTITY,LEFT(PUT(BILL,4.)),BLACK,0,0,.7,TRIPLEX,9)
23                    END;
24                    WHEN (10) DO;
25
%LABEL(YEAR,QUANTITY,LEFT(PUT(BILL,4.)),BLACK,0,0,.7,TRIPLEX,3)
26                    END;
27                    WHEN (25) DO;
28
%LABEL(YEAR,QUANTITY,LEFT(PUT(BILL,4.)),BLACK,0,0,.7,TRIPLEX,6)
29                    END;
30                    WHEN (50) DO;
31
```

Figure 20.24 (part 1): The creation of the Annotate data set. The Annotate macros do not accept variables for most of their arguments. That is the reason for using the SELECT statement and all those %LABEL calls. The used GOPTIONS create a PostScript file, which can be downloaded and printed on a PostScript printer.

```
2                       The SAS System (6.08) - KLM
                                              21:20 Thursday, July 7, 1994
%LABEL(YEAR,QUANTITY,LEFT(PUT(BILL,4.)),BLACK,0,0,.7,TRIPLEX,6)
32              END;


33              WHEN (100) DO;
34
%LABEL(YEAR,QUANTITY,LEFT(PUT(BILL,4.)),BLACK,0,0,.7,TRIPLEX,6)
35              END;
36              WHEN (250) DO;
37
%LABEL(YEAR,QUANTITY,LEFT(PUT(BILL,4.)),BLACK,0,0,.7,TRIPLEX,3)
38              END;
39              WHEN (1000) DO;
40
%LABEL(YEAR,QUANTITY,LEFT(PUT(BILL,4.)),BLACK,0,0,.7,TRIPLEX,6)
41              END;
42            END;
43          END;
44          RUN;

NOTE: The data set WORK.ANNO has 7 observations and 18 variables.
NOTE: The DATA statement used 0.53 CPU seconds and 2343K.

45          PROC PRINT;

NOTE: The PROCEDURE PRINT printed page 1.
NOTE: The PROCEDURE PRINT used 0.02 CPU seconds and 2397K.

46          PROC GPLOT DATA=BANKNOTE ANNO=ANNO GOUT=GEN.ENG_GRPH;
47          PLOT QUANTITY*YEAR=BILL  /HAXIS = AXIS1 NOLEGEND NAME='PLOTAN';
48          TITLE1 F=TRIPLEX H=1.5
49                  'BANKNOTE CIRCULATION IN THE NETHERLANDS';
50          TITLE2 F=TRIPLEX H=1 'Quantity in millions';
51          SYMBOL1 I=JOIN V=NONE L=2  C=BLACK;
52          SYMBOL2 I=JOIN V=NONE L=14 C=BLACK;
53          SYMBOL3 I=JOIN V=NONE L=33 C=BLACK;
54          SYMBOL4 I=JOIN V=NONE L=8  C=BLACK;
55          SYMBOL5 I=JOIN V=NONE L=43 C=BLACK;
56          SYMBOL6 I=JOIN V=NONE L=3  C=BLACK;
57          SYMBOL7 I=JOIN V=NONE L=1  C=BLACK;
58          AXIS  VALUE=(A=45 F=SIMPLEX H=.8) ORDER=(1976 TO 1992 BY 2)
59              LABEL=NONE;
60          run;

NOTE:  1078 RECORDS WRITTEN TO DOWN.
63          quit;

NOTE: The PROCEDURE GPLOT used 0.16 CPU seconds and 3200K.

NOTE: The SAS session used 1.00 CPU seconds and 3200K.
NOTE: SAS Institute BV, 1217 KR Hilversum, The Netherlands
```

Figure 20.24 (part 2): To use the created Annotate data set, simply add the ANNO= option in the PROC GPLOT statement. The option NAME= in the PLOT statement names the entry in the GOUT catalog.

```
                        The SAS System, Version 6.08                      1
                                            21:20 Thursday, July 7, 1994

OBS  YEAR  BILL   AMOUNT   QUANTITY  FUNCTION  COLOR   STYLE    XSYS  YSYS

 1   1991  1000  15598.6    15.599    LABEL    BLACK  TRIPLEX    2     2
 2   1991   100  13904.4   139.044    LABEL    BLACK  TRIPLEX    2     2
 3   1991    25   1737.7    69.508    LABEL    BLACK  TRIPLEX    2     2
 4   1991    10    743.2    74.320    LABEL    BLACK  TRIPLEX    2     2
 5   1991     5     62.0    12.400    LABEL    BLACK  TRIPLEX    2     2
 6   1991    50   1562.4    31.248    LABEL    BLACK  TRIPLEX    2     2
 7   1991   250   4267.7    17.071    LABEL    BLACK  TRIPLEX    2     2

OBS  HSYS  WHEN  POSITION    X       Y      ANGLE  ROTATE  SIZE  TEXT

 1    4             6       1991    15.599     0      0     0.7  1000
 2    4             6       1991   139.044     0      0     0.7  100
 3    4             6       1991    69.508     0      0     0.7  25
 4    4             3       1991    74.320     0      0     0.7  10
 5    4             9       1991    12.400     0      0     0.7  5
 6    4             6       1991    31.248     0      0     0.7  50
 7    4             3       1991    17.071     0      0     0.7  250
```

Figure 20.25: This is how the Annotate data set of figure 20.23 and 20.24 looks.

Replay and Template facility

SAS/GRAPH software output is created in two phases: first an interim output is created which is independent of the terminal or printer used ('device independent'). Next, this interim output is converted into a series of plot commands for the device involved. The device independent output is stored in a catalog. The default catalog is WORK.GSEG, but with the GOUT= option in the PROC statement, the output can be assigned to any other (possibly permanent) catalog, as in:

```
    PROC GPLOT DATA=... ANNO=... GOUT=libref.catalog;
```

In principle output is always appended to the catalog. But with the option GOUTMODE=REPLACE (the counterpart of the default option GOUTMODE=APPEND) *all* earlier catalog entries are replaced. A more flexible alternative for replacing catalog entries is to use PROC CATALOG, the CATALOG window of the Display Manager or the catalog option in PROC GREPLAY.

The entries in the GOUT catalog are named by the procedure automatically. You can however also name the entry yourself. This is done by the

NAME= option in the PLOT or chart (VBAR etc.) statements. Figure 20.24 shows how.

The graphics in a GOUT catalog can be reused with PROC GREPLAY. With this the output can eventually be sent to another output medium. So you can first examine a graph on a terminal and then, after having assessed it, decide whether you want to send it on to a printer or a plotter.

Extra functionality when using prebuilt graphics is provided by the Template facility. This enables you to place multiple graphics side by side on the same page.

PROC GREPLAY

PROC GREPLAY takes prebuilt graphics from a catalog and can redisplay them, send them to another catalog or to another output medium. The form is:

```
PROC GREPLAY IGOUT=libref.catalog
                < GOUT=libref.catalog >
                < TC=libref.catalog >
                < TEMPLATE=template >
                < FS|NOFS >;
```

The IGOUT option indicates the catalog which contains the prebuilt graphics, GOUT designates the catalog to which the output is to be sent after the replay operations. TC and TEMPLATE are both related to the Template facility, about which more follows shortly. The options FS and NOFS, respectively, determine whether GREPLAY operates in full screen mode. If you work interactively with the SAS System, the default for PROC GREPLAY will be full screen mode and all commands are given through windows and "fill in the blanks" panels. With NOFS (default for noninteractive operation of the SAS System) the replay commands are given in the form of specification statements.

Template facility

The Template facility enables you to display 1 to 999 graphics together. The kernel is the Template. The template consists of numbered PANELS, each of which can contain a graphic. Each panel can in principle have its own size and design. They do not necessarily have to be rectangular. The graphic to be displayed in the panel will be adapted to the dimensions and the design of the panel.

Templates are stored in catalogs. There is no default catalog, so a template catalog must always be designated using the TC option. To get started, the SAS System provides a number of standard templates in the catalog SASHELP.TEMPLT. Making templates is easiest in full screen mode. This is demonstrated in figure 20.26 and 20.27.

If PROC GREPLAY is started up in full screen mode, you first of all come to the main screen. This screen (figure 20.26) shows the graphics which are available in the input catalog (IGOUT= option). From this main GREPLAY screen, the template catalog is opened using the TC command. This displays a list of available templates. Existing templates can be modified from this screen by typing the option E (Edit) on the appropriate line. A new template can be constructed by typing 'EDIT template-name' on the command line, for example EDIT PERSPECT. Following this, the template design window is displayed, where all attributes, the panels and their coordinates and so on can be entered (figure 20.27). The coordinates go from bottom left (0,0) to top right (100,100). The panel numbers will later be used to put the correct graphic in the correct panel. In the example all other components are left in their default settings. To see if the values entered have the desired effect, issue the PREVIEW command on the command line. The borders of the panels will then be visible on the screen. When you leave the window, the new or updated template will be put back in the catalog and from that moment it is available for use.

Full screen mode

The fundamentals of PROC GREPLAY in full screen mode have already been set out. The execution of a replay starts from the main screen. For this the command S (Select) is placed on the line with the desired graphic. Putting a sequential number after the S establishes the order in which multiple graphics can be replayed one after the other. Putting only a number on the desired line indicates that the replay is to take place through a template. The specified number corresponds to the number of the panel as defined in the template.

Thanks to the fact that in the GSEG catalog graphics are independent of the apparatus and device driver used, the destination of the output can still be changed on the main screen. You can also assign another template.

```
+PROC GREPLAY-----------------------------------------------------------------+
| Command ===>                                                                |
|                                                                             |
| IGOUT: GEN.ENG_GRPH       GOUT: _____        Device: IBM3192     |
| TC:    GEN.TEMPLATE       Template: PERSPECT           Scroll: PAGE        |
| CC:    _____    Cmap: _____                                  |
|                                                                             |
|                                                                             |
| Sel  Name       Type    Description                          Created       |
|                                                                             |
|  ___  GCHART     I       VBAR CHART OF YEAR                   07/07/94      |
|  ___  GCHART1    I       PIE CHART OF BILL                    07/07/94      |
|  ___  GSLIDE     I       OUTPUT FROM PROC GSLIDE              07/07/94      |
|  ___  PLOTAN     I       PLOT OF QUANTITY * YEAR = BILL       07/07/94      |
|                                                                             |
|                                                                             |
|                                                                             |
|                                                                             |
|                                                                             |
+--------------------------------------------------------- R --------+
```

Figure 20.26: The main screen of PROC GREPLAY. It displays some general information and also the graphics that are present in the IGOUT catalog. You select the graphics for replay from this list. The TC command leads you from here to the template catalog and the template design window.

```
+GREPLAY: DIRECTORY GEN.TEMPLATE (E)------------------------------------------+
| Command ===>                                                                |
|                                                                             |
|    Name      Type     Description                          Updated         |
| +PROC GREPLAY: TEMPLATE DESIGN----------------------------------------------+
| | Command ===>                                                             |
| |                                                                          |
| | TEMPLATE: PERSPECT                          TC: GEN.TEMPLATE            |
| | DESC: 4 panels in perspectief               Scroll: PAGE               |
| |                                             Device: IBM3192            |
| | Panel Clp Color      L-left U-left U-right L-right  Scale  Xlate  Rot  |
| |                                                                        |
| |  1    _  _____ X:   0.0    0.0   25.0   25.0  X: ____  ____   __   |
| |                   Y:   0.0  100.0   80.0   30.0  Y: ____  ____        |
| |                                                                        |
| |  2    _  _____ X:  25.0   25.0   75.0   75.0  X: ____  ____   __   |
| |                   Y:  30.0   80.0   80.0   30.0  Y: ____  ____        |
| |                                                                        |
| |  3    _  _____ X:  75.0   75.0  100.0  100.0  X: ____  ____   __   |
| |                   Y:  30.0   80.0  100.0    0.0  Y: ____  ____        |
| |                                                                        |
| |                                                                        |
| |                                                                        |
| +--------------------------------------------------------- R --------+
+                                                                             +
```

Figure 20.27: This is the Template design window. The key elements are the sequence number (the panel number) and the coordinates of the four corners of the panel.

Line mode

In the noninteractive use of PROC GREPLAY (thus in a batch environment or with the NOFS option, the SAS documentation speaks of 'Line
Mode'), the whole processing of the procedure has to be given with
specification statements. The two most important statements are: RE-
PLAY and TREPLAY, respectively for simply redisplaying a graphic
from the input catalog and displaying one or more graphics from the
input catalog using a template. In the REPLAY statement simply the
name of the graphic to be displayed is given. In the TREPLAY statement
that must be expanded with the number of the panel in which the graphic
is to be displayed. See the following example for the syntax.

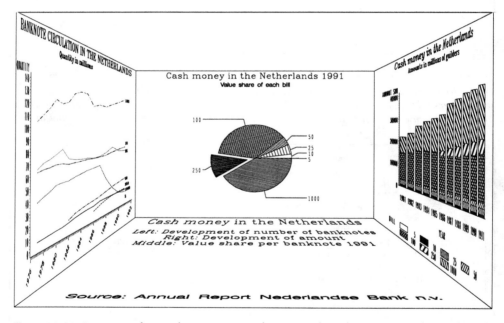

*Figure 20.28: By means of a template you can combine several graphics into one. The used graphs
are already known from (from left to right) figure 20.23, 20.16 and 20.14.*

Example of the Template facility

In this example we bring together a few of the graphics we created earlier
into the template defined in figure 20.27. The first panel contains the
graphic with the number of bills per type (see figure 20.23); the second
panel contains the pie chart as in figure 20.16; the third panel contains
the value of the banknotes as in figure 20.14. The last panel is used for

text created with PROC GSLIDE. The required PROC GREPLAY statements (in line mode) are:

```
PROC GREPLAY IGOUT=libref.GSEG TC=libref.TEMPLATE
             TEMPLATE= PERSPECT NOFS;
    TREPLAY 1:PLOTAN 2:GCHART1 3:GCHART 4:GSLIDE;
RUN;
```

The graphic names used correspond to the entry names as in figure 20.26. The result of this replay is printed in figure 20.28.

Exercises

1. The SAS data set BANKNOTE contains the value of banknote circulation in the Netherlands, by bill type. Graph these values for the year (X-Y diagram). Connect the graph points with a fluid line.

2. Put the number of banknotes and the value they represent for 1991 side by side in a vertical histogram.

   Hint: do a selection in a DATA step. With this make a new variable which at one time contains the total value and at another time the number of bills. A second new variable indicates which of the two values the first new variable contains. Output an observation for both situations. Use the GROUP option in PROC GCHART.

Appendices A-N

Appendix A: Solutions to the exercises

Chapter 2

1.   NAME   correct

1.	NAME	correct
	AGE	correct
	RESIDENCE	wrong: more than 8 characters
	RESID.	wrong: period not allowed
	2ND_SCOR	wrong: first position numeric
	SCORE	correct
	QTR ONE	wrong: no space allowed

2.	Data set name:	CARDATA
	Variables:	KM LITERS MILEAGE
	Numeric variables:	all
	Number of observations:	60
	Output page 3:	result of PROC MEANS

3.	Variables:	CITY UNEMPL MARKET COST INCOME
	Observations:	all data for one city
	Number of observations:	10

or:

	Variables	ENTITY CITY1 CITY2 ... CITY10
	Observations:	a certain entity for all cities, e.g. unemployment
	Number of observations:	4

In most cases the first variant will be the best approach. There are, however, situations where the second structure is more appropriate.

Chapter 3

1a.	NAME :	IAN	
	AGE:	292165	
	SALARY:	63	
	DEPT:	.	("missing value")
	JOINDATE:	.	("missing value")

b. NAME: IAN
    AGE: 29
    SALARY: 2165
    DEPT: 63
    JOINDATE: 07MAR08

c. NAME: IAN
    AGE: 29
    SALARY: 2165
    DEPT: 63
    JOINDATE: 07MAR84

2. ALPHA   wrong: INFILE must precede INPUT
    BETA   wrong: INFILE or CARDS missing
    GAMMA   wrong: SAS does not read back to front
                     (12-11)
    DELTA   wrong: no fileref in INFILE
    EPSILON   wrong: either CARDS or INFILE, not both
                     (unless INFILE CARDS statement)
    ITHA   wrong: variable should be between pointer
                     and format

3. INPUT A $ 3 B $ 6; reads columns 3 and 6 (column input)
    INPUT A $ 3. B $ 6.; reads from position 1 variable A (length 3),
    then variable B (length 6) (pointer input).

Chapter 4

1a.
```
FILENAME F1 'SOURCE.DATA';
DATA SALES;
INFILE F1;
INPUT   @1 SALESREP $15.  @16 DEPT $8.
        @24  PRICE  5.;
```

b.
```
PROC PRINT;
```

c.
```
PROC PRINT;
      ID SALESREP;
      VAR PRICE;
```

d.
```
PROC SORT;
     BY SALESREP DESCENDING PRICE;
PROC PRINT;
     BY SALESREP;
```

```
     e.    PROC CONTENTS DATA=SALES;


2a.    DATA WATER;
             INPUT    @1 CLIENT $8. @9 PREVIOUS 6.
                      @15 LAST 6. @21 MONTH $3.
                      @24 YEAR 4. @28 INVOICE 5.;
             LABEL    CLIENT   = 'Client code'
                      PREVIOUS = 'Previous reading'
                      LAST     = 'Last reading'
                      MONTH    = 'Month of reading'
                      YEAR     = 'Year of reading'
                      INVOICE  = 'Invoice amount';
          CARDS;
             (input rows)


  b.   PROC PRINT LABEL;
             ID CLIENT;
             SUM INVOICE;
```

Chapter 6

```
1.     REPMNTH=INTNX('MONTH',TODAY(),-1);
       * This statement determines the first day of the month for the
       report;
       IF JOBDATE LT REPMNTH THEN DELETE;
```

You could of course combine these two statements:

```
       IF JOBDATE LT INTNX('MONTH',TODAY(),-1) THEN DELETE;
```

2 a.   yes
  b.   no, N is missing

```
3 a.   FILENAME DD1 'WEATHER.DATA';
          DATA STATS;
             INFILE DD1;
             INPUT      @1 STATE $2 @3 MONTH $3. @6 RAINFALL 5.
                        @11 MAXTEMP 5.1 @16 MINTEMP 5.1
                        @21 AVETEMP 6.2;
```

b.   ```
RANGE=MAXTEMP-MINTEMP;
```

c.     ```
* Be careful: rainfall was specified in millimeters;
IF RAINFALL / 10 LT 5
   THEN MODE = 'DRY';
   ELSE MODE = 'WET';
```

d.   ```
IF AVETEMP GT 23 AND MAXTEMP GT 30
   THEN CLIMATE = 'TROPICAL';
ELSE DO;
   IF AVETEMP GT 18 AND AVETEMP LT 23
                       AND MINTEMP GT 15
                       AND MAXTEMP LT 30
      THEN CLIMATE = 'HOT';
   ELSE DO;
      IF AVETEMP GT 10 AND AVETEMP LT 18
         THEN CLIMATE = 'MILD';
      ELSE DO;
         IF MINTEMP GT 0 AND MAXTEMP LT   15
               THEN CLIMATE = 'COOL';
         ELSE DO;
            IF MINTEMP LT 0 OR MAXTEMP LT 5
               THEN CLIMATE = 'COLD';
            END;
         END;
      END;
   END;
```

An alternative would be to start with the coldest qualification and work your way up to warmer qualifications. In that case you don't need the nesting.

# Chapter 7

1a.    Variables: ID_NO RATE1 RATE2 RATE3 AVE1 AVE2

b.     ID_NO:   03
       RATE1:   6
       RATE2:   6
       RATE3:   6
       AVE1:    6
       AVE2:    6

c.     There are three passes through the DATA step
```

d. AVE1 and AVE2 are equal to each other as long as RATE1-RATE3 are not "missing". If any of the RATE variables has a missing value then AVE1 is also missing.

e. `HIGHEST=MAX(OF RATE1-RATE3);`
    insert between INPUT and CARDS

If you interpreted the exercise as "the highest value in any observation", you could do it this way:

```
RETAIN HIGHEST;
HIGHEST=MAX(OF RATE1-RATE3,HIGHEST);
```

2.

```
a,g.    DATA  EXCEPT   PROFIT(KEEP=NET_REV);
a,f,g.      INFILE INPTF END=LAST; * Points to inputfile;
            INPUT @1 DATE DDMMYY8.
                  @9 REP 2.
                  @11 PROD 4.
                  @15 DEFECT 4.
                  @19 MACHINE $1.;
a.          IF DEFECT/PROD GE .1 THEN OUTPUT EXCEPT;
b.          IF PROD LE 0 THEN LIST;
c.          TOT_REP+REP;
            IF MACHINE='A'
               THEN DO;
d.                 A_REP+REP;
                   PROFIT_A+(PROD-DEFECT)*.55;
                   LOSS_A+DEFECT*.23;
                 END;
            IF MACHINE='B'
               THEN DO;
d.                 B_REP+REP;
e.                 PROFIT_B+(PROD-DEFECT)*.35;
                   LOSS_B+DEFECT*.21;
                 END;
            IF MACHINE='C'
               THEN DO;
d.                 C_REP+REP;
e.                 PROFIT_C+(PROD-DEFECT)*.19;
                   LOSS_C+DEFECT*.11;
                 END;
f.          IF LAST
               THEN DO;
```

```
                NET_REV = PROFIT_A + PROFIT_B +
                PROFIT_C - LOSS_A - LOSS_B - LOSS_C;
                LOSS_PRC = (LOSS_A + LOSS_B + LOSS_C) /
                           (PROFIT_A + PROFIT_B + PROFIT_C)*100;
                OUTPUT PROFIT;
        g.      END;
```

Chapter 8

1a.

OBS	ID	X	Y	Z
1	1	12	11	.
2	2	15	.	.
3	1	.	.	4
4	3	17	.	6
5	3	18	.	.

b.

OBS	ID	X	Y	Z
1	1	.	11	4
2	3	17	.	6

Note: In one pass through the DATA step, you execute a SET statement for A and a SET statetement for B. If either A or B reaches end-of-file, the DATA step finishes execution.

c.

OBS	ID	X	Y	Z
1	1	12	11	.
2	1	.	.	4
3	2	15	.	.
4	3	17	.	6
5	3	18	.	.

d.

OBS	ID	X	Y	Z
1	1	.	11	4
2	3	17	.	6
3	3	18	.	.

e.

OBS	ID	X	Y	Z
1	1	.	11	4
2	2	15	.	.
3	3	17	.	6
4	3	18	.	.

f.

OBS	ID	X	Y	Z
1	1	12	11	4
2	2	15	.	.
3	3	18	.	6

g.

OBS	ID	X	Y	Z
1	1	12	11	4
2	3	17	11	6
3	3	18	11	.

Note: Variables read from a SAS data set are automatically RETAINed. Y has only be read at the first observation and keeps it`s value from then on.

h.

OBS	ID	X	Z
1	3	17	6
2	3	18	.

i.

OBS	ID	X	Z
1	3	17	6
2	3	18	.

j.

OBS	ID	X	Y	Z
1	1	.	11	4

2a.
```
PROC SORT DATA=CANDIDAT;
    BY NAME;
PROC SORT DATA=ELECTION;
    BY NAME;
DATA A;
    MERGE ELECTION(IN=E) CANDIDAT;
    BY NAME;
    IF E;
PROC PRINT;
    VAR NAME PARTY STATE YEAR;
    TITLE
    'Winner of the election with party and state';
```

b.
```
PROC SORT DATA=ELECTION OUT=ELECT2;
    BY LOSER YEAR;
DATA B;
    MERGE ELECTION ELECT2(IN=IN_2 DROP=NAME
                          RENAME=(LOSER=NAME));
    BY NAME YEAR;
    IF LAST.NAME THEN DO;
        IF IN_2 THEN RESULT='LOSER  ' ;
        ELSE RESULT='WINNER';
        OUTPUT;
    END;
PROC PRINT;
```

```
               VAR NAME YEAR RESULT;
               TITLE 'Last election and result for per cantidate';
```

c.
```
         DATA C;
               MERGE CANDIDAT ELECTION(IN=E);
               BY NAME;
               IF FIRST.NAME THEN COUNT=0;
               COUNT+E; *E is numeric variable, value 0 or 1!;
               IF LAST.NAME THEN OUTPUT;
         PROC PRINT;
               VAR  NAME COUNT;
               TITLE 'Number of times that each candicate won';
```

d.
```
         DATA LOSER;
                SET ELECTION(DROP=NAME RENAME=(LOSER=NAME));
         PROC SORT;
                BY NAME;
         DATA D;
                MERGE LOSER(IN=L) ELECTION(IN=E);
                BY NAME;
                IF L AND E;
         PROC PRINT;
                VAR NAME;
                TITLE 'Candidates that both won and lost';
```

3.
```
         DATA WGHTMEAS;
               MERGE WEIGHING MEASURE;
               BY IDENT;
               WGT_MEAS = MEASRMNT * WEIGHT;
         RUN;
```

Note: The measured value cannot be multiplied directly with the weight factor as shown below:

```
DATA WRONG;
      MERGE WEIGHING MEASURE;
      BY IDENT;
      MEASRMNT = MEASRMNT * WEIGHT;
RUN;
```

As mentioned the SAS System retains variables read from a SAS Data set. When processing the second weight factor on the same measurement, the variable MEASRMNT is already changed by the multiplication with the first weight factor. The disastrous result can be seen in the following output:

	MEASURE			WEIGHING	
IDENT	MEASRMNT		IDENT		WEIGHT
1	3		1		5
2	5		1		8
			1		3
			2		10
			2		12

WRONG		
IDENT	WEIGHT	MEASRMNT
1	5	15
1	8	120
1	3	360
2	10	50
2	12	600

Chapter 9

1a.
```
PROC FORMAT;
    VALUE CODE
        0='NOT AVAILABLE'
        1='AVAILABLE';
    PICTURE AMNT
        LOW-HIGH='000.000.009,--'
                        (PREFIX= '$ ' MULT=1);
PROC PRINT DATA=REALEST.HOUSES;
    FORMAT GARAGE FIREPL CELLAR CODE.;
    FORMAT PRICE AMNT.;
```

b.
```
DATA _NULL_;
    SET REALEST.HOUSES;
    FILE PRINT;
    PUT @1 'City:'  @9 CITY  $15.
        @40 'Street:'  @48 STREET $15.;
    PUT @1 'Type:'  @9 TYPE $12.
        @40 'Price:'  @48 PRICE AMNT.;
    PUT / @1 'Land:' @9 LAND 6. @40 'Sq. feet';
    PUT / @1 'Number of rooms:' @20 ROOMS;
    PUT @1 'Type of bathroom:' @20 BATHROOM $6.;
    PUT / @1 'EXTRA''S:' @;
    IF FIREPL THEN PUT @30 'Fireplace';
    IF GARAGE THEN PUT @30 'Garage';
    IF CELLAR THEN PUT @30 'Cellar';
    PUT _PAGE_;
```

2a. PROC CONTENTS will tell you which variables exist and what their attributes (labels, formats and so on) are. Combined with PROC PRINT just some of the observations, and you will have a fair impression of the data at hand.

b. Assumptions:

Dataset DEPTMENT (libref F1) contains the variables NAME and DEPTCODE and other.

Dataset PHONE (libref F2) contains the variables NAME FONENBR and other.

```
* Sort and copy to WORK;
PROC SORT DATA=F1.DEPTMENT OUT=DEPTMENT;
   BY NAME;
PROC SORT DATA=F2.PHONE OUT=PHONE;
   BY NAME;
DATA _NULL_;
   MERGE DEPTMENT(KEEP= DEPTCODE NAME)
         PHONE(KEEP= FONENBR NAME);
   BY NAME;          * matching variable  ;
   RETAIN L 5;       * initial value = first line of
                       names from top of page;
   RETAIN C 1;       * initial value: first column;
   LENGTH BEG $3 INIT $1 LAGINIT $1;
   FILE PRINT N=PS HEADER=PAGEHD;
   BEG=SUBSTR(NAME,1,3);
   INIT=SUBSTR(NAME,1,1);
   LAGINIT=LAG(SUBSTR(NAME,1,1));
   IF INIT NE LAGINIT THEN DO;
      * This signals start of new first character;
      IF L GT 47 THEN LINK NEWCOL;
      * NEWCOL starts new column;
      IF L=5 AND C=1 THEN PUT #2 @90 INIT;
      * This is a new page, print first character;
      * in upper right corner;
      IF L GT 5 THEN L+3; * Skip three lines;
      PUT #L @C INIT; * print new first character;
      L+2;
   END;
   IF L=5 AND C=1 THEN PUT #2 @90 BEG;
   ELSE PUT #2 @96 BEG;
   * This way you have always the last name in the
```

```
                    * upper right hand corner of the page;
                    PUT #L @C NAME @C+20 DEPTCODE @C+30 FONENBR;
               L+1;
               IF L=56 THEN LINK NEWCOL;
               RETURN; * This ends the main program;
               NEWCOL: * Subroutine to start a new column or page;
                    C+40; L=5;
                    IF C GT 81 THEN DO;
                         PUT _PAGE_;
                         C=1;
                    END;
               RETURN;
               PAGEHD: * Subroutine to print page header;
                    DO C=1, 41, 81;
                         PUT #3 @C 'NAME' @C+20 'DEPTMENT'
                                   @C+30 'FONE';
                    END;
               RETURN;
```

Chapter 10

1. Assume that the library with the ELECTION dataset has been
    assigned with libref ELECTLIB.

    ```
    PROC DATASETS LIBRARY=WORK;
       COPY IN=ELECTLIB OUT=WORK;
       SELECT ELECTION;
       RUN;
       CHANGE ELECTION=ELECT2;
       RUN;
       MODIFY ELECT2;
            RENAME NAME=NOT_USED LOSER=NAME;
         * You cant do a DROP!;
    RUN;
    QUIT;
    ```

2. The creation of a data library is system dependent. More informa-
    tion is in the system appendices (H - M).

    ```
    LIBNAME MYLIB 'datalibrary-name';
    PROC  CATALOG CAT=WORK.FORMATS;
          COPY OUT=MYLIB.FORMATS;
          SELECT PHONENBR/ENTRYTYPE=FORMAT;
    RUN;
    QUIT;
    ```

Chapter 11

1a.
```
PROC MEANS  DATA=REALEST.HOUSES
    MEAN MIN MAX;
    VAR PRICE;
```

b.
```
PROC FREQ  DATA=REALEST.HOUSES;
    TABLE TYPE;
```

c.
```
PROC FREQ  DATA=REALEST.HOUSES;
    TABLE TYPE*ROOMS/ NOFREQ NOROW NOCOL;
```

d.
```
PROC SORT DATA=REALEST.HOUSES OUT = HOUSES;
    BY TYPE FIREPL;
PROC MEANS DATA=HOUSES NOPRINT;
    VAR PRICE;
    BY TYPE FIREPL;
    OUTPUT OUT=PRICE MEAN=MEAN_PR;
PROC FREQ DATA= HOUSES;
    TABLE TYPE*FIREPL / OUT=FIRE;
DATA RESULT;
    MERGE PRICE FIRE;
    BY TYPE;
PROC PRINT;
```

e.
```
PROC SORT DATA=REALEST.HOUSES OUT=HOUSES;
    BY TYPE FIREPL;
PROC MEANS MEAN N NOPRINT;
    VAR PRICE;
    BY TYPE FIREPL;
    OUTPUT OUT=MEANDATA N=COUNT MEAN=MEAN_PR;
PROC PRINT;
```

Chapter 12

1.
```
PROC FORMAT;
    VALUE GAR
        0='No garage'
        1='Garage present';
    VALUE FP
        0='No fireplace'
        1='Fireplace present';
PROC TABULATE;
    CLASS TYPE ROOMS GARAGE FIREPL;
    VAR PRICE;
```

```
TABLE TYPE*ROOMS,GARAGE*PRICE*MEAN
      FIREPL*N;
FORMAT GARAGE GAR.;
FORMAT FIREPL FP.;
KEYLABEL N='Quantity' MEAN = 'Average price';
```

Chapter 13

1a.
```
PROCSORT DATA=INPUT.STATS;
    BY STATE;
PROC PLOT;
    PLOT MAXTEMP*MONTH='+' MINTEMP*MONTH='-'
      / OVERLAY HAXIS='JAN' 'FEB' 'MAR' 'APR' 'MAY'
    'JUN' 'JUL' 'AUG' 'SEP' 'OCT' 'NOV' 'DEC';
    BY STATE;
```

b.
```
PROC CHART;
    VBAR CLIMATE/MIDPOINTS='TROPICAL' 'HOT'
    'MILD' 'COOL' 'COLD';
```

c.
```
PIE CLIMATE/TYPE=PCT;
```

Chapter 14

1a.   `DROP  &VAR1 - &VAR3 ;      (unresolved)`
 b.   `DROP  DATE1 - DATE3 ;`

2a.   prints variables X and DATE7
 b.   prints variable X with format DATE7.
 c.   same as b.

 a.   prints variable X with format DATE7.
 b.   results in "invalid statement": PUT X DATE7..;
 c.   results in "invalid statement": PUT X DATE7..;

3.   `PROC PRINT DATA=&SYSLAST(FIRSTOBS=100 OBS=200);`

          You could off course also use _LAST_ as data set specification!

4.   a. `%LET GRAND=TOTAL;`
          b. GRAND TOTAL

5a.   INPUT is a reserved word and cannot be used as macro name. Change for example into: INPUTRTN

b.
```
%INPUTRTN(TEMP,F1,NAME,ADDRESS,CITY)
```
generates:

```
DATA TEMP;
    INFILE F1;
    INPUT NAME ADDRESS CITY;
PROC SORT DATA=TEMP OUT=RESULT;
    BY CITY NAME ADDRESS;
```

6.
```
%MACRO PROCED(DATA,PROC=PRINT);
    PROC &PROC DATA=&DATA;
    RUN;
%MEND PROCED;
```

To print data set DS, you would call this macro with:
%PROCED(DS)
To execute PROC MEANS, it would be:
%PROCED(DS,PROC=MEANS)

7.
```
%MACRO PROCED(DATA,VAR=_ALL_,PROC=PRINT);
    PROC &PROC DATA=&DATA;
            VAR &VAR;
    RUN;
%MEND PROCED;
```

You could also replace the VAR statement by:

```
%IF &VAR NE %THEN VAR &VAR; ;
```

Note: Use two semicolons. The first closes the %IF statement, the second either terminates the generated VAR statement or it forms a dummy statement. A more elegant alternative would be:

```
%IF &VAR NE %THEN VAR &VAR %STR(;) ;
```

8.
```
%MACRO COUNT(STRING);
    %LET N=0;
    %DO %UNTIL (&WORD =);
        %LET N=%EVAL(&N+1);
        %LET WORD=%SCAN(&STRING,&N,%STR( ));
        %LET W&N=&WORD;
    %END;
```

```
              %* N is now 1 too high;
              %LET N=%EVAL(&N-1);
              %PUT The number of found words is: &N;
          %MEND TEL;
```

9.
```
              %MACRO PLOTREF(DATA, YVAR, XVAR);
              PROC MEANS NOPRINT DATA=&DATA;
                  VAR &YVAR;
                  OUTPUT  MEAN=MEAN STD=STD;
              DATA _NULL_;
                  SET;
                  CALL SYMPUT('MEAN',LEFT(PUT(MEAN,8.)));
                  CALL SYMPUT('LOW',LEFT(PUT(MEAN-STD,8.)));
                  CALL SYMPUT('HIGH',LEFT(PUT(MEAN+STD,8.)));
              PROC PLOT DATA=&DATA;
                  PLOT &YVAR*&XVAR/VREF=&MEAN &LOW &HIGH;
              %MEND PLOTREF;
```

Chapter 15

1.
```
              DATA NULLS;
                  SET MISSING;
                  ARRAY MISSINGV {*} _NUMERIC_;
                  DO N=1 TO DIM(MISSINGV);
                          IF MISSINGV(N)=. THEN MISSINGV(N)=0;
                  END;
```

Note: It is customary to place ARRAY statements at the start of a
DATA step. In the situation above this is not possible. The
variables in the data set are not yet known in the Program Data
Vector before the SET statement is compiled. Therefore, the
dimension of the array would be zero.

2.
```
              DATA OPTION;
                  ARRAY ACTION {8 } $1;
                  ARRAY CNTRY  {10} $2;
                  ARRAY OPTION {8 } $15
                      ('POPULATION ','AREA','CURRENCY',
                       'NAT. PRODUCT','GOVERN.BUDGET',
                       'OFF. INTEREST %','TAX %','NAT. INCOME');
                  WINDOW CHOICE
                      #2 @2 ACTION{1} ATTR=UNDERLINE
                              +1 OPTION{1} PROTECT=YES
                          +2 ACTION{2} ATTR=UNDERLINE
                              +1 OPTION{2} PROTECT=YES
```

```
                         +2 ACTION{3} ATTR=UNDERLINE
                            +1 OPTION{3} PROTECT=YES
                         +2 ACTION{4} ATTR=UNDERLINE
                            +1 OPTION{4} PROTECT=YES
                     #3 @2 ACTION{5} ATTR=UNDERLINE
                            +1 OPTION{5} PROTECT=YES
                         +2 ACTION{6} ATTR=UNDERLINE
                            +1 OPTION{6} PROTECT=YES
                         +2 ACTION{7} ATTR=UNDERLINE
                            +1 OPTION{7} PROTECT=YES
                         +2 ACTION{8} ATTR=UNDERLINE
                            +1 OPTION{8} PROTECT=YES
                     #5 @5 CNTRY{1} ATTR=UNDERLINE
                         +5 CNTRY{2} ATTR=UNDERLINE
                         +5 CNTRY{3} ATTR=UNDERLINE
                         +5 CNTRY{4} ATTR=UNDERLINE
                         +5 CNTRY{5} ATTR=UNDERLINE
                     #6 @5 CNTRY{6} ATTR=UNDERLINE
                         +5 CNTRY{7} ATTR=UNDERLINE
                         +5 CNTRY{8} ATTR=UNDERLINE
                         +5 CNTRY{9} ATTR=UNDERLINE
                         +5 CNTRY{10} ATTR=UNDERLINE;
      DISPLAY CHOICE;
      * Shift specified countries to begin of array;
      CNTR_SP = 0; * counts specified countries;
      DO X = 1 TO DIM(CNTRY);
          IF CNTRY{X} NE ' ' THEN DO;
          * Country specified in this location;
          CNTR_SP +1;
          * Shift it to first free location;
          CNTRY{CNTR_SP} = CNTRY{X};
          END;
      END;
  DO X=CNTR_SP+1 TO DIM(CNTRY);
      * Clean the remainder of the array;
      CNTRY{X} = ' ';
  END;
      * Generate observations for chosen options;
  DO X=1 TO DIM(ACTION);
      IF ACTION{X} NE ' ' THEN DO;
      SELECT = OPTION{X};
      OUTPUT;
      END;
  END;
  STOP; * Don't display window again;
RUN;
```

```
3.      SELECT;
            WHEN (AVETEMP GT 23 AND MAXTEMP GT 30)
                    CLIMATE = 'TROPICAL';
            WHEN (AVETEMP GT 18 AND AVETEMP LT 23
                    AND MINTEMP GT 15 AND MAXTEMP LT 30)
                CLIMATE = 'HOT';
            WHEN (AVETEMP GT 10 AND AVETEMP LT 18)
                    CLIMATE = 'MILD';
            WHEN (MINTEMP GT 0 AND MAXTEMP LT 15)
                    CLIMATE = 'COOL';
            WHEN (MINTEMP LT 0 OR MAXTEMP LT 5)
                    CLIMATE = 'COLD';
            OTHERWISE CLIMATE=' ';
        END;
```

Chapter 16

1.
```
DATA _NULL_;
    IF 0 THEN SET DATASET POINT=POINT NOBS=NOBS;
    CALL SYMPUT('NOBS',LEFT(NOBS));
STOP;
```

2a.
```
PROC DATASETS LIBRARY=libref;
    MODIFY BOOKS;
    INDEX CREATE AUTHOR;
```

b.
```
DATA SELECT;
    SET libref.BOOKS;
    WHERE NAME IN ('Mailer','Vidal');
```

c.   Sort the BOOKS data set by ISBN number. With a binary search, you can select the ISBN very fast.

d.
```
%LET ISBN=0-917382-65-X; * Makes it easy to change!;
DATA ISBN;
     BASE=1;
    TOP=NOBS;
    POINT=INT(BASE+TOP)/2);
    DO WHILE (TOP-BASE >2);
        SET LIB.BOOKES POINT=POINT NOBS=NOBS;
        IF ISBN="&ISBN" THEN LEAVE;
        IF ISBN LT "&ISBN"
            THEN BASE=POINT+1;
            ELSE TOP=POINT-1;
        END;
```

```
* If the number exist it cannot be further than;
* one observation away;
* Check within limits of the data set;
DO P=MAX(POINT-1,1) TO MIN(POINT+1,NOBS);
    SET LIB.BOOKS POINT=P;
    IF ISBN="&ISBN" THEN OUTPUT;
END;
STOP; * Necessary with POINT option;
```

3.
```
DATA INDEX(KEEP= ID F_OBS L_OBS);
    RETAIN F_OBS;
    SET B;
    BY ID;
    IF FIRST.ID THEN F_OBS=_N_;
    IF LAST.ID THEN DO;
        L_OBS=_N_;
        OUTPUT;
    END;
RUN;
DATA N2M(DROP= F_OBS L_OBS);
    MERGE A INDEX;
    BY ID;
    DO PT=F_OBS TO L_OBS;
        SET B POINT=PT;
        OUTPUT;
    END;
RUN;
```

Note: This time you do not have to use the STOP statement as you normally would when working with the POINT option. End-of-File signaling takes place through the MERGE statement.

Chapter 17

1. This is the code that is needed for the desired report. If you created the report interactively you could use the LIST option of the LOCALS menu to compare the results.

```
PROC REPORT LS=76  PS=20  SPLIT="/" CENTER ;
COLUMN  STATE MONTH,( MINTEMP MAXTEMP );
DEFINE  STATE / GROUP FORMAT= $2. WIDTH=5 SPACING=2
   LEFT "state" ;
DEFINE  MONTH / ACROSS FORMAT= $3. WIDTH=3 SPACING=2
   LEFT ORDER=DATA  ">month<" ;
```

```
DEFINE  MINTEMP / MEAN FORMAT= BEST4. WIDTH=4
    SPACING=2 RIGHT  "min. temp" ;
DEFINE  MAXTEMP / MEAN FORMAT= BEST4. WIDTH=4
    SPACING=1 RIGHT "max. temp" ;


RBREAK AFTER   / DOL SUMMARIZE ;
```

Chapter 18

1a.
```
FILENAME TEMP 'temporary data set';
    FILENAME CURRENCY 'input data set';
    DATA _NULL_ ;
        INFILE CURRENCY END=EOF ;
        INPUT @01 CURRCODE $3 @04 RATE 6.;
        FILE TEMP NOPRINT ;
        IF _N_ = 1 THEN DO ;
            PUT 'PROC FORMAT LIBRARY = libref;' ;
            PUT 'VALUE $RATE ';
        END ;
        PUT CURRCODE $3. " = '" RATE 6. "'" ;
        IF EOF THEN PUT "OTHER = '.';" ;
    RUN;
    %INCLUDE TEMP ;
    RUN;
```

You could of course also read the file into a SAS data set according the CNTLIN specification and then call PROC FORMAT with the CNTLIN option.

b.
Assume that the amount in foreign currency is in AMNTX, the used currency in **CURRENCY** and the result in AMNT_USD:

```
AMNT_USD = AMNTX*PUT(CURRENCY,$RATE.);
```

This construction will however lead to the warning: "character value converted to numeric ..." because the PUT function returns a character result. To suppress that warning, you could read the output of the PUT function again with an INPUT function:

```
AMNT_USD =
    AMNTX*INPUT(PUT(CURRENCY,$RATE.),6.);
```

The cleanest solution, however, would have been to define a

numeric informat with the INVALUE statement of PROC FORMAT. For information about the INVALUE statement you are referred to the Procedures Guide.

2.
```
PROC SORT DATA=libref.PROJECT;
    BY PROJECT;
DATA INTERIM(DROP=TOT);
    SET;
    BY PROJECT;
    OUTPUT; * Write the original observation;
    IF FIRST.PROJECT THEN TOT=0;
    TOT + WEEKS;

    IF LAST.PROJECT THEN DO;
        WEEKS=TOT;
        DEPT='TOT';
        OUTPUT; * Write extra observation with total;
    END;
PROC TRANSPOSE;
    BY PROJECT;
    VAR WEEKS;
    ID DEPT;
PROC PRINT;
    VAR PROJECT A B C D TOT;
```

3.
```
LIBNAME GEN 'data library name';
DATA GEN.DIYCOMBI/VIEW=GEN.DIYCOMBI;
    SET GEN.DEPT1 GEN.DEPT2 GEN.DEPT3;
    BY ART_NBR;
RUN;
DATA;
    MERGE GEN.DIYCOMBI GEN.ART_DES;
    BY ART_NR;
RUN;
```

Chapter 19

1. You should take the following steps:

```
PROC FSEDIT NEW=libref.HOUSES;
```

Next, you fill in the variables. Refer to exercise 1 of chapter 9 (page 172) for their description. After leaving this screen you will see the standard FSEDIT screen. The MODIFY command will bring you to the "Screen modification mode". The adaptation of the screen is self-explanatory.

Chapter 20

1.
```
     PROC   GPLOT DATA=BANKNOTE;
            PLOT AMOUNT*YEAR=NOTE;
            SYMBOL1 I=SPLINE COLOR=BLACK V=SQUARE;
            SYMBOL2 I=SPLINE COLOR=BLACK V=DIAMOND;
            SYMBOL3 I=SPLINE COLOR=BLACK V=TRIANGLE;
            SYMBOL4 I=SPLINE COLOR=BLACK V=STAR;
            SYMBOL5 I=SPLINE COLOR=BLACK V=HASH;
            SYMBOL6 I=SPLINE COLOR=BLACK V=PLUS;
            SYMBOL7 I=SPLINE COLOR=BLACK V=X;
```

You could, of course, expand this with different line types, axis definitions, legend, et cetera.

2.
```
     DATA Y1991;
          LENGTH TYPE $ 8 ;
          SET GEN.BANKNOTE(WHERE=(YEAR=1991));
          VALUE=AMOUNT;
          TYPE='Amount';
          OUTPUT;
          VALUE=QUANTITY/10000;
          TYPE='Quantity';
          OUTPUT;
          RUN;
     PROC GCHART;
          VBAR NOTE/SUMVAR=VALUE GROUP=TYPE DISCRETE;
     RUN;
```

A scaling factor of 10000 is applied to QUANTITY to create comparable response axis values for both AMOUNT and QUANTITY.

Appendix B: Symbol coding and number systems

Introduction

This appendix deals with a number of technical aspects of the coding of symbols in a computer and the way in which computers do calculations. This knowledge is not needed to work with the SAS System. It is only included here for curiosity's sake.

Bits and Bytes

Every symbol (letter, digit or special symbol) is coded in a computer as a so-called 'byte'. A byte, the unit of memory, consists of 8 bits. A bit is the smallest unit of information in a computer: a 0 or a 1. 8 bits can make a total of 256 combinations, from 00000000 to 11111111. Each combination has a specific meaning. In the EBCDIC code on an IBM mainframe (for example, a 4300 or a 3090) 11000001 stands for the letter 'A'. In the same system the digit 2 is coded 11110010. On minicomputers and microcomputers a different coding is used: the ASCII code. In ASCII the letter 'A' is 01000001 and '2' is 01100010. Usually the bits in a byte are not written out in zeros and ones as we have done here, but in so-called 'hexadecimal digits': groups of 4 bits.

Number systems

From our first day in school we have learned to calculate in the number system with base 10: the decimal system. To find the value of a certain figure we have to multiply the digits with powers of 10: 10^0 (=1) for units, 10^1 for decades, 10^2 for hundreds and so on. This is illustrated in figure B.1.

In principle any number, not just 10, can be used as base for a number system. In computers two number systems are used: the binary and the hexadecimal. In the decimal system we use the digits 0 through 9. In the binary system the base is 2 and, therefore, we have only the digits 0 and 1, perfectly suited for a bit. Every next position in a binary number is the next power of 2: the last position is the unit position 2^0. The next-to-the-last position has the value 2 (2^1), before that 4 (2^2), then 8 (2^3), then 16 (2^4). The binary number 0101 is thus equal to decimal 5 (= 0x8 + 1x4 + 0x2 +1x1). The hexadecimal system uses 16 as a base, and its digits are thus 0 through 15. Since it is easier to count with digits of one position, hexadecimal digits from 10 on are usually represented as A B C D E F. Binary 1111 has the decimal value 15, thus F in hexadecimal, the highest digit in the system. Thus we see that 4 bits together can be represented as a single hexadecimal digit. A byte in hexadecimal notation is 2 digits. The binary number 11000101 can be written as C5. Since this is much more convenient than binary notation, we almost always see hexadecimal notation with computers.

Henceforth wherever necessary, a number's base will be given as a subscript, as in 75_{16} (=117_{10}, =01110101_2).

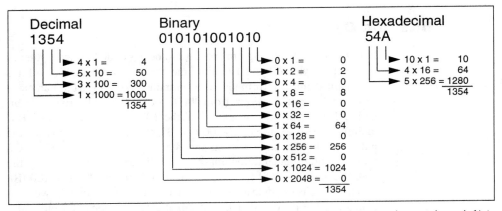

Figure B.1: The decimal system uses 10 as base. Each next digit (moving from right to left) is multiplied by a next power of 10 to determine its value. In principle any number can be used as the basis for a number system. For comparison to the usual decimal system the above also shows the binary and hexadecimal system.

Numbers in a computer

All of this gives us a method for recording numbers in a computer. Instead of the (ASCII or EBCDIC) codes for digit symbols, we can store binary or hexadecimal numbers. In one byte we can count to 255, with 2 bytes to 65535. This increases rapidly as we add more bytes. Usually, however, the first bit position of a number is not used for the value of the number but for a sign, so that negative numbers can also be recorded. For example 12710 is 7F16 and 01111111_2. However, 128_{10} is not 80_{16} in a single byte, but 0080_{16}, 2 bytes, in order to keep the first position on 0.80_{16} would mean -128_{10} because the first bit is now at 1. Taking these limitations into account, with 2 bytes we can count from -32768 to 32767.

Floating Point numbers

The above method is easy to work with and very efficient from a computer standpoint. It has only one significant disadvantage: it can only work with whole numbers; 0.75 cannot be recorded. For this another technique is used: the 'floating point' technique.

A whole number such as 15 can also be written as 0.15×10^2. In like manner 158.63 can be written as 015863×10^3. You can see that in this notation there is actually no difference between a whole number and a fraction. To work with floating point numbers the computer stores the matissa (the fraction component) and the exponent of the multiplication factor. (In the computer these principles are applied in base 16. The principle is the same, so here for simplicity we will continue with the decimal example.) Thus 158.63 is recorded as 15863e3. Only advantages? No: it has the important disadvantage that precision is limited by the number of decimals of the mantissa which can be recorded. Say that we can record 5 decimals; then 68352 can be recorded exactly (68352e5), but 152382 cannot be recorded (becomes 15238e6). There are also fractions which by their nature cannot be recorded exactly, such as 1/3 (33333e0). The range of numbers which can be stored is very wide and is only limited by the space available for the exponent. (The usual working range is from -64 to +64 in base 16. Therefore the multiplication factor can vary from $1:16^{64}$ to 16^{64}.) It will be clear from the above that the largest whole number that can be recorded with the 'floating point' method is determined by the number of positions reserved for the mantissa. In computer systems this length can often be set by the user, so that no more decimals are processed than necessary.

The SAS System uses this 'floating point' method for all numeric variables and calculations. The largest whole number that can be returned exactly is, in the IBM mainframe environment, 72,057,594,037,927,935. Other system environments can have other limits.

Appendix C: Examples of PROC TABULATE

Introduction

This appendix presents a number of simple examples in an attempt to make PROC TABULATE easier to use. The examples are based on a data set with personnel data, which looks like this:

OBS	EMPLOYEE	DEPARTM	SAL_GRP	SALARY	SEX
1	EMPL01	A	GROUP1	2350	M
2	EMPL02	A	GROUP1	2475	M
3	EMPL03	A	GROUP2	2930	M
4	EMPL04	B	GROUP1	6500	M
5	EMPL05	B	GROUP3	3250	M
6	EMPL06	A	GROUP1	2100	F
7	EMPL07	A	GROUP1	2320	F
8	EMPL08	B	GROUP1	2580	F
9	EMPL09	B	GROUP1	2750	F

In the examples only the used TABLE statements and their results are shown. The composition of the VAR and the CLASS statements is left to the reader.

Questions

Number of employees per department

A simple count, only one dimension and no analysis variable.

```
TABLE DEPARTM*N;
```

```
-----------------------------------
|              DEPARTM            |
| ------------------------------- |
|      A       |       B          |
| ------------------+------------- |
|      N       |       N          |
| ------------------+------------- |
|         5.00|          4.00|    |
-----------------------------------
```

Number of employees per department and salary costs per salary group

Two questions which are in fact separate from each other. Everything in 1 dimension; concatenation of the two questions takes place.

```
TABLE DEPARTM*N SAL_GRP*SALARY*SUM;
```

```
-------------------------------------------------------------------------
|                              |                     SAL_GRP             |
|                              |-----------------------------------------|
|         DEPARTM              |   GROUP1   |   GROUP2    |   GROUP3      |
|------------------------------+------------+-------------+---------------|
|    A      |      B           |   SALARY   |   SALARY    |   SALARY      |
|-----------+------------------+------------+-------------+---------------|
|    N      |      N           |    SUM     |    SUM      |    SUM        |
|-----------+------------------+------------+-------------+---------------|
|       5.00|           4.00|      21075.00|      2930.00|        3250.00|
-------------------------------------------------------------------------
```

Average salary costs per department divided by salary group

Division points to nesting. KEYLABEL statement is used to suppress the subtitle MEAN.

```
TABLE DEPARTM*SAL_GRP* SALARY*MEAN;
KEYLABEL MEAN=' ';
```

```
-----------------------------------------------------------------------
|                             DEPARTM                                 |
|---------------------------------------------------------------------|
|              A               |               B                      |
|------------------------------+--------------------------------------|
|           SAL_GRP            |            SAL_GRP                     |
|------------------------------+--------------------------------------|
|   GROUP1    |    GROUP2      |    GROUP1     |     GROUP3            |
|-------------+----------------+---------------+----------------------|
|   SALARY    |    SALARY      |    SALARY     |     SALARY           |
|-------------+----------------+---------------+----------------------|
|      2311.25|        2930.00|        3943.33|          3250.00|
-----------------------------------------------------------------------
```

Average salary per salary group set off against departments

Two magnitudes set off against each other points to 2 dimensions. The first dimension is the row dimension, the second the column dimension.

```
TABLE DEPARTM, SAL_GRP* SALARY=' '*MEAN;
KEYLABEL MEAN=' ';
```

```
-----------------------------------------------------------------
|                   |                    SAL_GRP                  |
|                   |--------------------------------------------|
|                   |   GROUP1   |   GROUP2   |   GROUP3   |
|-------------------+------------+------------+------------|
|DEPARTM            |            |            |            |
|-------------------|            |            |            |
|A                  |    2311.25|    2930.00|           .|
|-------------------+------------+------------+------------|
|B                  |    3943.33|          .|    3250.00|
-----------------------------------------------------------------
```

Average salary per department and salary group, divided by male/female.

Two dimensions, with a nesting in the row dimension.

```
TABLE DEPARTM=' '*SEX=' ',
      SAL_GRP=' '*SALARY=' '*MEAN;
KEYLABEL MEAN=' ';
```

```
---------------------------------------------------------------
|            |       |   GROUP1   |   GROUP2   |   GROUP3   |
|------------+-------+------------+------------+------------|
|A           |M      |    2412.50|    2930.00|           .|
|            |-------+------------+------------+------------|
|            |F      |    2210.00|          .|           .|
|------------+-------+------------+------------+------------|
|B           |M      |    6500.00|          .|    3250.00|
|            |-------+------------+------------+------------|
|            |F      |    2665.00|          .|           .|
---------------------------------------------------------------
```

Average salary for male/female personnel per department with totals

Two dimensions. Concatenation with the 'universal class variable' ALL to create totals column and totals row.

```
TABLE DEPARTM=' ' ALL,(SEX=' ' ALL)*SALARY=' '*MEAN;
KEYLABEL MEAN=' ' ALL='TOTAL';
```

```
---------------------------------------------------------------
|                   |     M      |     F      |   TOTAL    |
|-------------------+------------+------------+------------|
|A                  |    2585.00|    2210.00|    2435.00|
|-------------------+------------+------------+------------|
|B                  |    4875.00|    2665.00|    3770.00|
|-------------------+------------+------------+------------|
|TOTAL              |    3501.00|    2437.50|    3028.33|
---------------------------------------------------------------
```

Personnel composition per department (percentage male/female), description in top left compartment.

Two dimensions. Percentage male/female indicates that an explicit denominator must be used: percentages for SEX must total 100%. Place text with BOX option.

```
TABLE DEPARTM=' ',SEX*PCTN<SEX>=' '/
   BOX='PERSONEL COMPOSITION PER DEPARTMENT';
```

```
-----------------------------------------
|PERSONEL             |         SEX         |
|COMPOSITION          |---------------------|
|PER DEPARTMENT       |    M     |    F      |
|---------------------+----------+----------|
|A                    |    60.00|     40.00|
|---------------------+----------+----------|
|B                    |    50.00|     50.00|
-----------------------------------------
```

Appendix D: Examples of PROC CHART

Introduction

This appendix gives a number of examples of VBAR statements. The graphics which follow are derived from the same SAS data set as in appendix C. The graphics are the 'bald' PROC CHART output.

Frequency counting

Show the number of employees per salary group

A simple frequency count, no options needed.

```
VBAR SAL_GRP;
```

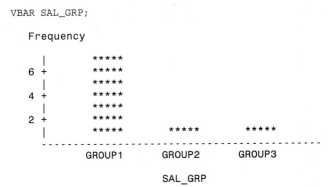

Show the cumulative number of employees per salary group

Each bar is as high as the previous one plus its own value. The first bar then corresponds to group 1, the second to group 1 + group 2 and the third to group 1 + group 2 + group 3.

```
VBAR SAL_GRP/TYPE=CFREQ;
```

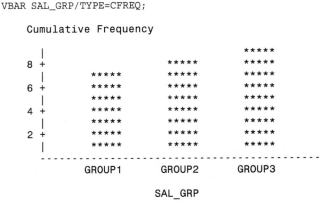

Percentage charts

Number of employees per salary group, but printed as a percentage.

A TYPE option must always be present for percentage charts.

```
VBAR  SAL_GRP/TYPE=PERCENT;
```

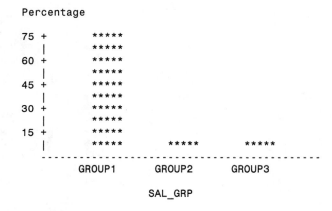

```
  Percentage

  75 +        * * * * *
     |        * * * * *
  60 +        * * * * *
     |        * * * * *
  45 +        * * * * *
     |        * * * * *
  30 +        * * * * *
     |        * * * * *
  15 +        * * * * *
     |        * * * * *     * * * * *     * * * * *
     -------------------------------------------------
              GROUP1        GROUP2        GROUP3

                        SAL_GRP
```

Number of employees per salary group, as a cumulative percentage.

The last bar now reaches 100%.

```
VBAR  SAL_GRP/TYPE=CPERCENT;
```

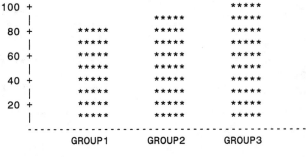

```
  Cumulative Percentage

  100 +                                   * * * * *
      |                     * * * * *     * * * * *
   80 +        * * * * *     * * * * *     * * * * *
      |        * * * * *     * * * * *     * * * * *
   60 +        * * * * *     * * * * *     * * * * *
      |        * * * * *     * * * * *     * * * * *
   40 +        * * * * *     * * * * *     * * * * *
      |        * * * * *     * * * * *     * * * * *
   20 +        * * * * *     * * * * *     * * * * *
      |        * * * * *     * * * * *     * * * * *
      -------------------------------------------------
               GROUP1        GROUP2        GROUP3

                         SAL_GRP
```

Group totals

Total salary per salary group

Now a second variable enters the game: the sum variable. This determines the height of a bar by adding all values of the variable.

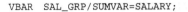

```
VBAR   SAL_GRP/SUMVAR=SALARY;
```

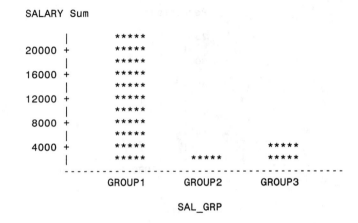

Average salary per salary group

By adding TYPE=MEAN the total salary sum is not calculated, but the average salary per group is calculated.

```
VBAR   SAL_GRP/SUMVAR=SALARY  TYPE=MEAN;
```

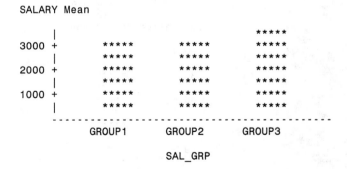

Show the salary per group for each department

The salary determines the height of the bars and is thus used as SUMVAR variable. There must be a set of bars for each department. Consequently, DEPARTM goes in the GROUP option.

```
VBAR  SAL_GRP/SUMVAR=SALARY  GROUP=DEPARTM;

SALARY Sum

12000 +                             *****
      |         *****               *****
 8000 +         *****               *****
      |         *****               *****
 4000 +         *****               *****           *****
      |         *****     *****     *****           *****
      - - - - - - - - - - - - - - - - - - - - - - - - - - - - - - - - - - -
           GROUP1   GROUP2   GROUP3     GROUP1   GROUP2   GROUP3     SAL_GRP

          |- - - - - - - A - - - - - - - -|     |- - - - - - - B - - - - - - - -|     DEPARTM
```

Subdividing the bars

Show for each group how the salary sum per department is composed

Here a subdivision is done, so the SUBGROUP option should be used.

```
VBAR  SAL_GRP/SUMVAR=SALARY
               SUBGROUP=DEPARTM;

SALARY Sum

20000 +         BBBBB
      |         BBBBB
10000 +         AAAAA
      |         AAAAA         AAAAA         BBBBB
      - - - - - - - - - - - - - - - - - - - - - - - - - - - - - - - - - - -
                GROUP1        GROUP2        GROUP3

                SAL_GRP


       Symbol DEPARTM      Symbol DEPARTM

          A    A              B    B
```

Appendix E: Binary Search macro

Introduction

In chapter 16 the principle of the binary search technique was introduced as a way of quickly locating observations in a data set. A general routine like this lends itself to being recorded in a macro. That way you can always use it, without any complex programming. The macro described here makes a selection from a data set similar to what you could make using SUBSETTING IF statements or WHERE clauses. A prerequisite for using the binary search is that the data set be sorted according to all variables which are to be used as keys.

Using the macro

The macro replaces the combination of a SET statement and the necessary selection statements. The structure is given in figure E.1; a practical example is shown in figure E.2. Normally the macro automatically sends the output to the data set to be created. If you want to do it yourself, because a number of selections are still to come after the binary search, you have to declare OUTPUT=NO (YES is the default for this parameter). If you want to make additional selections, you must not specify SUBSETTING IF or DELETE statements. This would interfere with the search mechanism.

```
DATA libref.dataset;
    %BINSET( SET= libref.inputdataset,
             VAR= selectionvariable-1
                  selectionvariable-2
                  ...
                  selectionvariable-n,
             KEY= value 1st sel. var.
                  value 2nd sel. var.
                  ...
                  value n-th sel. var.,
             OUTPUT=YES|NO
             )
    * Here follow possible further tests and calculations;
```

Figure E.1: The macro %BINSET, explained in this appendix, combines a set statement with a collection of selection criteria. The keywords are chosen for easy recognition.

```
DATA SUBSET;
    %BINSET( SET=libref.CARSALES,
             VAR=MAKE MODEL YEAR,
              KEY='CHRYSLER' 'SARATOGA' 1992,
             OUTPUT=NO)
    IF COLOR='RED' THEN OUTPUT;
```

Figure E.2: The data set CARSALES contains a survey of carsales over the years. It is sorted by manufacturer (MAKER), type (MODEL) and year of construction (YEAR). It is not sorted on COLOR, so we cannot make the selection on COLOR in the macro. That is why we use OUTPUT=NO in combination with an OUTPUT statement.

The macro source code

```
%MACRO  BINSET(SET=,VAR=,KEY=,OUTPUT=YES);
```

First come some initializations. The help variable BASE is initialized to 1 and the variable TOP to NOBS, the number of observations in the data set. These variables are not written to the data set.

```
BASE=1;
TOP=N_OBS;
DROP BASE TOP;
```

Then follows the SET statement, with the POINT option (access to observation number) and the NOBS option (number of observations in the data set). The POINTER variable points to the middle of the data set.

```
DO WHILE (TOP-BASE GE 2);
    POINTER=INT((TOP+BASE)/2);
    SET &SET POINT=POINTER NOBS=N_OBS;
```

Now generate the statements to compare the found observations with the declared key values. Keep a count of the number of key variables in macro variable NVAR.

```
%LET NVAR=1;
```

The key variables reside in the macro variable VAR, separated by spaces. They can be separated with the %SCAN function. We must go on searching until VAR is 'exhausted'.

```
%DO %WHILE (%SCAN(&VAR,&NVAR,%STR( )) NE );
```

We run a test using the SELECT statement. In the conditions we must always compare a variable (from VAR) with the corresponding key value from KEY. If the value in the observation is lower than that in the key, a new observation must be fetched higher up in the data set; if the value in the observation is higher, do the opposite. This is done by updating either BASE or TOP. If the values in the observation correspond to the key value, then the next variable should be analyzed. This is done by generating a subsequent (nested) SELECT statement in the OTHERWISE task.

```
SELECT;
    WHEN (
        %SCAN(&VAR,&NVAR,%STR( )) LT
        %SCAN(&KEY,&NVAR,%STR( ))
          ) BASE=POINTER+1;
    WHEN (
        %SCAN(&VAR,&NVAR,%STR( )) GT
        %SCAN(&KEY,&NVAR,%STR( ))
          ) TOP=POINTER-1;
    OTHERWISE DO;

    %LET NVAR=%EVAL(&NVAR+1);
%END;
```

If the OTHERWISE branch is even valid for the last variable, then we force an end to the DO-WHILE loop. Do this by making BASE and TOP equal each other.

```
TOP=BASE;
```

Then all SELECT statements and the DO statements in the OTHER-WISE branches have to be closed. This means two END statements for each variable. At this time NVAR has the value of the number of selection variables +1.

```
%DO N=1 %TO ((&NVAR-1)*2);
    END;
%END;
```

Finally, the DO-WHILE loop has to be closed.

```
END;
```

If there are observations in the input data set which fulfill the selection criterion, they will be at the location where we last fetched an observation. We now go backwards through the data set step by step, until the selection criterion is no longer fulfilled (or until we are at observation 1), in order to localize the first qualifying observation. The UNTIL condition must have the form VAR1 NE KEY1 OR VAR2 NE KEY2 OR VARn NE KEYn OR POINTER=0

```
DO UNTIL (
    %DO N=1 %TO %EVAL(&NVAR-1);
        %SCAN(&VAR,&N,%STR( )) NE
        %SCAN(&KEY,&N,%STR( ))  OR
    %END;
    POINTER=0
    );

        POINTER + (-1);
        IF POINTER GT 0 THEN
            SET &SET  POINT=POINTER;
END;
```

Now that we have gone through until the key no longer fits, we must move one observation forward to the fetch of the first good observation (if there are any good observations).

```
POINTER+1;
```

From the point where we now are, we must step forward until we are past the selection. This will not work with a DO WHILE; we must first execute the SET statement before we can test the condition. The routine is analogous to the backward stepping routine.

```
DO UNTIL (
    %DO N=1 %TO %EVAL(&NVAR-1);
        %SCAN(&VAR,&N,%STR( )) NE
        %SCAN(&KEY,&N,%STR( )) OR
    %END;
    POINTER GT N_OBS
    );
    SET &SET POINT=POINTER;
```

Now we must test whether the observation we have selected fulfills the criterion. There does not have to be an observation which fulfills the condition.

```
IF
    %DO N=1 %TO %EVAL(&NVAR-1);
        %SCAN(&VAR,&N,%STR( )) =
        %SCAN(&KEY,&N,%STR( ))
```

```
        %IF &N LE &NVAR-2 %THEN AND;
    %END;
    THEN DO;
```

Now we do a LINK to the end of the macro. Any SAS statements placed after the macro will then be executed. The end of the DATA step works like a RETURN, meaning that we will come back here.

```
    LINK TAIL;
    %IF %UPCASE(&OUTPUT)=YES %THEN
        OUTPUT %STR(;);
```

When using the POINT option the SAS System must be explicitly told when it should stop the DATA step. The RETURN statement makes a break between the macro and the statements which follow it. These will be executed by the LINK TAIL statement.

```
    STOP;
    RETURN;
    TAIL:

%MEND BINSET;
```

Appendix F: ISO week number macro

Introduction

This macro calculates an ISO week number from a given SAS date value. To be able to figure out the ISO week number correctly, you have to take the year into consideration: the first few days of the year are often counted as week 52 (or 53) of the previous year and the last days of the year as week 1 of the following year. Under the ISO norm, Monday is day 1 of the week and week 1 of the year is the week in which the first Thursday of the year falls.

The macro generates a single complex expression, which can be used as if it were a function. One or two arguments can be given. The first argument is always the input date and the second argument the separator which goes between year and week number. Default is '/'. The result is a text string of seven positions. For example:

```
DATE = '15MAR92'D;
LENGTH ISO_WK $7;
ISO_WK = %ISOYRWK(DATE);
PUT ISO_WK=;                * prints: ISO_WK=1992/11 ;
DATE = '02JAN93'D;
ISO_WK = %ISOYRWK(DATE,"#");
PUT ISO_WK=;                * prints: ISO_WK=1992#53 ;
```

Construction of the macro

The core of the macro contains an expression which looks like:

```
INTNX('WEEK1.2',
       INTNX('WEEK1.6',MDY(1,1,YEAR(&DATE)),0),1)
```

This nested combination of INTNX functions determines day 1 of week 1 of a year. The MDY function determines the SAS date for the first of January. The inner INTNX then determines the last Friday before 1 January. (Not Thursday! Only if 1 January falls on a Friday, Saturday or Sunday is the first day of the year counted as part of week 52 or 53 of the previous year.) Then the outer INTNX function steps forward to the next Monday. If there is a Monday between 1 January and that Friday, then the last days of the old year count as part of the new year; if there is no Monday in between, then the first days of the new year count as the last days of the old year.

You will find several variants of this expression, but the basic working is the same.

The macro source code

```
%MACRO ISOYRWK( DATE, SEP );
%IF &SEP EQ %STR( ) %THEN %LET SEP= '/' ;
```

The first part determines the year. You have to subtract 1 if the input date comes before day 1 of week 1 of the year; you have to add 1 if the date comes on or after day 1 of week 1 of the next year. The calculation is carried out with a 'boolean expression', based on the fact that in the SAS System TRUE has the value 1 and FALSE has the value 0.

```
PUT(  YEAR(&DATE)
      -
      (INTNX('WEEK1.2',
              INTNX('WEEK1.6', MDY(1,1,YEAR(&DATE))),0),
              1) GT &DATE)
      +
      (INTNX('WEEK1.2',
              INTNX('WEEK1.6', MDY(1,1,YEAR(&DATE)+1),0),
              1) LE &DATE), 4.)
```

The separator needs no further explanation.

```
|| &SEP ||
```

Thereafter follows the calculation of the week number. This too will be built all together into a PUT function.

```
PUT(
```

If the date comes before day 1 of week 1 of the current year, then the number of weeks will be calculated with respect to week 1 of the previous year. The first half of the following expression is again boolean (0 or 1) dependent on this condition. The second half is the calculation of the number of weeks.

```
(INTNX('WEEK1.2',
        INTNX('WEEK1.6', MDY(1,1,YEAR(&DATE))),0),
        1) GT &DATE)
*
```

```
INTCK('WEEK1.2',
         INTNX('WEEK1.2',
           INTNX('WEEK1.6',MDY(1,1,YEAR(&DATE)-1),0),1),
         &DATE)
      +
```

If the input date comes after day 1 of week 1 of this year, then the number of weeks is calculated with respect to the beginning of this year. The structure is analogous to the one above.

```
(INTNX('WEEK1.2',
        INTNX('WEEK1.6', MDY(1,1,YEAR(&DATE)),0),1)
         LE &DATE)
      *
INTCK('WEEK1.2',
        INTNX( 'WEEK1.2',
             INTNX('WEEK1.6',MDY(1,1,YEAR(&DATE)),0),1),
         &DATE)
      -
```

If the last day of the year belongs to week 1 of the following year, the result can be 52 weeks too high (1 was already added to the year). Thus if the input date comes after day 1 of week 1 of the following year, 52 is subtracted again.

```
(INTNX('WEEK1.2',
        INTNX('WEEK1.6', MDY(1,1,YEAR(&DATE)+1),0),1)
         LE &DATE)
      * 52
```

Now we have to deal with the familiar '1-off' error (10 posts in a fence imply 9 spaces in between), meaning that the calculated result has to be increased by 1.

```
      +1,
```

Finally the calculated value is put into the result with a 'leading zero'. The expression is not followed by a semicolon, to preserve the function nature of the macro: you must be able to use the macro as a component in a more elaborate expression.

```
      Z2.)
      %MEND ;
```

Appendix G: Ternary diagram macros

Introduction

The Ternary diagram is a diagram that is frequently used in the process industry for the graphic representation of mixtures consisting of three components. The three components together make up 100% of the mixture. In the Ternary diagram then, three axes are used, at 60° angles to each other. The diagram has the shape of an equilateral triangle.

Because there is no ready-made procedure in SAS/GRAPH software for creating this type of diagram, we construct it ourselves with the Annotate facility and, for the sake of convenience, we will make it into a macro. The macro %TERNARY draws the proper diagram and the macro %TERN_X_Y draws in the points in the diagram.

Using the macros

The principle

Figure G.1 shows schematically a program in which the macros are used. %TERNARY is called just once, %TERN_X_Y for each observation to be plotted.

Practical example

The data set LAB contains the results of a number of mixture measurements. The variables for the left and right components are respectively A and B. The diagram will be 5 x 5 inches and will have ten reference lines per axis. The program in figure G.1 can be literally followed if you substitute: %TERNARY(5,10), or %TERNARY(5) since 10 is the default number of reference lines, and %TERN_X_Y(A,B). LAB, of course, comes in the SET statement.

```
DATA ANNO;
   IF _N_=1 THEN DO;
       %TERNARY(afmeting,reflijnen)
   END;
   SET libref.dataset; *the input data set;
   %TERN_X_Y(left,right)
   OUTPUT;
PROC GANNO ANNO=ANNO;
RUN;
```

Figure G.1: The use of the two macros for Ternary diagrams. %TERNARY defines the diagram, %TERN_X_Y draws the measuring points. The arguments of %TERN_X_Y are the left and the right component. The third always adds up to 100%.

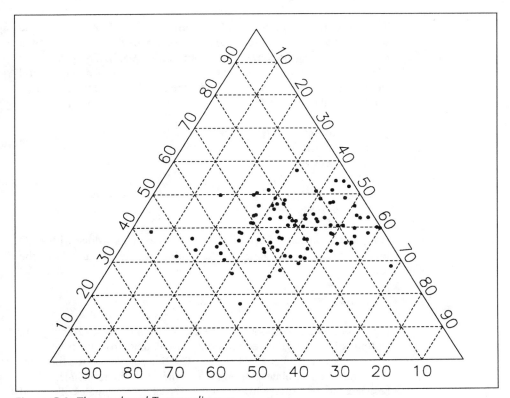

Figure G.2: The produced Ternary diagram.

The %TERNARY macro source code

The macro has two arguments: the dimensions of the diagram (in inches) and the number of reference lines. The latter has a default value of ten. In the macro we need the size of the steps between the reference lines.

```
%MACRO TERNARY(SIZE,STEP);
%IF &STEP NE %THEN %LET STEP=%EVAL(100/&STEP);
              %ELSE %LET STEP=10;
```

We begin by defining the Annote variables and initializing the coordinate system.

```
LENGTH FUNCTION COLOR STYLE $8;
LENGTH XSYS YSYS HSYS WHEN POS $1;
XSYS='5'; YSYS='5'; HSYS='4'; COLOR='BLACK';
RETAIN XSYS YSYS HSYS COLOR;
```

Then we define a square area of the correct size (SIZE parameter) and we draw the triangle. The bottom left vertex of the triangle goes at coordinates (5,5), bottom right at coordinates (95,5). The side of the triangle is therefore 90 units long. Since the height of an equilateral triangle is $1/2\sqrt{3}$ x the length of a side, the coordinates of the top vertex can be calculated $(50 , 45\sqrt{3} + 5)$.

```
GOPTIONS HSIZE=&SIZE VSIZE=&SIZE;
FUNCTION='MOVE'; X=5;Y=5; OUTPUT;   * start at lower left;
FUNCTION='DRAW'; SIZE=1;LINE=1;
X=50;Y=45*SQRT(3)+5;OUTPUT;         * top;
X=95 ;Y=5;OUTPUT;                   * lower right;
X=5;Y=5;OUTPUT;                     * back to lower left;
```

Now comes the definition of the reference lines. This is done with a DO loop. The macro variable STEP determines the index variable of the loop.

```
DO N=&STEP TO 100-&STEP BY &STEP;
```

Figure G.3 helps to show how the coordinates of the beginning and ending points of the lines come about. We calculate from the base of the triangle. A line begins at 5 + 0.9*N. The line running to the top right forms again an equilateral triangle, together with the remainder of the base and the right side, with side 90 - 0.9*N. The coordinates of the end point can easily be calculated (see figure G.3).

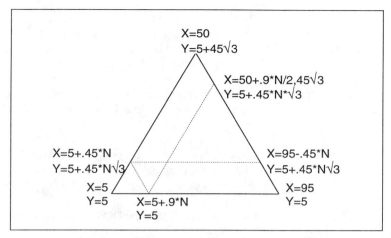

Figure G.3: The start and end coordinates of the reference lines.

The start and end coordinates of the other reference lines are calculated in a similar manner.

It is clear that in many places the values 0.45*N and 0.45*N√3 are needed. Therefore these values are calculate beforehand and stored in a separate variable. This is also done with the variable which goes along the axis.

```
M=.45*N;  O=M*SQRT(3);  L=PUT(N,2.);
```

The first line runs to top right. Line type 2 is a dotted line. The value is placed along the axis outside the triangle, at each end coordinate. The font size is influenced by the number of reference lines.

```
FUNCTION='MOVE';  X=5+.9*N;  Y=5;  OUTPUT;
FUNCTION='DRAW';  X=M+50;  Y=45*SQRT(3)-O+5;
    SIZE=1;  LINE=2;  OUTPUT;
FUNCTION='LABEL';  X=M+52;  Y=45*SQRT(3)-O+7;
    ANGLE=-60;ROTATE=0;  TEXT=L;  POS='2';
    STYLE='SIMPLEX';  SIZE=MIN(1,&STEP/10);  OUTPUT;
```

From the same starting coordinate also stems the line to top left. This piece of code also prints the value along the base of the triangle, however from right to left!

```
FUNCTION='MOVE';  X=5+.9*N;  Y=5;  OUTPUT;
FUNCTION='DRAW';  X=M+5;  Y=O+5;SIZE=1;  OUTPUT;
FUNCTION='LABEL';  X=95-.9*N;  Y=3;  ANGLE=0;  ROTATE=0;
    SIZE=MIN(1,&STEP/10);  OUTPUT;
```

Next follow the horizontal reference lines. These begin where the line to top left ends. For this line the label is placed on the leftside.

```
FUNCTION='MOVE';  X=M+5;  Y=O+5;  OUTPUT;
FUNCTION='DRAW';  X=95-M;  Y=O+5;SIZE=1;  OUTPUT;
FUNCTION='LABEL';  X=M+3;  Y=O+7;  ANGLE=60;  ROTATE=0;
    SIZE=MIN(1,&STEP/10);  OUTPUT;
```

The work is done. Close the DO loop and terminate the macro.

```
END;
%MEND;
```

The %TERN_X_Y macro is much simpler. This translates the values from the first two Ternary coordinates into the X and Y coordinates of the graph and puts a point at that spot. On some devices a single point is so thin that you would like to plot the points somewhat bigger. For that reason there is a third argument. If that argument has the value BOLD, then we draw a miniscule circle.

```
%MACRO  TERN_X_Y(LEFT,RIGHT,STYLE);
   %IF %UPCASE(&STYLE) EQ BOLD %THEN %DO;
        FUNCTION='PIE';  COLOR='BLACK';
        LINE=0;ROTATE=360;SIZE=.1;STYLE='SOLID';
   %END;
   %ELSE FUNCTION='POINT';
     X=5+.9*(.5*&LEFT+&RIGHT);
     Y=5+.45*&LEFT*SQRT(3);
     OUTPUT;
   %MEND;
```

Appendix H: The SAS System under the Windows operating systems

Introduction

This appendix covers briefly a few specific aspects of the SAS System under Microsoft's Windows operating system. This is not, however, an installation manual for the SAS System under Windows, nor a Windows manual. The reader is assumed to be familiar with Windows and with the basic principles of the SAS System (at least chapters 1 - 5 of this book). The current version of the SAS System under Windows is 6.10. Base SAS software of Version 6.10 is virtually identical, functionally, to Version 6.08 on which this book is based.

The operation of the SAS Software under Windows

Starting a SAS session

Under Windows, the SAS System can be used both interactively and in batch mode. In both modes Windows has to be active. You start via a 'program group window'. The SAS System must be declared as a program item in such a window. This is a Windows function. If the SAS System has been declared, a double click on the SAS icon starts up a SAS session. In case the SAS System has not been declared in a program group, it can still be started via the RUN option in the FILE menu. Type in the complete name (including directory path and extension) of the SAS System in the RUN dialog box, as in:

```
C:\SAS\SAS.EXE
```

Clicking OK starts up the SAS System.

The SAS System can also be started from a DOS prompt. Because the SAS System will always be operating in a Windows environment, the SAS command is entered in the WIN command. This is also the proper way to start up batch programs.

During start up, the SAS System consults a configuration file CONFIG.SAS. In the CONFIG.SAS file are a number of essential options for using the SAS System. You can add your own frequently used options. See chapter 18 for the possible options. During installation of the SAS System a standard CONFIG.SAS is created in the !SASROOT directory (see section "Required directories').

Display Manager

The Display Manager operates as described in chapter 5, however in principle the Display Manager does not start up with a command line but with pop-up and pull-down menus.

The text editor in the PROGRAM window can function in two ways: normally as a standard Windows editor, similar to the Notepad editor (no line numbers, editing done with 'copy & paste'), but also as the SAS editor, as described in chapter 5.

The assignment of function keys deviates from what is described in chapter 5. Bringing up the KEYS window shows directly how each key has been programmed. In the KEYS window these assignments can be adjusted as needed.

Batch mode

Starting up the SAS System in batch mode proceeds from a DOS prompt. For this the file with the program source is given as an option in the start up command, as in:

```
C:\WINDOWS\WIN C:\SAS.SAS.EXE -SYSIN C:\dir\file.SAS
```

in which 'dir' and 'file' are the directory path and the name of the program to be started up. The extension .SAS is a standard extension for SAS source files. In batch processing the SAS log and list are output to files in the working directory with the name of the source file and, respectively, the extensions .LOG and .LST.

SAS options

The options described in chapter 18 are also valid for the SAS System under Windows. In addition there are a few options of special importance for the Windows environment. These are listed in figure H.1. Options can be declared in an OPTIONS statement, in the CONFIG.SAS file or as options in the SAS startup command. In the last two cases the options are preceded by a dash (-). So in the CONFIG.SAS file they would be:

```
-NOCENTER
-LINESIZE 72
```

Be careful not to write LINESIZE=72, the way this option appears in the OPTIONS statement. The same options should be entered in the SAS command as:

```
C:\SAS\SAS.EXE -NOCENTER -LINESIZE 72
```

If the same option (but with different setting) appears in both places, then the option in the SAS command takes precedence over the option in the CONFIG.SAS file. Likewise, settings in the command are over-ruled by settings in an OPTIONS statement.

SET variable directory<\file>	Equivalent of the DOS SET command to define an "environment variable". If the variable points to a data library, it can be used as libref. If the path points to external files, you can use the variable as fileref.
SYSIN	Path + file name for SAS source file to be used in batch mode.
PRINT destination	Destination of procedure output, specified as directory path and eventually a file name or a standard address such as LPT1:.

Figure H.1: Next to the general SAS options as discussed in chapter 18 the above are specific for the WINDOWS environment.

Printing

The SAS System makes use of the standard Windows print monitor. The Windows dialog boxes for printer setup are also available. The default printer address is 'LPT1:'. If a different address is desired, this can be declared via the OPTIONS statement or in the CONFIG.SAS file, as shown here for addressing a serial printer:

```
OPTIONS SYSPRINT='COM1: <driver>';
```

In the CONFIG.SAS file it reads:

```
-SYSPRINT 'COM1:' <driver>
```

The optional driver name specfies the Windows print driver that you want to use.

A printer can also be designated via a FILENAME statement, in an analogous manner. Then you use PROC PRINTTO or the FILE state-ment to direct the output to the designated file (in this case a printer).

Interrupting a SAS session

If you need to interrupt the execution of an SAS program, for example in response to an error message, use a CTRL-Break combination. This also applies to a batch program: the CTRL-Break is given in the status window.

Executing DOS commands

The X command on a command line of the Display Manager temporarily transfers you to a DOS environment. At this time any legal DOS command can be given, such as DIR, MKDIR and so on. Typing EXIT after the DOS prompt returns you to the SAS environment.

If only one command needs to be executed, this can be given directly in the X command, for example:

```
X 'CD A:\THEDATA'
```

This X command can also be used as a statement (of course, followed by ';'). It is a global statement, just as, for example, the TITLE statement. It cannot therefore be used conditionally in a DATA step. For this, use the CALL SYSTEM routine:

```
IF ... THEN CALL SYSTEM('DOS-command');
```

Ending a SAS session

You can end a SAS session under Windows in several ways. You can type BYE or ENDSAS on a Display Manager command line; you can submit an ENDSAS statement or use the various standard Windows methods for closing a program, such as 'End Task' from the Task list or Exit SAS under the File menu.

Directory and file structure

Required directories

During the installation process of the SAS System under Windows a number of directories are created and the environment variable !SASROOT is defined. !SASROOT refers to the SAS root directory, usually called SAS. All other SAS directories go within this root directory. The table in figure H.2 gives a summary of the directories which are created. Also the CONFIG.SAS file normally goes in this root directory. During startup the SAS System also creates the WORK data library. This goes in the 'working directory'. Usually this is the same as the root directory.

```
!SASROOT\CORE\SASINST          (installation files)
!SASROOT\CORE\SASDLL           (general system files)
!SASROOT\product\SASEXE        (program files)
!SASROOT\product\SASHELP       (help files + catalogs)
!SASROOT\product\SASMACRO      (autocall macros)
!SASROOT\product\SASMSG        (message files)
!SASROOT\product\SAMPLE        (sample programs)
!SASROOT\product\SASTEST       (test programs)
```

Figure H.2: When installing the SAS System, a number of directories are created, all within the !SASROOT directory (usually C:\SAS) The first two directories are always there, the others are created for each licensed product.

File names

A file name in the DOS environment generally has an extension of three positions, which describe the type of file it is. The SAS System has its own standard for file extensions under Windows. These extensions are listed in figure H.3. Changing extensions can have the effect that the files can no longer be accessed.

.SD2	SAS data set (Memtype=DATA)
.SI2	Index data set, created in a DATA step with INDEX data set option or with INDEX CREATE in PROC DATASETS
.SC2	SAS catalog
.SS2	Stored program (Compiled data step, ref. chapter 15)
.SV2	Data view, for example created with the DATA step view facility (ref. chapter 18) or with PROC SQL (not discussed)
.SA2	ACCESS descriptor file, created with SAS/ACCESS (not discussed)
.DAT	Any data file (for use in INFILE or FILE statement)
.SAS	SAS source file
.LOG	SAS log file, during background processing
.LST	SAS list file (procedure output), during background processing

Figure H.3: Summary of the file name extensions that are used by the SAS System.

SAS data libraries

In the Windows environment a SAS data library is a subdirectory. All files in the subdirectory which are recognized by the SAS System as SAS files (via the extensions) and which can be accessed with the same engine together form the data library. In principle, a data library can be made of a collection of subdirectories, but considering the confusion that this can cause in locating input data sets and placing output data sets, this is not recommended.

Autoexec processing

At startup the SAS System looks for a file AUTOEXEC.SAS. If this exists, then the SAS statements in this file will be processed. The SAS System looks for the AUTOEXEC.SAS in the following places (and in this order): the working directory, directories listed in the DOS PATH command and finally in the root directory. Should the autoexec file have a different name, or exist in a different location, then this must be declared in the AUTOEXEC option at SAS System startup, as in:

```
C:\SAS\SAS.EXE  -AUTOEXEC  C:\SAS\INITPGM.SAS
```

If an AUTOEXEC.SAS file exists and you do not want it executed, give the NOAUTOEXEC option at startup.

Allocations

Host system allocation

Windows gives you the possibility to allocate files with DOS SET commands. With the DOS SET command you define an 'environment variable' which contains the directory path and eventually the file name of the file that you want to allocate. If the environment variable contains only one directory, this can be used as libref for SAS data libraries or as fileref for all files in the directory. The individual files can then be named as 'members' in, for example, INFILE and FILE statements:

```
INFILE  MYFILES(RAWDATA);
```

When using environment variables, no engine can be specified. Thus if you use an environment variable as a library name, it is always processed with a default engine (see chapter 10).

The SET commands must take place before you start Windows and the SAS System.

As an alternative, there is also a SAS SET system option (not to be confused with a SET statement!) with which environment variables can be defined during SAS System startup. It works like the DOS SET command.

The examples which follow, work both for DOS and SAS SET commands. MYLIB addresses a directory which functions as a SAS data library, MYFILES refers to a directory with input files, and MYDATA refers to a particular file.

```
SET MYLIB  C:\SAS\PERMLIB
SET MYFILES  C:\SAS\DATADIR
SET MYDATA  C:\SAS\DATADIR\RAWDATA.DAT
```

The following statements show how these references can be used. Be careful that a reference to an environment variable in Windows is normally preceded by an exclamation mark. Not however when used as fileref or libref.

```
DATA MYLIB.SASDATA;
...
INFILE MYFILES(RAWDATA);
...
INFILE MYDATA;
```

FILENAME statement

The form of the FILENAME statement is:

```
FILENAME fileref <device> <'file name'> <options>;
```

The fileref cannot be CON, since under Windows this is a 'reserved name'. The device only needs to be used if a destination other than a disk file is allocated. The possible device types are listed in figure H.4.

The file name is a complete DOS name, including path, or only a directory path, in which case the individual files within the directory are declared in the INFILE or FILE statement. Standard addresses can also be given as COM1:, LPT1:, and so on. If you give a device type, specifying a file name is often not necessary.

Among the options, MOD is particularly important; with this option new information can be appended to an existing file.

COMMPORT	Assigns a COMM port. Instead of the file name, you specify the port you want to use (e.g. FILENAME port COMMPORT 'COM1:';)
DDE	Use "Dynamic Data Exchange"
DISK	The default device. May be left out.
DRIVEMAP	Special option to find out which drives are available.
DUMMY	No output, DATA step works normal otherwise
PLOTTER	An eventual connected plotter for SAS/GRAPH output
PRINTER	Printer (printer port assigned as file).

Figure H.4: The device types which you can specify in the FILENAME statement. Notice that the decice types TAPE and TERMINAL are not available in the Windows environment.

The following statements are correct FILENAME statements (compare section 'Host system allocations' above):

```
FILENAME MYFILES 'C:\SAS\DATADIR';
FILENAME  MYDATA 'C:\SAS\DATADIR\RAWDATA.DAT';
```

In FILENAME statements (and also in LIBNAME statements) an environment variable can also be used as an address pointer. Then it should be preceded by an exclamation mark:

```
FILENAME  MYDATA '!MYFILES\RAWDATA.DAT';
```

LIBNAME statement

The LIBNAME has the form:

```
LIBNAME libref <engine> 'directory';
```

There are no specific Windows options. Since the engine only needs to be declared in special situations, we will not go into this any further. The following is thus a correct LIBNAME statement (compare section 'Host system allocations' above):

```
LIBNAME MYLIB 'C:\SAS\PERMLIB';
```

DDE (Dynamic Data Exchange)

DDE is one of the unique capabilities of Windows for the exchange of data among programs which are active under Windows. The SAS System supports DDE via special options in the FILENAME statement. Reading and writing data via the DDE link thus takes place in the DATA step with INPUT and PUT statements. The DDE option in the FILENAME statement consists of three parts. First of all the keyword DDE, which goes directly after the fileref, then the DDE file specification and finally any special DDE options. The DDE file specification can have two forms: a 'DDE triplet' or 'CLIPBOARD'. With the latter you read data from and write data to the Windows clipboard. The DDE triplet contains the definition of the data source or destination at the other side of the link. The precise form depends on the application on the other side, but in Microsoft's Excel for example it is: 'Application name|document!location', as in: 'Excel|PlanSheet!r5c30:r60c38'. The options are HOTLINK and NOTAB. HOTLINK will always signal if data has been changed to the other side of the link. With NOTAB, TAB characters are left out between variables.

The complete statement looks like this example:

```
FILENAME EXCEL DDE 'Excel|PlanSheet!r5c30:r60c38';
```

With this each INPUT statement reads a line from the designated spreadsheet, in which each variable is read from the following column, or vice versa: each PUT statement writes to a line, each variable going into its own column.

It is also possible via DDE to issue commands to Excel. Here, SYSTEM is given as destination:

```
FILENAME EXCELCMD DDE 'Excel|SYSTEM';
```

The commands which can be given via this link correspond with the commands from the Excel macro language, for example:

```
...
FILE EXCELCMD;
PUT '[SELECT ("R1C1:R1C20")]';
...
PUT '[SAVE()]';
```

Special functions

SLEEP function

The SLEEP function pauses the execution of a DATA step for a given number of seconds. The maximum number of seconds that can be given corresponds roughly to 46 days.

The following DATA step pauses the SAS program for one and one-half hours:

```
DATA _NULL_;
 X=SLEEP(3600*1.5);
RUN;
```

WAKEUP function

The WAKEUP function is more or less the complement of the SLEEP function: it sets up a time (possibly with date) at which the DATA step is to resume. The argument is a date/time constant, a time constant or a number. In the second case the SAS System waits until that time comes up (today or tomorrow) and in the third case the SAS System wakes up the given number of seconds after midnight.

```
X = WAKEUP('21JUN93:06:00:00'DT);
Y = WAKEUP('22:30'T);* may be tonight or tomorrow night;
Z = WAKEUP(7200);    * wakes up 2:00 AM tomorrow;
```

Appendix I: The SAS System under the OS/2 operating system

Introduction

This appendix briefly covers a few specific aspects of the SAS System under IBM's OS/2 operating system. The intention is to get the user started with the SAS System under OS/2, not to cover all attributes and options. OS/2 is technically a totally different system from Microsoft's Windows, but functionally both systems are very similar to each other. In this appendix then we will frequently be referring to what was described in appendix H, to avoid repetition.

The reader is assumed to be familiar with the basic principles of the SAS System (at least chapters 1 - 5 of this book).

The current version of the SAS System under OS/2 is 6.08.

The operation of the SAS System under OS/2

Starting up a SAS session

Under OS/2, the SAS System can be used both interactively and in batch mode. It is best to start up with the help of the Desktop Manager. For this you should load the SAS System as 'program entry' in a Program group window, for example in Group Main, during installation. Multiple program entries are possible, to have both the Display Manager and batch sessions available.

During start up, the SAS System consults the configuration file CONFIG.SAS. In the CONFIG.SAS file are a number of essential options for using the SAS System. You can add your own frequently used options. See chapter 18 for the possible options. During installation of the SAS System a standard CONFIG.SAS is created in the !SASROOT directory (see the section "Required directories').

Display Manager

In principle the Display Manager operates as described in chapter 5, however a number of things have been adapted to be in line with the guidelines for OS/2 applications. The standard method of operation is not with a command line but with pull-down menus, according to the Presentation Manager guidelines. Programs can be loaded in the PROGRAM window via the OPEN option of the FILE menu.

The assignment of function keys deviates from what is described in chapter 5. Calling the KEYS window shows directly how each key has been programmed. In the KEYS window these assignments can be adjusted as needed.

Batch mode

SAS System startup in batch mode can also be done from a 'Program Group Window' (for example Group-Main), but also from an OS/2 command prompt. For this either the SASROOT directory must be present in the OS/2 PATH command, or SASROOT is the working directory. The program source file is given as an option in the start command, as in:

```
SAS -SYSIN C:\dir\file.SAS
```

in which 'dir' and 'file' are the directory path and the name of the program to be started. The extension .SAS is a standard extension for SAS source files. In batch processing the SAS log and list are output to files in the working directory with the name of the source file and the extensions .LOG and .LST, respectively.

Batch mode programs can be run in the background under OS/2. Then the PC is available for other tasks. Background processing takes longer than foreground processing, because any foreground tasks always take precedence.

SAS options

The options described in chapter 18 are also valid for the SAS System under OS/2. The most important specific OS/2 options correspond with the options for the SAS System under Windows, see appendix H and specifically figure H.1.

Printing

Printing from Display Manager windows can be done with print options under the FILE menu. In batch mode SAS log and list are in principle sent to a file. It is also possible however to send output directly to a printer. The command:

```
SAS -SYSIN C:\SAS\SRC\MYPROG.SAS -ALTPRINT LPT1:
```

immediately sends a copy of the output to the LPT1: printer.

Also PROC PRINTTO (see chapter 18) can be used to get output to a printer:

```
FILENAME PRTOUT PRINTER;
PROC PRINTTO PRINT=PRTOUT;
```

From this point all output is directed to PRTOUT and thus to the printer.

Interrupting a SAS session

During execution a SAS program can be interrupted with CTRL-Break. A dialog gives various choices for the rest of the program.

Executing OS/2 commands

The X command on a command line of the Display Manager temporarily transfers you to an OS/2 environment. At this time any OS/2 command can be given, such as DIR, MD and so on. Typing EXIT after the OS/2 prompt brings you back to the SAS environment. The commands given at the OS/2 prompt are not applicable to the SAS session.

If only one command needs to be executed, this can be given directly in the X command, for example:

```
X 'CD A:\THEDATA'
```

This X command can also be used as a statement (of course followed by ';'). It is a global statement, just as for example the TITLE statement. It cannot therefore be given conditionally in a DATA step. For this, use the CALL SYSTEM routine:

```
IF ... THEN CALL SYSTEM('OS/2 command');
```

OS/2 commands which have been given directly in an X statement or by a CALL SYSTEM statement affect the SAS session.

Ending as SAS session

You can end a SAS session under OS/2 in several ways: typing BYE or ENDSAS on a Display Manager command line: submitting an ENDSAS statement or use the various standard OS/2 methods for closing a program, such as 'End Task' from the Task list or Exit SAS under the File menu.

Directory and file structure

Required directories

Installing the SAS System under OS/2 creates a number of directories and defines the environment variable SASROOT. SASROOT refers to the SAS root directory, usually called SAS. All other SAS directories are created within this root directory. The table in figure I.1 gives a summary of the directories which are created. Also the CONFIG.SAS file normally goes in this root directory.

During startup the SAS System also creates the WORK data library. This goes in the 'working directory'. Usually this is the same as the root directory.

```
SASROOT\CORE\SASINST          (installation files)
SASROOT\CORE\SASDLL           (general system files)
SASROOT\product\SASEXE        (program files)
SASROOT\product\SASHELP       (help files + catalogs)
SASROOT\product\SASMACRO      (autocall macros)
SASROOT\product\SASMSG        (message files)
SASROOT\product\SAMPLE        (sample programs)
SASROOT\product\SASTEST       (test programs)
```

Figure I.1: When installing the SAS System a number of directories are created, all within the SASROOT directory (usually C:\SAS). The first two directories are always there, the others are created for each licensed product.

File names

File name conventions under OS/2 correspond to Windows. The extensions used by the SAS System are also the same. For a summary refer to figure H.3. Changing extensions can have the effect that the files can no longer be accessed.

SAS data libraries

In the OS/2 environment a SAS data library is a subdirectory. All files in the subdirectory which are recognized by the SAS System as SAS files (via the extensions) and which can be accessed with the same engine together form the data library. Just as in Windows, a data library can be made up of a collection of directories rather than just one; this is not recommended.

Autoexec processing

At startup the SAS System looks for a file AUTOEXEC.SAS. If this exists, then the SAS statements in this file will be processed. The SAS System looks for AUTOEXEC.SAS in the following places (and in this order): the working directory, directories listed in the OS/2 PATH command and finally in the root directory. Should the autoexec file have a different name, or exist in a different location, then this must be declared in the AUTOEXEC option at SAS System startup, as in:

```
SAS  -AUTOEXEC  C:\SAS\INITPGM.SAS
```

If an AUTOEXEC.SAS file exists and you do not want it executed, give the NOAUTOEXEC option at startup.

Allocations

Host system allocation

OS/2 gives you the possibility to allocate files with host system commands. With the OS/2 SET command you define an 'environment variable' which contains the directory path and eventually the file name of the file that you want to allocate. If the environment variable contains only one directory, this can be used as libref for SAS data libraries or as fileref for all files in the directory. Individual files can then be named as 'members' in, for example, INFILE and FILE statements. Allocations done with SET commands must take place before SAS System startup.

As an alternative, there is also a SAS SET system option (not to be confused with a SET statement!) with which environment variables can be defined during SAS System startup. It works like the OS/2 SET command, although the syntax is a little different.

In the examples which follow MYLIB points to a directory which functions as a SAS data library, MYFILES points to a directory with input files and MYDATA points to a particular file.

OS/2 SET commands:

```
SET MYLIB=C:\SAS\PERMLIB
SET MYFILES=C:\SAS\DATADIR
SET MYDATA=C:\SAS\DATADIR\RAWDATA.DAT
```

SAS SET option

```
SET MYLIB C:\SAS\PERMLIB
SET MYFILES C:\SAS\DATADIR
SET MYDATA C:\SAS\DATADIR\RAWDATA.DAT
```

When using environment variables, no engine can be specified. Thus if you use an environment variable as library name, it is always processed with the default engine (see chapter 10).

The functioning of the SET command and system options is the same as in Windows. See appendix H.

FILENAME statement

The form of the FILENAME statement is:

```
FILENAME fileref <device> <'file name'> <options>;
```

You only have to declare the device if a different destination than a disk file is intended. The possible device types are listed in figure I.2.

DDE	Use "Dynamic Data Exchange" (later in this appendix).
DISK	The default device. May be left out.
DUMMY	No output, DATA step works normal otherwise.
NAMEPIPE	Reads/writes from/to an OS/2 "Named Pipe".
PIPE	Reads/writes from/to an OS/2 "Unnamed pipe".
PRINTER	Printer (printer port assigned as file).
TERMINAL	Reads/writes from/to the terminal.

Figure I.2: The device types which you can specifiy in a FILENAME statement. Notice that the standard device type TAPE is not available in the OS/2 environment.

The file name is a complete OS/2 name, including path, or only a directory path, in which case the individual files within the directory are declared in the INFILE or FILE statement. Standard addresses can also be given, such as COM1:, LPT1:, and so on. If you specify a device type, specifying a file name is often not necessary.

Most options are related to the use of OS/2 pipes. We will not discuss them here.

The following statements are correct FILENAME statements:

```
FILENAME MYFILES 'C:\SAS\DATADIR';
FILENAME MYDATA  'C:\SAS\DATADIR\RAWDATA.DAT';
```

LIBNAME statement

The LIBNAME has the form:

```
LIBNAME libref <engine> 'directory';
```

There are no specific OS/2 options. Since the engine only needs to be declared in special situations, we will not go into this any further. The following is thus a correct LIBNAME statement (compare section 'Host system allocations' above):

```
LIBNAME MYLIB 'C:\SAS\PERMLIB';
```

Interprocess Communication

OS/2 has various capabilities for exchanging data and commands among programs. These are known as 'named pipes', 'unnamed pipes' and DDE. Under the Presentation Manager is also, of course, the Clipboard available for transferring information.

DDE under OS/2 is similar to DDE under Windows. Refer to appendix H for further information.

Special functions

The SLEEP and WAKEUP functions are also implemented in the OS/2 version of the SAS System. For a description: see appendix H.

Appendix J: The SAS System under the UNIX environment

Introduction

This appendix briefly covers a few specific aspects of the SAS System under the UNIX environment. This environment has already existed for a long time and continues to enjoy a growing popularity. On a number of points UNIX has been a model for the later operating systems DOS and OS/2. Therefore much of the information from the preceding appendices applies here, with some minor adjustments. The problem is however that UNIX is not entirely standardized. There are many variants.

A fundamental difference between UNIX and most operating systems (Windows and OS/2 among others) is that UNIX is 'case sensitive', in other words the file 'MyFile' is different from 'MYFILE' and 'myfile'! In most UNIX environments you work mainly in lowercase letters. Therefore the rule under which we have operated so far -- 'copy uppercase letters, replace lowercase letters by specific information' -- does not apply for this chapter.

The reader is assumed to be familiar with the operation of the UNIX system in his own hardware environment and with the basic principles of the SAS System (at least chapters 1 - 5 of this book). The current version of the SAS System under UNIX is 6.09.

The operation of the SAS System under UNIX

Starting a SAS session

A UNIX system can operate both in the foreground and in the background. In the foreground you can choose between interactive and batch mode. In the background, usually only batch mode is used, because there is no direct connection between the terminal and the program being executed. However some UNIX shells have the capability of bringing a background program to the foreground. Then it might make sense to run an interactive program in the background. The program comes to the foreground when interactivity is needed, making interaction with the terminal possible. In every case (except when the program has to be placed in a batch Q) the SAS System is started with the SAS command after a UNIX prompt. The options declared at this time determine the type of session:

```
$ sas <program name> <SAS options> <&>
```

If a file name with source statements is specified (if necessary with directory path), a noninteractive session is started up. Without program name, but with the DMS option, an interactive session with the Display Manager is started up. Frequently used options are those for controlling output destinations (log and list). The options are declared with a dash before the option name, just as with Windows and OS/2, for example -LINESIZE 72. The & option indicates that background processing is desired.

If a SAS program has to be consigned to a batch Q or the 'time initiated Q', then the SAS command is given with the relevant UNIX command:

```
$ batch sas programname <options>
$ at 2a sas programname <options>
```

The use of the CONFIG.SAS file under UNIX is comparable to the use of these files under Windows and OS/2. Compare appendix H and I. A standard CONFIG.SAS file is created in the SASROOT directory during installation of the SAS System (see section 'Required directories').

Display Manager

The Display Manager operates under UNIX as described in chapter 5, with a few exceptions. Whether or not the Display Manager is automatically started up in an interactive session depends on the options in the CONFIG.SAS file.

If one of the X Window managers is used (for example OSF/Motif, AIX Window manager, OpenWindows), then the Display Manager will make use of them. Without such a manager, the SAS System will use its own window manager, which corresponds to that in chapter 5. Under X Windows, pull-down menus are standard; without X Windows, windows are opened with a command line. By means of a PMENU command, this can be converted to pull-down menus if required.

The assignment of function keys deviates from what is described in chapter 5. This is in large part determined by the function key capabilities of the terminal used. Calling the KEYS window shows directly how each key has been programmed. In the KEYS window these assignments can be adjusted as needed.

Batch mode

We have already covered starting up a SAS session in batch mode in the section 'Starting up a SAS session', since in fact with UNIX there is no difference between foreground and background with respect to interac-

tive and batch processing. The command below executes the program
MyReport.sas in the background (MyReport.sas resides in the default
directory):

```
sas MyReport &
```

The SAS log and list are output by batch processing to files with the
name of the source file and the extensions .log and .lst in the working
directory, unless other destinations are given with the options -print or
-log.

SAS options

The options described in chapter 18 are valid for the SAS System under
UNIX. There are a number of specific options for UNIX or with a
specific operation under UNIX, but the default setting is such that
normally no readjustment is needed.

Options can be declared under UNIX in a config.sas file, in the sas
command, but also in the special environment variable SAS_OPTIONS
(uppercase letters!) which must be entered before startup of the SAS
System, for example:

```
SAS_OPTIONS='-nocenter'
export SAS_OPTIONS
```

Printing

Print commands are sent from the Display Manager to the default
printer, as defined in the UNIX .profile file. In batch mode the SAS log
and list output are in principle sent to a file, with the name of the source
program but with extensions .log and .lst respectively. It is also possible
to use a FILENAME statement to address a printer. Under UNIX all
peripheral devices are treated as files. Thus for example:

```
FILENAME theprint PRINTER;
PROC PRINTTO LOG=theprint OUT=theprint;
RUN;
(rest of the program)
```

From this point all output is sent to theprint, and thus to the printer.

Interrupting a SAS session

The method of interrupting a SAS program under UNIX depends on the
operating method. To interrupt a SAS program in a standard (terminal)

UNIX environment, an interrupt signal must be given. This is done with the 'kill' command:

```
kill -INT PID
```

in which PID is the 'program identification number' of the SAS System (which can be queried with the 'ps' command). If the SAS System is operating in the foreground, an interrupt can also be forced, normally with CTRL-C or another CTRL-key combination. The proper combination can be found in the UNIX documentation. In an X Windows environment a SAS program can be interrupted with mouse button 2 in a SAS window.

Executing UNIX commands

The X command on a command line of the Display Manager temporarily transfers you to a UNIX environment. At that moment all possible UNIX commands can be given, such as 'ls', 'cd' and so on. After the commands have been executed, you can type an 'end of file' character (CTRL-D) to bring you back to the SAS environment. The commands which are given while working in the UNIX environment do not apply to the SAS session.

If only one command needs to be executed, this can be given directly in the X command, for example:

```
X 'cd users/maindir/data'
```

The 'cd', 'pwd' and 'setenv' commands given in this way are intercepted by the SAS System and do apply to the SAS session. The X command can also be used as an X statement (with a ';' after it, naturally). This is a global statement, just like TITLE, for example. It cannot be given conditionally in a DATA step. For this, use the CALL SYSTEM routine:

```
IF ... THEN CALL SYSTEM('UNIX command');
```

Ending a SAS session

Ending a SAS session under UNIX is done with a 'quit' signal. It can also be done with a 'kill' command, or with CTRL-\ (check whether using an 'stty' command is legal in your UNIX environment). A Display Manager session is ended by typing BYE or ENDSAS on a Display Manager command line or submitting an ENDSAS statement. The SAS session can also be ended by means of the Exit option under the File menu.

Directory and file structure

Required directories

When the SAS System is installed under UNIX the required directories are created in /usr/lib/sas, but it is also possible to set them up in another location in the file system. An environment variable 'sasroot' is defined, which refers to the SAS root directory. All other SAS directories go in this root directory. The table in figure J.1 gives a summary of the directories which are created. Also the config.sas file normally resides in the root directory.

sas	(command file to start SAS)
config.sas	(configuration file)
autoexec.sas	(initialization file)
terminfo	(directory with terminal definitions)
sasexe	(program files)
sashelp	(help files + catalogs)
sasmacro	(autocall macros)
sasmsg	(message files)
samples	(sample programs)
sastest	(test programs)

Figure J.1: Some of the Files and directories which are created during the installation of SAS within the sasroot directory (usually /usr/lib/sas).

File names

Figure J.2 gives a summary of the file name extensions which the SAS System uses under UNIX. Changing these extensions can have the effect of making the files no longer accessible. Under UNIX a suffix of two digits is attached to the extensions for SAS files to make them unique in a network environment. As a user you do not take much notice of this, since the management of individual members of a data library is still done by the SAS System.

SAS data libraries

In the UNIX environment a SAS library is formed through a subdirectory. All files in the subdirectory which are recognized by the SAS System as SAS files (via the extensions) together form the data library.

.ssd*nn*	SAS data set (Memtype=DATA).
.snx*nn*	Index data set, as created in a DATA step with the INDEX data set option or with INDEX CREATE in PROC DATASETS.
.sct*nn*	SAS catalog.
.ssp*nn*	Stored program (Compiled DATA step, refer to chapter 15).
.ssv*nn*	Data view, e.g. created with the DATA step view-facility (refer to chapter 18) or with PROC SQL (not discussed).
.ssa*nn*	ACCESS descriptor file, created with SAS/ACCESS (not discussed).
.dat	Any data file (for use in INFILE or FILE statement).
.sas	SAS source file.
.log	SAS log file, during background processing.
.lst	SAS list file (procedure output), during background processing.

Figure J.2: Summary of the file name extensions as used by the SAS System under UNIX. The suffix nn represents a number which is used to make file names unique in a network environment. In single user installations this is normally 01.

Autoexec processing

At startup the SAS System looks for a file autoexec.sas. If this exists, then the SAS statements in this file will be processed. The SAS System looks for the autoexec.sas in the following places (and in this order): the current directory, the home directory and finally in the sasroot directory. Should the autoexec file have a different name, or exist in a different location, then this must be declared in the AUTOEXEC option at SAS startup, as in:

```
$ sas -autoexec /usr/sas/initpgm.sas
```

If an AUTOEXEC.SAS file exists and you do not want it executed, give the noautoexec option at startup.

Allocations

Host system allocation

Allocating files with UNIX system commands is done by defining and exporting an 'environment variable'. Be careful here: the environment variable must be in uppercase letters!

```
MYLIB=/users/maindir/test
export MYLIB

...

PROC PRINT DATA=MYLIB.RESULT;
RUN;
```

The contents of the environment variable exists of the complete directory path and therefore begins with a '/'. If the environment variable contains only a directory, this can be used as libref for SAS data libraries or as fileref for all files in the directory. Individual files can then be named as 'members' in, for example, INFILE and FILE statements.

In the following examples MYLIB points to a directory which functions as a SAS data library, MYFILES to a directory with input files and MYDATA to a particular file.

```
MYLIB=/users/maindir/test
export MYLIB
MYFILES=/users/maindir/results
export MYFILES
MYDATA=/users/maindir/results/rawdata.dat
export MYDATA
```

When using environment variables, no engine can be given; they are always processed with a default engine (see chapter 10).

FILENAME statement

The form of the FILENAME statement is:

```
FILENAME fileref <device> <'file name'> <options>;
```

The device needs to be used only if another destination than a disk file is given. The possible device types are listed in figure J.3.

DISK	A general disk file.
DUMMY	A file which behaves as a disk file, but it will not be created. Especially for testing purposes.
PIPE	A UNIX "PIPE", via which you can issue UNIX commands and via which you can read the results of a UNIX-command.
PRINTER	A printer file, hence a printer.
TAPE	A tape file.
TERMINAL	To read and write to/from a terminal.

Figure J.3: UNIX device types which can be specified in the FILENAME statement. If no device type is specified DISK is assumed.

The file name is a complete UNIX name, path + file name, or only a directory path. In case only a directory path is given with a disk, the individual files in the directory can be designated in the INFILE or FILE statement. With the PIPE device type, the file name is replaced by a UNIX command.

Of the options, MOD and NEW are of particular importance; MOD appends new information to an existing file and NEW creates a new file. If the file declared with NEW already exists, it will be removed and set up again. The OLD option is equivalent to the NEW option.

The following statements are correct FILENAME statements (compare section 'Host system allocations' above):

```
FILENAME MYFILES '/users/maindir/results';
FILENAME MYDATA  '/users/maindir/results/rawdata.dat';
```

With the device PRINTER the printer name is specified as the file name. To address the printer with the name 'dept3', do this:

```
FILENAME MYPRT PRINTER 'dept3';
```

In the specification of the directory path a number of special symbols can be given to prevent from having to specify the whole path over and over. ~/ at the beginning means the path is specified from the $HOME/ directory; a period indicates the current working directory, two periods indicate the directory one level higher in the hierarchy and !sasroot indicates the sasroot directory.

LIBNAME statement

The LIBNAME has the form:

```
LIBNAME libref <engine> 'directory';
```

There are no specific UNIX options. Since the engine only needs to be declared in special situations, we will not go into this any further. The following is thus a correct LIBNAME statement (compare section 'Host system allocations' above):

```
LIBNAME MYLIB '/users/maindir/test';
```

Appendix K: The SAS System under the VMS operating system

Introduction

This appendix briefly covers a few specific aspects of the SAS System under Digital Equipment Corporation's VMS operating system. VMS is an advanced multi-user operating system with extensive on-line and batch processing capabilities. A window oriented environment is available under the name DECwindows for workstations. The reader is assumed to be familiar with VMS and with the basic principles of the SAS System (at least chapters 1 - 5 of this book). The current version of the SAS System under VMS is 6.08.

The operation of the SAS System under VMS

Starting a SAS session

Under VMS the SAS System can be used both interactively and in batch mode. In both cases you start up with a SAS command after the VMS prompt:

```
$ SAS</option/option/option....> <program name>
```

The system manager will have set up a configuration file in the system. In it, a number of system options have been set. These will include the setting for whether or not the SAS System will start up in Display Manager mode by default. If so it also contains a specification for which window environment to use and which terminal driver to use. In the VMS environment, in principle multiple configuration files can be present, for example at the system and at the branch level. During startup the SAS System looks for the logical name SAS$CONFIG. If this is linked to a file, then the options in that file will be installed.

By declaring a program name in the SAS command, a noninteractive session is started. Under VMS the SAS System can also work in the background, so that the terminal is not blocked during execution.

Display Manager

The Display Manager functions under VMS as described in chapter 5, with a few exceptions.

If DECwindows is active on the workstation, then the Display Manager will make use of it; otherwise the SAS System will use its own window manager, which corresponds to that in chapter 5.

If the terminal type being used has not already been indicated in the configuration file, it should be specified in the SAS command:

```
$  SAS/FSDEVICE=terminaltype
$ SAS/DECWINDOWS
```

Under DECwindows pull-down menus are standard; without DECwindows, windows are opened with the command line. By means of a PMENU command this can be converted to pull-down menus if required.

The assignment of function keys deviates from what is described in chapter 5. This is in large part determined by the function key capabilities of the terminal used. Calling the KEYS window shows directly how each key has been programmed. In the KEYS window these assignments can be adjusted as need be.

Batch mode

The SAS System can operate interactively both in the foreground and in the background. In the foreground you startup the SAS System with the SAS command, in which you give the program to be executed (see section 'Starting a SAS session' earlier in this chapter). For background processing you start up a SAS program with a SUBMIT command.

The $SAS command and any necessary $DEFINE commands are given in a 'command procedure file'. This file would look similar to:

```
$   DEFINE MYLIB DISK:[directory]
<   possible other DEFINE commands >
$   SAS/LINESIZE=72/PAGESIZE=60/NOCENTER-
_$  [HOME.SUBDIR]MYPROG.SAS
```

in which MYLIB for example addresses the data library to be used and MYPROG.SAS contains the SAS program to be executed. The command procedure file can be executed with a SUBMIT command. Say that the file has been given the name SUBSAS.COM, then the SUBMIT command looks like:

```
$ SUBMIT/NOTIFY SUBSAS.COM
```

It is also possible to put the DCL statements in the same file as the SAS program. This takes the form:

```
$ DEFINE MYLIB DISK:[directory]
$ SAS/LINESIZE=72/PAGESIZE=60/NOCENTER SYS$INPUT
PROC  PRINT  DATA=MYLIB.TESTDATA;
RUN;
```

SAS options

The options described in chapter 18 are also valid for the SAS System under VMS. Of the specific VMS options, the most important is DECWINDOWS (and NODECWINDOWS), used to instruct the Display Manager to use DECwindows. The options can be declared in an OPTIONS statement, in the configuration file(s) or as options at SAS System startup. At SAS system startup the options to be used are listed after one another, separated by a "/", as shown above.

If the same options (but with different settings) appear at multiple locations, then the options in the SAS command prevail over options in the configuration file(s). Settings in an OPTIONS statement in turn prevail over those in the SAS command.

Printing

When the SAS System is being used noninteractively, in principle print output is sent to the SYS$PRINT printer. If you want to designate a different print destination, it is often easiest to redefine SYS$PRINT to the desired printer.

You can also address a printer with a FILENAME statement. The QUEUE= option sets up a queue for print output. Here the PROC PRINTTO or the FILE statement can be used to ensure that output is sent to the designated printer.

Interrupting a SAS session

SAS programs and sessions in the foreground of VMS can be interrupted with a VMS attention command: CTRL-Y or CTRL-C. After this command the SAS System asks whether to resume execution or end the session.

Executing VMS commands

The X command on a command line of the Display Manager transfers you temporarily to a VMS environment. This VMS environment forms a subprocess of the SAS System. The standard VMS prompt at that moment is SAS_$. Subsequently, in the VMS environment, all legal

VMS commands can be given, for example the definition of logical names. To return to the SAS System, give a LOGOFF command. Be careful: logical names which are defined in a subprocess are not available in the parent (SAS) process. When the VMS command is declared in the X command directly then the result is available.

The X command can also be used as an X statement (naturally, with a ';' after it). This is a global statement, just as for example TITLE. It can therefore be used inside and outside a DATA step, but not as a conditional statement, for example in an IF statement. For this, use the VMS function of the CALL SYSTEM routine:

```
RC = VMS(DCL commando);
CALL SYSTEM(DCL commando);
```

The DCL command can be given as text in quotation marks, as well as by a character variable which contains the command.

Ending a SAS session

The attention command mentioned earlier (CTRL-Y or CTRL-C) is also used to end a SAS session. In the Display Manager, of course BYE and ENDSAS can also be used.

Directory and file structure

Required directories

Installing the SAS System under VMS creates a variety of directories, most of which the user does not have to be concerned with. At the same time, the SAS System defines a great number of logical names, most of them beginning with 'SAS$', which are referred to in the default settings of many options. Those interested should refer to the *SAS Companion for the VMS Environment, Version 6, First Edition.*

File names

VMS knows the type of a file by its file type extension after the file name. The SAS System also uses these, and there is a set of standard extensions. These are listed in figure K.1. Changing extensions can have the effect that the files can no longer be accessed. As you can see, the engine name which belongs to the data library is recorded in the extension of the SAS files. The standard engine is called SASEB.

Data libraries

The SAS data library has a broad implementation in VMS. It is the set of all SAS files (data sets, catalogs, views and so on) which come under a single VMS directory and which are accessed with the same engine. As previously indicated, we see this interpretation in the filename extensions which the SAS System uses: the engine is mentioned.

.engine$DATA	SAS V6 data set (Memtype=DATA).
.engine$INDEX	Index data set, as created in a DATA step with the INDEX data set option or with INDEX CREATE in PROC DATASETS.
.engine$CATALOG	SAS catalog.
.engine$PROGRAM	Stored program (Compiled DATA step, ref. chapter 15).
.engine$VIEW	Data view, for instance created with the DATA step view facility (ref. chapter 18) or with PROC SQL (not discussed).
.engine$ACCESS	ACCESS descriptor file, as created in the SAS/ACCESS product (not discussed).
.SSD	SAS V5 data set.
.DAT	Any data file (for use in INFILE or FILE statements).
.SAS	SAS source file.
.LOG	SAS log file, during background processing.
.LIS	SAS list file (procedure output), during background processing.

Figure K.1: Overview of file name extensions as used by the SAS System under the VMS operating system. As you can see for SAS files the engine name is included. The default engine is SASEB, thus a complete extension for a SAS data set would be: SASEB$DATA.

Autoexec processing

At startup the SAS System looks for a file indicated by the logical name SAS$INIT. If this file is present, then the SAS statements in the file will be executed. You can enter SAS$INIT with the DEFINE command. Say that the name of the autoexec file is INITPGM.SAS, then:

```
$DEFINE SAS$INIT disk:[directory]INITPGM.SAS
$SAS
```

Alternatively you can use the AUTOEXEC option at SAS System startup. With the same file as above, it looks like:

```
$SAS/AUTOEXEC=disk:[directory]INITPGM.SAS
```

Allocations

Host system allocations

Under VMS, allocations are made with the VMS DEFINE command. With the DEFINE command both librefs and filerefs can be defined. The form is:

```
$ DEFINE logicalname [directory pad]
$ DEFINE logicalname [directory pad]filename.extension
```

in which the logical name must comply with the SAS rules for librefs and filerefs and the directory path can be the complete path, therefore ultimately including network node and device indicators, and can also be constructed from its own default directory, following the standard VMS rules. With only a specification of a directory the logical name can be used as libref for SAS data libraries or as fileref for all files in the directory, where the individual files can be declared as 'members' in, for example, INFILE and FILE statements. In case you want or need to give, besides the member name, the extension as well, put the whole thing in quotation marks, because otherwise a problem arises with breaking SAS syntax rules. Thus:

```
$ DEFINE MYFILES [directory]
...
INFILE MYFILES(MYINPUT) ... ;
```
or
```
INFILE MYFILES('MYINPUT.DAT') ... ;
```

If, when using a VMS logical name as libref, no engine can be specified: the default engine is always used (see chapter 10).

FILENAME statement

The FILENAME statement has the form:

```
FILENAME fileref <device> <'file name'> <options>;
```

As with the VMS logical name, here too you can specify just the directory, after which the individual members can be listed in an INFILE or FILE statement.

In the FILENAME statement, a device type can be given between the fileref and the file name. In figure K.2 is a summary of the possible device types.

DISK	Default device setting. May be left out.
DUMMY	No output, DATA step functions normally.
PLOTTER	Output file for a plotter.
PRINTER	Printer. Without specification the SYS$PRINT printer; otherwise specify the printer port as the file name.
TAPE	Reads/writes a tape file. If no destination is specified, the SAS System uses the unit which is specified in the logical name SASTAPE. Otherwise the file name should contain a valid tape address.
TERMINAL	Reads and writes from/to the terminal with logical name SYS$OUTPUT.

Figure K.2: The device types which can be specified in the FILENAME statement when working with the VMS operating system. DISK is the default and does not need to be specified.

There are various specific VMS options in the FILENAME statement including, among others, those for reading and writing RMS files. This is outside the scope of this brief introduction.

The following statements are correct FILENAME statements (compare section 'Host system allocations' earlier in this chapter):

```
FILENAME MYFILES 'disk:[directory]';
FILENAME MYDATA 'disk:[directory]MYINPUT.DAT';
```

LIBNAME statement

The LIBNAME has the form:

```
LIBNAME libref <engine> 'directory';
```

There are a few specific VMS options, however the default settings will usually suffice. The following is therefore a correct LIBNAME statement:

```
LIBNAME THELIB '[HOME.DATLIB]';
```

by which the data set RESULTS can be accessed as follows:

```
PROC PRINT DATA = THELIB.RESULTS;
```

Appendix L: The SAS System under CMS

Introduction

This appendix briefly covers a few specific aspects of the SAS System in IBM's CMS (Conversational Monitor System) system environment. CMS is a component of the VM (Virtual Machine) operating system. The reader is assumed to be familiar with CMS and with the basic principles of the SAS System (at least chapters 1 - 5 of this book). The current version of the SAS System under CMS is 6.08.

The operation of the SAS System under CMS

Starting a SAS session

Under CMS the SAS System is started up by means of the SAS command. This is a CMS EXEC routine written in REXX. The command is supplied by SAS Institute with installation files.

```
SAS <pogram name> <(option option .....>
```

The system manager can have changed the routine or even given it another name. You should therefore check with your system manager to find out exactly how the SAS System has been implemented in your installation.

In case a program name is given in the SAS command, a noninteractive SAS session is started: the program will be executed and after that the session will end. Without a program name, an interactive session will be started, in principle a Display Manager session.

Display Manager

The Display Manager operates under CMS as described in chapter 5, with a few exceptions.

Since in a VM environment you are usually working with terminals of the 3270 family, the function keys correspond reasonably well with what was said about this earlier. The KEYS window gives a definite answer.

Batch mode

The SAS System operates noninteractively both in the foreground and in the background. In the foreground you startup the SAS System with the SAS command, in which you indicate the program to be executed (see section 'Starting a SAS session' earlier in this appendix). A SUB-MIT command starts up the background processing. The SUBMIT command varies widely from installation to installation. This does not concern the SAS System, but has to do with the setup of the VM system. Consult your system manager about the use of the SUBMIT command.

SAS Options

The options described in chapter 18 are also valid for the SAS System under CMS. Specific CMS options are only important in a limited number of situations. For the most part the default settings supplied by SAS Institute will suffice.

Printing

Printing facilities in VM systems are strongly installation dependent. For the most part it comes down to a choice between local printers and central system printers. Consult your system manager to find out which printing facilities you have.

Interrupting a SAS session

A noninteractive SAS program can be interrupted if it is in RUNNING status. Keying Enter requests the attention of CMS. The HX command (Halt eXecution) then interrupts and terminates the SAS program. Interrupting a Display Manager session is dependent on the installation and the type of terminal being used. Consult your system manager for more information.

Executing CMS and CP commands

CMS and CP commands can be executed from the SAS System. The X command on a command line of the Display Manager transfers you temporarily to a CMS environment. At that moment various CMS and CP commands can be executed. The RETURN command gets you back to the SAS System. If only one command has to be executed, then the command can be given directly in the CMS or X command, for example:

```
CMS ERASE MYDATA DATA A
```
or
```
X ERASE MYDATA DATA A
```

The X command can also be used as an X statement (naturally with a ';' after it). This is a global statement, just as for example TITLE. It can go anywhere and will be executed whenever the SAS System reads it. That also means that this statement cannot be executed conditionally, in an IF statement for example, even if it is in a DATA step. For this you can use the CMS function. This will be executed during the execution of the DATA step:

```
RC = CMS('command');
```

The variable RC will now contain the return code from CMS upon completion of the command.

Directory and file structure

Required libraries

Installing the SAS System under CMS creates a variety of libraries, most of which the user does not have to be concerned with. The structure and contents of these libraries is only interesting for the system managers responsible for the installation.

File names

A file under CMS has a name consisting of 3 components: the file name, the type (file type) and the 'file mode'. The file mode indicates which minidisk the file is on and if it is available for read or read/write. For more information about the structure of file names under CMS, the role of file name components and naming conventions, refer to the CMS documentation.

Data libraries

Because of the different structure of file names under CMS, the construction of a SAS data library is different than with other operating systems. The CMS file type is used by the SAS System as libref, in other words: all files with the same file type belong to the same data library. Such a file therefore will always be accessed via the same libref. The CMS file name corresponds with the SAS data set name in the data library. Thus the CMS file

```
MYDATA MYFILES A
```

in the SAS System becomes

```
SET MYFILES.MYDATA;
```

By this linking of libref and file type, it is often not necessary to separately allocate a data library with a LIBNAME statement. Still you may want to use a LIBNAME statement, because now you can refer directly to a particular minidisk. The CMS naming structure also has another consequence: with most SAS files, the SAS System puts a code digit before the name as an indicator of the SAS file type (data set, view, catalog and so on). The consequence is that SAS file names under CMS can have only seven positions! The exception to this is an unindexed data set, but for the sake of uniformity it is sensible to use seven positions there as well.

Autoexec processing

An AUTOEXEC file can be addressed in two ways. The first possibility uses the CMS FILEDEF command. If you issue a FILEDEF with the name SASEXEC, then that file will be the autoexec file. The second possibility is declaring the autoexec file in the AUTOEXEC option at SAS System startup. In the option the complete CMS file name is given (name type mode), as in:

```
SAS (AUTOEXEC='INITPGM SASPGM A'
```

Allocations

Host system allocations

The CMS FILEDEF command can in principle be used for allocations. However this is not recommended. It is better to work with LIBNAME and FILENAME. We will not go into allocating with FILEDEF here.

FILENAME statement

The form of the FILENAME statement is:

```
FILENAME fileref <device> <'file name'> <options>;
```

The device has to be declared only if a different destination than a disk file is intended. The possible device types are listed in figure L.1.

The file name is a complete CMS name, consisting of file name, file type and file mode.

The following statement is a correct FILENAME statement to assign the file TESTDATA FILE on minidisk A:

```
FILENAME THEDATA 'TESTDATA FILE A';
```

TESTDATA FILE A is indicated by the name THEDATA in an INFILE or a FILE statement.

DISK	Default device. May be left out.
DUMMY	No output, DATA-step functions as normal.
PRINTER	Assigns a virtual printer. With the CP SPOOL and TAG commands you can control the destination of the print.
TAPE	Assigns a tape file. Consult your system manager for tape processing facilities and procedures.
TERMINAL	Reads and writes from/to the terminal.

Figure L.1: Device types that can be specified in the FILENAME statement when running under the CMS system. There exist also the devices MONI-TOR, PUNCH and READER. Consult your system manager for possibilities and applications.

LIBNAME statement

Because the file type of a CMS file is like a SAS libref, only the specification of the minidisk is still important. The libref works for all files on that minidisk with that file type. The following LIBNAME statement:

```
LIBNAME THELIB 'B';
```

therefore refers to all files on minidisk B with file type THELIB.

```
PROC PRINT DATA=THELIB.RESULTS;
```

therefore prints the SAS data set with CMS name RESULTS THELIB B.

Of course an engine name can also be given, but for simplicity's sake it will be assumed here that the default engine is sufficient.

Appendix M: The SAS System under the MVS operating system

Introduction

This book has been based on the SAS System under IBM's MVS operating system. This is also one of the most used platforms for the SAS System. All examples have been processed under MVS. Matters specific to MVS, however, have been avoided as much as possible.

The reader is assumed to be familiar with TSO and MVS and with the basic principles of the SAS System (at least chapters 1 - 5 of this book).

The current version of the SAS System under MVS is 6.08.

The operation of the SAS System under MVS

Starting a SAS session

The SAS System under MVS can be used both interactively and noninteractively; the noninteractive method can take place both in the foreground (TSO) and in the background (MVS batch processing). Starting up in the TSO environment is done with a SAS command. This starts a CLIST which is provided by SAS Institute with the installation files. The SAS command can be given with a number of options, as in:

```
SAS OPTIONS('LINESIZE=72 PAGESIZE=40')
```

Many installations use ISPF as user environment under TSO. In this case the SAS System is probably entered in one of the ISPF panels as a selection option. Selecting this option has the same effect as executing the CLIST. Consult your system manager for further information about starting up the SAS System in your installation.

Background processing is controlled by Job Control Language (JCL). See chapter 1 for some information on JCL. The JCL to be used normally contains many installation dependent adaptations, such as accounting information. Consult your system manager for the required JCL.

Display Manager

The Display Manager under MVS has been described in chapter 5.

A useful, specific MVS command in the Display Manager is the MEMLIST command:

MEMLIST 'PDS-name'

or

MEMLIST fileref

This opens the MEMLIST window in which the members of a partitioned data set (PDS) are displayed (figure M.1). If a fileref is attached to the PDS, then this can be used; otherwise the name of the PDS (in quotation marks) is entered directly in the command. In the IBM environment PDSs are often used for storing program source code: each program or program segment is then a 'member' of such a PDS. The MEMLIST command gives a quick summary of the various programs present.

```
+MEMLIST: TILANE.SASENGED.SASPGM-------------------------------------------+
| Command ===>                                                             |
|                                                                          |
|  Name         VV.MM  Created  Last Modified  Size   Init   Mod    ID     |
|                                                                          |
| _ BENZINE1    01.01 94/05/11 94/06/01 16:38    69      1     0  TILANE   |
| _ BENZINE2    01.00 94/06/01 94/06/01 17:14    68     68     0  TILANE   |
| _ BENZINE3    01.00 94/06/01 94/06/01 17:19    68     68     0  TILANE   |
| _ BENZINE4    01.03 94/06/01 94/06/05 11:54    91     88     0  TILANE   |
| _ CHART       01.01 94/06/09 94/06/09 21:07    23     23     0  TILANE   |
| _ CHECKOUT    01.02 94/06/17 94/06/17 11:32    64     62     0  TILANE   |
| _ COMPARE     01.01 94/06/13 94/06/13 13:14     5      4     0  TILANE   |
| _ DIYORDER    01.06 94/06/06 94/06/06 20:05    33     21     0  TILANE   |
| _ DIYREP1     01.02 94/06/11 94/06/11 22:03    62     52     0  TILANE   |
| _ DOLOOP      01.00 94/06/03 94/06/03 11:16    18     18     0  TILANE   |
| _ EXECUTE     01.02 94/06/10 94/06/10 21:58    17     15     0  TILANE   |
| _ FORMAT      01.01 94/06/13 94/06/13 12:13     8      8     0  TILANE   |
+--------------------------------------------------------------------------+
| 00002                                                                    |
| 00003                                                                    |
| 00004                                                                    |
| 00005                                                                    |
| 00006                                                                    |
+--------------------------------------------------------------------------+
```

Figure M.1: The MEMLIST command opens the MEMLIST window in the Display Manager. From there you can execute programs, copy them to the Program window or you can carry out several maintenance tasks.

In the MEMLIST window various support tasks can be performed, and you can also transfer members to the SAS environment. The tasks are set up by placing the command involved before the member. Figure M.2 gives the commands which can initiate actions in the MEMLIST window.

B	Browse the member.
E	Edit the member.
I	Include the member in the PROGRAM EDITOR window.
%	Submit the member for processing (%INCLUDE action).
R	Rename the member.
D	Delete the member. The SAS System will ask confirmation with the V (verify) command.
C	Cancel eventual rename or delete actions.

Figure M.2: The commands which can be specified in the MEMLIST window

Another useful command is the DSINFO command: this lists the system attributes of a data set: organization, size and so on. Here too the command can contain both a fileref and a file name:

```
DSINFO 'file name'|fileref
```

Batch mode

Noninteractive foreground processing of SAS programs under TSO is also started with the CLIST. For this, the program to be executed is entered in the INPUT parameter:

```
SAS INPUT('''program name''')
```

Be careful of the proliferation of quotation marks. This has to do with the manner in which this parameter is analyzed in the IBM environment. A background program is started up from a TSO terminal by means of a SUBMIT command. In the SUBMIT command the required JCL (sometimes a JOB statement, certainly an EXEC statement and often one or more DD statements) is declared to MVS. The JCL is followed by the SAS source or the JCL contains a DD statement that refers to the SAS source code:

```
//MYJOB    JOB  accounting information
//         EXEC SAS
//GEN      DD   DSN=data library,DISP=OLD
//SYSIN    DD   DSN=data set with SAS source,DISP=SHR
```

For the contents of the accounting information and file naming conventions, consult the system manager for your installation.

SAS options

Although there are dozens of special MVS options, you as a user will seldom have anything to do with them. The system manager will take care of the default settings, which will usually be sufficient.

Printing

The printing facilities also vary considerably from installation to installation, both for local printing and for central printing. Therefore here too we advise you to consult your system manager.

Interrupting a SAS session

SAS programs and sessions in the foreground can be interrupted with an attention command (sometimes PA1, other times ATTN). With this command the SAS System asks whether to proceed or end the session.

Executing TSO commands

The X command on a command line of the Display Manager transfers you temporarily to a TSO environment. You are then in the so-called TSO READY mode, even if you stated your session from an ISPF panel. In the TSO environment, any normal TSO commands can be given, such as for example a LISTC to call up a list of catalogued files. An END command returns you to the SAS System. A single TSO command can be entered with the X command on the command line.

The X command can also be used as an X statement (naturally with a ';' after it). It is a global statement, just as for example TITLE. It can go anywhere and will be executed whenever the SAS System reads it. That means that this statement cannot be executed conditionally. Conditional execution of TSO commands during execution of the DATA step is possible with the TSO function:

```
RC = TSO('command');
```

The variable RC will now contain the return code from TSO upon completion of the command.

Directory and file structure

Required libraries

Installing the SAS System under MVS creates a variety of libraries, most of which the user does not have to be concerned with. The structure and contents of these libraries is only interesting for the system managers responsible for the installation.

File names

File naming in an MVS environment is flexible. A file name consists first of all of a user/owner indicator. This is normally a department code or a TSO user ID or the like. Then the file's actual file name (possibly in several parts) and finally a type indicator. This is mainly to make it recognizable for the user, however, not for MVS. MVS recognizes the file type by the structure of the file, which is specified in the 'file attributes', in the DSORG and the RECFM attributes among others. Also the SAS System has no fixed file name extensions under MVS, but recognizes files by their organization.

Many installations do have guidelines for the contents of the last segment of the file name, often with particular provisions in the system attached. The different segments of the name are separated by periods.

Figure M.3 gives the conventions for the last segment of the file name as we have used them in this book.

The MVS file TILANE.GENERAL.SASLIB is therefore a SAS data library with the name GENERAL with user/owner indicator TILANE.

.DATA	A general data file, used as input or output (with INFILE or FILE statements)
.SASPGM	A data set with SAS source statements
.SASLIB	A SAS data library

Figure M.3: The dataset extensions as used by the author in the MVS environment. The .SASPGM files could be either a PDS or a sequential file.

TSO users are used to address files which are linked to their user ID without quotation marks and without declaring the user ID. In the SAS System quotation marks must always be used. However by putting a period before the file name, the SAS System knows that the user ID goes in front.

The MEMLIST command, which was called up in the window in figure M.1, could be declared in these two ways:

```
MEMLIST 'TILANE.SASENGED.SASPGM'
MEMLIST '.SASENGED.SASPGM'
```

Data libraries

The SAS data library under MVS has a concrete implementation. For MVS the data library is a single file (in V5 with a DSORG=DA and in V6 with DSORG=PS and RECFM=FS). All housekeeping within the data library is in the hands of the SAS System. Data libraries can be created by means of the LIBNAME statement or by means of MVS (or TSO) allocation commands.

Autoexec processing

At SAS System startup under TSO, an autoexec file can be given in the SAS command:

```
SAS AUTOEXEC('''program name''')
```

In the MVS batch environment, the SAS System looks for a file allocated with the DD name (fileref) SASEXEC:

```
//STEPNAME EXEC SAS
//SASEXEC  DD   DSN=program name,DISP=SHR
```

If necessary a different DD name can also be used. This must be declared in the AUTOEXEC option at SAS System start-up:

```
//STEPNAME EXEC SAS,OPTIONS=('AUTOEXEC=AUTOFILE')
//AUTOFILE DD   DSN=program name,DISP=SHR
```

Allocations

Host system allocations

The way MVS carries out allocations using host commands depends on the user environment. Under TSO allocations are done with the ALLOC command. For batch processing it is done with JCL DD statements. The data library referred to earlier, TILANE.GENERAL.SASLIB, could be allocated with the following command:

```
ALLOC FI(MYLIB) DA('TILANE.GENERAL.SASLIB') OLD
```

in which MYLIB is the SAS libref. The indicator OLD says that there is
an existing data library, and that read/write authority is required. If only
read authority is required, then OLD is replaced by SHR. If the first
segment of the data set name is the same as the user ID, it can be left out.
The quotation marks around the name are also left off in that case. See
the section 'File names' above. Therefore if TILANE is the user ID, the
ALLOC command below does the same as the one above:

```
ALLOC FI(MYLIB) DA(GENERAL.SASLIB) OLD
```

As a JCL DD statement this allocation looks like:

```
//MYLIB   DD   DSN=TILANE.GENERAL.SASLIB,DISP=OLD
```

and exclusively for read access:

```
//MYLIB   DD   DSN=TILANE.GENERAL.SASLIB,DISP=SHR
```

FILENAME statement

The form of the FILENAME statement is:

```
FILENAME fileref <device> <'file name'> <options>;
```

The device has to be declared only if a different destination than a disk
file is intended. The device types possible are listed in figure M.4.

DISK	Default device setting. May be left out.
DUMMY	No output, DATA step functions as normal.
PRINTER	Printer.
TAPE	Assign tape unit.
TERMINAL	Reads and writes from/to the terminal.

*Figure M.4: These device types can be specified in the FILENAME statement
in MVS.*

The file name is a complete MVS name. Under TSO a file whose name
begins with the TSO user ID can be specified without the user ID. Instead
the name is preceded by a period (see also the section 'File names above).

If an existing data set has been allocated, it is only necessary to give the DISP= option to indicate whether it is opened for reading (SHR) or for update (OLD). In the MVS batch environment the WAIT= option is also important: the SAS System will wait for the given amount of time (in minutes) until the requested file becomes available.

In an MVS batch environment, the FILENAME statement works as a dynamic allocation. By using FILENAME statements, the files no longer have to be listed in the JCL DD statements.

The FILENAME statement can also be used to set up new, temporary or permanent files. A temporary file is set up by putting a & sign before the file name:

```
FILENAME TEMPFILE '&TEMP';
```

Setting up a new permanent file is done with options. To begin, give: DISP=NEW. Then give the size of the file in the SPACE= option. This contains first of all the unit (for example TRK -tracks or BLK -blocks) and then the primary capacity followed by the secondary capacity, the space which (up to 16x) can be added if the space in the file is used up. In the following FILENAME statement:

```
FILENAME NEWFILE '.MYFILE.DATA'DISP=NEW
               SPACE=(TRK,(10,2));
```

a data set is set up beginning with the TSO user ID and then the name MYFILE.DATA. The initial size is 10 tracks, which can be expanded by increments of 2 tracks if necessary.

A FILENAME statement that addresses a PDS can address the PDS itself or a member of that PDS. In the first case for example, the member is addressed in the INFILE or FILE statement. The member RAWDATA in the PDS userID.MYDATA.DATA can therefore be read with the following combinations:

```
FILENAME MYFILES '.MYDATA.DATA';
...
INFILE MYFILES(RAWDATA);

FILENAME  MYDATA '.MYDATA.DATA(RAWDATA)';
...
INFILE MYDATA;
```

LIBNAME statement

The LIBNAME statement has the form:

```
LIBNAME libref <engine> 'directory' <opties>;
```

The operation and the options are similar to those of the FILENAME
statement, keeping in mind the difference of course: the FILENAME
statement is for external files, the LIBNAME statement is for SAS data
libraries.

With 'normal' data libraries, no engine is given. Only in special cases is
that necessary. See also chapter 10.

Of the following LIBNAME statements, the first two set up the previously stated userID.GENERAL.SASLIB (user ID is TILANE) and the
last two set up a new temporary and a new permanent data library (under
the user ID):

```
LIBNAME  MYLIB  'TILANE.GENERAL.SASLIB' DISP=OLD;
LIBNAME  MYLIB  '.GENERAL.SASLIB' DISP=SHR;
LIBNAME  TEMPLIB  '&TEMP' SPACE=(TRK,(5,5));
LIBNAME  PERMLIB  '.NEWLIB.SASLIB' DISP=NEW
                  SPACE=(TRK,(50,50));
```

Appendix N: Summary of SAS products and documentation

Introduction

This book introduced you to base SAS Software. It also gave you a short introduction to two of the more specialized SAS software products: SAS/FSP software (chapter 19) and SAS/GRAPH software (chapter 20). This appendix gives a listing and short synopsis of other products that together form the SAS System.

SAS Institute documentation is extensive. Making the proper choice from the dozens of books is not always simple. Therefore this appendix lists a number of books which are of general importance for the serious SAS user.

SAS software products

Base SAS

Base SAS is the foundation of the SAS System. Without it you can't do anything. It provides data access and management, analysis, presentation capabilities and a powerful applications development environment.

SAS/ACCESS

Interfaces to various database management systems;including IMS, DB2, SQL/DS, Rdb/VMS, ORACLE, INGRES, AS/400 data, OS/2 DB server, dBASE DBF files, Lotus DIF files.

SAS/AF

Shell around the SAS System for constructing complete (menu driven and window oriented) applications. In applications which are to be constructed under the SAS/AF umbrella all other parts of the SAS System can be used.

SAS/ASSIST

A menu driven shell around the SAS System to lead users to a result, without SAS statements having to be written directly. SAS code is generated based on user responses to menu choices.

SAS/CALC

A multiplatform electronic spreadsheet. Advantages over most common PC based spreadsheet packages are that all formulas are concentrated in one point, rather than being spread all over the cells, and that a direct link is possible to SAS data sets.

SAS/CONNECT

Communication facility to let SAS sessions on different system platforms communicate with each other.

SAS/CPE

A collection of ready made programs and procedures for computer performance evaluation. It allows system managers to collect, analyze and report performance data and system resource usage from a menu driven environment.

SAS/DMI

Interface to IBM's ISPF, making it possible to use the SAS System as a development tool for building ISPF applications.

SAS/EIS

Object oriented expansion for the development of Executive Information Systems. Provides facilities like 'drill down', 'traffic lighting' and so on. Forms a 'seamless' link with other SAS products, through which data access (weak spot in many EIS systems) is optimal.

SAS/ENGLISH

A "natural language" shell to translate English-language queries into SQL (Structures Query Language) commands and to present the retrieved data or answers to the user in the SAS/ASSIST environment.

SAS/ETS

A collection of procedures and functions in the area of econometrics and time series analysis. It also covers forecasting techniques and planning models.

SAS/FSP

Online, full screen data entry and data retrieval facilities. It also handles computerized mailings.

SAS/GRAPH

Many-faceted graphics package. From 'business graphics' to maps.

SAS/IML

An interactive matrix oriented programming language. Simultaneous execution of operations on whole matrices of numbers. Has being described by some people as a 'legible version of the APL programming language'.

SAS/INSIGHT

Interactive package for statistical analysis. Especially for gaining an insight into statistical attributes of a set of data.

SAS/LAB

Interactive environment for setting up and executing simple statistical analyses. The user is lead by means of questions and answers to the correct statistical analysis for his/her work.

SAS/OR

Procedures in the field of Operations Research. It contains tools for linear programming, network optimalization, 'critical path' project planning and 'resource planning'.

SAS/PH-Clinical

Routines and procedures for processing test results in the pharmaceutical and biotechnical sciences and industries.

SAS/QC

Procedures for process monitoring and quality control. Fits in the concepts of Total Quality Management.

SAS/RTERM

Terminal emulator software capable of producing hardcopy graphics with a personal computer.

SAS/SESSION

Special interface to offer access to all the functionality and power of the SAS System from the CICS environment.

SAS/SHARE

Facility for simultaneously accessing SAS data sets and the like by multiple users.

SAS/STAT

The 'Classic-SAS': the statistical procedures, from simple linear and nonlinear regressions to complex multivariate analysis. The Cadillac of statistical analysis software.

SAS/TOOLKIT

A collection of routines which can be used as an interface for adding your own procedures and/or functions to the arsenal of SAS software. The procedures and functions are written in programming language like PL/1 or C.

SAS documentation

Every SAS user should have access to the following three books

* *SAS Language Reference, Version 6, First Edition*
  ISBN 1-55544-381-8, SAS order number A56076

* *SAS Procedures Guide, Version 6, Third Edition*
  ISBN 1-55544-378-8, SAS order number A56080

* *SAS Technical Report P222: Changes and Enhancements to Base SAS Software, Release 6.07*
  ISBN 1-55544-466-0, SAS order number A59139

The need to acquire other books depends on the area of application and the complexity of the problems you want to solve using the SAS System. SAS Institute semiannually publishes the *Publications Catalog* with a summary of all available books.

The books listed below are valuable supplements to the information given on individual subjects in this book:

- *SAS Guide to TABULATE Processing, Second Edition*
  ISBN 1-55544-416-4, SAS order number A56095

- *SAS Guide to Macro processing, Version 6, Second Edition*
  ISBN 1-55544-382-6, SAS order number A56041

- *Guide to the REPORT procedure: Usage and Reference, Version 6, First Edition*
  ISBN 1-55544-422-0, SAS order number A56088

The following book contains many practical tips for efficient programming in the SAS System:

- *SAS Programming Tips: A Guide to Efficient SAS Processing*
  ISBN 1-55544-431-8, SAS order number A56150

For more information on the operation of the SAS System in your system environment, get hold of the relevant system companion. That will contain a complete description of the system-dependent aspects of the SAS OPTIONS and the FILENAME and LIBNAME statements, of the SAS file management in that system environment and system-dependent aspects of various functions and procedures and so on.

- *SAS Companion for the MVS Environment, Version 6, First Edition*
  ISBN 1-55544-398-2 , SAS order number A56101
  +
  SAS Technical Report P218, Changes and Enhancements to the SAS System, Release 6.07, for the MVS Environment
  ISBN 1-55544-467-9, SAS order number A59135

- *SAS Companion for the OS/2 Environment, Version 6, Second Edition*
  ISBN 1-55544-517-9, SAS order number A56111

- *SAS Companion for the UNIX Environment and Derivatives, Version 6, First Edition*
  ISBN 1-55544-420-2, SAS order number A56107

- *SAS Companion for the Microsoft Windows Environment, Version 6, First Edition*
  ISBN 1-55544-527-6, SAS order number A56110

- *SAS Companion for the VMS Environment, Version 6, First Edition*
  ISBN 1-55544-392-3, SAS order number A56102
  +
  SAS Technical Report P220, Changes and Enhancements to the SAS System, Release 6.07, for the VMS Environment
  ISBN 1-55544-462-8, SAS order number A59137

- *SAS Companion for the CMS Environment, Version 6, First Edition*
  ISBN 1-55544-399-0, SAS order number A56103
  +
  SAS Technical Report P219. Changes and Enhancements to the SAS System, Release 6.07, for the CMS Environment
  ISBN 1-55544-464-4, SAS order number A59136

- *SAS Companion for the AOS/VS Environment, Version 6, First Edition*
  ISBN 1-55544-407-5, SAS order number A56104

- *SAS Companion for the PRIMOS Environment, Version 6, First Edition*
  ISBN 1-55544-406-7, SAS order number A56105

- *SAS Companion for the VSE Environment, Version 6, First Edition*
  ISBN 1-55544-525-X, SAS order number A56109

For a summary of the reference guides for the various SAS software products, refer to the *Publications Catalog* mentioned earlier. You can order all books and the *Publications Catalog* by writing to your local SAS subsidiary or representative or to:

SAS Institute Inc.
Publications Division
SAS Campus Drive
Cary, NC 27513
USA

Phone:(919) 677-8000

Index